APPROACHING THE LAND OF BLISS

BUDDHIST TRADITION SERIES

VOLUME 58

APPROACHING THE LAND OF BLISS

Religious Praxis in the Cult of Amitābha

Edited by
RICHARD K. PAYNE
KENNETH K. TANAKA

MOTILAL BANARSIDASS PUBLISHERS
PRIVATE LIMITED • DELHI

*First Indian Edition: Delhi, **2008***
First Published by the University of Hawai'i Press, 2003

ISBN: 978-81-208-3194-0

MOTILAL BANARSIDASS
41 U.A. Bungalow Road, Jawahar Nagar, Delhi 110 007
8 Mahalaxmi Chamber, 22 Bhulabhai Desai Road, Mumbai 400 026
203 Royapettah High Road, Mylapore, Chennai 600 004
236, 9th Main III Block, Jayanagar, Bangalore 560 011
Sanas Plaza, 1302 Baji Rao Road, Pune 411 002
8 Camac Street, Kolkata 700 017
Ashok Rajpath, Patna 800 004
Chowk, Varanasi 221 001

For Sale in South Asia only

Printed in India

BY JAINENDRA PRAKASH JAIN AT SHRI JAINENDRA PRESS,
A-45 NARAINA, PHASE-I, NEW DELHI 110 028
AND PUBLISHED BY NARENDRA PRAKASH JAIN FOR
MOTILAL BANARSIDASS PUBLISHERS PRIVATE LIMITED,
BUNGALOW ROAD, DELHI 110 007

To the memory of my father,
Perley Baldwin Payne, Jr., 1914–2002.

RICHARD K. PAYNE

To LaVerne Sasaki Sensei,
for getting me started on the academic path.

KENNETH K. TANAKA

Contents

Acknowledgments

WE WISH to thank the contributors for their cooperation, and for their patience. Like many such collections of essays, this one has a long and complex textual history.

Kenneth K. Tanaka organized a conference entitled "A Cross-Cultural Study of Pan–Pure Land Buddhist Practices: Roots of Japanese Amida Tradition," which was held at the Institute of Buddhist Studies in Berkeley on June 17–18, 1995. Participants included Roger Corless, Hee-soo Jung, Allan Andrews, Eva Neumaier-Dargyay (in absentia), Mark Blum, Todd T. Lewis, Cuong Nguyen, Whalen Lai, and Richard K. Payne. Alfred Bloom and Kenneth K. Tanaka acted as discussants. A follow-up panel was organized by Richard Jaffe for the 2000 Association for Asian Studies Conference in San Diego: "Varieties of Pure Land Practice in China and Japan." Presenters at this panel were Charles B. Jones, Charles D. Orzech, James H. Sanford, and Richard Jaffe, with a response by Richard K. Payne. Other essays included here were solicited specifically for the collection by Richard K. Payne.

The editors wish to express their deepest appreciation to Peter Gregory and the rest of the Kuroda Institute's editorial committee, and to the two anonymous reviewers for their assistance in giving this volume its current shape. In addition, we are indebted to the Buddhist Churches of America's Ministers Association Research and Propagation Committee and the Buddhist Churches of America's Fraternal Benefit Association Legacy Fund for substantial subventions toward the publication of this collection. We also want to thank the excellent staff of the University of Hawai'i Press, and especially Patricia Crosby, who provided both guidance and encouragement at critical times.

Foreword

Ernst Steinkellner
Alexander Van Rospatt

The history of Buddhism covers more than 2300 years and a vast area extending from the Afghan region in the west to Japan in the east. Given the great variety of Buddhist source languages and the immense diversity of cultural and historical contexts in which Buddhism found (and finds) itself embedded, it is only natural that there is considerable compartmentalisation in the academic study of this religion. Generally, scholars specialize in the Buddhism of a particular region and its literature, be it the Indian subcontinent, Tibet, China, Japan, or another part of Central, East or Southeast Asia. While the study of certain textual and doctrinal traditions straddles such regional divides, few attempts have been undertaken to examine how particular forms of Buddhist practice play out in different areas.

The present volume addresses the dearth of such studies by pursuing the cult of Amitābha in various parts of the Buddhist world. It brings together the contributions of a conference on this theme held on Berkeley in 1995 and of a follow-up panel organized five years later in San Diego, and supplements this with further contributions specifically commissioned for this volume. From the papers on the Tibetan and Newar tradition by Kapstein and Lewis, it emerges that the cult of Amitābha initially was not a sectarian movement, but a form of practice that captured the popular imagination of large circles of Buddhist practitioners and laity. Daniel Gertz' re-examination of the patriarch Shenghchang (959-1020) suggests likewise that Pure Land practice in the Chinese tradition was initially less sectarian than commonly assumed. Naturally, the focus of the studies assembled here is on Japan where the cult of Amitābha was taken to its furthest extreme. They deal with particular forms of Pure Land Buddhist practice there, and in the process touch upon important aspects of religious life such as "deathbed practices" and address pertinent issues such as gender and salvation.

Together these studies convey an impression of the stunning range of Japanese Pure Land traditions.

The papers published here are authored by leading authorities in their field. They are not only case studies that are of interest for the specialist, but collectively they also demonstrate how a particularly important form of Buddhist devotional practice, namely the cult of the Buddha Amitābha with its concomitant aspiration to be reborn in his paradise, assumed varying forms and guises in different traditions. In this way the present collection of papers gives an idea of the continuity and discontinuity of particular forms of practice across the Buddhist world and thereby enhances our understanding of the dissemination and workings of the world religion that Buddhism is.

Introduction

Richard K. Payne

The discourse of Buddhist studies has predominantly been structured by two themes: texts and nations. One doubts, however, that these reflect in any significant way the organizing themes of most Buddhists. In contrast, the cultic practices associated with particular buddhas and bodhisattvas would probably be much more representative of the way Buddhist adherents themselves conceive of their relation to the tradition. This collection draws together recent research on the cult of Amitābha.

Several authors have attempted to break out of the standard categories that structure our academic discourse.[1] In his introduction to a special issue of the *Journal of the International Association of Buddhist Studies* devoted to the topic of the mandala, Frank Reynolds writes: "For many years Buddhist Studies has been dominated by research that has focused on particular 'national' traditions on the one hand, and on written texts and textual traditions on the other." His own interest in the theme of mandalas was "an attempt to move beyond the limitations on our understanding that the dominance of these two components of the received Buddhological orthodoxy has imposed."[2]

Similarly, Todd Lewis comments here on the split between the philological–textual approach to studying Buddhism and the ethnographic approach, which focuses only on the activities and beliefs of the laity. This split creates a lacuna into which the living Buddhist religious professionals who put the teachings found in the texts into effect in the lives of the laity disappear. A broad concern with cultic praxis avoids this methodological blind spot.

The problematic organization of our knowledge of Buddhist history is also apparent in the "three countries" model, that is, seeing the history of Buddhism as a movement from India to China to Japan. Even with the emendation of Tibet and the creation of a "four countries" model, this organizing principle implicitly makes the Japanese forms of the various lineages and traditions into the culmination of Buddhist history.[3] In other words, such a trajectory suggests that Japanese Pure Land, Zen, or Shingon is the most highly developed form of each tradition, and that the history of Buddhism is properly organized as a set of sectarian histories. It can also truncate the ongoing historical development in, for example, China, once the focus of attention shifts with the transmission to Japan.[4]

Other authors have also attempted to move beyond the limitations of defining Buddhism in terms of its textual corpus or nation-states. One strategy has been to deploy emic categories, such as Buddha, dharma, sangha. Although such an approach has its appeal and value as an attempt to represent the categories employed by Buddhists themselves, it does limit the possibility of drawing comparisons between Buddhism and other religious traditions. The approach taken in this volume is to focus on cult and praxis, which have comparative possibilities and represent—if not a category per se—at least a type of religious phenomenon that Buddhists would recognize.

Key Terms

Cult

By "cult" we mean what more classically trained scholars meant by the Latin *"cultus"*—the set of practices identified with the worship of a particular deity.[5] Although frequently described as if necessarily communal in nature, the cultic practices we consider here include individual practices as well.[6] Cult as cultus is to be distinguished from the sociology of religion's use of the word as a category of religious organization, like that of church, sect, and so on.[7] Much less is the term intended in the pejorative sense found in popular journalism, where it is simply a sloppy shorthand for "cult of personality." Its use here allows for the idea of cult as a religious entity that exists over time and can be carried across cultural boundaries. As such, cults do not exist as pristine, ahistorical, unchanging, logically coherent, systematized sets of practices. Indeed, as several of the essays here indicate, cults are deeply enmeshed in the political, economic, and historical conflicts of the societies in which they exist.[8] As S. R. F. Price has noted, it is necessary that we "analyse and avoid the difficulties which derive from our own cultural background . . . and of these the most pervasive is our assumption that politics and religion are separate areas."[9]

By organizing our inquiry around the category of cults, we avoid inadvertently introducing the problematic distinction between popular and elite. The Pure Land traditions are often identified as popular, on the basis that some of them developed the idea that Amitābha's vows provide an "easy path," contrasted with the "path of sages." A frequently repeated analogy—attributed to Nāgārjuna—equates following the path of sages with walking to awakening, while depending on the vows of Amitābha is like riding in a boat.

This idea of the two paths seems to have been a powerful one, creating a widespread following for Pure Land Buddhism in late medieval Japan, for example. However, this is not the same as the distinction between popular and elite as commonly used in the academic literature. The ambiguity of the term "popular" to mean both "widespread" and "of the general populace" has contributed to this confusion, creating opportunities for anachronisms, such as sectarian apologetics that equate the "easy path" with a democratic impulse. Despite being "one of the most basic distinctions made by the modern study of Buddhism," Malcolm David Eckel has identified this distinction between popular and elite as needing reexamination.[10] He points out that despite their status as learned monks, both Bhāvaviveka and Xuanzang were also without contradiction pilgrims and devotees, sharing as a common language the stories and symbols "gleaned from Buddhist sacred sites."[11]

Praxis

The term "praxis" is used here to mean the totality of practice and belief, theory, or ideology.[12] "Praxis" is distinguished from "practice" in that the latter term identifies specific activities, such as a ritual, meditation, or visualization. Use of "praxis" in contemporary cultural studies derives from the early Marx. In his discussion of the relation between human nature and human history, Marx presents the "core of human nature . . . as the ability to consciously transform the environment. Humans therefore live in a world that they have built, and they continue to rebuild and change. It is through this practical engagement with the world (this praxis) that humanity can come to understand itself."[13]

The world is built in a variety of senses—in the structuring of the human environment, in the creation and maintenance of social institutions, and in the production of ways of thinking about one's own identity and relations to others, and to the world.[14] The building of the world is a dialectic interplay between practice and ideology, and it is this interplay that is identified by "praxis." This use of "praxis" denotes "a dialectic of the material and the symbolic, the real and the perceived, the structure and the act."[15]

Praxis has been introduced into contemporary religious studies discourse largely through the theoretical reflections of Catherine Bell. In this part of her work she refers particularly to the anthropological theories of Pierre Bourdieu.[16] David Morgan summarizes the value of this approach, remarking that it "stresses that thinking, wanting, deciding, speaking, and looking, as well as ritual performance and gift-giving, are all part of the concrete world-making activities that constitute social behavior. These are not mindless actions but embodied forms of cognition and collective memory that reside in the concrete conditions of social life."[17]

One of the presumptions found throughout Western intellectual and religious culture is that thought (belief, theory, or ideology) is the basis on which action is taken. This intellectualist presumption that ideology is foundational is probably a consequence of the common Protestant assertion that for salvation belief is more important than action. The pervasive quality of this doctrine is particularly evident in the study of religion, where so much attention is given to belief systems that the importance of ritual and other religious practices in the lives of adherents is obscured. Rhetorically, one might ask, why not focus on the comparative study of monastic rules as the main topic of inquiry and teaching?

Although contemporary use of the term "praxis" in cultural studies is rooted in Marxist thought, the concept of praxis also corresponds to the way in which—at least some, and arguably many—Buddhists themselves did not make the distinction between theory and practice that is presumed in Western academic discourse, including the academic discourse about Buddhism. This is another issue that Eckel has raised in relation to Bhāvaviveka:

> When Bhāvaviveka's "theorizing" is viewed as Bhāvaviveka himself saw it—as an inclusive system for the discipline of thought rather

> than as a piecemeal presentation of individual arguments—it is much closer to the *theoria* of Plato's contemplation of the Good than it is to "theory" in the modern distinction between theory and practice. It is not a pale shadow of reality but a direct confrontation with reality itself.[18]

Essay Summaries

Pure Land in Tibet

Matthew Kapstein's contribution to this collection, "Pure Land Buddhism in Tibet?" locates the cult of Amitābha as an integral part of the Mahāyāna Buddhist tradition of Tibet. Amitābha is central both to the mythohistorical creation of a Tibetan identity and to Tibetan Buddhist praxis, including tantra. As in East Asian Pure Land traditions, the goal of Sukhāvatī was promoted in Tibet as particularly important because of its accessibility. Other buddha realms may be limited to advanced practitioners, but Amitābha assured even common foolish people *(pṛthagjana)* access to Sukhāvatī. Kapstein outlines some important differences, however, between the Tibetan cult of Amitābha and Japanese Pure Land. While certain strains developed an antinomian interpretation in Japan, Kapstein's Tibetan material consistently emphasizes the need for moral effort. The exclusivist orientation to Amitābha and Sukhāvatī that characterizes what James Sanford in this collection identifies as the normative mainstream of Japanese Pure Land appears to be absent in Tibet.[19] Also missing is the sectarian identity that emerged in Japan in conjunction with this exclusivistic stance. As Kapstein notes, "there is no evidence that sectarian identity was ever peculiarly tied to the Pure Land of Amitābha. This was an inclusive cult, embracing Tibetan Buddhists overall." The fluidity of Buddhist iconography is also apparent in the differences between Tibetan and East Asian representations. Kapstein mentions that in Tibet Amitābha is matched with Avalokiteśvara and Padmasambhava, while Mahāsthāmaprāpta is identified with Vajrapāṇi. Kapstein's essay clearly suggests that Amitābha and Sukhāvatī held a privileged position in the imaginal worlds of Tibetan religion.

Deconstructing the Patriarchal Lineage

In his "Shengchang's Pure Conduct Society and the Chinese Pure Land Patriarchate," Daniel Getz examines the identification of

Shengchang as one of the Pure Land patriarchs. Following his review of the earliest records, Getz locates Shengchang more firmly in a Huayan context and views the purpose of his society not so much as propagating Pure Land praxis, but rather as a means of modifying the anti-Buddhist sentiments that Song dynasty literati had inherited from Han Yü.

The importance of the ways in which lineages were created in East Asia is highlighted in Getz's work. Early records regarding Shengchang and the society he established make only passing reference to Amitābha and the goal of birth in Sukhāvatī. These suggest a religious culture in which, as Gregory Schopen has discussed for Indian Mahāyāna, Sukhāvatī functioned as a generalized goal shared by many but without specific sectarian affiliation. After Shengchang two centuries would pass before Pure Land patriarchal lineages identifying Huiyuan as the founder and Shengchang as his lineal descendant were compiled.[20]

Uncritical acceptance of these "late Song and subsequent biographies" has been the basis of more recent scholarship. According to Getz, this has led to the impression that Pure Land had more sectarian identity and coherence than can be supported by examining materials closer to Shengchang's own period: "The silence of the sources in this regard suggests the absence of a distinct autonomous and continuous Pure Land tradition for Shengchang and the members of his society."

At the Time of Death

Religious associations were also known in medieval Japan, and Jacqueline Stone begins her study of the practice of reciting nenbutsu at the time of death with a discussion of the Samādhi Assembly of Twenty-Five established on Mt. Hiei in 986. Unlike Shengchang's society, this one was explicitly formed to assist its members with dying while uttering the nenbutsu as their last act. Genshin is one of the key figures responsible for codifying the practices of this group. Nenbutsu recitation at the time of death is often noted in passing as having been rejected by Hōnen, but Stone gives us an understanding of both the practices themselves and the logics that motivated them. For example, one view held that a final utterance of the nenbutsu at the moment of death could overcome the negative karma accumulated over a lifetime.

Many needed the assistance of a final nenbutsu to qualify for birth in Sukhāvatī, but the worst of the "evil people" were warriors. Not only did they engage in killing, but they were particularly in danger of dying in a state of anger or fear, making a final thought of the Buddha impossible. Camp priests assisted the dead and dying in the battlefield by chanting nenbutsu with or for them.[21]

The dangers attendant upon failing to hold the nenbutsu in mind at the last moment led to extreme acts of merit accumulation. For example, if one recited the nenbutsu thousands of times a day, one would be better able to keep Amitābha in mind while dying. Even more extreme were attempts to avoid the vagaries of death by committing religious suicide. Dying at a time of one's choosing increased the possibility of a good death. However, once deathbed practices had become routinized, they also became increasingly subject to contestation. Thus we have Hōnen's suggestion that one should depend on the vow of Amitābha rather than on the ritualized recitation of nenbutsu while awaiting death.

Esoteric Pure Land

About a century after Genshin and the establishment of the Samādhi Assembly of Twenty-Five, the "Esoteric Explication of Amida" appeared. Its author, Kakuban, was the founder of the one major "schism" in the history of the Shingon tradition, the New Doctrine school. Kakuban held a radically non-dualist view, which extended to asserting not only such familiar identities as samsara and nirvana, but also the identity of Mahāvairocana and Amitābha.[22]

James Sanford places Kakuban into a typology of Japanese Pure Land thought. He identifies the first category as the normative mainstream—that set of conceptions that derives from the work of Hōnen and Shinran, and includes the familiar emphasis on exclusive practice of recitative nenbutsu and exclusive dependence on Amitābha. Sanford suggests that the lineages deriving from Hōnen (other than Shinran's) form a second strain of Pure Land thought. A third is found among a group known as *hijiri* (holy men), who were often itinerant, such as Ippen.[23] Nenbutsu practices within Japanese esoteric Buddhism, or "secret nenbutsu," constitute a fourth form, and this is where Sanford locates Kakuban. The variety of "heresies" to mainstream Pure Land thought constitutes the fifth strain, while the presence of Pure Land thematics in other traditions such as Tendai and Zen makes up the sixth.

Like Kapstein's examination of Amitābha in Tibetan tantric traditions, Sanford's translation demonstrates the importance of Amitābha in the Japanese tantric traditions. Although East Asian Buddhism is generally not considered strongly scholastic in character, the four kinds of *dharmakāya* discussed by Sanford indicate the scholasticism of East Asian Buddhism that is deserving of further research.

Mothers and Daughters

The cult of Chūjōhime, which Hank Glassman examines in his contribution to this collection, constitutes what might be called a "subsidiary cult," meaning, one that derives from the cult of Amitābha but grows to such importance that its central figure actually displaces Amitābha as the focus of worship. The technology that produced the cult included preaching performances illustrated by a *mandara* that itself held the status of a relic.[24] The origins of these preaching performances have been traced back to Indian practices.[25]

Chūjōhime's cult focused on women's salvation. The etiological myth of the cult concerns a daughter whose mother dies while she is an infant and includes a manifestation of Amitābha as a nun. The famous Taima *mandara,* which is central to the tale, visually recounts the story of Queen Vaidehī, and nuns played the central role in propagating the cult. The problematics of women's birth in Sukhāvatī are directly confronted in the story's finale: At the time of Chūjōhime's death, she is taken in her own body by Amitābha directly to Sukhāvatī; she does not need to be reborn first as a man.

The role of relics in authenticating the cult is matched by the importance of geography in locating the story in the physical reality of medieval Japan. Viewing the relics and hearing the story of Chūjōhime had the ability to establish a karmic affiliation that assured one of birth in Sukhāvatī. Similarly, locating the events of the saint's life in the local geography made her much more accessible than Amitābha in Sukhāvatī or Śākyamuni in India.

Transgression

In his examination of what he calls "radical Amidism," Fabio Rambelli discusses a variety of different forms of Japanese Pure Land thought, which, as suggested by Sanford, constitutes divergences from the mainstream or normative forms. Avoiding the fixed categories of orthodox and heterodox, he describes instead a cycling between center and periphery in which interpretations by one group are reinterpreted by another in light of its own interests, and these latter return to be reinterpreted again.[26]

The divergent forms discussed by Rambelli almost all share one version or another of the fundamental concept of the efficacy of a single thought *(ichinengi)* in achieving birth in Amida's Pure Land. Not surprisingly, these movements drew on other strains of thought found in medieval Japanese Buddhism. The two Rambelli finds most influential are the concept of original enlightenment *(hongaku)* found in Tendai and a pansexualism found in some strains of Shingon, especially the little-studied Tachikawaryū.[27]

From the perspective of mainstream Pure Land in Japan, one of the key heretical concepts was the notion of "licensed evil," which threatened to bring the entire movement into disrepute and repression. From Rambelli's perspective, however, "licensed evil" is part of a carnivalesque reversal of social and religious norms. This reversal is a critique of the repressive social order, including the dominant religious institutions.

Purification and the Politics of Lineage

As in China, sitting meditation and nenbutsu recitation in Japan were propagated by teachers who saw them as complementary practices. Richard Jaffe examines the work of Ungo Kiyō, who sought to match the kind of teaching he provided to the needs and capacities of his disciples. The poem Jaffe translates here was composed for the widow of one of Ungo's daimyo supporters who had become a nun. The model of Queen Vaidehī as precedent served Ungo in this project, just as she played an important role in the Chūjōhime cult discussed by Glassman.

Ungo's interpretation of nenbutsu practice is clearly in keeping with Zen notions of the path to awakening. He describes the goal of practice as an "unattached, nondiscriminating nenbutsu"—in other words as an object of meditation similar to some uses of mantra. Also, Ungo's understanding of the Pure Land is immanentalist and clearly comparable to Kakuban's as discussed here by Sanford. Despite what one might expect from such a stance, Ungo resisted any tendency toward antinomian interpretations. His emphasis on the importance of the precepts is fully compatible with the attitudes of the Tibetan authors discussed by Kapstein—and fully at variance with the carnivalesque antinomianism found in Rambelli's radical Amidist groups.

Where Rambelli examines the societal processes by which orthodoxy is defined, Jaffe explores the role of institutional politics in defining "true Rinzai." When Ōbaku was introduced from China, it carried the panache of coming from the country that many Japanese considered to be the source of the most important developments in Buddhism. This created the feeling that it was necessary to contrast existing Rinzai with the more inclusive Ōbaku. By examining one of the specific locations where our contemporary understanding of Zen has been formed, Jaffe's work highlights the historically conditioned character of our own expectations of what is proper to each of these traditions. As Helen Baroni notes: "It is from the retrospective view that the greatest contrast exists between Ōbaku and the rest of Japanese Rinzai in terms of Pure Land practice, as 'purity' became a major issue only in the later Tokugawa and modern periods."[28]

Death in Nepal

Todd Lewis opens his essay on Sukhāvatī beliefs in Nepal by noting some of the ways in which partial information about the history of the cult of Amitābha has created misleading expectations. Specifically he calls attention to his own expectation that devotion to Amitābha was exclusively an East Asian phenomenon (though having its origins in northwest India) and therefore not to be found in Nepal.

However, Lewis did discover that—as with the importance of the "Sukhāvatī orientation" Kapstein uncovered in Tibet—the hope for birth in Sukhāvatī is found in many different forms in Nepal. As in Tibet (but not Japan), this phenomenon does not constitute a separate sectarian identity. Attention to the cultic life of the Kathmandu valley reveals the goal of birth in Sukhāvatī to be an important stream of belief that might otherwise have been obscured. Lewis highlights the importance of understanding that rituals are integral to Buddhism. Western religious historiography is informed by the rhetoric of decadence, according to which rituals are at best merely vulgar concessions to the religious needs of the ignorant folk, or at worst manipulative creations of a venal priesthood.[29] He emphasizes the pedagogic role of ritual as a means of acculturating people to the Buddhist path.

Lewis finds traces of the desire for birth in Sukhāvatī in four different cultic practices: in stupa worship, in cultic devotions to Avalokiteśvara, in the founding story of the greatest Buddhist temple and festival of Kathmandu, and in a variety of lay Buddhist rituals. Interestingly, the *bhajan* style of group devotional singing imported from India within the last century has been adapted to Newari Buddhist use, albeit within the context that "Sukhāvatī rebirth remains an unsystematically articulated goal, merely one of many associations linked to venerating the stupas and bodhisattvas of the country."

Seeking the Land of Bliss in Taiwan

Contemporary Taiwan provides an example of the way in which the cult of Amitābha continues in present-day East Asia. Charles Jones gives us a "thick description" of a one-day recitation retreat that is paradigmatic for longer retreats as well. In the course of his discussion, Jones highlights the understanding of Pure Land Buddhism as an "easy path" in contemporary Taiwan—a path that is in fact very strenuous. This understanding contrasts markedly with what Sanford identifies as the normative form of Japanese Pure Land thought, wherein the rhetoric of "self power" *(jiriki)* versus "other power" *(tariki)* has led to questioning the entire concept of practice per se.

Jones calls attention to the problematics of appropriating the concept of grace as a way of describing the workings of Amitābha's vows *(praṇidhāna)*. The theological connotations of grace (it is a freely given gift of the Creator to his creation) are radically different from those resulting from Dharmākara's accumulation of merit, which works automatically, without Amitābha's active involvement.[30]

Jones brings an issue of great importance in contemporary discussions of epistemological issues: the "ambiguity and interpretability of religious experience." His discussion implies not only that experience can be interpreted in a variety of ways after the fact, but also—citing Clifford Geertz—that an experience can itself be constructed according to one's expectations and the content of one's practice. Far from providing an epistemologically irreducible ground, experience, whether "religious" or not, dissolves like every other construct. As Ivan Strenski has noted, "intuitions are not self-authenticating."[31]

Conclusion

Four themes that run throughout this volume are important in the field of Buddhist studies: first, the place of Amitābha and Sukhāvatī in the broad range of Mahāyāna and Vajrayāna Buddhism; second, the variety of practices directed toward Amitābha and Sukhāvatī; third, the importance of the way in which conceptions of orthodoxy and heterodoxy are created; and fourth, the sociohistorical locatedness of religious practice.

Although commonly associated with the Japanese Pure Land sects deriving from Hōnen and Shinran, Amitābha is actually found throughout the Mahāyāna and Vajrayāna. The essays collected here open up the cult of Amitābha in Nepal, Tibet, China, and Taiwan, as well as new aspects of Japanese Pure Land.[32] They also indicate the historical depth of the cult. The cult of Amitābha involves a wide variety of practices other than simply devotional recitation of the name (invocational nenbutsu). There are many ways of "keeping the Buddha in mind" *(buddhānusmṛti),* and many ways of understanding why one would do so.

The construction of orthodoxy is more than simply a matter of historical interest. Our own contemporary understanding of Buddhism has been informed by these orthodoxies, and it is important in our own critical reflection that we understand the historically conditioned nature of such conceptions—they were created as attempts to respond to particular challenges. Seen in that fashion it should be clear that they do not constitute an ahistorical essence that can be used to define any particular tradition within Buddhism over the course of its entire development.

Notes

1. One example of an attempt to employ an emic structure is Roger J. Corless, *The Vision of Buddhism: The Space Under the Tree* (New York: Paragon House, 1989), which uses the twelve acts of the Buddha Śākyamuni as recounted in Aśvaghoṣa's *Buddhacarita.*

2. Frank Reynolds, preface to special issue "On Maṇḍalas," *Journal of the International Association of Buddhist Studies* 19, no. 2 (Winter 1996): 177.

3. As much as I might like to claim this critique as my own, it was a comment made by one of the participants at an American Academy of Religion panel on the *Lotus Sūtra* in, I think, Kansas City. Unfortunately, none of the participants I have contacted can remember who made the comment, so I am unable to give credit where it is properly due.

4. The importance of avoiding this kind of truncated history is made evident in Peter N. Gregory and Daniel A. Getz, Jr., eds., *Buddhism in the Sung*, Kuroda Institute Studies in East Asian Buddhism, no. 13 (Honolulu: University of Hawai'i Press, 1999).

5. See, for example, W. Brede Kristensen, *The Meaning of Religion: Lectures in the Phenomenology of Religion,* trans. John B. Carman (1960; reprint, The Hague: Martinus Nijhoff, 1971). For instances, see Stephan Beyer, *The Cult of Tārā: Magic and Ritual in Tibet,* Hermeneutics, Studies in the History of Religions, no. 1 (Berkeley, Los Angeles, and London: University of California Press, 1973); Gananath Obeyesekere, *The Cult of the Goddess Pattini* (Chicago and London: University of Chicago Press, 1984); and Alf Hiltebeitel, *The Cult of Draupadī,* esp. vol. 2, *On Hindu Ritual and the Goddess* (Chicago and London: University of Chicago Press, 1991).

6. Regarding the implication of communality of practice, see *The HarperCollins Dictionary of Religion* (San Francisco: HarperSan Francisco, 1995), s.v. "cult."

7. For this usage, see, for example, Wouter J. Hanegraaff, *New Age Religion and Western Culture: Esotericism in the Mirror of Secular Thought* (1996; reprint, Albany: State University of New York Press, 1998), 14–18.

8. On the involvement of cults in the societal conflicts of their times, see, for example, Raymond Jonas, *France and the Cult of the Sacred Heart: An Epic Tale for Modern Times* (Berkeley, Los Angeles, and London: University of California Press, 2000); B. Robert Kreiser, *Miracles, Convulsions, and Ecclesiastical Politics in Early Eighteenth-Century Paris* (Princeton: Princeton University Press, 1978); David M. Guss, *The Festive State: Race, Ethnicity, and Nationalism as Cultural Performance* (Berkeley, Los Angeles, and London: University of California Press, 2000); and Emmanuel Le Roy Ladurie, *Carnival in Romans,* trans. Mary Feeney (New York: George Braziller, 1979).

9. S. R. F. Price, *Rituals and Power: The Roman Imperial Cult in Asia Minor* (Cambridge: Cambridge University Press, 1984), 2.

10. Malcolm David Eckel, *To See the Buddha: A Philosopher's Quest for the Meaning of Emptiness* (1992; reprint, Princeton: Princeton University Press, 1994), 5–6.

11. Ibid., 6.

12. "Ideology" refers here to something more inclusive than is usually meant by the perhaps more commonly used categories of "belief" and "theory." "Belief" often carries the implication of a systematized set of beliefs, a formal set of truth claims. "Theory" is, perhaps, better restricted to more specific assertions, such as scientific theories. "Ideology" as it is used here is more in keeping with Mannheim's understanding than Marx's: "For Mannheim, there is then no single truth against which all ideologies can be judged. Each ideology will have its own standards of truth and accuracy, dependent upon the social circumstances within which it is produced" (Andrew Edgar, "Ideology," in *Cultural Theory: The Key Concepts,* eds. Andrew Edgar and Peter Sedgwick (1999; reprint, New York: Routledge, 2002), 191.

13. Edgar, "Praxis" in *Cultural Theory,* 309.

14. See Peter Berger and Thomas Luckmann, *The Social Construction of Reality: A Treatise in the Sociology of Knowledge* (1966; reprint, New York: Anchor Books, 1967); and John R. Searle, *The Construction of Social Reality* (New York: The Free Press, 1995).

15. Catherine Bell, *Ritual Theory, Ritual Practice* (New York and Oxford: Oxford University Press, 1992), 76. Bell identifies this view with critiques of classic Marxist thought for being exclusively concerned with the material pole of the dialectic, as exemplified in the work of Marshall Sahlins.

16. Ibid., ch. 3; Pierre Bourdieu, *Outline of a Theory of Practice,* trans. Richard Nice (Cambridge: Cambridge University Press, 1977); and Pierre Bourdieu, *The Logic of Practice,* trans. Richard Nice (Stanford: Stanford University Press, 1990). Note that both Bell and Bourdieu use the term "practice" rather than "praxis," though with the same meaning. The use of the latter term here highlights the distinction between "praxis" as the interplay of the two poles of the dialectic (such as thought and activity) and the more casual use of "practice" to simply identify activities such as ritual, meditation, and visualization.

17. David Morgan, *Visual Piety: A History and Theory of Popular Religious Images* (Berkeley, Los Angeles, and London: University of California Press, 1998), 4.

18. Eckel, *To See the Buddha,* 5. For further discussion of this issue, see Pierre Hadot, *Philosophy as a Way of Life,* ed. Arnold I. Davidson, trans. Michael Chase (Oxford, England, and Cambridge, Mass.: Blackwell, 1995); Pierre Hadot, *What Is Ancient Philosophy,* trans. Michael Chase (Cambridge, Mass.: Harvard University Press, 2002); Sara Rappe, *Reading Neoplatonism: Non-discursive Thinking in the Texts of Plotinus, Proclus, and Damascius* (Cambridge: Cambridge University Press, 2000); and Michael McGhee, *Transformations of Mind: Philosophy as a Spiritual Practice* (Cambridge: Cambridge University Press, 2000).

19. The characteristic of exclusive devotion to Amitābha commonly associated with Pure Land Buddhism per se is actually only found in the sects deriving from the thought of Hōnen. Most Japanese Buddhists probably held an inclusive view comparable to the one discussed by Kapstein. See, for example, James L. Ford, "Jōkei and Hōnen: Debating Buddhist Liberation in Medieval Japan—Then and Now," *Pacific World: Journal of the Institute of Buddhist Studies* 3, no. 3 (2001), 199–217.

20. On Huiyuan, see Kenneth K. Tanaka, *The Dawn of Chinese Pure Land Buddhist Doctrine: Ching-ying Hui-yüan's Commentary on the* Visualization Sutra (Albany: State University of New York Press, 1990).

21. Contrary to the present-day association of warriors with Zen, which appears to have been created in the West by D. T. Suzuki's romanticized image of samurai and Zen, medieval *bushi* seem to have been strongly attracted to Amitābha and the possibility of birth in Sukhāvatī.

22. Kakuban's non-dual view is effectively identical to those held in other tantric Buddhist traditions, including some Tibetan traditions. See, for example, Janet Gyatso, *Apparitions of the Self: The Secret Autobiographies of a Tibetan Visionary* (Princeton: Princeton University Press, 1998).

23. See Dennis Hirota, trans., *No Abode: The Record of Ippen,* rev. ed. (Honolulu: University of Hawai'i Press, 1997).

24. On the importance of relics in medieval Japan, see Brian D. Ruppert, *Jewel in the Ashes: Buddha Relics and Power in Early Medieval Japan* (Cambridge and London:

Harvard University Press, 2000). See also Kevin Trainor, *Relics, Ritual, and Representation in Buddhism: Rematerializing the Sri Lankan Theravāda Tradition* (Cambridge: Cambridge University Press, 1997).

25. See Victor H. Mair, *Painting and Performance: Chinese Picture Recitation and Its Indian Genesis* (Honolulu: University of Hawai'i Press, 1988).

26. The malleable character of the categories of orthodox and heterodox is discussed by Jamie Hubbard in his *Absolute Delusion, Perfect Buddhahood: The Rise and Fall of a Chinese Heresy* (Honolulu: University of Hawai'i Press, 2000).

27. See Jacqueline I. Stone, *Original Enlightenment and the Transformation of Medieval Japanese Buddhism,* Kuroda Institute Studies in East Asian Buddhism, no. 12 (Honolulu: University of Hawai'i Press, 1999).

28. Helen Baroni, *Obaku Zen: The Emergence of the Third Sect of Zen in Tokugawa Japan* (Honolulu: University of Hawai'i Press, 2000), 106–107.

29. For the rhetoric of decadence, see Richard K. Payne, introduction to *Re-Visioning "Kamakura" Buddhism,* ed. Richard K. Payne, Kuroda Institute Studies in East Asian Buddhism, no. 11 (Honolulu: University of Hawai'i Press, 1998), 9–11.

30. The concept of grace also entails—in at least some theological conceptions—the idea that it is only "mediated through a specific historical community," i.e., a church (Claude Welch, *Protestant Thought in the Nineteenth Century* [New Haven and London: Yale University Press, 1972], 1:82). There does not seem to be any corollary to this in Pure Land thought.

31. Ivan Strenski, *Religion in Relation: Method, Application and Moral Location* (Columbia: University of South Carolina Press, 1993), 26.

32. Cuong Tu Nguyen, one of the presenters at the original conference from which this volume grew, has discussed Amitābha in Vietnamese Buddhism. For a brief discussion of Zen and Pure Land practice in Vietnam, see his *Zen in Medieval Vietnam: A Study and Translation of the* Thiền Uyển Tập Anh, Kuroda Institute Classics in East Asian Buddhism (Honolulu: University of Hawai'i Press, 1997), 94.

1

Pure Land Buddhism in Tibet?

From Sukhāvatī to the Field of Great Bliss

MATTHEW T. KAPSTEIN

IN THE AUTUMN of 1973, while trekking in Nepal with a group from the University of California at Berkeley, we were obliged to halt for some days in the village of Be-lding in the Rol-ba-gling valley. Heavy rains had closed the passes before us. I took advantage of our forced sojourn to make the acquaintance of Dge-slong Pa-sangs, an elderly monk who lived above the village temple and was the main religious teacher in the region. A young ex-monk from the village, who now worked as a mountaineering guide, on learning that I read Tibetan gave me a small xylographic booklet as a gift and suggested that it might be an appropriate text to read with the teacher. The booklet was the renowned "Prayer of the Pure Field of Great Bliss" (Rnam dag bde chen zhing gi smon lam, or Bde-smon) by the seventeenth-century master Karma Chags-med (Rāga-a-sya), and Dge-slong Pa-sangs was indeed delighted when I asked him to teach it to me.[1] As we sat in his small house during the seemingly interminable late monsoon downpour, he enthusiastically elaborated on Karma Chags-med's descriptions of the many blessings to be gained through birth in the Pure Land of the Buddha Amitābha. "It's perfectly flat, not all hills and ravines like you have here. No passes to cross, so you wouldn't have to be stuck in this village if we were there! How's it in America? It's mostly a plain, too, isn't it? That must be very pleasant!"[2]

At that time there was a band of poachers hunting musk deer in the dense forest in the lower part of the Rol-ba-gling valley. They provoked quite a bit of fear among the local inhabitants, for there had recently been a rash of burglaries in the village and it was generally believed that the poachers, who were of course armed and therefore dangerous, were responsible. One afternoon, as I was reading with Dge-slong Pa-sangs, a village woman excitedly burst into the house. "There's been another robbery," she cried, stifling her tears, but visibly quite shaken. The old monk calmed her, and after she had taken some tea with us and gone off, he turned to me with an odd expression of weariness and bemusement and said, "You'd never have this sort of trouble in Sukhāvatī." I understood his words as expressing the three things every New Yorker is supposed to know about real estate: "location, location, location." Rebirth in Sukhāvatī, he taught me, was a move to a much better neighborhood. Sukhāvatī was an actual destination, to which, after a life of back-breaking labor and hardship in what only foreign trekkers took to be a paradise, you aspired if you had any sense at all. The liturgies and prayers for rebirth in Amitābha's realm were part of an elaborate marketing campaign, highlighting the inconveniences of one's present circumstances, and promising in their stead a gentle land, with such amenities as hot and cold running water,[3] wishing trees, birds singing dharma-songs,[4] and offering goddesses in place of (heaven forbid!) human women.[5]

Though there can be no question of a tradition or school of Tibetan Buddhism that advocates the aspiration for rebirth in Amitābha's paradise as the uniquely appropriate expression of Buddhist practice, it is nevertheless clear that Sukhāvatī has long been an important focal point for much of Tibetan devotion. In the eastern and southern regions of the Tibetan world, and in particular wherever the Rnying-ma-pa and Bka'-brgyud-pa orders are preeminent, that is, in places much like Rol-ba-gling, the trinity of Amitābha, Avalokiteśvara, and Padmasambhava is universally revered, and lay religious practice turns almost exclusively on these figures, who are regarded as the three embodiments (*sku-gsum,* Skt. *trikāya*) of a single buddha.[6] We may be entitled, therefore, to propose that, even in the absence of a "Pure Land Sect" of Tibetan Buddhism, there was nevertheless an important Pure Land orientation in Tibet, just as there is in contemporary Nepal.[7] In the present chapter, I shall seek to delineate not a thoroughgoing history of this orientation, but rather a number of particular motifs and moments that are of special importance to it and so convey some of its chief characteristics.

According to some accounts, the Rol-ba-gling valley mentioned above is itself a "hidden land" *(sbas-yul),* that is, a terrestrial pure land. In such realms, neither the inhabitants nor their visitors are necessarily aware of the special status and character of the place; its hiddenness is as much a matter of religious vision as of geography, and what is thus hidden stands revealed only to those of pure vision *(dag-snang)*. The most famous of the terrestrial pure lands is perhaps the mythical land of Śambhala, whose exact location is a mystery, but many identifiable places, including Sikkim and the region of Padma-bkod, near the great bend of the Brahmaputra river, are known as hidden lands as well. Mt. Potalaka, the paradise of Avalokiteśvara, and the Copper-Colored Mountain (Zangs-mdog dpal-ri) on Camaradvīpa, where Padmasambhava resides until the end of the aeon, are also located within our world of four continents encircling Mt. Meru. Beyond our world, pure lands are scattered throughout the universe, like galaxies in contemporary cosmology.

The theme of the pure land in Tibetan Buddhism, therefore, is a vast one, and one can readily enumerate prayers for rebirth in Tuṣita, Abhirati, Alakāvatī, Mt. Potalaka, the Copper-Colored Mountain, Śambhala, and so on, as well as an entire panoply of myths, beliefs, and practices that focus on one pure realm or another.[8] Indeed, the entire Tibetan practice of pilgrimage is wrapped up in such conceptions.[9] A broad consideration of the pure land *(dag-pa'i zhing-khams)* as one of the fundamental organizing themes in Tibetan religion would, therefore, be desirable, but that is not what I shall attempt to provide here. What follows will be for the most part restricted to a consideration of the cult of Amitābha and his Sukhāvatī realm, as befits this volume overall. This is, of course, a sufficiently large topic in itself; a recent two-volume collection of Tibetan texts pertaining to the aspiration for birth in Sukhāvatī, for instance, includes, in addition to a selection of the major canonical and paracanonical sources, some fifty aspirational prayers by various Tibetan authors of the twelfth through twentieth centuries, together with seven commentarial works.[10] And this is merely an anthology, by no means a complete collection of pertinent materials.

We must consider, too, the significance of the Tibetan Pure Land orientation for our understanding of Tibetan religious culture in general. The recent study of Tibetan Buddhism, particularly in the United States, has tended to emphasize the rarified domain of scholastic philosophy, while popular writings in English stress such topics as ethical advice on the bodhisattva's path and meditations on the nature of mind. The foregrounding of these interests has obscured in large measure the religious phenomena that were and still are predominant in traditional Tibetan settings, phenomena such as donative merit-making and contrition for sin, purposeful rituals of many kinds, devotion, and prayer.[11] The Tibetan Pure Land orientation has therefore received but scant attention to date.[12] There is no doubt some analogy with the Western study of Japanese Buddhism and its general neglect of "Amidism" relative to, for instance, Zen meditation—a bias that has been recently discussed at length by Galen Amstutz.[13]

The Emergence of the Pure Land Orientation

Tibetan Buddhist funerary rites found at Dunhuang, dating to the period of the old Tibetan empire and its immediate aftermath (eighth to tenth centuries), place much emphasis on the importance of securing rebirth in a divine realm in which the Buddhist teaching is available, for instance in Tuṣita. I have discussed elsewhere the "teaching of the path to the gods' realm" *(lha-yul-du lam bstan-pa),* according to which the deceased must journey through several paradises before seeking the attainment of perfect nirvana.[14] It may be useful, nevertheless, to repeat here a few lines from that work, which is presented as a postmortem itinerary to be recited to the deceased:

> From this Rose-Apple Continent, there is in the north Mt. Meru. It is the king of mountains, made of four sorts of precious gems. On its summit is the gathering place of the gods of the excellent religion, where the lord of the gods, Indra, and his thirty-two ministers open the way and show the paths of gods and men and of the world. There that king of the gods will teach the instructions of the doctrine to you, O worthy son, and the power of [your] merits will be emptied. O worthy son! then on the northern summit of Mt. Meru, there is the palace called Alakāvati, where the transcendent lord, glorious Vajrapāṇi dwells with a retinue of many wrathful ones. Worthy son, he will confer empowerment upon you, granting all desires to your heart's content. Then, worthy son, owing to the blessing of Vajrapāṇi, continue your journey, and in the divine abode of Tuṣita there is the religious regent of Buddha Śākyamuni, who is called sublime Maitreya. His retinue includes the bodhisattvas Vasumitra and Siṃhāntara, the nine-hundred ninety-six bodhisattvas of the Auspicious Aeon, and others, as well as numberless godlings. In a jewelled palace, with flowing godly robes, the enjoyment of varied musical instruments, and other such things unimaginable, the perfect provisions of happiness, in that holy, divine land may you be cautious about those many joys![15]

It is only after attaining this paradise that the deceased may aspire to attain nirvana (hence, the caution above, not to become too attached to heaven's pleasures!). As readers of the so-called *Tibetan Book of the Dead* will no doubt recognize, this is a path that differs to some degree from that taught in many of the later Tibetan *bar-do* traditions, which emphasize the necessity of avoiding both divine and infernal realms alike and searching for liberation alone.[16] Nevertheless, as will be made clear in what follows, with the emergence of a religious orientation focusing on rebirth in Sukhāvatī and the incorporation of paradise into the path that this entailed, the eschatological vision that had characterized such early Tibetan Buddhist funerary rites as the "teaching of the path to the gods' realm" was in essence forever retained.

The Dunhuang Tibetan documents, together with the evidence of the eighth- and ninth-century Tibetan translations of Buddhist canonical texts, further establish that Amitābha and the Sukhāvatī realm were well known to Tibetan Buddhists of the Tibetan imperial period.[17] This may be seen, for instance, in a famous Dunhuang Tibetan collection of benedictory prayers commemorating the construction and consecration of the temple of De-ga G.yu-tshal:

> Installed [in the temple] is the image of Buddha Amitābha, whose field is supreme among those of all buddhas, so that even the names for the three evil destinies and the eight obstacles are unknown. Being adorned with all the adornments of divine enjoyment, even the name for passing beyond sorrow [nirvana] cannot be known there! For it is a field adorned with all and perfect world-transcending happiness. Because [Amitābha] is especially compassionate on behalf of beings, by just reciting his name all sins are purified and one is blessed to be born in that buddha-field.[18]

It seems sure, however, that to the extent that rebirth in Sukhāvatī was emerging as a soteriological goal for Tibetan Buddhists, it was by no means an exclusive goal or one that was decisively preeminent in relation to other important Buddhist ends. In the text just cited, Amitābha is mentioned as but one of three primary icons installed in the temple and is neither central in his position in the overall iconographical scheme nor exalted above the others (namely, Vairocana and Maitreya) in the trio of divine figures extolled by the authors of our text.[19]

During the period following the fall of the Tibetan empire during the mid-ninth century and the subsequent renewal of Indian Buddhist contact with Central Tibet in the eleventh and twelfth centuries, we find occasional references to Sukhāvatī in the biographies of famous masters, though it is not always clear whether this reflects new Indian influences or tendencies established in earlier Tibetan Buddhism (and no doubt influenced by earlier developments in China).[20] As an example, we may cite the hagiographers' description of events preceding the death of the tantric master Khyung-po Rnal-'byor (d.c. 1140), founder of the Shangs-pa Bka'-brgyud line of teaching:

> After his disciples asked, "To which realm is our guru going? Where should we direct our prayers?" he replied, "Since I am going to be a Buddha in Sukhāvatī, direct your prayers there. Do not harbor doubts or ambivalence about it." This he recited three times.[21]

Khyung-po Rnal-'byor had also identified his preceptor Glang ri-thang-pa Rdo-rje-seng-ge (1054–1123), a famed figure in the early Bka'-gdams-pa order under whom he had received his *bhikṣu* ordination, as an emanation of Amitābha, an identification that remained current in later Tibetan historical tradition.[22] As will be seen below, tantric teachers of several lineages during the twelfth century were also promoting the aspiration for Sukhāvatī, a development that was no doubt further reinforced by the great expansion of the Tibetan Avalokiteśvara cult, which reached its apogee during the same age.[23]

Nevertheless, although a certain prominence was given to the conception of rebirth in Sukhāvatī, other Buddhist paradises are also much in evidence in the hagiographical traditions of the early second millennium.[24] What then accounts for the special emphasis on Sukhāvatī that we begin to find in some sources? There are, I think, two closely interrelated stories to be told here. On the one hand, practical soteriological concerns have begun to be rather sharply felt. There is a strong sense, frequently reflected in post-eleventh century Tibetan religious literature, that this is a degenerate age, and that the Tibetan people are sinful and unworthy.[25] Under these circumstances, one must accept that, even if one aspires to them, many of Buddhism's goals will be simply unattainable for any but the most exceptional adepts. Amitābha's vows to save those of little merit, however, are preeminent among teachings that appear to offer hope, even to benighted persons far removed in both place and time from the Buddha of our world-age, Śākyamuni. Such concerns are very much in evidence in a passage attributed to the renowned *yoginī* and founder of the Gcod tradition of tantric teaching, Ma-cig Lab-kyi sgron-ma (1055–1145/1153):

> For those who wish to become buddhas swiftly, it is necessary to pray for [rebirth in] a pure buddha-field. There are differing fields beyond number, and it has been declared that they are difficult to delimit in speech. Among them, in order to be born in the other superior fields excepting Sukhāvatī, you must attain at least the eighth station *(bhūmi)*, having entirely cut off the two obscurations. Even to be born in the middling fields, you must entirely cut off even the most subtle aspects of the obscuration of the afflictions *(kleśāvaraṇa)* and attain at least the first [moment] on the path of contemplative cultivation *(bhāvanāmārga)*. And for even the least of the fields, you must cut off attachment to self from the roots, and attain the path of seeing *(darśanamārga)*, that is, selflessness, the real truth. Until you've attained the path of seeing, though you pray [for rebirth in a buddha-field], you'll not achieve it. But even without attaining the path of seeing, should you strive at prayer, while not engaging even in the most subtle disciplinary faults with respect to your commitments and moral training, and purifying sins and gathering the profits of virtue, you may just be born in some of the trifling fields such as Tuṣita, and even that will be difficult.[26] Because in those fields there is no room for the births of common, ordinary persons *(pṛthagjana)*, who wallow in the afflictions *(kleśa)*, from now on you must pray at length! Therefore, it would seem that afflicted, common persons will not be born in the field of a buddha. Nevertheless, through the power of Buddha Amitābha's prayers, birth in the Sukhāvatī field has been vouchsafed by lord Amitābha himself, for which reason you must by all means [lit., "through all gates"] strive at prayer for rebirth in Sukhāvatī! Without doubt, suspicion, laziness, or irresolution, and by means of certainty and with ardent exertion you must pray, while recollecting the array of the Sukhāvatī field and its qualities. Because even common, ordinary persons, who are burdened with the afflictions, may be born in Sukhāvatī, it is exceptional. And having been born there, all of your wishes will be realized just as soon as you conceive them, and you will not be tainted by the merest obscuration of affliction. Moreover, because you are permitted to journey to whichever among the buddha-fields you wish, it is exceptional; and it is exceptional because buddhahood is swifter than in the other fields. Because there is nowhere another field that is closer to being attained than Sukhāvatī, which is endowed with the aforementioned and other qualities beyond all conception, it is exceedingly important that you strive in prayer for birth in Sukhāvatī.[27]

In the seventeenth century, Karma Chags-med would cite this passage at least twice in his writings, treating it as a dictum of near-canoncial authority.[28] In it, Tibetan Buddhism comes closest to elaborating a conception of salvation by Amitābha's unique grace, as is often associated with some varieties of Pure Land faith in East Asia.

The second and, over the long term, perhaps more important reason for Tibetan concern for rebirth in Sukhāvatī was the crystallization, during the eleventh to thirteenth centuries, of a mythologized construction of Tibet's earlier history in which Amitābha emerged as, to all intents and purposes, the patron Buddha of Tibet. The key figures in the drama of Tibet's adoption of Buddhism were now the seventh-century monarch Srong-btsan-sgam-po, regarded as the emanation of Avalokiteśvara, and the supreme guru Padmasambhava, tantric master of the emperor Khri Srong-lde'u-btsan (742–c. 797).[29] Both, however, are very closely associated with Amitābha and frequently regarded as his emanations. Thus, for instance, in the *Bka'-chems ka-khol-ma,* a cardinal work for the Avalokiteśvara traditions,[30] we find the following discussion taking place in Sukhāvatī itself, as the time of Śākyamuni's decease approaches in our world:

> Encouraged by light-rays emanating from Avalokiteśvara, who dwelt as Amitābha's attendant and was of his very essence, Amitābha spoke to him thus: "Son of my clan! If you proceed from here to the east, for as many aeons as there are sands of the Ganges, there is a world-system called Sahā. There, the Tathāgata named Śākyamuni dwells as a Buddha and teaches the Dharma. I perceive that he has resolved upon his [final] nirvana, though his intentions remain unfulfilled. Therefore, won't you go there to pray that the Lord not pass into nirvana?"
>
> Avalokiteśvara responded saying, "I will go there to pray."
>
> Amitābha spoke again, "You should go there, and in the kingdom of snows [Tibet] you must pray that the Lord not pass into nirvana and that he turn the Dharma-wheel!"[31]

With the redaction, during the same period, of the legends of Padmasambhava, we find a similar emphasis on the preeminence of Amitābha, and the formation of a clear conception of the trinity of which he is the first member. Consider in this regard the opening passage of the earliest of the great narrations of Padmasambhava's career, the popular Zangs-gling-ma, revealed by first major "treasure finder" *(gter-bton)* of the Rnying-ma-pa tradition, Nyang-ral Nyi-ma-'od-zer (1124–1192):

> Dharmakāya Amitābha,
> Sambhogakāya Avalokiteśvara,
> Nirmāṇakāya Padmasambhava—
> I bow before the divine Trikāya!

> Among all fields, the most exalted is the western Sukhāvatī field. There, the Buddha called Amitābha—in order that Ārya Avalokiteśvara might tame Oḍḍīyāna, India, and especially all the realms of snowy Tibet, in the southern Rose-Apple Continent (Jambudvīpa), in the field of the Nirmāṇakāya Śākyamuni, the Sahā realm—emanated the Nirmāṇakāya Padmasambhava in order to fulfill the goals of living beings.[32]

The mythologized constructions we are considering were much elaborated and widely promulgated in works redacted throughout the twelfth through fourteenth centuries, above all by Rnying-ma-pa authors, and came to form the mythological framework for much of later Tibetan historiography. The prominence of Sukhāvatī in the visions of Rnying-ma-pa masters at this time may be illustrated by the hagiographical account of Dam-pa Bde-gshegs (1122–1192), the founder of Kaḥ-thog monastery, an important Rnying-ma-pa center in far eastern Tibet (now Sichuan), of whom it is related:

> Katokpa [Kaḥ-thog-pa Dam-pa Bde-gshegs] could always gaze on the Buddha-field of Akṣobhya, Sukhāvatī, the buddha-field of Bhaiśajyaguru, and others. . . . He obtained the prophecy that in his following life he would dwell in Sukhāvatī as the bodhisattva Matisāra *(blo-gros-snying-po),* and obtain the actual realisation of the eighth level; and that then, in the future, in the aeon called "Star-like Array," he would become the Sugata Amitāyus.[33]

Dam-pa Bde-gshegs's visions of Sukhāvatī inspired him, too, to compose a prayer for rebirth in that realm and a tantric sādhana for the visualization of Amitābha in accord with the Rnying-ma-pa Mahāyoga system, which he transmitted to his disciple and regent Gtsang-ston-pa (1126–1216).[34] The latter's own hagiography also tells us of his special connection with Amitābha's field:

> [O]nce in a vision of Akṣobhya's buddha-field all the bodhisattvas in the retinue were buzzing with the news that this doctrine master was the bodhisattva Maṇigarbha *(nor-bu'i snying-po),* in which form he would be reborn in Sukhāvatī in his next life.[35]

Despite the fundamental role played by the Rnying-ma-pa in elaborating the mythohistorical framework for the Tibetan Pure Land orientation, however, it must be stressed that this development was by no means uniquely tied to a particular Tibetan Buddhist order. The following section will illustrate some of the ways in which a similar orientation became established throughout the Tibetan Buddhist sectarian traditions overall.

Devotional and Ritual Traditions

Tibetan prayers for rebirth in Sukhāvatī are so numerous that they form an identifiable subgenre among liturgical works, most often called Bde-smon, the acronym for Bde-ba-can-gyi smon-lam, "prayerful aspirations of [that is, for rebirth in] Sukhāvatī."[36] These were in the first instance modeled on well-known canonical verses such as *Saddharmapuṇḍarīka sūtra,* 24.29–33, and *Bhadracaryāpraṇidhānaraja,* 57–60 (in *Gaṇḍavyūha sūtra,* ch. 56).[37] Prayers of this type with clear attributions of authorship began to appear by about the twelfth century, though anonymous works along these lines had also been composed much earlier.[38] One of the earliest by a named author is the brief Bde-smon of Kaḥ-thog-pa Dam-pa Bde-gshegs, which we considered above.

The prayer liturgies were just one aspect of the Amitābha and Sukhāvatī cults as they unfolded in Tibet. Of particular importance, and great complexity, was the role of tantric approaches to contemplation and yoga. The Buddha Amitābha, as one of the Conquerors of the Five Families *(rgyal-ba rigs-lnga),* is ubiquitous within the Buddhist tantric milieu. His presence as the primary deity of a mandala or *sādhana,* however, appears to be rather uncommon, though his counterpart Amitāyus emerges early on as an important tantric divinity.[39] The enormous elaboration of the Tibetan cult of Amitāyus is of very great interest for the study of longevity techniques and alchemy, but as that subject would take us far from our present concerns it will not be considered here.[40]

Despite this, Amitābha and the Sukhāvatī field did acquire a special association with one very important technique of tantric yoga in Tibet, transference *('pho-ba),* whereby one's consciousness at the moment of death may be forcefully projected to a suitable realm of rebirth. The practice of transference causes the consciousness of the dying individual to depart suddenly from the body through a forced opening at the crown of the skull and travel immediately to a pure land, in which enlightenment will be swiftly attained. Because adepts of transference are believed also to be able to direct the consciousness of a dying or recently deceased individual to a blessed realm, the technique became not only an essential aspect of personal religious practice, but equally the stock in trade for ritual specialists called on to assist at the time of death and for subsequent funeral rites, so that the performance of transference became a major source of religious revenue.[41]

After the technique was introduced from India to Tibet, probably during the eleventh century, transference became particularly prominent within the Bka'-brgyud-pa traditions. No firm connection with Sukhāvatī is evident in the earliest Bka'-brgyud-pa instructions for the practice of transference with which I am at present familiar. One is told instead to direct one's consciousness to the "buddha-field to which one has devotion."[42] We may suppose that the strong association between the transference technique and the goal of rebirth in Sukhāvatī that did emerge over the centuries was due to the confluence of this particular injunction with the general development of the Sukhāvatī orientation within early-second-millennium Tibetan Buddhism. The idea of propelling one's consciousness to a pure land that enjoys a particularly welcoming relationship with our much-less-than-pure realm would perhaps have seemed very attractive to some. In later times, indeed, an important pilgrimage and public teaching of the 'Bri-gung Bka'-brgyud-pa order would make this connection fully explicit.[43]

In all events, that the Bka'-brgyud-pa hierarchs did actively promote faith in the vows of Amitābha is quite clear. Their encouragements for the aspiration for rebirth in his field are fully in evidence in the many Bde-smon liturgies authored by leading Bka'-brgyud-pa masters, and it was this tradition with which Karma Chags-med was himself formally affiliated. The Bde-smon composed by the fifth Karma-pa De-bzhin-gshegs-pa (1384–1415) and the fourth Rgyal-dbang 'Brug-pa Padma-dkar-po (1527–1592) remain prayer-texts for obligatory memorization by monks within their respective orders and formed models for Karma Chags-med's work.[44] Among the earliest of the Bka'-brgyud-pa Bde-smon is a very short example of the genre, written by the revered founder of the 'Bri-gung Bka'-brgyud-pa order, 'Bri-gung skyob-pa 'Jig-rten gsum-mgon (1143–1217). It is imbued with the sentiments of fervent devotion and hope for salvation that characterize the Bde-smon texts in general:

> I beseech you, Conqueror Amitābha!
> Gaze on me compassionately, venerable Avalokiteśvara!
> Bless me, O Conquerors' son, Mahāsthāmaprāpta!
> Lead me by gnosis to that field of light!
> Lead me by compassion to that field of light!
> Lead me by skilled action to that field of light!
> Lead me by prayer to that field of light!
>
> In the famed field of great bliss, the Conqueror's field,
> Before the feet of the victorious lord, Amitābha
> And Matisāra, father with your disciples,[45]
> May I and others be born when life has passed.
>
> There, having reached the culmination of contemplative intentions,
> The Dharmakāya being disclosed, may I fulfill the wishes
> Of those needing training in accord with their spirits,
> And by limitless deeds free all beings!
>
> From here in the western direction,
> Is Amitābha's field.
> May all those who adhere to his name
> Be born in that supreme field!
>
> Like the lotus unsoiled by the mire,
> Unsoiled by the three worlds' taint,
> Sprung from the lotus of being,
> May we be born in Sukhāvatī![46]

The Bde-smon liturgies are not the only explicit examples of the devotion to Amitābha and his realm that was emerging in Tibet during the period with which we are here concerned. A variety of contemplative and ritual traditions, for instance, also focusing upon Amitābha and Amitāyus became widely transmitted after the eleventh century, and some of these are traced to the celebrated Indian philosopher Jetāri (who is no doubt better known to contemporary scholars of Buddhism for his contributions to epistemology than to tantrism!). In our present context, the most pertinent of these is no doubt a tantric contemplative exercise to be practiced just before falling asleep, whose final aim is rebirth in Sukhāvatī. It appears to have been popularized primarily in the Sa-skya-pa order, and the most famous of the Sa-skya hierarchs, Sa-skya Paṇḍita Kun-dga'-rgyal-mtshan (1182–1251), composed a brief Amitābha Meditation Topic (Snang-ba-mtha'-yas bsgom-don) describing it:

Homage to the guru and to Mañjuśrī!
It says in the *Bhadracaryāpraṇidhānarāja* [verses 57–58ab]:

> When I come to the time of my death,
> May all obscurations be removed,
> And seeing Amitābha directly
> May I go to Sukhāvatī field.
> Arriving there, may all of these, my prayers,
> Be manifestly fulfilled, none excepted!

Based on this, the meditation on Amitābha is as follows:

At night, when going to sleep, lie down upon your right side. Perform the refuge and cultivation of bodhicitta, and thinking to yourself that this very place is the Sukhāvatī field, visualize yourself as your favored meditational deity. Visualize that before you, atop a lotus and lunar disk, sits Amitābha, red in color, his hands resting in an even gesture and holding a begging bowl filled with ambrosia. He sits in the cross-legged [vajra-]posture and is adorned with varied jewel-ornaments. Think that he is surrounded by the gurus. Then, thinking that all around them are the Buddhas and bodhisattvas, mentally perform three prostrations. Recite three times either the sevenfold service of the *Bhadracaryāpraṇidhānarāja* [verses 1–12], or, if not that, the "Ten Religious Practices" that I have composed.[47] Then, together with your exhalations, imagine that your mind dissolves into the heart of the Conqueror, indivisibly merging with the Conqueror's Heart. When you inhale, imagine that light comes forth from the Conqueror's Heart, and entering by the path of your speech, it dissolves into your heart, so that the Conqueror's Mind *(thugs)* and your mind *(sems)* indivisibly merge. After practicing that for three cycles [of breath], imagine that the buddhas and bodhisattvas dissolve into the gurus and the gurus then into Amitābha. Amitābha melts into light and dissolves into yourself. And you, in turn, dissolve into light, thinking the trinity of Buddha, meditational deity, and your own mind to be indivisibly intermingled. Then recite this prayer [*Bhadracaryāpraṇidhānarāja,* v. 59]:

> In that fine and delightful mandala of the Conqueror,
> Born from a sacred, most beautiful lotus,
> May I obtain there directly
> The prophecy of Amitābha the Conqueror!

Having recited that prayer, go to sleep in that state, without letting your thoughts wander. It is taught in the *Ratnakuṭa* that by practicing this, in the future, sloughing off this body like a serpent's skin, you will be miraculously born from a lotus in Sukhāvatī in the west, and hear the dharma preached by Amitābha.[48]

The so-called "sleep meditation" *(nyal-bsgom)* of Amitābha continues to be transmitted among the Sa-skya-pa and other orders, and a number of important doctrinal authors have written texts explaining it, and liturgies for its practice, that remain popular at the present time.[49]

Sa-skya Paṇḍita was not alone among the major Tibetan scholastic masters to have contributed to the development of the Pure Land orientation. Dol-po-pa Shes-rab-rgyal-mtshan (1292–1361), the founder of the controversial *gzhan-stong* (extrinsic emptiness) teaching of the Jo-nang-pa order,[50] authored two prayers for rebirth in Sukhāvatī.[51] Beyond this, he appears to have had a special interest in the sūtras that are the sources for this aspiration. His collected works include both an interesting text extracted from the *Adhyāśayasaṃcodana sūtra* concerning the relationship between the tenfold cultivation of *bodhicitta* and the conditions for attaining Sukhāvatī,[52] and a commentary on the larger *Sukhāvatīvyūha sūtra* itself, entitled *Rang gzhan bde ba can du skye ba'i thabs mchog* (The supreme means whereby self and others may be reborn in Sukhāvatī).[53] This interesting work consists of a detailed topical outline on the text of the sūtra, followed by this response to skeptical criticism of the sūtra's intentions:

> Now this must be said to remove error and doubt: about this [sūtra] some *kalyāṇamitras* hold, "Because ordinary persons are not born in Sukhāvatī, the present ordinary persons who exist will not be born there despite their efforts." But this will harm sentient creatures, for it gives rise to error and doubt where these are not appropriate. For among the *bhikṣu*-bodhisattva Dharmākara's forty-nine vows, the eighteenth rightly dispels [such doubts].[54] How so? Because it makes clear that when an individual reaches the time of death, the Buddha Amitābha, together with his retinue, will appear before him, whereupon with joyful confidence [that individual] will go to Sukhāvatī. As the Buddha Śākyamuni has declared this, [such persons] will come to be exalted individuals (Ārya) during the intermediate state at the moment of death. This has the same significance as does the passage in the *Buddhāvataṃsaka* that begins:
>
> When I come to the time of my death.
> May all obscurations be removed,
> And seeing Amitābha directly
> May I go to Sukhāvatī field.
>
> Again, there are some who say, "In the *Gāthādvayavyākhyāna* [Peking 5503], composed by Ācārya Sundaravyūha, and in the *Sūtrālaṃkārabhāṣya* [Peking 5527] and the *Sūtrālaṃkāravṛttibhāṣya* [Peking 5531], the statement that by praying one may be born in Sukhāvatī is said to be an example of a temporally displaced intention [whereby "rebirth" may refer to a birth many lifetimes removed], so

> even if you were to practice in accord with what is stated in this sūtra, you will not be born in that field in the next life." But this also harms sentient creatures by becoming the basis for the rejection of the doctrine and doubt. It is to be dispelled by this monk's [Dharmākara's] nineteenth vow. How does that dispel it? It is because it says here that it is not enough to have prayed, but that one must also have parted far from the [five] deeds bringing immediate retribution and from the rejection of the doctrine, and have engendered the enlightened attitude tenfold[55]—it says thus that [rebirth in Sukhāvatī] will not be achieved by prayer alone. And it is because it exemplifies a temporally displaced intention only inasmuch as the intention is directed to prayer alone [that is to say, if prayer is taken as the sole relevant factor, the rebirth in Sukhāvatī may be many lifetimes removed]. Therefore, there is no contradiction whatsoever here, and the intentions [of the sūtra and of the aforementioned commentaries] are in accord.
>
> Further, consider whether or not that monk's forty-nine vows were realized or not. If they were realized, then because the eighteenth and nineteenth must have also been realized, it is not appropriate to harbor error and doubt about them. But if they were not realized, that would contradict [Buddha Śākyamuni's] declaration that since that monk had become manifestly and perfectly awakened in Sukhāvatī ten aeons had passed,[56] and also contradict the [declaration of Amitābha's] names and characteristics that were forthcoming when [Ānanda inquired] whether or not he had realized [buddhahood].[57] And it would contradict the assertion that the great sons of the Conqueror [the bodhisattvas], without having fulfilled the three special objectives, do not disclose the genuine limit.[58]
>
> Therefore, suspecting that error about this would arise, the Buddha Śākyamuni well instructed the Conquerors' son Ajita in many ways regarding the faults of harboring doubt, with significant examples and so on, and declared that numberless and immeasurable buddhas of the ten directions spoke similarly. For this reason, having abandoned those faults [of error and doubt], you should believe in just what [the Buddha] has declared and, having once and again accumulated many immeasurable roots of virtue, perform pure prayers once and again. Thus, you must strive decisively. If you do this, there can be no doubt that you will be born miraculously in a lotus in Sukhāvatī, where doubtlessly you will come to possess many virtues in accord with [Dharmākara's] forty-nine vows.[59]

Dol-po-pa's argument makes it clear, I think, just why the Tibetan religious intelligentsia, even while energetically promulgating faith in Amitābha and the aspiration for rebirth in his realm, could not countenance a conception of salvation by grace alone. On purely dogmatic grounds, held to be derived from the larger *Sukhāvatīv-*

yūha sūtra itself, such a teaching was deemed untenable. Rather, Amitābha's unusual grace required the moral effort—and not only the prayer—of the aspirant in order to take effect. Dol-po-pa's selection culled from the *Adhyāśayasaṃcodana sūtra,* which accompanies *The Supreme Means Whereby Self and Others May Be Reborn in Sukhāvatī,* was clearly intended as a proof-text in support of this view.

Before closing this survey of the unfolding of the Pure Land orientation within the major Tibetan Buddhist orders, we must mention briefly the contribution of Rje Tsong-kha-pa Blo-bzang-grags-pa (1357–1419), founder of the Dge-lugs-pa order that has dominated Tibet in recent centuries. His celebrated tract called *Bde-smon zhing mchog sgo 'byed* (The Sukhāvatī prayer—Opening the gate to the supreme field) recapitulates in much detail the larger sūtra's descriptions of Sukhāvatī and the benefits that accrue from rebirth therein.[60] The devoted recollection of these qualities and freedom from all doubt should inform the practice of the prayer for rebirth, and it is Tsong-kha-pa's much elaborated prayer that occupies the final section of the text.

The figures I have discussed in this section were of unparallelled importance for the development of Buddhism in Tibet and their writings would prove to be exceptionally influential down to the present day. The foregoing examples make clear, I think, that without promoting faith in Amitābha and his Pure Land as an exclusive practice for Tibetan Buddhists, all of them—and hence the monastic orders that owed them allegiance—nevertheless gave their support to the conception of Sukhāvatī as an especially appropriate focal point for devotional striving. Devotion in Amitābha, and the prayers and meditations directed to him were thus promulgated with the sanction of Tibet's leading religious authorites. Still, for the most part we have been concerned here with the writings of masters who, though of great importance for Tibetan religious history, were closely studied primarily by the monastic elite, though some of their prayer-texts and other works did become very widely known. It may be, therefore, difficult to judge precisely the extent to which their writings on Sukhāvatī reflect a more generalized orientation in the religious life of Tibet during their time.[61] As suggested earlier, the growing traditions of Avalokiteśvara and Padmasambhava probably did impart some impetus to a popular Pure Land orientation, and it is moreover clear that the masters we have considered here were by no means cut off from such trends in Tibetan Buddhism, though their primary interests often lay in other areas. However this may be, with the seventeenth-century revelations of the tantric *Gnam-chos Bde-chen zhing-sgrub* (The means for the attainment of the field of great bliss, [according to] the celestial doctrine), we do find certain evidence for a broad, popular promulgation of the teaching of salvation in Amitābha's realm.

The Treasures of the "Celestial Doctrine"

The crucial development for the popular Pure Land orientation in Tibet was certainly the revelation, in the form of rediscovered treasures *(gter-ma)*, of tantric texts focusing on Sukhāvatī. Though the revelation of the treasures was a phenomenon that characterized primarily the Rnying-ma-pa tradition, they played some role among the other Buddhist orders as well, above all the Bka'-brgyud-pa.[62] These texts included works concerned with the yogic practice of the transference of consciousness, which was described above. Besides this, the revealed treasures also included liturgical/contemplative cycles known as Bde-chen zhing-sgrub (Means for the Attainment of the Field of Great Bliss), which employ elaborate visualization exercises in which Sukhāvatī itself is conceived as the mandala. It is not yet clear to me just when and where the first Bde-chen zhing-sgrub revelations made their appearance. As we have remarked earlier, during the twelfth century, the Rnying-ma-pa master Kaḥ-thog-pa was inspired to compose a tantric *sādhana* focusing on Amitābha, and it is possible that this work, which I do not believe is yet available, anticipates the Bde-chen zhing-sgrub rites. Certainly, it would not be astonishing to learn of the appearance of works of this type from the twelfth century on.[63]

However questions regarding the origins and development of the genre may be eventually resolved, the most celebrated version of the Bde-chen zhing-sgrub dates only from the seventeenth century, and belongs to the Gnam-chos (Celestial Doctrine) revelations of the child prodigy Mi-'gyur-rdo-rje (1645–1668), which were redacted by the latter's tutor Karma Chags-med, the author of perhaps the most renowned of the Bde-smon prayers.[64] Karma Chags-med provides an account of the origin of the Celestial Doctrine's *Means for the*

Attainment of the Field of Great Bliss in his introduction to the instructions on the transference of consciousness that are found therein (text 13 in the collection described in note 64) and included in most editions of these revelations:

> If you ask, what is this doctrine's history in brief? In the *Rgyal po bka'i thang yig* (The testimonial record of the king), which is included in the *Bka' thang sde lnga* (The five testimonial records), it says that during the end of the age [the period of degeneration] thirty-three Vidyādharas, masters of secret mantra, will arrive. In the prophecy of their supreme enlightenment it says:
>
> In the field of Śākya[muni], called Mdo-khams,
> A yoginī who practices the Mahāyāna of secret mantra,
> The master of mantra [named] Rdo-rje-drag-po will arise.
> Transferring from that [lifetime], he will practice extensively.
> To the north of this trichiliocosm,
> In the pure field called Sandalwood Grove,
> He will become a Tathāgata, a conductor of persons,
> Protecting an assembly of three thousand teachers of the
> Unsurpassed [Yoga],
> And called the Conqueror Jñāna-Samantabhadra.
>
> Thus, the emanational embodiment Mi-'gyur-rdo-rje was prophesied in this and many other treasures. In essence, he was the combined emanation of the great translator Vairocana [of Pa-gor, eighth century] and Shud-pu Dpal-seng, and, practicing the conduct of enlightenment, will be the future Buddha called Jñāna-Samantabhadra. In his thirteenth year, the Golden Pendant year (*gser-'phyang, hemalamba* = 1657), on the seventh day of the month of Vaiśakha, he actually beheld the countenances of the trinity of buddha Amitābha and his foremost attendants [the bodhisattvas Avalokiteśvara and Mahāsthāmaprāpta], limitlessly splendorous and exceedingly great, the size of a mountain. [Amitābha] actually bestowed on him the *Bde-chen zhing gi sgrub thabs* (The *sādhana* of the field of great bliss, text 3), *Rmi lam du bde chen zhing mjal thabs* (The means to encounter the field of great bliss in dreams), *Snang ba mtha' yas kyi tshe sgrub* (The longevity rites of Amitābha, appended to text 3), *Bde-chen zhing gi 'pho ba* (The transference [of consciousness at death] to the field of great bliss, text 13), *Bde-chen zhing gi gsol 'debs* (The reverential petition of the field of great bliss, text 1), *Bde-chen zhing gi smon lam* (The prayer of the field of great bliss, included in text 3), and the *Bde-chen zhing gi dbang* (The empowerment of the field of great bliss, text 11). Again, that evening, when he once again beheld Buddha Amitābha and his attendants, they bestowed on him both the *Rmi lam gzung ba'i gsol 'debs* (The reverential petition for grasping [one's] dreams) and the *Rmi lam gzung ba'i zhal gdams* (The oral instructions for grasping [one's] dreams).[65]

Karma Chags-med, as the redactor of Mi-'gyur-dro-rje's revelations, expanded them to include a number of ancillary works, such as instructions on the visualizations to be practiced with the *sādhana* (texts 5 and 10) and rites for funerals and cremations (texts 10 and 11). These latter were to become particularly popular mortuary texts throughout the Tibetan world, and their spread no doubt both reflected and reinforced the close association between the Tibetan cult of Amitābha and the rites of the dead.[66] Similar remarks apply to the cycle's *Transference of Consciousness at Death to the Field of Great Bliss,* which has enjoyed a very widespread promulgation among works of this type.[67] In later times, the fourteenth Karma-pa hierarch Theg-mchog-rdo-rje (1799–1869) added to the cycle a ritual for the communal feast (*tshogs-mchod,* Skt. *gaṇapūjā,* text 7), to be performed in tandem with the basic *sādhana* (text 3). As the latter is the linchpin of the cycle as a whole, my remarks here will focus primarily on it.

The practitioner is to begin by taking refuge in the Three Jewels and in the Three Roots of tantric practice (guru, deity, and *ḍākiṇī*), followed by the recitation of an abbreviated formula for the blessing of the offerings.[68] The offerings may be visualized, for the text specifies that it is not necessary to install a physical mandala or votive offering cake *(gtor-ma).*[69] With these simple preparations, the visualization practice may begin.[70]

One is to visualize oneself as a white bodhisattva, which Karma Chags-med in his commentaries (texts 5 and 10) specifies to be the seated four-armed Avalokiteśvara. One faces Amitābha, visualized as seated in meditational posture on a lotus, red in color and holding a begging bowl in his two hands. He is accompanied by the standing bodhisattvas Avalokiteśvara, to his right, and Vajrapāṇi, in the form of Mahāsthāmaprāpta, to his left.[71] The former is white, four-armed, with two hands pressed together in prayer and a second pair of hands holding a rosary and lotus. Mahāsthāmaprāpta is blue, two-armed, and holds the *vajra* and bell. They are surrounded by innumerable buddhas, bodhisattvas, and arhats. Rays of light pour forth from the head-, throat-, and heart-centers of the three principle deities and, proceeding to Sukhāvatī, invite Amitābha and his retinue to enter into and to bless the visualized assembly. After requesting that the Buddha and his accompanying divinities remain present, the practitioner salutes them with an appropriate verse of homage. Light once again pours forth, this time inviting the Jinas of the five families to grant *abhiṣeka*. When this is conferred Amitābha is adorned with Amitāyus on his crown.

In the main body of the *sādhana* that follows, the practitioner worships Amitābha with a visualized series of offerings, described in a lyrical series of verses, ranking among the finest examples of Tibetan popular devotional poetry. It is important, I think, to recall that during the past three centuries these verses have no doubt most often been sung by monks and nuns of humble status and by lay devotees, who have enjoyed relatively little in the way of material luxury. The offerings begin with the classical Indian hospitality bestowed on a welcome guest:

> *Hūṃ!* To Amitābha's body I offer a bath
> Of fragrant, perfumed water.
> Though divinities possess no taint,
> May this be the coincidence for purifying our sins!
> *Oṃ sarba ta thā ga ta a bhi ṣe ka te sa ma ya śrī ye hūṃ!*[72]
>
> *Hūṃ!* To Amitābha's body I offer a towel
> Of white cotton, soft and scented.
> Though his body possesses no taint,
> May this be the coincidence for our freedom from pain!
>
> *Hūṃ!* To the Conqueror's body I offer clothing,
> These beauteous ochre robes.
> Though his body catches no chill,
> May this be the coincidence for the growth of our vital glow!
>
> *Hūṃ!* To the bodies of the Conqueror's two sons I offer
> These beautiful adornments of gems.
> Though their bodies are without ornamentation,
> May this be the coincidence for magnifying our splendor!
>
> *Hūṃ!* To the mouths of the Conqueror and his sons I offer
> This refreshing water, excellent in eight ways,[73]
> Though their mouths never know thirst,
> May this be the coincidence for our freedom from pain!
>
> *Hūṃ!* To them I offer perfumed bathing water
> To cleanse Amitābha's feet.
> Let my ordinary body
> Be visualized as the yellow goddess of bathing waters,
> And offer worship at his feet.

The series of offerings continues according to the same pattern, the practitioner visualizing in turn the goddess of flowers to delight the eye, of perfumes for the nose, of lamps to be held in the hand, of unguents for the body, of delicacies for the taste, and of musical instruments for the ear. The final offering in this series is the beautiful wisdom goddess (Vidyā) herself, conferring delight. Each of these verses is to be chanted melodiously, to the accompaniment of bells and drums, as one visualizes the bestowal and acceptance of the offering. A second series of visualized offerings follows, including the eight auspicious emblems and substances, the jewelled mandala of Mt. Meru, and the "esoteric offerings" *(nang-mchod)* of nectar-ambrosia, votive cakes, and transsubstantiated menstrual blood *(rakta)*. This segment of the worship-service is brought to a conclusion with hymns in praise of Amitābha's body, speech, and mind, together with contrition for those acts whereby the practitioner may have violated his or her initiatory commitments (Skt. *samaya*, Tib. *dam-tshig*). In its development so far, the Bde-chen-zhing-sgrub adheres closely to the pattern of Buddhist tantric services of the type frequently known as *Gurupūjāvidhi (Bla-ma-mchod-pa'i cho-ga)*, "rites for the worship of the guru."[74] With the completion of the worship-service, one requests the blessings of Amitābha and his retinue and then, maintaining the visualization, settles into the recitation of his mantra, *Oṃ Amidhewa Hrīḥ!*

In concluding the session of practice, it is usually the custom to perform the brief longevity rites of Amitābha that were also revealed in Mi-'gyur-rdo-rje's visions. The Karma-pa's ritual for the communal feast may be performed as well, particularly on the tenth and twenty-fifth days of the lunar month. After these rites are completed, the visualization is dissolved and the practitioner rests in the contemplation of the coalescence of clarity and emptiness *(gsal-stong-zung-'jug)*.[75] The service is brought to a close with dedicatory prayers, most often including Karma Chags-med's *Bde-smon*.

The same ritual, up to the performance of the mantra, is used also as the introduction to the appropriate funerary or cremation rites, as may be required. One of the admonitions here addressed to the deceased well epitomizes the standpoint of what I have been calling the Tibetan Pure Land orientation:

> *Hūṃ!* You who are deceased!
> The western field of Sukhāvatī
> Is the field of greatest advantage
> And hence is the sole pure abode.
>
> In the southwestern land of cannibal ogres,
> Dwells Guru Padmasambhava.
> You'll be easily born there, but to little advantage.[76]

Apart from that are other buddha-fields,
Realms of the Conquerors of the four families.[77]
It's difficult to be born in them, so forget it!
Go to Sukhāvatī instead![78]

No doubt it will seem to some readers that here we do have an exhortation to an exclusive faith in Amitābha and his realm. Nevertheless, it is clear that the Celestial Doctrine revelations, constituting a vast ritual corpus focusing on the cults of Padmasambhava and many other divinities, do not in fact seek to underwrite an exclusivism of this kind.[79] The exhortation we find here must be explained, I think, by its context: the deceased, thought to be now wandering among the phantasmagoria of the *bar-do,* requires nothing so much as a point of clear and certain focus. Under such circumstances, Sukhāvatī must be considered far and away the best destination.

It is apparent from these descriptions that the Bde-chen zhing sgrub rites adopt tantric means to fulfill the conditions required for effective prayer. As Ma-cig had said, "with ardent exertion you must pray, *while recollecting the array of the Sukhāvatī field and its qualities.*" Rje Tsong-kha-pa's detailed descriptions of Sukhāvatī must also be understood in this light. Clearly the *sādhana* we have considered greatly intensifies that recollection and reinforces the practitioner's assurance that he or she may enter into a direct and palpable communion with Amitābha and his circle. For one who can achieve this, ardent devotion comes easy. Indeed, devotional practice and tantrism here clearly go hand in hand. As Buddhist tantrism in general speaks of attaining enlightenment "in one life and one body" *(tshe gcig lus gcig),* so, with the rise of the Bde-chen zhing sgrub teachings, a means has been found to anticipate rebirth in Sukhavatī by realizing its presence here and now.[80]

Sukhāvatī and the Progressive Path

Not long ago I published an edition of the works of Glag-bla Bsod-nams-chos-'grub (1862–1944), a well-regarded recent Rnying-ma-pa master, who had been active and influential earlier in this century in Khams, far eastern Tibet (modern Ganze district, Sichuan province).[81] I had first heard of Glag-bla during the early 1970s, when I was studying with the late Mkhan-po Sangs-rgyas-bstan-'dzin

(1924–1990) of Ser-lo-dgon-pa, Nepal. Mkhan-po Sangs-rgyas-bstan-'dzin's excellent personal collection of the writings of Khams-pa masters associated with the so-called Ris-med (nonpartisan) movement of the nineteenth century included Glag-bla's extensive commentary on the *Bde-smon* of Karma Chags-med. The tantrism of the Bde-chen zhing sgrub according to Mi-'gyur-rdo-rje's Celestial Doctrine had always been closely associated with the promotion of the normative ethical concerns of the Vinaya and the Mahāyāna path, and Karma Chags-med's *Bde-smon* played an important role in this; for that work transforms the aspiration for rebirth in the field of Great Bliss into the occasion for a careful review of the path and its commitments. Glag-bla's treatise, which was also among his few works to have appeared outside of Tibet (it was published at least twice in India during the 1970s), seemed to suggest that Glag-bla, like Chags-med himself, had a special interest in reaching beyond the restricted circle of scholars in the monastic colleges and bringing the teaching to a broader range of common monks and laypersons. On the basis of the *Bde-smon,* Glag-bla had elaborated a comprehensive guidebook to the path in a style that lent itself to public discourse and preaching.

It was only when I was able to collect, in 1992, all of Glag-bla's available writings that the broader context of his commentary on the *Bde-smon* became apparent, for the fifth and final volume of his collected writings contains his commentary on Chags-med's prayer accompanied by an associated ritual for the realization of Amitābha's Pure Land, and Glag-bla's own abbreviated version of the *Bde-smon* and further commentary on that as well. Together these writings constitute a complete system for study and ritual/contemplative practice, focusing on the goal of rebirth in Sukhāvatī immediately following this lifetime.

Given what we have seen, however, it would seem that Glag-bla's project was by no means entirely unprecedented. What perhaps distinguishes it from earlier contributions to what I have called the Pure Land orientation in Tibetan Buddhism is the extent and clarity of his elaboration of a complete program of spiritual training in which Sukhāvatī remains the central focus throughout. In order to appreciate better the contribution made by his expansive commentary on Karma Chags-med's *Bde-smon,* we need to review briefly the structure of that work.

The *Bde-smon* is traditionally analyzed as a composition in four major sections: (1) the repeated recollection of the array of the realm [of Sukhāvatī]; (2) the accumulation, by various means, of limitless roots of virtue; (3) engendering the will to supreme enlightenment; and (4) dedicating those roots of virtue to be the basis for birth in Sukhāvatī.[82] The first section (verses 2r1–3r8, following Peter Schwieger's numbering) sets the stage for the prayer as a whole, briefly describing the Sukhāvatī field, with Buddha Amitābha surrounded by his retinue, including Avalokiteśvara and Mahāsthāmaprāpta. It is referred to as a "repeated" recollection, not owing to any repetition in the text itself, but because it is understood that the devotee must repeatedly strive to imagine Sukhāvatī, to visualize the very presence of Amitābha as the prayer is performed.

The section that follows (verses 3r9–7r5) is very much elaborated and is based on the sevenfold worship service that, with few variations, is pervasive in the devotional literature of the Mahāyāna: salutations, offering, contrition, sympathetic joy, encouraging the turning of the wheel of the dharma, prayers that the buddhas not pass into final nirvana, and the dedication of merits.[83] Each of these is described in detail, making this portion of Karma Chags-med's prayer in fact a richly developed Mahāyāna liturgy. The cultivation of the enlightened attitude is then the subject of three four-line verses; the fourth and final section, the dedication for rebirth in Sukhāvatī (verses 7v2–12v12), returns to the description of the paradise to which one aspires, closely recapitulating the depiction of its attributes in the larger *Sukhāvatīvyūha sūtra.*

What is perhaps most remarkable about Glag-bla's commentary on all this is the great emphasis he gives to the details of the sevenfold service that constitutes part two. In fact, he uses this section of the prayer as the basis for setting forth what is, in effect, a relatively thorough, general introduction to the Mahāyāna path, such as one finds developed in a somewhat more technical manner in the Lam-rim literature, the Tibetan genre devoted to the progressive path of Mahāyāna practice. Glag bla, in short, bears out Gregory Schopen's suggestion, in connection with the cult of Sukhāvatī in Indian Buddhism, that Sukhāvatī is better regarded as an idealized goal of Mahāyāna practice in general than as the crystallization of a particular sectarian adherence.[84]

The Place of the Pure Land in Tibet

The Tibetan Sukhāvatī orientation, while nevertheless exhibiting elements of the devotional character often attributed to East Asian Pure Land traditions, also clearly reveals, to varying degrees, the synthetic tendencies of Tibetan Buddhism. Thus, as we have just seen, the progressive path of the Mahāyāna, which was normative in Tibet, informed well-known prayers for rebirth in Sukhāvatī, and this is made fully explicit in the commentaries on them. Similarly, ritual and visualization texts such as the *Means for the Attainment of the Field of Great Bliss* and the innumerable rites of transference demonstrate that the aspiration for the realization of Sukhāvatī was fully assimilated within tantric milieux as well. Further evidence of the same tendency I am describing may be found in a prayer from the revelations of the great nineteenth-century Rdzogs-chen master, Khrag-'thung Bdud-'joms-rdo-rje:

> *E-ma-ho!*
> In the self-manifest, pure expanse that is the real Akaniṣṭha,
> The magical field that is gnosis arrayed,
> Is the Dharmakāya of the ground, the Conqueror Amitābha,
> Resplendent among the assemblies of bodhisattvas,
> who are his own expressive play.
> By the expressive power of evident wisdom and gnosis,
> At that time when appearances transform [at death],
> May I, reaching the limit of supreme, primordial confidence,
> Conclusively fulfill both ends, and disclose the four embodiments.[85]

In these verses, we find devotion to Amitābha fully harmonized with the Rdzogs-chen teachings of the *bar-do.* Sukhāvatī is here identified with Akaniṣṭha *('og-min),* which is itself no longer the name of a particular paradise, but rather a metonymic expression for the primordial ground in which the Buddha's gnosis is disclosed. From the position we have now reached, it becomes evident that Sukhāvatī is not, for Tibetan Buddhists, the goal of an exclusive allegiance to a particular sectarian strain of the Mahāyāna, but is, rather, an encompassing end that embraces all the possible goals of the Mahāyāna and so accords with all approaches to the path, tantric and non-tantric.

Pure Land Buddhism is frequently thought to be a peculiarly East Asian development, in which devotion to Amitābha and the aspiration for rebirth in his field came to have established cultic identities quite apart from other aspects of the Mahāyāna, a tendency that finally crystallized in Japan with the emergence of a separate and distinctive sectarian trend. By contrast, what I have shown here is that in Tibet, while there was indeed a powerful devotional current that maintained a comparable orientation, the Pure Land orientation developed in a manner that was fully integral to other major facets of Tibetan Buddhism. Though this process did of course involve Tibetan sectarian developments to some extent, there is no evidence that sectarian identity was ever peculiarly tied to the Pure Land of Amitābha. His was ever an inclusive cult, involving Tibetan Buddhists overall.

Nevertheless, as I have suggested earlier, there is some reason to hold that Amitābha and Sukhāvatī did enjoy privileged positions in the Tibetan religious imagination. The questions we must pose, but which can only be answered in outline given the available materials, concern the role of the Pure Land orientation in Tibetan social history generally. As I have shown above, there is some reason to believe that certain of the Tibetan Pure Land teachings were addressed primarily to common monks and laypersons rather than the learned monastic elites (who, however, did play authorial and pastoral roles here, as did Karma Chags-med and Glag-bla Bsod-nams-chos-'grub). And my own, somewhat informal, observations over the years suggest that liturgies such as the *Means for the Attainment of the Field of Great Bliss* of the Celestial Doctrine revelations enjoyed a great grassroots popularity.

In reflecting on this, my thoughts inevitably return to my meetings with Dge-slong Pa-sangs during the monsoon rains in Rol-ba-gling almost thirty years ago, and to the sense he conveyed to me of Sukhāvatī as a concrete destination. Taking our lead from Steven Collins' suggestive analysis of Buddhist conceptions of "felicity" in traditional, agrarian societies, it seems clear that the ideal of Sukhāvatī succeeded in Tibet precisely because it captured the real aspirations of the peasants and nomads, who knew all too well toil and hardship from cradle to grave. For Tibet, far from being the earthly paradise of the Western popular imagination, was, like other premodern societies, one in which the vast majority had to labor for their existence with backs bent and for that of their social superiors as well. A vision of ease, if one was available, was preeminently the gift of religion.[86]

From the Tibetan Buddhist clerical point of view, too, the more or less "natural" fit between the ideal of Sukhāvatī and the common wish for happiness, set over and against a life of trials, was felicitous from at least two perspectives. On the one hand, most religious were, after all, products of Tibetan society generally, and so shared many of the aspirations of their countrymen. Indeed, among them, the vision of the lay life as one of almost unbroken misery was systematically reinforced in the elaborated teachings on suffering found in the elementary manuals of all sectarian traditions.[87] In the first instance, therefore, Sukhāvatī embodied and focused the proper orientations of the religious vocation; Sukhāvatī served, in effect, as the cosmological projection of Tibetan Buddhist monasticism. But, on the other hand, for those whose religious journeys had taken them into the stratospheric heights of abstraction—whether through the philosophical investigations of a Tsong-kha-pa or the Rdzogs-chen meditations of a Bdud-'joms-rdo-rje—Sukhāvatī supplied both an organizing metaphor and a bridge, whereby the insights gleaned at the farthest reaches of the path might yet be articulated in resonance with the hopes and fears that impelled them to embark on the path at the outset.

Notes

1. The remarkable popularity of this prayer is demonstrated by the numerous manuscript and xylographic editions one encounters throughout the Tibetan world. The edition I was given in Rol-ba-gling was struck from blocks carved at Dung-srung Gu-ru Lha-khang in the Darjeeling area of West Bengal in about 1926. For an edition and translation of Karma Chags-med's *Rnam dag bde chen zhing gi smon lam,* see Peter Schwieger, *Ein tibetisches Wuschgebet um Wiedergeburt in der Sukhāvatī* (St. Augustin: VGH Wissenschaftsverlag, 1978). I shall refer to this edition throughout this chapter, though using the Wylie transcription system in favor of that employed by Schwieger. The author Karma Chags-med is often referred to by his "Sanskrit" pen name Rāga-a-sya (which Western scholars sometimes give as Rāgāsya, as if this made the Sanskrit any better!).

2. Cf. Schwieger, *Ein tibetisches Wuschgebet,* 66: *rin chen sa gzhi khod snyoms lag mthil ltar,* "The bejewelled ground is even and flat, like the palm of the hand." Here and in the notes that immediately follow, Karma Chags-med's images are of course derived directly from the larger *Sukhāvatīvyūha sūtra.*

3. Cf. ibid., 67: *bdud rtsi'i rdzing dang chu klung de rnams kyang/ dro grang gang 'dod de la de ltar 'byung,* "Those ambrosia ponds and streams, moreover, flow hot or cold, just as you wish."

4. Cf. ibid.: *bya dang ljon shing chu klung rol mo sogs/ thos par 'dod na snyan pa'i chos sgra sgrogs,* "The birds, wishing trees, waters, musical instruments, and so on, proclaim the sweet words of the Dharma whenever you wish to hear them."

5. Cf. ibid.: *bud med med kyang sprul pa'i lha mo tshogs / mchod pa'i lha mo du*

mas rtag tu mchod, "Though there are no women, there is an assembly of emanational goddesses, many offering goddesses perpetually bestowing their offerings."

6. The most popular female divinity in Tibet, Tārā, being an emanation of Avalokiteśvara, is equally a member of the same "family." The epic hero Gesar, being an emanation of Padmasambhava, is often assigned here as well.

7. See Todd T. Lewis, "From Generalized Goal to Tantric Subordination: Sukhāratī in the Indic Buddhist Traditions of Nepal," in this volume.

8. Selections of such prayers for rebirth are usually included in the collections known as *Chos-spyod* (dharma-practice [manuals]) that contain the main recitation texts for a given order or monastic community.

9. See now especially Toni Huber, *The Cult of Pure Crystal Mountain: Popular Pilgrimage and Visionary Landscape in Southeastern Tibet* (New York: Oxford University Press, 1999).

10. *Bde-smon-phyogs-bsgrigs,* 2 vols. (Chengdu: Si-khron-mi-rigs-dpe-skrun-khang, 1994).

11. Convenient introductions to these and other "popular" aspects of Tibetan religion may be found in Donald Lopez, Jr., ed., *Tibetan Religions in Practice* (Princeton: Princeton University Press, 1997).

12. Nevertheless, as Jonathan Silk has kindly brought to my attention, there has been a body of Japanese scholarship devoted to "Tibetan Pure Land thought" *(Chibetto no Jōdo Shisō).* Among the authors who have contributed in this regard, he notes Akamatsu Kōshō, Kajihama Ryōshun, Munekawa Shūman, Nakamura Hajime, Odani Nobuchiyo, Onoda Shunzō, Tokiya Kōki, and a Tibetan scholar resident in Japan, Tshul khrims skal bzang. Some of the material I consider in the present chapter has been discussed in the writings of these scholars, though, because I do not read Japanese, it is impossible for me to review their work beyond the general descriptions I have been given. Despite this, the material I am presenting here is largely new to anglophone readers, refers to some texts that have not, to my knowledge, been considered elsewhere (even by the Japanese Pure Land scholars), and offers what I hope is a novel synthesis concerning the general question of "Pure Land Buddhism in Tibet."

13. Galen Amstutz, *Interpreting Amida: History and Orientalism in the Study of Pure Land Buddhism* (Albany: State University of New York Press, 1997). A similar bias in Western views of Tibetan Buddhism has been noted in Peter Bishop, *Dreams of Power: Tibetan Buddhism and the Western Imagination* (London: The Althone Press, 1993), 87: "The one-sided technocratic fantasy about Tibetan Buddhism can also be seen in the comparative failure of Pure Land Buddhism to stimulate the Western imagination. Despite the overwhelming popularity of Pure Land beliefs in Tibet (and in all other Mahayana countries), it has received very little emphasis in Western commentary. This may be because such Buddhism is not readily reduced to a technique, nor is it conducive to scientific status, and in addition it relies almost totally upon faith. Hence Pure Land beliefs do not easily fit the dominant scientific image that the West seems to want from Buddhism."

14. Matthew T. Kapstein, *The Tibetan Assimilation of Buddhism: Conversion, Contestation, and Memory* (New York: Oxford University Press, 2000), 7–8.

15. Pelliot tibétain 239, translated in Kapstein, *The Tibetan Assimilation of Buddhism,* 8.

16. For a translation, see W. Y. Evans-Wentz, ed., *The Tibetan Book of the Dead*, trans. Kazi Dawa-Samdup (1927; reprint, London: Oxford University Press, 1960). Also Francesca Freemantle and Chogyam Trungpa, *The Tibetan Book of the Dead* (Boston and London: Shambhala Publications, 1987). Chap. 2 of Donald S. Lopez, Jr., *Prisoners of Shangri-la: Tibetan Buddhism and the West* (Chicago and London: The University of Chicago Press, 1998), provides an interesting and thorough account of the history of the reception of the "Tibetan Book of the Dead" in the West.

17. Refer to Jonathan A. Silk, *The Virtues of Amitābha: A Tibetan Praise Poem from Dunhuang* (Kyoto: Ryukoku University, 1993).

18. Pelliot tibétain 16, 1.27b.2–28a.1 (reproduced in Ariane Macdonald and Yoshiro Imaeda, *Choix de documents tibétains* [Paris: Bibliothèque Nationale, 1978]):

> *sangs rgyas snang ba mtha' yas thams kyïs* [sic?] *sangs rgyas thams cad kyï zhïng gï mchog ngan song gsum dang bgegs brgyad kyï myïng myï gragste/ lha'ï longs spyod kyï rgyan thams cad kyïs brgyan pa na/ mya ngan las 'da' ba'ï myïng myị srid pa na bzhugs shïng 'jïgs rten las 'das pa'ï skyid pa phun sum tshogs pa thams cad kyis brgyan pa'i zhïng na/ sems can gyï don mdzad cing lhag pa thugs rje che bas mtsan brjod pa tsam kyis sdïg pa thams cad 'byang la sangs rgyas kyï zhïng der skye bar byïn kyïs rlobs pa'ï sku'ï gzugs brnyan bzhugs par gsol pa dang.*

19. The De-ga G.yu-tshal temple and its Dunhuang documentation are the subjects of a study in progess, tentatively entitled, "The Tibetan Treaty Temple of De-ga G.yu-tshal: Identification and Iconography," in Matthew T. Kapstein, ed., *Buddhism between Tibet and China* (forthcoming).

20. This, of course, raises the question of Song period contacts with Tibetan Buddhism and possible influences. All in all, it must be said that, based on evidence currently available, direct Song interaction with Tibet was rather slight and perhaps limited to local contact in the extreme eastern quarters of the Tibetan cultural sphere, where in any case Tibetan relations with China were largely mediated by the Xixia and Nanzhao kingdoms, to the northwest and southwest of China, respectively. In the absence of further evidence, it seems most prudent to withhold judgment regarding Song Buddhist influence on Tibetan developments.

21. *Shangs-pa bka'-brgyud bla-rabs-kyi rnam-thar,* Gangs-can rig-mdzod Series 28 (Lhasa: Bod-ljongs bod-yig dpe-rnying dpe-skrun-khang, 1996), 60; compare also pp. 57–58.

22. Ibid., 10, 35; G. N. Roerich, trans., *The Blue Annals,* 2d ed. (Delhi: Motilal Banarsidass, 1976), 271.

23. On the development of the Tibetan Avalokiteśvara cult during the period concerned, see Matthew T. Kapstein, "Remarks on the *Maṇi-bka'-'bum* and the Cult of Avalokiteśvara in Tibet," in *Tibetan Buddhism: Reason and Revelation,* eds. R. Davidson and S. Goodman (Albany: State University of New York Press, 1992), 79–93, 163–169; revised in Kapstein, *The Tibetan Assimilation of Buddhism,* chap. 8.

24. See, for example, the remarks below on Kaz-thog Dam-pa Bde-gshegs and his regent, Gtsang-ston-pa.

25. Kapstein, *The Tibetan Assimilation of Buddhism,* chap. 8, esp. pp. 149–150, 160–161.

26. This apparently derisive description of Tuṣita stems from the fact that it is a mundane paradise, whose status as a sort of pure land derives from the presence of the Buddha-to-be (in our age, Maitreya). In this it differs from those genuine pure

lands that transcend all mundane heavens and are generated entirely by the aspiration of a Buddha.

27. Ma-cig Labs-kyi sgron-ma, *Sras Rgyal ba don grub la mkha' 'gro'i gsang tshig tu gdams pa dam tshig nyi shu rtsa gcig pa,* quoted in *Zhing dbang,* (text 9 described in n. 64 below), folios 3b5–5b4:

> *sangs rgyas myur du thob par 'dod pa la: sangs rgyas kyi zhing khams rnam dag gcig tu smon lam gdab dgos: zhing khams mi 'dra ba bgrang gis mi longs shing: brjod pas mtha' chod dka' ba rnams yod tshul gsungs nas: de la bde ba can ma gtogs pa'i gzhan zhing khams rab rnams su skye ba la: sgrib gnyis ma lus pa chod nas: sa brgyad pa yan chod thob dgos: zhing khams 'bring du skye ba la yang: nyon mongs pa'i sgrib pa phra ba'i phra ba yang ma lus pa chod nas: sgom lam dang po yan chad thob dgos: zhing khams tha ma na yang bdag 'dzin rtsa ba nas chod cing: bdag med chos nyid kyi bden pa mthong lam thob dgos: mthong lam ma thob kyi bar du smon lam btab kyang mi 'grub: mthong lam ma thob kyang: dam tshig bslab bya'i tshul khrims rnams la skyon phra ba'i phra ba tsam yang ma zhugs shing: sdig pa'i dag shan dang: dge ba'i phogs rnams sgrub pa dang: smon lam la 'bad nu dga' ldan la sogs pa'i zhing khams chung ngu 'ga' zhig tu skye rung ba tsam yang yod par 'dug ste: de yang dka' bar gda'o: zhing khams de rnams su nyon mongs pa'i khrod na gnas pa'i: so so'i skye bo tha mal pa'i skye gnas ni ma yin pas: da rung smon lam ring du gdab par bya'o: de bas na tha mal pa'i gang zag nyon mongs pa can rnams ni: sangs rgyas kyi zhing du skye mi srid pa yin te: 'on kyang sangs rgyas 'od dpag med kyi smon lam gyi stobs kyis bde ba can gyi zhing khams de ru skye ba ni: mgon po 'od dpag med pa nyid kyis zhal gyis bzhes pa yin pas na: bde ba can du skye ba'i smon lam sgo thams cad nas 'bad dgos so: de yang the tshom dang: som nyi dang: le lo dang: spang blang med par: nges shes dang brtson 'grus drag po'i sgo nas: bde ba can gyi zhing bkod dang: yon tan rnams dran par byas la smon lam gdab par bya'o: bde ba can du tha mal pa nyon mongs pa dang bcas pa'i so so'i gang zag rnams kyang skye rung bas lhag pa yin pa dang: der skyes nas kyang ci bsam pa'i 'dod pa thams cad kyang bsam ma thag nas 'grub pa 'grub pa yin cing: nyon mongs pa'i sgrib pa phra ba tsam gyis kyang mi gos pa dang: gzhan yang sangs rgyas kyi zhing khams gang 'dod du 'gro bas chog pas lhag pa dang: gzhan gyi zhing khams las sangs rgyas pa yang myur bas lhag pa dang: de la sogs pa'i yon tan bsam gyis mi khyab pa dang ldan pa'i: bde ba can las zin thag nye ba'i zhing khams ni gzhan du med pas: bde ba can du skye ba'i smon lam la 'bad pa ni gal shin tu che: zhes gsungs so:*

On Ma-cig and her place in the development of Tibetan Buddhism, see Janet Gyatso, "The Development of the Gcod Tradition," in *Sounding in Tibetan Civilization,* eds. Barbara Nimri Aziz and Matthew Kapstein (New Delhi: Manohar, 1985), 320–342; Giacomella Orofino, *Contributo allo studio dell'insegnamento di Ma gcig lab sgron* (Naples: Instituto Universitario Orientale, 1987); Jérôme Edou, *Machig Labdrön and the Foundations of Chöd* (Ithaca: Snow Lion Publications, 1996).

28. The passage cited is itself introduced by Karma Chags-med with a statement of Ma-cig's certain authority. The second citation is found in his celebrated *Ri-chos mtshams-kyi zhal-gdams.* The passage in question is reproduced in *Bde-smon phyogs-bsgrigs,* 2.320.

29. Chap. 8 of Kapstein, *The Tibetan Assimilation of Buddhism,* describes the early

elaboration of the Tibetan traditions of Avalokiteśvara and Padmasambhava, and details previous contributions to this area of research.

30. *Bka'-chems ka-khol-ma* (Lanzhou: Kan-su'u mi-rigs dpe-skrun-khang, 1989). According to tradition, this work is a *gter-ma,* revealed by Atiśa in Lhasa during the mid-eleventh century. However this may be, versions of the work appear to have been in circulation by about the mid-twelfth century. See Helmut Eimer, "Die Auffindung de *bKa' chems ka khol ma:* Quellenkritische Uberlegungen," in *Contributions on Tibetan Language, History and Culture,* eds. Ernst Steinkellner and Helmut Tauscher (Vienna: Arbeitskreis fur Tibetische und Buddhistische Studien Universität Wien, 1983), 45–51.

31. *Bka'-chems ka-khol-ma,* 13–14.

32. *Slob-dpon Padma'i rnam-thar zangs-gling-ma* (Chengdu: Si khron mi rigs dpe skrun-khang, 1989), 3.

33. Dudjom Rinpoche, Jikdrel Yeshe Dorje, *The Nyingma School of Tibetan Buddhism: Its Fundamentals and History,* trans. Gyurme Dorje and Matthew Kapstein (Boston: Wisdom Publications, 1991), 1:691.

34. *Bde-smon-phyogs-bsgrigs,* 1.159–163. On the Mahāyoga system of the Rnying-ma-pa, as presented doctrinally, see Dudjom Rinpoche, *The Nyingma School of Tibetan Buddhism,* 1:275–283.

35. Dudjom Rinpoche, *The Nyingma School of Tibetan Buddhism,* 1:693.

36. Throughout this chapter I generally render Tib. *smon-lam,* which is the translation equivalent to Skt. *praṇidhāna,* as "prayer." However, in many canonical contexts it is more accurately interpreted as meaning "vow." "Prayerful aspiration" in fact best captures the sense of the Tibetan, but in most cases I have opted to retain just "prayer" so as to avoid wordiness, as well as to underscore the clearly devotional connotations of the term when used to refer to a genre of liturgical text.

37. P. L. Vaidya, ed., *Saddharmpuṇḍarīkasūtram,* Buddhist Sanskrit Texts Series, no. 6 (Darbhanga: Mithila Institute, 1960), 256; P. L. Vaidya, ed., *Gaṇḍavyūhasūtram,* Buddhist Sanskrit Texts Series, no. 5 (Darbhanga: Mithila Institute, 1960), 435–436.

38. Silk, *The Virtues of Amitābha.*

39. See, for instance, the entry "Amitābha" in Marie-Thérèse de Mallman, *Introduction à l'iconographie du tântrisme bouddhique* (Paris: Adrien Maisonneuve, 1986), 94–96.

40. Particularly prominent here is the entire ritual genre known as *tshe-sgrub* (Skt. *āyuṣ sādhana*), "means for the attainment of longevity."

41. Cf. my remarks on this in "The *Sprul-sku's* Miserable Lot: Critical Voices from Eastern Tibet," in *Amdo Tibetans in Transition: Society and Culture in the Post-Mao Era,* ed. Toni Huber (Leiden: E. J. Brill, 2002).

42. Mar-pa lo-tā-ba and Dpal-'byor-don-grub, *Rtsa rlung 'phrul 'khor* (Chengdu: Si khron mi rigs dpe skrun khang, 1995), 437.

43. See Matthew T. Kapstein, "A Tibetan Festival of Rebirth Reborn: The 1992 Revival of the Drigung Powa Chenmo," in *Buddhism in Contemporary Tibet: Religious Revival and Cultural Identity,* eds. Melvyn C. Goldstein and Matthew T. Kapstein (Berkeley: University of California Press, 1998).

44. *Bde-smon-phyogs-bsgrigs,* 1.192–197, 207–211.

45. We have seen above that Matisāra *(blo-gros snying-po)* was the name by which Kaḥ-thog-pa Dam-pa Bde-gshegs, who was 'Bri-gung skyob-pa's senior contempo-

rary, would be known as a bodhisattva in Sukhāvatī. I have not yet determined whether this is the reference intended, or if there were wider traditions concerning a bodhisattva so named.

46. *Bde-smon-phyogs-bsgrigs,* 1.171–172.

47. Sa-skya Paṇḍita Kun-dga'-rgyal-mtshan, *Sa paṇ kun dga' rgyal mtshan gyi gsung 'bum,* Gangs-can rig-mdzod Series, no. 25 (Lhasa: Bod-ljongs bod-yig dpe-rnying dpe-skrun-khang, 1992), 3:520–521.

48. Ibid.

49. See, for example, *Sgrub thabs kun btus,* vol. 5 (Dehra Dun, U. P.: G. T. K. Lodoy, N. Lungtok, and N. Gyaltsan, 1970).

50. On Dol-po-pa and his teaching, refer to Cyrus Stearns, *Buddha from Dolpo* (Albany: State University of New York Press, 1999); and Kapstein, *The Tibetan Assimilation of Buddhism,* 106–119.

51. *Bde-smon-phyogs-bsgrigs,* 1.172–181; and *The 'Dzam-thang Edition of the Collected Works of Kun-mkhyen Dol-po-pa Shes-rab-rgyal-mtshan,* vol. 7 (series vol. 10), collected and presented by Matthew Kapstein (New Delhi: Shedrup Books and Konchhog Lhadrepa, 1992–1993), 891–896.

52. *Lhag bsam skul ba'i mdo'i lung btus,* in *The 'Dzam thang Edition,* 7:874–877.

53. *Rang gzhan bde ba can du skye ba'i thabs mchog ces bya ba bde ba can gyi mdo'i spyi don, The 'Dzam-thang Edition,* 7:877–891.

54. Usually forty-seven or forty-eight vows are enumerated. The eighteenth referred to here corresponds to the eighteenth in the Sanskrit and the nineteenth in the Chinese version of the longer *Sukhāvatīvyūha sūtra.* Refer to Luis O. Gómez, *The Land of Bliss, The Paradise of the Buddha of Measureless Light: Sanskrit and Chinese Versions of the Sukhāvatīvyūha Sutras* (Honolulu: University of Hawai'i Press, 1996).

55. This corresponds to the nineteenth vow in the Sanskrit, and the eighteenth in the Chinese.

56. Gómez, *The Land of Bliss,* 85, par. 51.

57. Ibid., 80ff.

58. Dol-po-pa is here referring to the authority of the *Pañcaviṃṣatisāhasrikā Prajñāpāramitā:* "Without having fulfilled their prayers, without having ripened beings, and without having purified buddha-fields, [the bodhisattvas] are not to disclose the genuine limit." The text is cited by Haribhadra near the beginning of his *Sphutartha* commentary on the *Abhisamayālaṃkāra,* the Tibetan text of which is given in Hirofusa Amano, *A Study on the Abhisamaya-alaṃkāra-kārikā-śāstra-vṛtti* (Tokyo: Japan Science Press, 1975), 11: *smon lam yongs su rdzogs par ma byas pa dang sems can rnams yongs su smin par ma byas pa dang sangs rgyas kyi zhing yongs su ma sbyangs par de dag gis yang dag pa'i mtha' mngon sum du mi bya'o.* For the Sanskrit text of this passage, see Corrado Pensa, *L'Abhisamayālaṃkāravṛtti di Ārya-Vimuktisena, Primo Abhisamaya,* Serie Orientale Roma, no. 37 (Rome: Is. M. E. O., 1967), 12: *na cānena bhūtakoṭiḥ sākṣātkartavyā aparipūrya praṇidhānam aparipācya sattvān apariśodhya buddhakṣetram /*

59. *The 'Dzam-thang Edition,* 7:883–886:

> *da ni log rtog the tsom bsal ba yang brjod par bya ste/ 'dir dge ba'i bshes gnyen la la dag/ bde ba can du so so'i skye bo mi skye bas da lta so so'i skye bor yod pa rnams kyis 'bad kyang der mi skye'o/ zhes 'dod pa ni/ log rtog dang the tsom skye*

ba'i gnas ma yin pa la skye bar 'gyur bas sems can la gnod par 'gyur te/ de ni dge slong byang chub sems dpa' chos kyi 'byung gnas kyi smon lam bzhi bcu rtsa dgu'i nang nas bco brgyad pas legs par bsal te/ ji ltar bsal zhe na/ gang zag te 'chi ba'i dus byed pa'i tshe/ sangs rgyas 'od dpag med pa/ 'khor dang bcas pa mdun du byon pa'i snang ba shar nas dga' zhing dang ba dang bcas te/ bde ba can du 'gro bar gsal la/ sangs rgyas shākya thub pa kyang de dang mthun pas bka' stsal pas 'chi ka bar do'i gnas skabs der 'phags par 'gyur ba'i phyir ro// 'di ni sangs rgyas phal po che'i mdor/ bdag ni 'chi ba'i dus byed gyur pa na/ bsgrib pa thams cad dag ni phyir bsal te/ mngon sum snang ba mtha' yas de mthong nas/ bde ba can kyi zhing der rab tu 'gro/ zhes sogs gsung ba dang yang don gcig go// yang la la dag na re/ tshigs su bcad pa gnyis pa'i 'grel pa slob dpon mdzes bkod kyis mdzad pa dang/ mdo sde rgyan gyi 'grel pa dang 'grel bshad du/ bde ba can du smon lam btab pas skye zhes pa ni dus gzhan la dgongs pa'i dpe brjod du gsungs pas/ mdo 'di nas gsungs pa bzhin bsgrubs kyang tshe phyi mar zhing der skye ba ma yin no// zhes smra ba yang chos spong gis las dang the tsom gyi rgyur 'gyur ba'i phyir sems can la gnod pa yin te/ de ni dge slong 'di ni smon lam bcu dgu pas bsal ba yin no/ ci ltar bsal zhe na/ 'di nas kyang smon lam btab pas mi chog par 'tshams med pa dang dam pa'i chos spong ba'i las las ring du gyur pa dgos shing dge ba'i rtsa ba tha na'ang sems bskyed pa'i 'gyur ba bcu dgos par gsungs pa smon lam tsam gyis mi 'grub par gsungs pa'i phyir dang/ dus gzhan la dgongs pa'i dpe byas pa de yang smon lam tsam la dgongs pa'i phyir ro// des na 'di la 'gal ba cung zad tsam kyang med kyi dgongs pa mthun pa yin no// gzhan yang dge slong de'i smon lam bzhi bcu rtsa dgu po thams cad grub 'am ma grub/ grub na ni bco brgyad pa'ang/ bcu dgu pa yang grub pas de dag la log rtog dang the tsom byar mi rung la/ ma grub na ni dge slong de bde ba can du mngon par rdzogs par sangs rgyas nas skal pa bcu lon par bka' stsal pa dang 'gal zhing/ 'grub mi 'grub brtag pa'i tshe 'grub pa'i mtshan rtags shar ba dang yang 'gal la/ rgyal sras chen po rnams dmigs gsal gsum po ma rdzogs par yang dag pa'i mtha' mngon du mi mdzad par gsungs pa yang 'gal ba yin no/ de'i phyir 'di la log rtogs dang the tshom skyes kyis dogs nas sangs rgyas shākya thub pas the tsom yod mod kyi skyon dang dpe don la sogs pa rnam pa mang pos rgyal sras ma pham pa la legs par gdams shing phyogs bcu'i sangs rgyas grangs med dpag tu med pas kyang de ltar gsung bar bka' stsal pa'i phyir nyes pa de dag spangs nas gsal bas ci ltar bka' stsal pa la yid ches par bya ste dge ba'i rtsa ba mang po dpag tu med pa yang dang yang du bsags nas smon lam rnam dag yang dang yang du sgrubs pa la bsam pa thag pa nas 'bad par bya'o// de ltar byas na bde ba can du pad ma la brdzus te skye bar the tsom med cing smon lam bzhi bcu rta dgu dang mthun pa'i yon tan mang po 'thogs par yang the tsom med do//

[I have left the sometimes irregular orthography of the text as it is.]

60. Tsong-kha-pa Blo-bzang-grags-pa, *Rje Tsong kha pa chen po'i bka' 'bum thor bu* (Xining: Mtsho sngon mi rigs dpe skrun khang, 1987), 156–182; *Bde-smon-phyogs-bsgrigs,* 2.334–365.

61. In the case of Rje Tsong-kha-pa's *Bde-smon zhing mchog sgo 'byed,* for example, because the Dge-lugs-pa monastic system came to be very widespread, this Sukhāvatī prayer at least would have been known to the broad range of even minimally educated monks. Even with this assumption, however, we have little basis for infer-

ences regarding the religious life of the Tibetan population at large. It is possible that a close reading of biographical sources, with a view to assembling full historical documentation of references to teachings and practices relating to Sukhāvatī, would allow us to form a better picture of the Pure Land in Tibetan religious life generally, but that vast project lies beyond the scope of the present essay.

62. Karma Chags-med, the redactor of Mi-'gyur-rdo-rje's "Celestial Doctrine" revelations, is himself seen as the fountainhead of the Gnas-mdo Bka'-brgyud suborder of the Karma Bka'-brgyud and, at the same time, as one of the founding figures in the lineage of the Rnying-ma-pa monastic center of Dpal-yul.

63. One puzzle we encounter here concerns the shift in the name of Amitābha's realm from *Bde-ba-can* (Sukhāvatī), "Blissful," to *Bde-chen* (Mahāsukha), "Great Bliss." As seen above, this phrase was already used by 'Bri-gung skyob-pa, though it seems to predominate only in the Bde-chen zhing-sgrub texts. There are three factors that may explain this terminological transformation. One is no doubt the possible influence of the Chinese translation of Sukhāvatī as "Supreme Bliss" *(ji le)*. In the Tibetan religious milieu, however, there were also no doubt strong associations due to the common characterization of the goal of the tantric path as *mahāsukha,* so that Sukhāvatī came to be in some sense identified with the aspirations of tantric practice. Lastly, we must not forget that *Bde-ba-can,* in its abbreviated form *Bde-can,* is pronounced as a near, and in some dialects exact, homonym of *Bde-chen.* The orthographic and semantic shift, therefore, was to all intents and purposes overdetermined.

64. Editions of the Gnam-chos Bde-chen-zhing-sgrub cycle are very numerous, and there are many variations among them, though the central *sādhana* of the field of Great Bliss (no. 3 below) is always an essential component. The edition I have used here, a xylograph from the old 'Ja'-sa temple of Solu district, Nepal, is a typical version, and is a relatively complete redaction of the cycle in 103 folios, omitting only the texts concerned with dreams. It very closely follows the arrangement found in *Rin-chen gter-mdzod,* vol. 32 (Paro: Ngodrup and Sherap Drimay, 1976), and its contents are as follows:

1. *Bde chen zhing sgrub kyis* [sic!] *gsol 'debs* (1 folio)
2. *Gnam chos thugs kyi gter kha snyan brgyud zab mo gu ru zhi ba'i skor las rtsa gsum spyi yi sngon 'gro* (1 folio)
3. *Gnam chos thugs kyi gter kha snyan brgyud zab mo'i skor las bde chen zhing gi sgrub thabs 'don cha* (10 folios)
4. *Bkra shis gtso bo rdzas brgyad* (1 folio)
5. *Zhing sgrub zin bris kyi lhan thabs nyung bsdus* (5 folios)
6. *Bde chen zhing sgrub kyi bka' bsrung gsol mchod bkrigs chags su bris pa* (4 folios)
7. *Tshogs mchod byin rlabs char 'bebs* (6 folios)
8. *Bkra shis rtags brgyad kyi dbang* (3 folios)
9. *Gnam chos thugs kyi gter kha snyan brgyud zab mo'i skor las. bde chen zhing sgrub kyi byang chog thar lam dkar po* (10 folios)
10. *Bde chen zhing gi ro sreg cho ga ngan song gnas 'dren sdug bsngal mtsho skem gtan bde rab 'bar* (16 folios)

11. *Gnam chos bde chen zhing sgrub kyi dbang 'grig chags su bkod pa* (17 folios)

12. *Gnam chos thugs kyi gter kha las bde chen zhing sgrub kyi zin bris* (10 folios)

13. *Gnam chos thugs kyi gter kha las: bde chen zhing du 'pho ba'i gdams pa rgyas par bsgrigs pa* (17 folios)

14. *Dbang bsdus* (2 folios)

65. Text 13, 1b3–3a4:

chos 'di'i lo rgyus zur tsam zhu na: bka' thang sde lnga'i nang tshan rgyal po bka'i thang yig las: dus kyi mtha' la gsang sngags kyi bdag po rig 'dzin sum cu rtsa gsum 'byon par gsungs nas: de dag kyang byang chub mchog tu lung bstan pa'i skabs: shākya'i zhing khams mdo khams zhes bya na: gsang sngags theg chen spyod pa'i rnal 'byor pa: sngags kyi bdag po rdo rje drag po 'byung: de nas 'phos te spyod pa rlabs chen mdzad: stong gsum 'jig rten 'di yi byang phyogs su: zhing khams rnam dag tsandan nags zhes su: de bzhin gshegs pa skyes bu kha lo sgyur: bla med ston pa sum stong 'dus pa skyong: rgyal ba ye shes kun bzang zhes pa 'byung: zhes lung bston [sic!] *pa la sogs pa gter kha du ma nas lung bstan pa'i sprul sku mi 'gyur rdo rje zhes: lo chen bai ro tsa na dang shud pu dpal seng gnyis ka'i sprul pa gcig tu 'dus pa'i ngo bo: ma 'ongs pa'i sangs rgyas ye shes kun bzang zhes bya ba byang chub kyi spyod pa spyad bzhin pa de: dgung lo bcu gsum pa gser 'phyang gi lo sa ga zla ba'i tshes bdun nyin sangs rgyas 'od dpag tu med pa gtso 'khor gsum sku shin tu che ba ri bo tsam gzi brjid dpag tu med pa dngos su zhal gzigs te: bde chen zhing gi sgrub thabs: rmi lam du bde chen zhing mjal thabs: snang ba mtha' yas kyi tshe sgrub: bde chen zhing gi 'pho ba: bde chen zhing gi gsol 'debs: bde chen zhing gi smon lam: bde chen zhing gi dbang de rnams dngos su gnang ngo: slar yang de'i dgong mo sangs rgyas 'od dpag med 'khor dang bcas pa zhal gzigs na: rmi laṃ gzung ba'i gsol 'debs dang zhal gdams gnyis gnang ba'o:*

As noted above, the texts on dreams are not found in the 'Ja'-sa redaction.

66. Cremation *(ro-sreg)* was reserved exclusively for persons of high status throughout much of Tibet, though it was more widely practiced on the Tibetan frontiers, and in wooded districts was sometimes nearly universal. I have not yet established whether or not there was a particularly close correspondence between the distribution of the *Gnam-chos Bde-chen-zhing-sgrub* and the practice of cremation in the Tibetan world.

67. Thus, for example, Rdza Dpal-sprul Rin-po-che (1808–1887) incorporates its instructions into his *Kun-bzang-bla-ma'i zhal-lung,* far and away the most popular account, throughout the past century, of the fundamental practices of the Rnying-ma-pa tantric path.

68. Though I refer to the practitioner *(sgrub-pa-po)* in the singular throughout, one should recall that the ritual I describe here is particularly popular for congregational practice.

69. Text 3, 1b1: *dkyil 'khor med cing gtor ma med. Gtor-ma* (Skt. bali) in Tibet are usually conelike sculptures of flour and butter, often elaborately designed and decorated, that may serve either as offerings or as the deity's receptacle.

70. In actual practice a slightly more elaborate preparatory routine is followed, involving prayers to Padmasambhava and the performance of the litugies given in texts 1 and 2 of the cycle.

71. This identification appears to be universal in Tibet, and it is owing to Mahāsthāmaprāpta's identity with Vajrapāṇi that he may be said to have a sort of cultic following there (in contrast to East Asia, where he seems to have a separate identity).

72. This mantra, in Tibetan vulgar Sanskrit, invokes all the *tathāgata*s in connection with consecratory aspersion *(abhiṣeka)*.

73. For this stock list of the qualities of excellent drinking water, see Dudjom Rinpoche, *The Nyingma School of Tibetan Buddhism,* 2:160–161.

74. On these rites in general, refer to John Makransky, "Offering *(mChod pa)* in Tibetan Ritual Literature," in *Tibetan Literature: Studies in Genre,* eds., Roger R. Jackson and José Ignacio Cabezón (Ithaca: Snow Lion Publications, 1995), 312–330.

75. Cf. Silk, *The Virtues of Amitābha,* vv. 51–59.

76. It is considered somewhat risky to seek rebirth with Padmasambhava, as one might easily wind up an ogre instead of a Vidyādhara.

77. I.e., the four families (Buddha, Vajra, Ratna, and Karma) besides the Padma family of Amitābha.

78. Text 9, 9a3–6.

79. Like many other *gter-ma* cycles, the Gnam-chos revelations include rites dedicated to all of the major meditational divinities of the Rnying-ma-pa tradition. Though the preeminence of Padmasambhava no doubt reinforces the position of Amitābha within the *gter-ma* traditions, the accentuation of Sukhāvatī that we find in the Bde-chen-zhing-sgrub cycles does not seem to flow axiomatically from this.

80. The popularity these teachings attained is well reflected by the elaboration of Bde-chen-zhing-sgrub rites in many *gter-ma* celebrated cycles, including the *Klong-chen snying-thig* of 'Jigs-med-gling-pa (1730–1798) and the *Gter-gsar* of Bdud-'joms-gling-pa (1835–1904).

81. *The Collected Writings of Glag-bla Bsod-nams-chos-'grub: The 1991 Dkar-mdzes Edition,* 5 vols. (Delhi: Konchhog Lhadrepa, 1996).

82. Rdza Dpal-sprul O-rgyan 'Jigs-med chos-kyi dbang-po, in *Bde-smon-phyogs-bsgrigs,* 2.447–451.

83. Cf. Suniti Kumar Pathak, ed., *Āryabhadracaripraṇidhānarāja,* Sanskrit and Tibetan (Gangtok, Sikkim: Namgyal Institute of Tibetology, 1961), vv. 1–12.

84. Gregory Schopen, "Sukhāvatī as a Generalized Religious Goal in Sanskrit Mahāyāna Sūtra Literature," *Indo Iranian Journal* 19 (1977): 177–210.

85. *Bde-smon-phyogs-bsgrigs,* 1.274.

86. Steven Collins, *Nirvana and Other Buddhist Felicities* (Cambridge: Cambridge University Press, 1998).

87. For an excellent example, see Chap. 3 on suffering in *The Words of My Precious Teacher,* trans. Padmakara Translation Group (New York: HarperCollins, 1994).

2

Shengchang's Pure Conduct Society and the Chinese Pure Land Patriarchate

DANIEL GETZ

IN 991 C.E., the Chinese Buddhist monk Shengchang (959–1020) formed an association of laymen and monks at the Zhaoqing monastery on Hangzhou's West Lake. Shengchang established this group with the express intention of emulating the celebrated coterie of scholar hermits that had gathered around the charismatic scholar-monk Huiyuan (334–416) on Mt. Lu almost six centuries earlier.[1] Dedicated to meditation on the Buddha Amitābha and to the attainment of rebirth in this Buddha's Pure Land, Huiyuan's fraternity later came to be known as the White Lotus Society (Bailian she), a title that Shengchang adopted for his own association. Shengchang's White Lotus Society came into being at the beginning of the Northern Song (960–1126), a period in which the figure of Huiyuan enjoyed renewed popularity in official circles and in which societies dedicated to birth in Amituo's Pure Land began to make their appearance in increasing numbers.[2]

It was ostensibly for Shengchang's revival of Huiyuan's legacy in the Song and for his society's precedence among other Song societies that his name was included in a Pure Land patriarchate created more than two centuries later, during the Southern Song (1127–1279), by the Tiantai historians Zongxiao (1151–1214) and Zhipan (fl. 1258–1269). In attempting to present comprehensively the development of Pure Land in China, Zongxiao and Zhipan both created a patriarchal lineage that they entitled the Lotus Society Patriarchs (Lianshe zu). Zongxiao initiated this process at the turn of the thirteenth century by creating a group of six patriarchs of the Lotus Society for his anthology of Pure Land, the *Compendium of the Land of Bliss (Lebang wenlei)*.[3] In this patriarchate, Zongxiao accorded Huiyuan the title of Founding Patriarch *(shizu)*, while he assigned Shengchang to the fourth position of the five succeeding patriarchs *(jizu)*.[4] Zhipan followed this basic schema in his *Comprehensive History of the Buddhas and the Patriarchs (Fozu tongji)* published in 1265. In a three-fascicle section of this history comprised of Pure Land biographies, Zhipan created a list of seven Patriarchs of the Lotus Society in which Huiyuan was honored as the founder and Shengchang was given the final position.[5] Differences of number and order aside, both histories present patriarchal lists predicated on the model of the White Lotus Society initiated by Huiyuan, and both honor Shengchang as an heir and promulgator of that model.

Since that time, largely on the basis of these late Song and subsequent biographies, Shengchang has continued to be cited as an important figure in the history of Chinese Pure Land.[6] Shengchang's society, the first recorded in the Song, is customarily presented in modern studies as the forerunner of all subsequent Song Pure Land societies.[7] Japanese scholars portray Shengchang's White Lotus Society as an association engaged in the Pure Land practice of reciting Amituo's name *(nianfo)*, thus referring to it as the Nianfo Pure Practice Society (Nembutsu jōgyōsha). Moreover, they credit Shengchang with the Song revival of the Lotus Society *nianfo* practice *(rensha nembutsu)*.[8] These sources helped shape an image of Shengchang as a Pure Land devotee who, by zealously promoting the cult of Amitābha, was responsible for reviving Pure Land in the Song, thus earning a rightful place in Zongxiao and Zhipan's patriarchates.

Heretofore, this traditional image of Shengchang, the Pure Land figure, has not been questioned. If, however, we depart from the standard biographies on which the traditional assessment was based and examine sources that were contemporary with Shengchang and his society, questions arise regarding the validity of this well-established evaluation and the long-held assumptions about the practice of Pure Land in China that led to this evaluation. These alternate sources provide the basis for a somewhat different interpretation of Shengchang's mission and accomplishment: Shengchang's primary intellectual, devotional, and liturgical orientation was grounded not in the cult of Amitābha but in the Huayan tradition. His motivation for founding this society, then, derived from a wish to spread devotion to the Huayan scripture and a desire to justify and disseminate Buddhist belief among scholar-officials. These sources suggest that even though Pure Land belief was undoubtedly an element in the group that Shengchang organized, devotion to Amitābha and hope for rebirth in his Pure Land did not play a paramount role in this society's purpose and function as suggested in the version presented by later historians.

What is ultimately at stake in the reevaluation of Shengchang's role suggested above is not simply a question of biographical accuracy but larger issues pertaining to the significance and validity of the Pure Land patriarchate, the nature of Pure Land societies, and place of Pure Land within Chinese Buddhism. The creation of a Pure Land patriarchate by Zongxiao and Zhipan in the thirteenth century has left an impression for many later historians that an autonomous Pure Land tradition existed from the time of Huiyuan. Such a view of the Chinese Pure Land tradition, as constituting an exclusive practice, an independent religious community, and a distinct lineage, has held wide currency until very recently.[9] The critical study of Shengchang's biography offers one among many possible challenges to this traditional view, allowing a much more nuanced understanding of the many different modes in which Pure Land belief and practice functioned in China.

In view of the preceding discussion, the present study has two related aims. The primary focus, to be addressed in the main section of this paper, is the extent to which Pure Land played a role in Shengchang's society. This section will critically examine a number of sources relevant to Shengchang's society and will offer evidence for the alternate interpretation of Shengchang's role suggested above. The second issue, which will be briefly treated in the conclusion, is the significance of this reassessment for our understanding of Pure Land in Chinese Buddhism.

The use of the term "Pure Land" in this chapter will be largely confined to signifying Amitābha's realm and the cultic tradition in China associated with it. This by no means is to suggest that Amitābha's was the only pure land aspired to by Chinese Buddhists throughout history. However, in light of the central concern of the present volume with the tradition that focused on Amitābha's Sukhāvatī, the discussion of alternative soteriological options is a worthy topic that must wait for treatment elsewhere.

Critical Evaluation of the Sources

At the outset, an initial survey of the sources on Shengchang's society currently available requires a confession of limitations. The fact is, we do not possess all of the documents originally written on Shengchang's society. The loss of materials contemporary to the founding of the society, particularly a three-fascicle work by Shengchang himself entitled *Record of the West Lake Pure Society (Qiantang Xihu Jingshe lu),* hampers our ability to assess fully Shengchang's religious orientation as well as the nature and workings of his society.[10] Thus we are prevented from categorically dismissing the traditional view of Shengchang as a premier Pure Land devotee. While keeping in mind this limitation, the evidence to be considered below nevertheless strongly points to a view of Shengchang that digresses from the hagiographies.

The enlistment of some of the most prominent literati officials of the late tenth and early eleventh centuries insured Shengchang's society a place in official historical memory. In the decade following its inauguration, the society's founding was commemorated by a stele inscribed by Song Bo (936–1012), a member of the Hanlin Academy, whose *Stele Inscription on Forming a Society at the Zhaoqing Monastery on Hangzhou's West Lake (Da Song Hangzhou Xihu Zhaoqing si jieshe beiming)* recounts important details of Shengchang's life and the founding of the society. The posterior face of this stele displayed an inscription by the literatus Sun He (961–1004) whose *White Lotus Hall Record (Bailiantang ji)* provides yet more details on the society's beginnings. The appearance of the society also inspired a collection of poetry created by officials from all over who had sought through their literary contributions to become members of the society.[11] The preface for this collection was written by Ding Wei (966–1037), one of the most prominent literary figures of this period. In 1009, these inscriptions and prefaces were evidently gathered into a compilation, *Anthology of the West Lake Zhaoqing Monastery's Pure Conduct Society (Xihu Zhaoqing si jie Jingxing she ji),* which was prefaced by Qian Yi (n.d.), another outstanding literary talent. Except for Sun's inscription, which is included in the *Zhaoqing Monastery Gazeteer (Zhaoqing si zhi),* the other documents are all preserved in the *Wonjong munllyu,* a compendium containing a trove of documents brought back to Korea by the illustrious pilgrim-scholar Ŭich'ŏn (1055–1107), who visited China in the 1080s.[12] Besides these valuable contemporary sources, we also have the *Stele Inscription for the Head of the Qiantang White Lotus Society (Qiantang Bailian shezhu bei),* written by the Tiantai scholar Zhiyuan (976–1022) shortly after Shengchang's death in 1020.[13]

What is striking from the outset in these documents is the paucity of reference to Pure Land themes and aspirations. Qian Yi's preface to the collection on the society contains no discernable allusion to Pure Land. While summarizing the details on the founding of the society, he declares "the [society's] nomen, 'White Lotus' is a continuation of Lufu [Lushan]."[14] Yet this reference to Huiyuan's society on Mt. Lu contains no mention of the original group's soteriological aspiration to rebirth or of its practice of visualizing Amitābha. Most telling, however, is the fact that Qian Yi begins his account on the founding of the society by referring to Shengchang's association as the "Huayan Pure Society."[15] This title reveals not only this society's cultic focus at its founding but also, more fundamentally, the nature of its founder's training and spirituality.

Born to a Hangzhou family named Yan, Shengchang entered the monastery at the age of seven, was tonsured at fifteen, and received the full precepts when he was seventeen.[16] Song Bo recounts that by the age of twenty Shengchang thoroughly understood the "nature teaching" *(xingzong),* no doubt a reference to his conversance with Huayan doctrine.[17] When Shengchang was twenty-one, the governor of Hangzhou, Zhe Shousu (922–992), invited him to lecture on the *Dasheng qixin lun* (The awakening of faith), a text central to the Huayan tradition.[18]

Song Bo's biographical account indicates that sometime in Shengchang's early career he studied the "mind-only doctrine" with the Fayan Chan monk Zhifeng (909–985).[19] Although the term "mind-only" designates a number of different doctrinal traditions, the context strongly suggests that the Huayan tradition was the intended referent. Zhifeng was the disciple of the most eminent monk in WuYue Buddhism, Tiantai Deshao (891–972), who was instrumental in the Song revival of Tiantai Buddhism and whose legacy was insured through the fame of his prolific disciple Yanshou (904–975). Yanshou's career reflected the unique orientation of the Fayan lineage of Chan, which emphasized not only a wide range of cultivational practices but also broad and intensive doctrinal study. Given the prominence of Huayan texts and ideas in Yanshou's broad erudition, it would not have been unusual for Zhifeng as a fellow disciple to show a marked interest in the *Huayan jing*. Zhifeng's familiarity, and perhaps identification, with the Huayan tradition is manifest in one of the lengthiest accounts in his biography, a conversation with students in which he likens himself to the monk Meghaśri (Deyun biqiu), the first of fifty-three sages visited by the seeker Sudhana (Shancai) in the Gaṇḍhavyūha section *(Ru fajie pin)* of the *Huayan jing.*[20] Zhifeng's devotion to the *Huayan jing* is further suggested by his retirement to the Huayan Practice Hall *(daochang)* on Mt. Wuyun, outside of Hangzhou.[21] It was here that Shengchang visited the master and received the mind-only teaching.[22]

Shengchang's connnection with the Huayan tradition received confirmation in the 980s, when he had a dream in which a celestial monk appeared to him as Mañjuśrī.[23] From this point, Shengchang sought to convert the Buddhist community to conform thoroughly with "the marks *(xianghao)* of Wutai."[24] Although the exact nature of his activity in this regard is not clearly stated, the allusion to Mt. Wutai, which was both the cultic center of Mañjuśrī veneration grounded in the *Huayan jing* and a seminal site in the development of the Huayan school, leaves little doubt regarding Shengchang's doctrinal and devotional orientation.[25]

Evidence of Shengchang's commitment to the Mañjuśrī cult and to the Huayan tradition culminates in the details of White Lotus Society's founding at the Zhaoqing si.[26] Song Bo relates that Shengchang personally produced a copy of the *Jingxing pin* (The chapter on pure conduct) of the *Huayan jing,* using ink mixed with his blood.[27] After writing each character, he performed three obeisances, made three circumambulations, and invoked three times the Buddha's name. On completing the manuscript, he employed an artisan to reproduce his copy on a woodblock from which a thousand copies of the scripture were printed. These he distributed to clerics and laypeople alike. Shengchang also commissioned the sculpting of a sandalwood image of the Buddha Vairocana, and gathered an assembly of eighty monks to form a society. The details of this society's founding clearly point to the nature of the scriptural and cultic tradition from which the founder drew his inspiration.

The Huayan orientation adopted by Shengchang's society was by no means a new phenomenon. More than a century and a half earlier, Hangzhou had witnessed the creation of a similar group by the monk Nancao (n.d.), who called his new association The Society for the Recitation of the *Huayan jing.*[28] Nancao's intention was to enlist one hundred thousand monks and laypersons who would dedicate themselves to the *Huayan jing* and each would in turn enlist one thousand more members to recite the sūtra. The society was scheduled to meet four times a year for vegetarian feasts at which Nancao would offer incense before an image of Vairocana and recite the following vow:

> May I and every member of the society be reborn before Vairocana in his paradise within the Golden Wheel of Precious Lotus, floating in the Great Ocean of Fragrant Waters in the Lotus-Womb World [Padmagarbhadhātu]. Then I would be satisfied.[29]

Although the soteriological goal of Nancao's vow differed from Shengchang's, as will be seen shortly, the two societies shared a common iconographic and textual orientation. The memory of Nancao's society in Hangzhou could well have survived into the Song, inspiring Shengchang to spread the devotion to the Huayan through the establishment of a new society.[30]

We do not know what part of the *Huayan jing* Nancao singled out for devotion. Such uncertainty does not extend to Shengchang, who embraced "The Chapter on Pure Conduct" as a devotional and cultivational compass for the members of his society.[31] The chapter is a discourse in verse by Mañjuśrī addressed to the bodhisattva Zhishou.[32] It lists one hundred forty different wishes for the spiritual and physical well-being of all sentient beings. Each of these expressions is linked to one of a bodhisattva's myriad daily activities. This chapter is regarded as an articulation of an ideal for householder bodhisattvas, although many of the activities described therein are specific to monastic life.[33] The text has no visible connection to Pure Land belief, nor does it appear to have been generally perceived as containing a Pure Land message. It was not included in the first fascicle of the *Compendium of the Land of Bliss,* which contains a wide variety of passages from sūtras and commentaries that were thought to have a Pure Land orientation. The centrality of this text in Shengchang's society is reflected in the substitution of "Pure Conduct" for "White Lotus" in the society's title.[34] Thus the association came to be generally referred to as the Pure Conduct Society *(Jingxing she)* and its members were designated as Pure Conduct Disciples *(Jingxing dizi).*[35] For his part in promoting Huayan, Shengchang was acclaimed "Master of the Huayan Society" *(Huayan shezhu).*[36]

Shengchang's choice of cultic image as related by Song Bo was no less indicative of the master's devotion to Huayan. As the central buddha of the *Huayan jing* Vairocana signified a harmonious iconic counterpart to the society's textual focus on "The Chapter on Pure Conduct." Song Bo's account, however, is challenged by Zhiyuan's inscription, which states that Shengchang had a statue of the Buddha Amitāyus (Wuliangshou) carved because he believed that this buddha was the object of veneration *(yangzhi)* for a multitude of living beings.[37]

There are certain facts to commend the validity of Zhiyuan's observation. Zhiyuan was a scholar-monk versed in a wide range of Buddhist literature and practice. As Shengchang's neighbor on the West Lake, it stands to reason that he had an accurate view of the cultic objects in Shengchang's monastery. Furthermore, producing a devotional image of Amituo better corresponds with the precedent set by Huiyuan's society, which Shengchang was seeking to imitate.

Zhiyuan's evidence, however, is undermined by the fact that his inscription contains no other mention of Amituo or any further indication that Shengchang or the members of his group engaged in customary Pure Land practices such as *nianfo* or visualization of Pure Land.[38] Furthermore, Zhiyuan's document produced in 1020 is further removed in time than Song Bo's, which was written roughly a decade after the society's founding in 991. Although Song Bo as a member of the Shengchang's society would presumably have had firsthand knowledge of the society's cultic focus, there is no evidence that Zhiyuan was a member in Shengchang's association. Lastly, the carving of an image of Vairocana would appear to be a much more sensible accompaniment to a text from the *Huayan jing* than an image of Amituo. If, then, the choice is between one or the other of these two accounts, the evidence tilts in favor of Vairocana as the society's cultic focus.[39]

In the preceding discussion, I have sought to demonstrate Shengchang's primary religious orientation within the Huayan tradition and to emphasize the curious absence of Pure Land themes and allusions within the documents related to Shengchang's society. All of this is not to say, however, that Pure Land devotion was entirely absent from this group. Song Bo reports that on completion of the text and image and the convening of the society, Shengchang made a vow that contains several explicit Pure Land elements. Kneeling down and folding his hands, he vowed:

> Henceforth, together with eighty monks and one thousand members of the great assembly, I will give rise to inspiration to achieve enlightenment *(bodhicitta)* and will cultivate the bodhisattva practice all the way into the future. When [this] body of retribution *(baoshen)* is exhausted, I seek to be reborn in the Country of Peace and Sustenance (Anyang guo, that is, the Pure Land), to make sudden entrance into the Dharmadhātu, and to perfectly realize the [doctrine] of nonarising. I will cultivate the ten *pāramitā*s and will associate with countless virtuous companions. With the light from my body illuminating all quarters, I will lead all sentient beings to obtain the *nianfo sanmei,* just like Mahāsthāmaprāpta. Hearing cries [of distress] and saving [those calling] from suffering, I will help all sentient beings acquire the fourteen qualities of fearlessness, just like Avalokiteśvara. I will cultivate the oceanlike vow of the broad limitless practices, just like Samantabhadra. I will open the gate of subtle and profound wisdom, just like Mañjuśrī. My enlightened wisdom will permeate the realm of the Buddha-in-waiting, just like Maitreya. When I achieve Buddhahood, both in body and in land I will resemble Amituo, and I will individually bestow predictions upon each of these eighty monks and one thousand members of the great assembly that they will all attain enlightenment. Today I make this vow universally for all sentient beings. As sentient beings are incalculable, so is the breadth of my vow.[40]

Unlike Nancao, who, as mentioned earlier, directed his vow to Vairocana in hope of being reborn in the Lotus-Womb World of the Huayan scripture, Shengchang created a vow that diverged from his society's textual and iconographic focus on Huayan. Shengchang's aspiration to birth in the Pure Land reveals that Pure Land praxis occupied at least one corner of Shengchang's personal spiritual universe. This vow represents the strongest evidence of the existence of Pure Land belief in Shengchang's society. Yet the position of that tradition in his religious life was most certainly subsumed under the overarching canopy of the Huayan tradition. Furthermore, although some of the figures (such as Amituo, Mahāsthāmaprāpta, and Avalokiteśvara) invoked in the vow are central in the Pure Land tradition, the general thrust of the evocation of their names was to reproduce the bodhisattva path trod by these great figures. Finally, even though we can conclude that Pure Land praxis played some part in Shengchang's spiritual life, the degree to which that consciousness was imparted to other members of his society remains a question given the documents produced by the lay members of this society.

Among these documents, Sun He's *Bailian tang ji* affords us a valuable window for viewing a scholar-official's perspective on Shengchang and his society. Sun He was a renowned poet and writer in his time. In literary circles his name was commonly associated with Ding Wei, the aforementioned author of the preface of the poetry anthology generated by members of Shengchang's society.[41] Sun's record provides invaluable information on the lay membership of the Pure Conduct Society. He lists the names of seventeen eminent literati who joined the society, among them ministers of state, governors, and other high-ranking officials.[42] These men, together with Shengchang, constituted an assemblage of eighteen members, consciously fashioned after the purported eighteen-member cadre that made up the core of Huiyuan's White Lotus Society.[43] At the head of Shengchang's group *(sheshou)* was Wang Dan (Wang Wenzheng, 957–1017), who later was to become one of the most renowned Grand Councillors of the Song.[44] Other members on this list, which reads like a *Who's Who* of scholar-officials at the beginning of the eleventh century, were also to attain high positions in the Song government.[45]

Ding Wei's preface to the poetry produced by this talented group makes clear that most if not all of these men were enlisted by Shengchang from afar.[46] Responding to an invitation sent out by Shengchang, these scholar-officials responded with contributions of poetry that served as contracts in forming the society. It must be kept in mind, then, that this group was removed from the ritual and communal matrix that informed and nurtured the members of the society residing in Hangzhou. The question thus arises: To what extent were the members of this scattered association capable of reflecting the beliefs and ideals promoted by Shengchang? Despite their distance from the society's cultic center, it is safe to assume that if Shengchang had been intent on transmitting Pure Land belief and practice to these men, he would have done so effectively in his communication with them and they accordingly would have given some hint of this in their writings. Such a reflection, however, is not to be found.

Although not part of this original august cadre, Sun He joined the society later. His observations on Shengchang are instructive, showing how the master was viewed by these scholar-officials:

> Venerable Chang's (Chang Gong) power of meditative concentration is steadfast. He possesses a heart that he has made sincere and bright. He has perfectly attained to the Dharma-nature *(yuantong faxing)*.

> He has an exhortation that doing good is the greatest joy. He seeks to make people cultivate scrupulous conduct *(mixing)* and householders to imitate Vimalakīrti (Jingming). Upon viewing the image they give rise to the conditions of compassion. Upon reading the text they produce an intention to benefit [other sentient beings], to transport the masses [caught in] illusion leading them into nirvana (literally, the Land of Purity and Coolness, *qingliang zhi xiang*).[47] [His activities] are capable of mustering successors *(houlai)* and guiding the eminent predecessors *(xianjue)* to abide in the First Principle *(diyi yidi)* and to enter into the doctrine of non-duality *(buer famen)*.[48]

The portrait of this society presented here is a familiar, though not particularly extraordinary, description of a Buddhist monk proselytizing educated laymen. Except for the mention, although not by name, of the image and the text that constituted important elements of Shengchang's society, the description seems formulaic, drawing from a standard repertoire of phrases. The message is a generic Mahāyāna Buddhist one with no hint of Pure Land themes. One explanation for Sun He's silence with regard to Pure Land might be that he was not one of the original members of the society. Because his record was written a decade after the founding of the society, he was perhaps vague about the nature of this society and therefore depicted it in the most general of terms. This, however, seems unlikely since the society was still in existence when he wrote this piece. Furthermore, Sun He knew Shengchang personally and probably had read the texts and poems that he reported were written upon the society's inception by the literati members, some of whom were his close acquaintances. If Pure Land devotion were the preeminent element in Shengchang's proselytization as is suggested in the later Pure Land biographies, then Sun He's document should have provided at least a slight reflection of that reality.

For evidence of Pure Land belief to be missing in documents written by people once removed from the original membership of the society is one thing. For it to be absent in the consciousness of one of its original members—particularly in the experience of death, where Pure Land belief exercises its greatest influence—is a matter of another magnitude. As stated above, the future Grand Councillor Wang Dan was the head member in the group of scholar-officials who joined the Pure Conduct Society. Zongxiao's *Supplement to the Compendium of the Land of Bliss (Lebang yigao)* cites an excerpt from the mid-eleventh century *Xiangshan Record (Xiangshan yelu)* by Wenying (n.d.) in which Wang Dan vowed before dying that he wished to be reborn in the next life as monk, seated in meditation in a forest, taking joy in contemplating the mind.[49] This is a most curious aspiration for someone who at one point in his life had purportedly been instructed in the soteriological promises of Pure Land belief.

Wang Yücheng (954–1001), another member of the original group, appeared equally oblivious of Pure Land soteriology. Wang's poem, which is the only surviving work of the entire collection, makes allusions to the planting of lotuses in the Eastern Grove at Mt. Lu but is devoid of Pure Land imagery.[50] Ding Wei's preface reinforces this impression, making ample reference to Huiyüan and his society but none to the Buddha Amituo nor to rebirth in his Pure Land.[51] We are left, then, with serious doubt as to whether Wang Dan, Wang Yücheng, or any of their other comrades for that matter, had received any instruction in Pure Land from Shengchang when he wrote to invite them to contribute poems upon the society's founding.

This question of the religious consciousness possessed by the lay participants of Shengchang's society brings us to the issue of Shengchang's motivation in establishing this association in the first place. The details of his biography and the founding of the society discussed earlier make clear that Shengchang sought to promote a cultic observance derived from the Huayan tradition among both monastics and laics. Yet alongside this narrowly focused cultivational ideal, his work with scholar-officials reveals a broader evangelistic intent. Zhiyuan quotes Shengchang as saying to his students:

> Since the beginning of the dynasty, high officials have pursued their learning by revering the ancients *(zonggu)*. For the most part they have modelled themselves after the conduct of Tuizhi (Han Yu), their intention being to oust the Buddhists. I have therefore drawn upon Venerable Yuan's (Huiyuan's) legacy to assist in forming a society. [These high officials] are often converted by me and have accumulated stele inscriptions and amassed verses as vows of refuge praising the Buddhadharma. Such are sufficient to censure heterodox paths and protect our teaching. This age does not understand me. It takes me to be someone who performs wonders in order to spread my own reputation. I am not of that ilk.[52]

Shengchang's intention, as articulated here, had little to do with devotion to Huayan or aspiration to Pure Land. Rather, his goal in founding the society was expressly apologetic, seeking to offset the anti-Buddhist sentiment that literati in the first decades of the Song had inherited from Han Yü, the famous Tang official and renowned promoter of the Confucian cause who had written a scathing memorial against Buddhism and the Buddhist practice of worshiping the Buddha's relics.[53] Such views were embraced by literati-officials of the *guwen* movement during the early decades of the Northern Song. High officials such as Liu Kai (954–1000) and the aforementioned Wang Yücheng attributed a perceived decline in Chinese culture to the foreign influence of Buddhism and sought to renew society through a return to Confucian values and classical literary models *(guwen)*.[54]

The Buddhist response to this Confucian challenge was varied. On the one hand, Buddhist scholars such as Zanning (919–1001), Zhiyüan, and later Qisong (1007–1072) dealt with the literati on their own terms, demonstrating through their broad erudition how Buddhist scholarship was an integral part of China's literary tradition. Other Buddhists sought to convert literati to Buddhist practice. Among these latter was Shengchang, who through his society sought to tap into Huiyuan's revered status among the scholar class and particularly the nostalgic aura surrounding the White Lotus Society to bring literati to Buddhist belief and practice. His success can be measured in part by the eminence of the officials (including *guwen* proponents such as Wang Yücheng) who joined the society.

There is no suggestion in the above-cited passage or elsewhere in Zhiyuan's inscription that Shengchang also adopted Huiyuan's soteriological goal of rebirth as a primary doctrine to be conveyed to lay members. The instructional emphasis for these literati, as manifested in the nature of the text that he chose as the basis for this society, was on spotless conduct *(jingxing)*, a concern that certainly had more appeal to the rational ethical sensibilities of the scholar class than the otherworldly orientation of Pure Land. This conclusion, of course, does not mitigate the fact that many scholar-officials through the Song wholly dedicated themselves to Pure Land devotion.

Before concluding this overview of materials concerning Shengchang and his society, an examination of his later inclusion in Pure Land biographies is instructive in exploring the question of how he came to be viewed as a premier promoter of Pure Land. The first Pure Land biography produced in the Northern Song was Zunshi's *Brief Biographies of Rebirth in the Western Realm (Wangsheng Xifang luezhuan).*[55] This work appeared in 1017, too early to include Shengchang, who was still alive.[56] The next two Pure Land biographies were produced later in the eleventh century: Jiezhu's *Biographies of Rebirth in Pure Land (Jingtu wangsheng zhuan)* in 1064 and Wang Gu's *Newly Revised Biographies of Rebirth (Xinxiu wangsheng zhuan)* in 1084.[57] Although both of these works include early Song Pure Land figures, neither contains Shengchang's biography. This absence is not surprising in Jiezhu's work, which relied on Zanning's *Song Biographies of Eminent Monks (Song gaoseng zhuan)* and apparently did not go beyond it, concluding with the Tiantai patriarch Wuen, who died in 986. To the biographies of Song monks included in Jiezhu's biography, Wang Gu's collection adds the lives of Zunshi, who died after Shengchang, and Yanshou, who, like Shengchang, was not perceived as a Tiantai figure. It would seem, then, with our limited knowledge of Wang Gu's work that if Shengchang had been perceived as an important Pure Land personage, there was nothing barring his inclusion in Wang Gu's collection. In 1155 Lu Shishou supplemented Wang Gu's biography with his *Pure Land Collection of Treasured Pearls (Jingtu baozhu ji).*[58] Unfortunately, all that survives of the original eight-fascicle work is a single fascicle that only covers Pure Land figures into the Tang period. We therefore have no way of knowing if Shengchang was included by Lu Shishou. Shengchang's biography does not make an appearance in extant materials until Zongxiao's *Compendium of the Land of Bliss,* which was produced in 1200, almost two centuries after Shengchang's death. This source in fact gives very little biographical information on Shengchang. It primarily lists the materials written upon the founding of the society, occasionally citing one or two phrases from them. It concludes with a comparison between Huiyuan and Shengchang. There is no evidence of explicit Pure Land activity in the biography except at the beginning, where it states that at the Zhaoqing si Shengchang exclusively cultivated "pure actions" *(jingye),* a term with strong Pure Land connotations, commonly referring to activity that serves as the main karmic condition for rebirth in Pure Land. The source for this declaration is unclear, but one cannot help but think of the similarity between the terms "pure action" *(jingye),* which most certainly refers to Pure Land activity, and "pure conduct" *(jingxing),* which signifies the taintless conduct of the bodhisattva and may or may not refer to Pure Land belief and practice. Our examination of the documents above has revealed that *jingxing* constituted a central principle in Shengchang's cultivation. However, to what degree we should assign Pure Land connotations to this term is a problem. We are left, then, with a question: Is it possible that biographers like Zongxiao, who were aware that Shengchang had engaged in "pure conduct," interpreted this term as signifying Pure Land activity, which they expressed through the term "pure actions"?

More than sixty years after the *Compendium of the Land of Bliss,* Zhipan produced a collection of Pure Land biographies, *The Establishment of the Pure Land Teaching Record (Jingtu lijiao zhi),* which became part of the *Comprehensive History of the Buddhas and the Patriarchs.*[59] Zhipan's biography of Shengchang is brief, relative to the biographies of other patriarchs, and essentially follows the limited facts provided in Zhiyuan's record. It speaks of the establishment of the Lotus Society but has no explicit evidence of Pure Land activity until the conclusion, which describes Shengchang's death and burial:

> In the twelfth day of the first month of 1020 [Shengchang], sitting erect, recited the Buddha's name. After a while, crying in a sharp voice, "The Buddha is coming!" he peacefully was transformed. The assembly saw the ground's color [turn] completely golden. Momentarily it receded.[60]

The invocation of Amituo's name, the vision of the Buddha's arrival at the moment of death as promised in scripture, and the miraculous transformation of the earth's color are the only elements in Shengchang's biography that distinctly point to Pure Land belief. Yet there is no indication where this information came from, and we are left with the nagging suspicion that the biography at this point might simply have been conforming to a standard convention found throughout Pure Land biographies in which the death narrative frequently describes miraculous events pointing to the advent of Amituo and rebirth in Pure Land. Of course, even if Shengchang did indeed invoke the Buddha's name at his death (this practice being commonplace in the Chinese monastic community), such an act does not lead to a valid inference that this practice had been central throughout his life, much less to the conclusion that Shengchang represents one of China's foremost Pure Land devotees.

Our doubts about the degree to which Shengchang's society was focused on Amituo or on his Pure Land are strengthened by yet another source. In the eleventh century the Vinaya Patriarch Yuanzhao, in two different passages, discussed the development of Pure Land in China.[61] In both passages he provides lists of names, starting with Huiyuan, of those considered major contributors to the Pure Land tradition. Shengchang's name is found in neither of these passages. In one of them Yuanzhao is more specific with regard to the geographical areas affected:

> Those in later periods speaking of Pure Societies necessarily regarded the Eastern Grove (Donglin, i.e., Mt. Lu) as its start. Thus after that Shandao and Huaigan greatly expanded [this teaching] in Chang'an; Zhijue (Yanshou) and Ciyun (Zunshi) made it prosper in Zheyou.[62]

Strictly speaking, the region of Zheyou covers only the area south and east (right) of the Zhe river (Zhejiang; now known as the Qiantang river) up to and including Kuaiji and not the city of Hangzhou, which lies to the north (left) of the river. Nevertheless, it would seem that Zheyou is being used in this passage as a reference to the Hangzhou area, where Yanshou and Zunshi were both active. Yuanzhao, who spent most of his life around Hangzhou, was well acquainted with the history of Pure Land there. That he did not include Shengchang's name in either of his accounts would strongly suggest that in Yuanzhao's eyes Shengchang was not a pivotal figure in the spread of Pure Land devotion during this period.

The doubts raised here about the importance of Pure Land in Shengchang's society can be formulated into a question that might be applied when encountering societies that have traditionally been labeled as Pure Land associations: Should we, on encountering the name "Lotus Society" or "White Lotus Society" or the term "pure conduct," immediately assume that a society or an individual possessed a predominantly Pure Land orientation? While "pure conduct" has already been shown to denote activity that had no necessary connection with Pure Land, the label "White Lotus Society" still requires closer scrutiny.

In examining the history of the White Lotus Sect of the Southern Song, it is quite clear that groups using "White Lotus" as a self-referent often had little if any Pure Land belief. For later periods, then, the term cannot be immediately assumed to signify the presence of Pure Land activity.[63] Does this same ambiguity apply to earlier periods as well, especially to the beginning of the Northern Song, when Shengchang was forming his society? The contrasting interpretations put forward to explain the provenance of "Lotus Society" *(Lianshe)* offered by Daocheng (n.d.) in his *Shishi yaolan* (completed in 1020) would seem to suggest that the conception of the term at this time was not solely bound to Pure Land connotations.[64] It is true that Daocheng begins by recounting that Huiyuan gathered a congregation for the purpose of cultivating Pure Land practices (*Xifang jingye;* literally, "Pure Activity of the West"). For Daocheng, there was no ambiguity regarding the nature of Huiyuan's society. Yet in his discussion of why this group was referred to as "*Lianshe,*" he hints that use of the term elicited images not necessarily linked to Pure Land. His first explanation for the name is that there were many white lotuses growing around the community on Mt. Lu. Another was that in receiving people into Amituo's Pure Land, lotuses were used to divide them into nine different categories according to their merit. Yet another interpretation was that the term was used to praise the members of Huiyuan's group for not being tainted by desire for reputation or personal benefit, just as lotus blossoms remain untainted by the mud in which they grow. Finally, Daocheng mentions the story of Fayao, a disciple of Huiyuan, who invented a water clock carved in the shape of a twelve-petaled lotus. Of these explanations, the second developed from lotus imagery in Pure Land, while the third was derived from the traditional Buddhist understanding of the lotus as a symbol for lay purity. While these two separate connotations in most cases coexisted in the minds of those founding and joining societies, there remains the possibility that for some people, particularly Confucian scholar-officials, the second meaning—that appealing to pure conduct—was foremost. Such people revered Huiyuan's society for the participation of lay intelligentsia who were able to rise above the corruption of the world, and they viewed the formation of a *Lianshe* as a project to recreate the spirit of that first group. In all probability such was the state of mind among many of the literati joining Shengchang's society. Shengchang, although clearly cognizant of the Pure Land connotations of "*Lianshe,*" was not primarily interested in reorienting the aspirations of scholar-officials joining his society.

Conclusion

The preceding critique of Shengchang's historically perceived role as Pure Land proselytizer and patriarch not only suggests a new interpretation of his life but also invites a reevaluation of broader issues in Chinese Pure Land regarding the validity of the Pure Land patriarchate, the functioning of Pure Land societies, and the very nature of Pure Land as a movement. While acknowledging that an adequate treatment of these issues must extend far beyond the present chapter, a few brief observations will be offered below on how an interpretation of Shengchang's life that departs from the traditional Pure Land hagiographies might influence our approach.

The case of Shengchang naturally invites a critical analysis of the Pure Land patriarchate created by Zongxiao and Zhipan. The new assessment of Shengchang's role presented above challenges the Pure Land patriarchate with regard to not only Shengchang's place in the list of patriarchs but also the very validity of the patriarchate and, by extension, the concept of the Pure Land tradition as an autonomous movement. An initial analysis of the patriarchal lists suggests membership in this venerable lineage was based on at least two conditions: that the individuals identified as patriarchs followed the example of Huiyuan in establishing White Lotus societies, and that they and their societies were preoccupied with the beliefs and practices of Pure Land.

Although Shengchang, by establishing a White Lotus Society, clearly met the first of these two conditions, the evidence presented in this chapter suggests that he and his society did not fulfill the second requirement—the primacy of Pure Land in consciousness or practice. The description of the society's founding in Hangzhou recounted above clearly shows that Shengchang's devotional and ritual focus was on Vairocana and the *Huayan jing*. His vow to be reborn in Pure Land appears subordinated to that focus. We have no way of knowing whether Shengchang's aspiration to Pure Land was shared by members of the society in Hangzhou, but the evidence above strongly suggests that consciousness of Pure Land was conspicuously absent in the eminent scholar-officials who joined the society from afar. This absence challenges Shengchang's reputation as a Pure Land proselytizer and calls into question his position in the patriarchate.

Beyond the issue of whether a certain individual belongs on the list of patriarchs lies the more fundamental question of whether the list itself has any validity at all. This question in turn is intimately related to the issue of sectarian identity and autonomy. The assignment of a patriarchate to a particular tradition suggests that the tradition in question possesses a certain degree of self-conscious identity vis-à-vis other traditions. Although this issue of sectarian identity, and by extension lineage, has been treated at length as far as other Chinese Buddhist traditions such as Chan and Tiantai are concerned, it has only recently begun to generate intensive discussion on Chinese Pure Land.[65]

Shengchang's life provides one possible entry into this discussion. The sources considered above do not reveal any self-consciousness or sense of unique identity on his part with regard to Pure Land practice. Nor do they mention Shengchang receiving his Pure Land belief from a master, his passing it on to a disciple, or even his communicating with other practitioners or communities of Pure Land believers. The silence of the sources in this regard suggests the absence of a distinct autonomous and continuous Pure Land tradition for Shengchang and the members of his society. It would seem that whatever Pure Land practice Shengchang might have engaged in, it functioned alongside other beliefs and practices. Examination of the wider context of Chinese Buddhism in this same period further reveals that while Pure Land activity abounded, it coexisted with other beliefs and functioned within other institutional settings.[66]

Although this lack of an autonomous identity is most extreme in Shengchang's case, it is largely applicable to all of the other figures proclaimed as patriarchs by Zongxiao and Zhipan.[67] In the end, then, we are left with a question that calls for further consideration: Might the Shengchang whose Pure Land appears to have been subsumed within other activities ultimately be a truer representative of the general following of Pure Land in Chinese Buddhism than one solely dedicated to Pure Land? This Shengchang, whose traditional role as patriarch would seemingly be diminished by such a question, might in fact be a truer representative of Pure Land belief and practice in tenth-century China.

Notes

1. Concerning the founding of Shengchang's society, see his biography in *Lebang wenlei* 3 (hereafter, *LBWL;* T 47.193b.29). This biography states that the society was formed during the Chunhua reign period (990–994). The annals of the *Fozu tongji* 43 (hereafter, *FZTJ;* T 49.400c.19–23) list the founding of the society under the year 991. With regard to Huiyuan and his society, see E. Zürcher, *The Buddhist Conquest of China: The Spread and Adaptation of Buddhism in Early Medieval China* (Leiden: E. J. Brill, 1959), 1:208–223.

2. One indication of Huiyuan's importance during this early part of the Song dynasty can be inferred from the conferral of the title "Yuanwu" (Perfectly Enlightened) on Huiyuan by the emperor Taizong in 978. See the *FZTJ* 43, T 49.397b.25. Concerning the proliferation of Pure Land societies during the Song, see Suzuki Chūsei, "Sōdai ni okeru Bukkyō kessha no kakudai to sono shōkaku," in *Chūgoku ni okeru kakumei to shūkyō* (Tokyo: Tokyō Daigaku shuppangai, 1974); Kasuga Reichi, "Sōdai no Jōdokyō kessha ni tsuite," *Shūgaku kenkyū* 18 (1941): 49–74; also Daniel A. Getz, Jr., "T'ien-t'ai Pure Land Societies and the Creation of the Pure Land Patriarchate," in *Buddhism in the Sung*, eds. Peter N. Gregory and Daniel A. Getz, Jr., Kuroda Institute Studies in East Asian Buddhism, no. 13 (Honolulu: University of Hawai'i Press, 1999).

3. See *LBWL* 3, T 47.193c.

4. Zongxiao's Pure Land Lineage is as follows:

1. Huiyuan (334–416)
2. Shandao (613–681)
3. Fazhao (fl. 785)
4. Shaokang (d. 805)
5. Shengchang (959–1020)
6. Zongze (fl. 1105)

5. See *FZTJ* 26, T 49.260c. Zhipan's list of patriarchs appears as follows:

1. Huiyuan
2. Shandao
3. Chengyuan (712–802)
4. Fazhao
5. Shaokang
6. Yanshou (904–975)
7. Shengchang

6. Shengchang's life was included in the Zhuhong's (1535–1615) Ming-era Pure Land biography, the *Wangsheng ji* (T 51.133c) and Peng Shaosheng's (1740–1796) *Jingtu shengxian lu* in the Qing.

7. For examples, see Mochizuki Shinkō, *Chūgoku Jōdokyōrishi* (1942; reprint, Kyoto: Hōzōkan, 1978), 390; Sasaki Kūjō, "Hyakurenja no fukkō undō," *Ryūkoku Daigaku ronsō* 261 (1925): 204–206; and Kasuga, "Sōdai no Jōdokyō kessha ni tsuite," 54–55.

8. See, for example, Kasuga Reichi, "Seiko no jiin to Jōdokyō," *Nikka Bukkkyō kenkyukai nempō* 2 (1937): 271; Kamata Shigeo, *Chūgoku Bukkyōshi jiten* (Tokyo: Tokyōdō shuppan, 1981), 160a.

9. A good example of this traditional interpretation of Pure Land in Western scholarship is Kenneth Ch'en's *Buddhism in China* (Princeton: Princeton University Press, 1972), which although outdated, remains a standard text in the teaching of Chinese Buddhism. Robert Sharf has mounted a substantial challenge to this interpretation in "What (If Anything) Is Ch'an/Pure Land Synchretism" (paper delivered at the Third Chung-Hwa Interntaional Conference on Buddhism, Taipei, July 1997).

10. The *Qiantang Xihu Jingshe lu* in three fascicles by Shengchang is listed in the *Yiwenzhi* section of the *Songshi* 158 (Shanghai: Zhonghua shuju, 1977), 15:5187a.

Can we assume, then, that it was still extant in the period when the *Songshi* was produced (1343–1345)?

11. Although the preface to this collection is still extant, the only poem that survives is by Wang Yücheng (954–1001), which is included in the *Zhaoqing si zhi,* 5.15a–b; see *Wulin zhanggu congbian,* vol. 2 (1883; reprint, Taipei: Tailian guofeng chubanshe, 1967).

12. The two main collections of evidence on Shengchang's society are Ŭich'ŏn, *Wonjong munllyu* 22, in *Han'guk pulgyo chonso* (Seoul: Tunguk University Press, 1980), 4.640b–643b; and the *Zhaoqing si zhi,* compiled by Zhuanyu in 1742 and now contained in the *Wulin zhanggu congbian,* vol. 2. The *Wonjong munllyu* contains the following relevant pieces:

1. Qian Yi, *Xihu Zhaoqing si jie Jingxing she ji*
2. Song Bo (936–1012), *Da Song Hangzhou Xihu Zhaoqing si jieshe beiming*
3. Su Yijian (958–997), *Jingxing pin xu* (Preface to the chapter on pure conduct in the *Huayan jing*)
4. Ding Wei (966–1037), *Xihu jieshe shi xu* (Preface of poetry for the West Lake Society)

One other document that was part of the original collection and is contained in the *Zhaoqing si zhi* is the *Bailian tang ji* (White Lotus hall record), written by Sun He (961–1004) in 1001 and inscribed in 1017 on the back side of a stele containing other texts related to the society. Sun He reported that Shengchang went to Suzhou (Gusu) in 1001 and stayed half a year. While there, he invited Sun He to compose an inscription for the posterior side of the stele commemorating the society. See *Zhaoqing si zhi,* 5.11b.

Concerning Qian Yi, see *Songren zhuanji ziliao soyin* (hereafter, *SRZJ*), 5.4060; on Song Bo, see *SRZJ* 1.735; Su Yijian, *SRZJ* 5.4338; Ding Wei, *SRZJ* 1.6–7; and Wang Yücheng, *SRZJ* 1.323–4.

13. See *Xianju bian* 33, *Manji Dai Nihon zokuzōkyō* 2.6.1, p. 74 *verso* a. This is also included in *LBWL* 3, T 47.183c. The latter will be the version cited below. According to *LBWL* 3 (T 47.193c.5), Zhiyuan also composed a biography of Shengchang *(xingye ji).* This work is not extant.

14. *Wonjong munllyu* 22, 4.640c.1.

15. *Wonjong munllyu* 22, 4.640b.15–16.

16. See *Da Song Hangzhou Xihu Zhaoqing si jieshe beiming,* in *Wonjong munllyu* 22, 4.642c.11–15.

17. The *Bukkyōgaku jiten* states that while traditions like Jushe (Kusha) and Faxiang (Hossō) are characterized as *xiangzong* (appearance teaching), the *xingzong* includes Sanlun (Sanron), Huayan (Kegon), and others. See *Bukkyōgaku jiten,* eds. Taira Raijun et al. (Kyoto: Hōzōkan, 1945), 264b. In light of the evidence provided below, I have interpreted this as a reference to the Huayan teaching.

18. On Zhe Shousu, see *SRZJ* 4.3313.

19. See Zhifeng's biography in *Zhingde chuandeng lu* 26, T 49.422b–432a.

20. *Jingde chuandeng lu* 26, T 51.422b.27–c.7. On Huayan sources in Yanshou's *Wanshan tonggui,* see Albert Welter, *The Meaning of Myriad Good Deeds: A Study of Yung-ming Yen-shou and the* Wan-Shan t'ung-kuei chi (New York: Peter Lang, 1993), 121–127.

21. On the Chan monastery at Mt. Wuyun, see *Zengaku daijiten,* 1.462b.

22. According to his biography, Zhifeng retired to Mt. Wuyun in 971 (T 51.422c.27). Shengchang's biography suggests that Shengchang studied with Zhifeng while Shengchang was still in his twenties, which would have been some time after 968.

23. *Da Song Hangzhou Xihu Zhaoqing si jieshe beiming,* in *Wonjong munllyu* 22, 4.642c.19–20. Sung Bo states that this dream occurred in the Yongxi era (984–987). An alternate, and perhaps more literal, reading of this passage might be that the monk revealed an image of Mañjuśrī to Shengchang. I have chosen a more direct manifestation as my interpretation of the passage.

24. What these marks are exactly is not clear to me. Are they the marks of Mañjuśrī? Was Shengchang seeking to bring about a liturgical reform oriented to Mañjuśrī in the Buddhist community?

25. On Mt. Wutai as a pilgrimage site in the Song, see Robert Gimello, "Chang Shang-yin on Wu-t'ai shan," in *Pilgrims and Sacred Sites,* eds. Susan Naquin and Chün-fang Yü (Berkeley: University of California Press, 1992), 89–149.

26. The Zhaoqing si was founded as the Puti yuan in 936 by the King of Wu Yue. It was restored by the Vinaya monk Yongzhi in 964, and in 978 an ordination platform was built. In 982 it was granted the name Da Zhaoqing lüsi. After Shengchang, Zunshi and Renyue came to the monastery to promote Tiantai doctrine *(jingjiao),* but shortly thereafter the monastery, which throughout its history time and again fell victim to the ravages of war and fire, burnt down for the first of six times. The famous Vinaya figure Yunkan rebuilt the monastery in 1042. The monastery's function as a place of ordination continued down through the Qing dynasty. On the Zhaoqing si, see *Zhaoqing si zhi,* 1.5b–6a.

27. *Da Song Hangzhou Xihu Zhaoqing si jieshe beiming,* in *Wonjong munllyu* 22, 4.642a.23–b, 4.

28. This society was commemorated by the great Tang literatus Bo Juyi (772–846) in 826. Bo's essay is contained in *Boshih changqing ji,* 59.7a–8b. His work is also excerpted in *FZTJ* 42, T 49.384c. Bo's record of this society is translated in Kenneth Ch'en, *The Chinese Transformation of Buddhism* (Princeton: Princeton University Press, 1973), 210–212. My thanks to Peter Gregory for this reference.

29. Translation from Ch'en, *The Chinese Transformation of Buddhism,* 210–211. See T 49.384c.21–23.

30. How long Nancao's society survived is not known, but Po Juyi wrote in 826 that the society, which had been meeting since 822, had met fourteen times to that point. See Ch'en, *The Chinese Transformation of Buddhism,* 210.

31. The *Jingxing pin* is the seventh chapter in the sixty-fascicle version of the *Huayan jing* and the eleventh in the eighty-fascicle version. It also exists as an independent sutra in two other works, the *Fo shuo pusa benye jing* (T 10, no. 281) and the *Zhu pusa qiu Fo benye jing* (T 10, no. 282).

32. I have been unable to ascertain Zhishou's Sanskrit name.

33. See *Bussho kaisetsu daijiten, Bekkan* 1, ed. Ono Gemmyo (1932–1935; reprint, Tokyo: Daitō shuppansha, 1975–1978), 9.411d.

34. *Da Song Hangzhou Xihu Zhaoqing si jieshe beiming,* in *Wonjong munllyu* 22, 4.642c.21.

35. *FZTJ* 26, T 49.265.13–14.

36. This title is found in Wang Yücheng's heading to his poem. See *Zhaoqing si zhi,* 5.15a–b.

37. *Qiantang Bailian shezhu bei,* T 47.184a.8–9.

38. We do find the term "Western Sage" *(xisheng),* which, at first glance, appears to refer to Amituo, employed twice in Zhiyuan's document. However, I believe the context of the first passage, in extolling the pure conduct and benevolent teaching of the Western Sage, as well as speaking of the spread of his teaching to China and those converted by him, more closely fits the person of Śākyamuni than the buddha Amitābha.

39. This of course leaves the possibility that two different images, one of Vairocana and one of Amituo, were carved in the course of the society's development. There is, however, no evidence to support this view.

40. *Da Song Hangzhou Xihu Zhaoqing si jieshe beiming,* in *Wonjong munllyu* 22, 4.642b.5–17; *Lushan Lianzong baojian* 4, T 47.324c.1–5.

41. On Ding Wei's relationship with Sun He, consult Ding Wei's biography in *Songshi* 283, 27:9566. Sun He's biography is *Songshi* 306, 29:10097–10101.

42. See *Qiantang Bailian shezhu bei,* T 47.184a.20–184b.1 for a discussion of this list.

43. Ding Wei's preface states that there were eighteen or nineteen officials who contributed poems but does not list their names. See his *Xihu jieshe shi xu* in *Wonjong munllyu* 22, 4.641c.12. Zhiyuan, reflecting another version of the composition of Huiyuan's White Lotus Society, states that 123 people joined Shengchang's society (T 47.184a.15). The term "Eighteen Notables" *(shiba xian),* referring to Huiyuan's core group, only appears for the first time in the mid-Tang. The membership of this group, some of whom could not possibly have belonged to the society, appears in the *Shiba xian zhuan.* The origins of this work are unclear, but it first appeared in edited form in Chen Shunyu's (?–1076) *Lushan ji* 3 (T 51.1039a–1042b). According to the *FZTJ* (T 49.268c.20–25), the monk Huaiwu later added more details in the Daguan era (1107–1110), and Zhipan definitively reedited it and included it in *FZTJ* 26 (T 47.265b–268c). See Tang Yongtong, *Han Wei liang Jin Nanbei chao Fojiao shi,* 366–369.

44. *LBWL* 3, T 47.265a.14.

45. A thorough study of this group, which has yet to be done, will require an exhaustive search through the works of these known members for allusions to this society and for evidence of their affiliation with Buddhism.

46. See *Xihu jieshe shi xu,* in *Wonjong munllyu* 22, 4.641c.10–15.

47. Although *qingliang* is a term used for nirvana (Nakamura, *Bukkyō go daijiten* [Tokyo: Tōkyō shoseki, 1961], 721b), it is also an alternate name for Wutai shan, the locus of Mañjuśrī to whom Shengchang directed his devotional practice. I am grateful to Robert Gimello for alerting me to this alternate possibility.

48. *Zhaoqing si zhi,* 5.13b.6–10.

49. *Lebang yigao* 2, T 47.247b.26. Wang Dan made this vow in the presence of Yang Yi (Yang Danian), the eminent court official and devout Buddhist who had close associations with the Linji branch of Chan and later tried to persuade the Tiantai monk Zhili not to commit suicide. In this case, Wang Dan requested that upon his death Yang Yi shave his head and dress him in monk's robes. Furthermore, Wang instructed that valuable items were not to be placed in his coffin and that he be cremated and a stupa erected.

50. See *Zhaoqing si zhi,* 5.15b.

51. See *Xihu jieshe shi xu,* in *Wonjong munllyu* 22, 4.641b–642a.

52. *Qiantang Bailian shezhu bei,* T 47.184a.10–14.

53. Concerning Han Yü's polemic, see Ch'en, *Buddhism in China,* 225–226; also, Stanley Weinstein, *Buddhism under the T'ang* (Cambridge: Cambridge University Press, 1987), 103–105.

54. On the *guwen* movment, see Peter Bol, *"This Culture of Ours": Intellectual Transitions in T'ang and Sung China* (Stanford: Stanford University Press, 1992).

55. This work, as mentioned previously, is no longer extant, but is cited in other sources.

56. The *Wangsheng Xifang luezhuan* is commonly regarded to have been written in 1017, when Zunshi was living in Hangzhou, but it could have been produced earlier. Takao Giken raises a doubt as to whether this work was produced in 1017. See his "Sōdai Jōdokyō tenseki to wag a kuni shoka no taido," in *Sōdai Bukkyōshi no kenkyū* (Kyoto: Hyakken, 1975), 170. Zunshi's biography in *FZTJ* 10 (T 49.207 c.29–208a.2) states that in that year he produced the *Wangsheng Xifang luezhuan* as well as the *Wangsheng jingtu jueyi xingyuan ermen* (T 47, no. 1969) for the governor of Qiantang, Ma Liang. However, Qisong's biographical record of Zunshi, the *Hangzhou Wulin Tianzhu si gu da fashi Ciyun Shi Gong xingye quji* (in *Tanjin wenji* 12, T 52.714c.16–18), only mentions Zunshi as having written the latter work for Ma Liang. Takao believes Qisong to be the more reliable of the two sources, perhaps because of his proximity in time to Zunshi.

57. The *Jingtu wangsheng zhuan* is T 51, no. 1071. Wang Gu's *Xinxiu wangsheng zhuan* was a three-fascicle work of which only the first and the last fascicles have survived. It is found in *Zoku Jōdoshū zensho,* vol. 16 (Tokyo: Sankibō Busshorin, 1974). Concerning the development of Song Pure Land biographies mentioned here, see Takao Giken, "Sōdai shakai to Jōdokyō" and "Sōdai Jōdokyō tenseki," in *Sōdai Bukkyōshi no kenkyū* (Kyoto: Hyakkaen, 1975), 115–117, 169–172; Ogasawara Senshū, "Ōjōden no kenkyū," in *Chūgoku Jōdokyōka no kenkyū* (Kyoto: Heirakuji shoten, 1951), 107–123; also Fukami Jikō, "Ōjōden, Kōsōden," in *Jōdoshū tenseki kenkyū,* ed. Asaji Kōhei (Tokyo: Sankibō Busshorin, 1975), 812–819. On Wang Gu in particular, see Sasaki Kūjō, "Ō Ko no *Shinshu Ōjōden,*" *Ryūkoku daigaku ronsō* 270 (1925), 31–41.

58. Lu Shishou's biography was supplemented in turn by Haiyin, who in 1236 wrote a twelve-fascicle biography, the *Jingtu wangsheng zhuan.* This work is not extant. See Takao, "Sōdai shakai to Jōdokyō," 116. We must also acknowledge here that there were two other Pure Land biographies written in the Song period, but because they are no longer extant we have no way of knowing if Shengchang was included in them: the *Wangsheng jingtu luezhuan,* written by the Tiantai monk Qingyue some time in the Southern Song, and the *Suiyuan wangsheng ji* by Feizhuo of the Liao dynasty in the middle of the eleventh century.

59. *FZTJ* 26–28.

60. *FZTJ* 26, T 49.265a.18–20.

61. See *Wuliang yuan Mituo xiang ji,* in *LBWL* 3, T 47.187a.22–23; also his *Guan Wuliangshou Fo jing yishu* 1, T 37.284a.23–25.

62. *Wuliang yuan Mituo xiang ji,* in *LBWL* 3, T 47.187a.22–23.

63. This has been demonstrated by Barend ter Haar in his *The White Lotus Teachings in Chinese Religious History* (Leiden: E. J. Brill, 1992).

64. See *Shishi yaolan* 1, T 54.263a.8–16.

65. On sectarian identity in the Chan tradition, see T. Griffith Foulk, "The Ch'an Tsung in Medieval China: School Lineage or What?" *The Pacific World,* n.s., 8 (1992): 18–31. Concerning the creation of Tiantai lineage, see Linda Penkower, "T'ien-t'ai during the T'ang Dynasty: Chan-jan and the Sinification of Buddhism" (Ph.D. diss., Columbia University, 1993), chaps. 6–14. For the issue of Pure Land as a school, see Tang Yongtong, *Sui Tang Fojiaoshi gao,* Tang Yongtong lunzhu ji, no. 2 (Beijing: Zhonghua shuju, 1982), 223; also Stanley Weinstein, "Buddhism, Schools of: Chinese Buddhism," in *The Encyclopedia of Religion,* ed. Mircea Eliade (New York: Macmillan Publishing Company, 1987).

66. See Daniel Getz, "Siming Zhili and Tiantai Pure Land in the Song Dynasty" (Ph.D. diss., Yale University, 1994), chaps. 8–12.

67. There is, for example, no evidence that Shandao established a Pure Land society, thus challenging his placement on the list. The same applies to Yanshou, who slightly preceded Shengchang in Zhipan's patriarchate. Yanshou's inclusion in the patriarchate might be further questioned in light of Albert Welter's study of Yanshou, which poses serious questions about the preeminence of Pure Land in Yanshou's career as presented by later biographers. See Welter, *The Meaning of Myriad Good Deeds.*

3

By the Power of One's Last Nenbutsu

Deathbed Practices in Early Medieval Japan

JACQUELINE I. STONE

RESEARCHERS IN THE FIELD of Japanese Buddhism have long noted the remarkable rise of Pure Land thought and practice in the late tenth through thirteenth centuries. Scholar-monks of the Heian period (794–1185), such as the Tendai prelates Senkan (918–983) and Genshin (942–1017), the Sanron masters Eikan (1033–1111) and Chinkai (c. 1091–1152), and the Shingon figure Kakuban (1095–1143), developed Pure Land doctrine within the framework of their respective schools. Distinctively Pure Land forms of art and architecture were sponsored by the aristocracy, while itinerant monks such as Kūya (or Kōya, 903–972) and Ryōnin (1072–1132) spread the chanted nenbutsu among people of all classes. And in the Kamakura period (1185–1333), independent Pure Land sectarian movements led by Hōnen (1133–1212), Shinran (1173–1262), and Ippen (1239–1289) emerged. Less well recognized, however, is the central role played in much of early medieval Pure Land Buddhism by deathbed practices and accompanying beliefs about the radical salvific power of one's last nenbutsu, whether understood as the contemplation of the Buddha Amitābha (or Amitāyus, Jpn. Amida) or the invocation of his name. Although Buddhism in general has held that the last moment of consciousness can influence one's postmortem fate, in the Pure Land tradition, "right mindfulness at the last moment" *(rinjū shōnen)* was deemed the essential prerequisite to experiencing the *raigō*—Amitābha's descent, together with his holy retinue, to welcome practitioners at the time of their death and escort them to his Pure Land. Since birth in the Pure Land *(ōjō)* was equated with the stage of non-retrogression on the bodhisattva path, dying with one's mind fixed on Amitābha was thought to release the practitioner once and for all from the round of samsara and to guarantee one's eventual Buddhahood. Early medieval concerns for a ritually correct death were not limited to Pure Land devotees; other Buddhists focused their postmortem aspirations on the Tuṣita heaven, where the future Buddha Miroku (Maitreya) dwells; or Mt. Fudaraku (Potalaka), home of the bodhisattva Kannon (Avalokiteś-vara); or Sacred Vulture Peak (Ryōjusen), where the eternal Śākya-muni Buddha constantly preaches. Overwhelmingly, however, people sought birth after death in Amitābha's Pure Land of Utmost Bliss (Skt. Sukhāvatī, Jpn. Gokuraku jōdo), countless world-spheres away to the west, and the medieval discourse of a death with right mindfulness was dominated by a Pure Land idiom. This chapter will briefly trace the major developments in Pure Land deathbed practices in early medieval Japan, along with concomitant ideas about the liberative power of one's dying thoughts of the Buddha.

Genshin and the Nijūgozanmai-e

On the twenty-third day of the fifth month, 986, a group of twenty-five monks of the Yokawa retreat on Mt. Hiei, the great Tendai center northeast of the imperial capital, met and put their names to an oath. It reads in part:

> We pledge together to be "good friends" to one another and, at life's last moment, to help one other contemplate the Buddha [Amitābha]. We hereby set the number of our society at twenty-five. If one among us should fall ill, then by the power of the vow uniting us, without concern for whether the day be auspicious or not, we shall go to him and inquire after him and encourage [his deathbed contemplation]. And if he happens to achieve birth in [the Pure Land of] Utmost Bliss, then—whether by the power of his own vow or by relying on the Buddha's supernatural powers, whether in a dream or in waking reality—he shall so communicate this to the society. Or, if he has fallen into the evil paths, he shall communicate that as well. Our society shall at regular times perform together with like mind those practices leading to the Pure Land. In particular, on the evening of the fifteenth day of each month, we shall cultivate the *samādhi* of mindfulness of the Buddha *(nenbutsu zanmai)* and pray that we may be able to complete ten reflections [on Amitābha] in our last moments.[1]

The newly formed association called itself the Nijūgozanmai-e, or Samādhi Society of Twenty-Five.[2] Two sets of rules were promulgated to govern the group. An original set of eight regulations, dated

986, has been attributed to Yoshishige no Yasutane (c. 931–1002), a scholar of Chinese studies who had recently been ordained as the monk Jakushin.[3] A revised set of twelve regulations, dated 988, is said to have been written by the monk Genshin, who was active in the society's later development. Although exhibiting some differences in style and orientation, both sets of regulations stipulate that the society should devote the fifteenth of each month to nenbutsu practice with the aim of achieving birth in Amitābha's Pure Land; perform the mantra of light *(kōmyō shingon)* empowering earth and sand, to be sprinkled on the corpses of deceased members; nurse any members of the society who should fall sick and remove them to a separate chapel called the Ōjōin (Chapel for Birth in the Pure Land), to be established for this purpose; and establish a gravesite for members and perform funerals, centering around nenbutsu practice.[4] As these regulations suggest, deathbed practice was part of a continuum that encompassed, at one end, one's habitual practice during ordinary times, and at the other, funerary rites conducted after one's death. Within that continuum, however, practice during one's last hours held a special place, as the potential of this liminal moment was deemed to set it apart from ordinary time and offer a unique opportunity for securing birth in the Pure Land.

The deathbed observances of the Nijūgozanmai-e as set forth in these regulations resonate with slightly earlier prescriptions given in Genshin's *Ōjō yōshū* (Essentials of birth in the Pure Land), completed in the fourth month of 985, the year before the society was established.[5] This work would come to exert a profound influence on the rise of Japanese Pure Land thought and practice. It is justly famous for its vivid opening descriptions of the hells and others of the six realms of deluded rebirth, toward which one is to cultivate aversion, and of the splendors of Amitābha's Pure Land, toward which one is to aspire. The heart of the text, however, is devoted to instructions for practice to achieve birth in the Pure Land, among which the contemplative nenbutsu—the visualization of Amitābha—holds a preeminent place. The sixth chapter, "On the Nenbutsu for Special Times," contains a set of detailed instructions for deathbed nenbutsu practice, the first ever compiled in Japan.[6]

In the first part of this section, dealing with deathbed ritual *(rinjū gyōgi)* itself, Genshin draws primarily on Chinese texts. He first cites a "Chinese transmission" *(zhongguo benzhuan)*, quoted in the commentary on the four-part *vinaya* written by Daoxuan (596–667), in a section on "Caring for the Sick and Sending off the Deceased" that purports to describe the care of the terminally ill at the Jetavana monastery in Śrāvastī in India. The sick person is removed to a "chapel of impermanence" *(mujōin),* so that the sight of his familiar surroundings and robe, bowl, and other possessions will not generate thoughts of attachment. There he should be placed behind a standing Buddha image to whose right hand has been affixed one end of a trailing five-colored pennant. The dying person should be made to grasp the other end of this pennant, to help him generate thoughts of following the Buddha to his pure realm. Those in attendance are to burn incense, scatter flowers, and promptly remove any vomit or excrement.[7] Alternatively, Genshin cites the recommendation of Daoshi (d. 668?) that the Buddha image should face east, and the sick person should be placed in front of and facing it.[8]

Genshin also cites the instructions by the Chinese Pure Land teacher Shandao (613–681) that the dying should face west, visualize the coming of Amitābha's holy retinue, and continually recite his name. Of particular importance to the later Japanese tradition is Shandao's insistence that those in attendance should write down any visions described by the dying:

> If the sick are unable to speak, then those caring for them should by all means ask from time to time what they are seeing. If they describe scenes of painful punishment, then those by their side should say the nenbutsu for them and assist them by performing repentance with them, so that they may eradicate all their sins without fail. And if their sins are thus eradicated, then the saintly host bearing the lotus pedestal will appear before them in accord with their thoughts. That also should be recorded as before.[9]

Genshin further quotes Shandao to the effect that relatives and other visitors who have recently consumed meat, alcohol, or the five pungent roots should be refused access to the dying. Otherwise, this might cause them to lose their correct concentration, allowing demons to confuse them and make them fall into the evil paths.[10]

Another Chinese Pure Land master cited by Genshin is Daochuo (562–645), who comments on the difficulty of sustaining the ten continuous thoughts of Amitābha in one's last moments, deemed necessary in order to achieve birth in the Pure Land:

> To have ten uninterrupted reflections in succession would not seem difficult. But most unenlightened individuals have a mind as untamed as a wild horse, a consciousness more restless than a monkey. . . .

> Once the winds of dissolution arise [at the moment of death], a hundred pains will gather in the body. If you have not trained prior to this time, how can you assume that you will be able to contemplate the Buddha on that occasion? Each person should thus make a pact in advance with three to five people of like conviction. Whenever the time of death approaches [for any of them], they should offer each other encouragement. They should chant the name of Amitābha for the dying person, desire that person's birth in the Pure Land, and continue chanting to induce [in him] the ten moments of reflection.[11]

In Japan, Daochuo's suggestion of a pact among like-minded practitioners to encourage one another's deathbed practice was first realized in the founding of the Nijūgozanmai-e.

The "ten uninterrupted thoughts" mentioned here refers, on one hand, to Amitābha's famous eighteenth vow, which promises birth in his Pure Land to all who aspire to this goal with sincerity and call him to mind "even ten times";[12] it also refers to a passage in the *Contemplation Sūtra,* which, in describing the lowest of the nine levels of birth in the Pure Land, says that even an evil person, if he encounters a good friend *(zenchishiki)* who instructs him at the hour of death so that he is able to sustain ten thoughts of Amitābha, shall, with each thought, erase the sins of eight billion *kalpa*s and be born in Amitābha's Pure Land.[13] By Genshin's time, the ten thoughts or ten reflections at the time of death had been subject to considerable interpretation, but he himself took them to mean chanting the nenbutsu ten times while single-mindedly focusing on Amitābha.

Following these instructions for deathbed observances, Genshin gives his own recommendations for encouragement to the dying. These consist of ten items of exhortation, centering on visualization of Amitābha's physical marks, his radiant light, and his descent, together with his holy retinue, to escort the practitioner to the Pure Land. As the moment of death approaches, the person in attendance is to say:

> Child of the Buddha, do you realize that now is your last thought? This single reflection [on the Buddha] at death outweighs the karmic acts of a hundred years. If this instant should pass you by, rebirth [in samsara] will be unavoidable. Now is precisely the time. Reflect on the Buddha single-mindedly, and you will surely be born on a seven-jewelled lotus pedestal in the pond of eight virtues in the subtle and wondrous Pure Land of Utmost Bliss in the west.[14]

The instructions for deathbed practice given in Genshin's *Ōjō yōshū* and in the regulations of the Nijūgozanmai-e mark the entry into

Japanese Buddhist discourse of a concern with dying in a state of right mindfulness and belief in the power of one's last thoughts, ritually focused, to determine one's postmortem fate. The *Ōjō yōshū* drew attention in court circles; Fujiwara no Michinaga (966–1027), the most powerful courtier of his day, kept a personal copy close at hand.[15] The idealized account of Michinaga's death given in the historical tale *Eiga monogatari* (A tale of flowering fortunes, c. 1092) is clearly based on Genshin's description of deathbed ritual. Michinaga is depicted as dying lying down facing west, calmly chanting the nenbutsu while holding cords attached to nine full-size images of Amitābha, representing the nine levels of birth in the Pure Land.[16]

Aspirations for the Pure Land as set forth in Genshin's *Ōjō yōshū* also stimulated developments in architecture, sculpture, and painting, giving rise to a distinctive Heian-period Pure Land visual culture. Personal chapels for Pure Land devotion *(Amida-dō)* were sponsored by the aristocracy, such as the Hōjōji, completed by Michinaga in 1022, and the even more famous Byōdōin at Uji, begun by his son Yorimichi in 1052. Similar structures were built in considerable numbers up until about the thirteenth century.[17] The late Heian period also saw the emergence of the *raigōzu,* a new form of painting depicting Amitābha descending with his retinue of bodhisattvas to welcome the practitioner at death. So closely were *raigōzu* associated with the Pure Land thought of the *Ōjō yōshū* that, by the twelfth century, it was believed that Genshin had introduced the genre.[18] *Raigōzu* were on occasion used in the deathbed setting, and some surviving examples have threads remaining where cords were once attached for the dying person to hold.[19]

Genshin is also credited with another sort of representation of Amida's descent, the *mukaekō,* or "welcoming rite," a ceremonial procession that actually enacted the descent of Amitābha and his retinue, performed by monks and young novices in costume and accompanied by music and nenbutsu chanting. The *mukaekō* may originally have been performed at the Kedaiin, a chapel established by Genshin at Yokawa, and spread to other locations. Unlike privately commissioned *raigōzu, mukaekō* performances were witnessed by people of a range of social classes. Genshin's biography in *Hokke genki* (Accounts of the wondrous powers of the *Lotus Sūtra,* compiled 1040–1044) says that those who witnessed the ceremony, "from the monks and laiety, old and young, down to the dissolute and those of false views, all wept spontaneously, forming the karma for *ōjō,* and prostrated themselves, planting the seeds of enlightened insight."[20] The monk Nōgu, a disciple of Genshin, is said to have dreamed of his deceased teacher being escorted to the Pure Land by a procession of monks and four gorgeously arrayed youths, "on the whole, like the welcoming rite of Yokawa"[21]—thus hinting at the power of such performances to shape the dreams and visions of the living concerning the *ōjō* of the deceased.

Instructions for Deathbed Ritual after Genshin

Genshin's *Ōjō yōshū* did much to inspire subsequent ritualization of the deathbed scene. The "deathbed practice" section of the *Ōjō yōshū* itself circulated in a somewhat modified, *kana* version as an independent text;[22] it also seems also to have been read on occasion to the dying. For example, Shōnen Ajari (d. 1015), a member of the Nijūgozanmai-e, when he fell ill, reportedly "requested that worldly matters not be discussed in his presence but solely had the *rinjū gyōgi* section of the *Ōjō yōshū* read to him, learning its admonitions." On the night of his death, he had his attendant monks recite it, along with the "Fathoming the Tathāgata's Lifespan" chapter of the *Lotus Sūtra.*[23]

The "deathbed practice" section of the *Ōjō yōshū* also formed the prototype for a number of subsequent *rinjū gyōgi* texts, or "deathbed manuals," as they might be termed, compiled during the latter Heian and Kamakura periods. These texts retain and elaborate on the basic features of Genshin's instructions: the removal of the dying to a separate place; the enshrinement of a Buddha image with a cord fastened to its hand for the dying person to hold; the offering of flowers and incense; the shielding of the dying person from talk of worldly affairs or the intrusion of those who have recently consumed meat, alcohol, or the five pungent roots, or of those who would be likely to arouse strong feelings, either of love or aversion; and the need throughout to create a quiet and dignified atmosphere conducive to contemplation in one's last hours. Genshin's exhortation to the dying person is frequently quoted: "You should not visualize any form except the features of the Buddha. You should not hear any sounds except the Buddha's words of Dharma. You should not speak of anything except the true teachings of the Buddha. You should not think of anything except birth in the Pure Land."[24]

Underscored above all is the decisive influence of the last moment in determining the dying person's postmortem fate, and hence, the vital role of the person or persons in attendance—variously referred to as the *kanbyō* (carer for the sick) or *zenchishiki (kalyāṇamitra),* often shortened to *chishiki* (literally, a "good friend" or religious guide)—in offering encouragement, guiding deathbed reflection and repentance, and chanting the nenbutsu. This shared framework, however, was quickly assimilated to a range of practices and doctrinal interpretations. An early example is the *Rinjū gyōgi chūki* (Annotations on deathbed practice), written by Tanshū (1066–1120?), a Kōfukuji monk learned in Hossō doctrine.[25] Tanshū identifies right thoughts at the last moment with the aspiration for enlightenment (Skt. *bodhicitta,* Jpn. *bodaishin*), which marks the beginning of the bodhisattva path; so long as one has aroused the *bodhicitta,* one will not suffer at the time of death, even if one should fall into the evil paths. Tanshū's instructions for deathbed observance reflect the eclectic and nonexclusive character of much Heian-period Pure Land practice. In addition to chanting the Buddha's name, he says, if death is not imminent, other measures may be taken: Someone versed in the *Lotus Sūtra* may expound its meaning for the dying person, or a companion in practice may read the *Daihannya rishubun* (Scripture on the guiding principle of great wisdom).[26] He also suggests having the bodhisattva precepts recited for the dying person to hear, as an unrivalled source of merit. Tanshū's instructions for deathbed practice allow for aspiration to sacred realms other than Amitābha's Pure Land: If the dying person seeks birth in the Tuṣita heaven, for example, then an image of Maitreya should be substituted for that of Amitābha, and the dying person should visualize being born there.[27]

A number of texts of deathbed ritual instruction were also produced by monks active in the development of the *himitsu nenbutsu,* or esoteric Pure Land tradition. The earliest example is the *Byōchū shugyōki* (Notes on practice during illness) by Jichihan (c. 1089–1144), which draws on elements from Genshin's *Ōjō yōshū* but reinterprets them in an esoteric mode, emphasizing the non-duality of Amitābha and the *shingon* practitioner.[28] For example, Genshin had stressed the visualization of the radiant light emanating from the white curl *(ūrṇā)* between Amitābha's brows. This light embraces the practitioner and enables him to eradicate sin, focus his deathbed contemplation, and achieve birth in the Pure Land. Jichihan suggests that the white curl should be visualized as a transformation of the letter *hūṃ,* endowed with Amida's four inseparable mandalas. He further equates the name "Amida" with three fundamental esoteric meanings of the letter "A": *A* indicating originally unborn, which is the middle Way; *mi,* the non-self that is the great self, which freely abides; and *da,* moment-to-moment accordance with suchness, which is liberation. Deathbed nenbutsu is for Jichihan a form of empowerment through ritual union with the three secrets of a cosmic buddha *(sanmitsu kaji):* the practioner's reverent posture corresponds to the secret of the Buddha's body; the chanting of his name, to the secret of his speech; and the contemplation of the name's meaning, to the secret of his mind. Another figure to develop *himitsu nenbutsu* practice in the deathbed context was Kakuban, revered as the founder of "new doctrine" *(shingi)* Shingon, whose synthesis of Pure Land and esoteric thought is discussed in James Sanford's essay in this volume. Kakuban's *Ichigo taiyō himitsu shū* (Esoteric collection of essentials for life's end), which explicitly draws on Jichihan's *Byōchū shugyōki,* also equates the deathbed nenbutsu with esoteric three secrets practice. Kakuban's text is sometimes regarded as embodying a more "orthodox" esoteric position than Jichihan's in explicitly defining Amitābha as an aspect of the cosmic Buddha Dainichi (Mahāvairocana), but the two are alike in stressing union with the Buddha as the focus of the *shingon* practitioner's deathbed contemplation. Kakuban writes:

> Amida is Dainichi's function as wisdom. Dainichi is Amida's essence as principle. . . . When one contemplates in this way, then, without leaving the *sahā* world, one dwells in [the Pure Land] of Utmost Bliss. One's own person enters Amida, and Amida, without transformation, is precisely Dainichi. One's own person emerges from Dainichi; this is the subtle contemplation for realizing buddhahood in this very body.[29]

The deathbed scene in Kakuban's instructions even appears to be arranged in a mandalic structure: four *chishiki* who assist the dying person's nenbutsu take up their positions around him so that together they reproduce the configuration of the five wisdom buddhas, the dying person occupying the central position of Dainichi.

Although Genshin had encouraged those in attendance to chant the nenbutsu together with the dying to help them focus their contemplation, in light of his *Ōjō yōshū,* it is ultimately the dying person's own deathbed practice that determines his or her success or failure in achieving the Pure Land. However, *rinjū gyōgi* texts of the late Heian and Kamakura periods take cognizance, as the *Ōjō yōshū* does not, of the fact that many people lapse into unconsciousness before dying, and these texts therefore increasingly stress the power of the *chishiki*'s nenbutsu to lead the dying person to the Pure Land.[30] Kakuban's instructions, for example, advise that, should the dying person lapse into unconsciousness, the *chishiki* are to observe his breathing carefully and match their breathing to his, chanting the nenbutsu in unison on the outbreath, for a day, two days, a week, or as long as necessary until death transpires. In this way, the dying person can be freed of sins and achieve the Pure Land, because the power of Amitābha's original vow must inevitably respond to the invocation of his name. Moreover, the *chishiki* are to visualize their nenbutsu, chanted on the outbreath, as the six syllables *Na-mu-a-mi-da-butsu* in Siddham letters, entering the dying person's mouth with the inbreath, transforming into six sun disks, and dispelling with their brilliance the darkness of the obstructions of sins associated with the six sense faculties. Here the deathbed chanting of the nenbutsu by the *chishiki* in attendance is assimilated to the visualization and breath meditations that were to figure largely in the esoteric nenbutsu tradition.[31]

A similar theme appears in the *Kanbyō yōjin shō* (also known as the *Kanbyō yōjin* or *Kanbyō goyōjin,* Admonitions for attending the sick), a very detailed set of deathbed instructions compiled by Nen'a Ryōchū (1199–1287), third patriarch of Hōnen's Pure Land sect.[32] Ryōchū places immense responsibility on the *kanbyō* to encourage the dying person's chanting of the nenbutsu with wholehearted reliance on Amitābha as the "foremost essential" and to let him hear the nenbutsu chanted when he himself can no longer chant it; so long as the aural faculty is still operative, Ryōchū suggests, hearing the nenbutsu alone can be sufficient to enable the dying to reach the Pure Land. The *kanbyō* must watch over the dying person with compassion, attentive to the exact moment at which life ends, and then continue chanting the nenbutsu for two to four hours after the person has died. "Perform the transfer of merit in all sincerity so that, by the virtue of this deed, the dead person will achieve *ōjō,* even from the interim state."[33] Ryōchū's emphasis on the *kanbyō*'s ritual influence over the dying person's passage to the Pure Land may seem at odds with the spirit of abandoning reliance on the power of one's own efforts and instead placing wholehearted trust in the "other power" of Amitābha's original vow, which is often associated with Hōnen's Pure Land thought. However, it must be borne in mind that Hōnen's disciples embraced widely varying understandings of his teaching, a point underscored by their divergent attitudes toward deathbed practice, to which we will return.

The thrust of such deathbed ritual instructions was to emphasize the authority of the *chishiki* or *kanbyō* as an emerging religious specialist. With him rested the ritual control of the final moment with its brief window onto the possibility of escape from samsaric suffering, and thus a large share in the responsibility for a dying person's success or failure in reaching the Pure Land. Kakuban stipulates that the chief *chishiki* should be a person of wisdom and aspiration for the Way; the sick person should look upon him as the bodhisattva Kannon come to lead him to the Pure Land.[34] Ryōchū for his part writes: "Without the compassionate encouragement of the *chishiki*, how could this sole great matter [of birth in the Pure Land] be achieved? Thus the sick person should look upon the *chishiki* as the Buddha, while the *chishiki* should extend compassion to the sick person, as though toward his only child."[35] The *chishiki*'s authority in turn worked to strengthen the larger religious networks, old and new, in which it was embedded: monastic fraternities; nenbutsu societies *(kessha)*, sometimes including laypeople; or the ties between lay patrons and the ritual specialists who served their religious needs. In the founding regulations of the Nijūgozanmai-e, the dying person and the attending *chishiki* are assumed to be fellow monks; later, deathbed ritual became a service also performed by monks for lay patrons. Hōnen and his disciples, for example, are known to have acted as *chishiki* to lay followers as well as fellow clerics.[36] A recent study by Jonathan Todd Brown analyzes how Ta'amidabutsu Shinkyō (1237–1319), successor to Ippen as leader of the Jishū, skillfully secured this fledgling movement an institutional base among the *bushi* of the eastern provinces by emphasizing how hard it is for those professionally engaged in the sin of killing to reach the Pure Land, and thus, the immense benefits to be gained by any warrior who supported a local Jishū practice hall, thus ensuring himself the presence of a *chishiki* in his last hours.[37] In later medieval times, as is well known, Jishū "camp priests" *(jinsō)* chanted the nenbutsu on the battlefield to ensure the *ōjō* of the fallen and dying—an extension of the *chishiki*'s role at the deathbed and of belief that, by hearing the chanted nenbutsu, the newly deceased could be guided to the Pure Land.[38]

Good and Bad Deaths

What was the ideal death supposed to look like? While *rinjū gyōgi* texts emphasize how deathbed scenes should be conducted, images of exemplary deaths were circulated in a very different sort of literature known as *ōjōden* (literally, accounts of *ōjōnin,* or persons who achieved birth in the Pure Land). The first of these, *Nihon ōjō gokurakuki* (A record of Japanese who achieved birth in [the Pure Land] of Utmost Bliss, c. 985), was compiled by Yoshishige no Yasutane, the scholar of Chinese learning and close associate of Genshin traditionally said to be the author of the Nijūgozanmai-e's initial regulations.[39] Yasutane was inspired by earlier Tang-dynasty accounts recording the ideal deaths of men and women believed to have reached the Pure Land, such as Jiacai's *Jingtu lun* (Treatise on the Pure Land, c. seventh century), whose sixth chapter contains twenty such biographies of both clergy and laity, and the *Wangsheng xifang jingtu ruiying zhuan* (Accounts of auspicious responses accompanying birth in the western Pure Land), compiled by Wenshen (n.d.) and Shaokang (d. 805), which contains forty-eight such accounts. Yasutane's own collection includes forty-two accounts that he discovered in older records and through personal inquiry, of individuals said to have died exemplary deaths. His collection was followed by five subsequent major and several minor *ōjōden* collections, chiefly written in the latter part of the Heian period.[40] Typically these include examples of the *ōjō* of monks, laymen, nuns, and laywomen, representing a range of social classes. In these accounts, the lives of *ōjōnin* tend to be summarized in a few sentences, as though mere headnotes to their deaths, which are often described in detail. The stated purpose of this literature, for both compilers and readers, was to form a karmic tie, or *kechien,* conducive to birth in the Pure Land by gathering or reading stories of those believed to have reached this goal. Yasutane quotes Jiacai on this point: "The wisdom of the beings is shallow, and they cannot understand the sagely intent [set forth in sūtras and treatises]. Unless one records examples of those who actually achieved *ōjō,* one will not be able to encourage them."[41] But in addition, *ōjōden* served to circulate images and thus, expectations, of what a death with "right mindfulness" should look like.

Where texts of instruction for deathbed practice tend to stress the importance and authority of the *chishiki,* the men and women whose stories are recounted in *ōjōden* are in most cases very much the principle agents in their own deathbed scenes. Death never takes them by surprise; they foresee it to the day and announce it to disciples or family. They bathe, put on clean clothes, then sit upright in the posture of meditation or lie down facing west. They die peacefully, as though sinking deep into contemplation or falling asleep. Though no doubt considerably idealized, such accounts provide a useful index to the range of deathbed practices carried out in the latter Heian period. Some *ōjōnin* are described as entering meditation in their last hours, but, for most, deathbed practice seems to have entailed some form of vocalization, whether of mantras, *dhāraṇīs,* sūtras, or other sacred texts. Most popular was the invocation of Amitābha's name, *Namu-Amida-butsu.* Genshin had recognized the value of the chanted nenbutsu as an aid to deathbed visualization, and although the emphasis on contemplative practice remains paramount in his Pure Land thought, he also argued that invoking the name of Amitābha in one's last moments carried an immense salvific potency that it did not possess at ordinary times.[42] In addition, contemplation was thought to be extremely difficult to practice in one's last moments, when the "winds of dissolution" *(danmatsuma no kaze)* were said to wrack the body with excruciating pain. Even for those trained in meditation, the chanted nenbutsu may well have proved more practicable at a time when one was greatly weakened and perhaps suffering. It was at least partly in the context of deathbed practice that the practice of chanting the nenbutsu spread.

Takagi Yutaka, tabulating the evidence from seven Heian-period *ōjōden* collections, found sixty-seven examples, dating from 951 to 1153, of people who died chanting the nenbutsu in their last hours. Most of these are concentrated after 1051.[43] The year 1052, of course, was widely thought to mark the beginning of the Final Dharma age *(mappō),* when sentient beings are said to be greatly burdened by ignorance and evil, and liberation becomes exceedingly difficult to achieve. Although consciousness of *mappō* has often been invoked uncritically as a convenient explanation for a range of complex religious phenomena, the growing popularity of the invocational nenbutsu may in part have stemmed from its reputation as a practice suited to benighted worldlings of the last age. Certainly it was accessible to people across the boundaries of class and level of education. The examples identified by Takagi of *ōjōnin* who chanted the nenbutsu as their deathbed practice include not only aristocrats and literati but also warriors of both high and low rank, as well as provincial officials and commoners.

A second form of deathbed practice, also aimed at achieving birth in Amitābha's Pure Land, was reciting the *Lotus Sūtra,* or individual chapters, verses, or phrases from the *Lotus Sūtra.* In the same survey of *ōjōden,* Takagi found examples of thirty-six individuals who chanted the *Lotus Sūtra* or some portion thereof on their deathbed. This is a much smaller percentage than those who employed the invocational nenbutsu and includes only seven laypeople. Reciting the *Lotus Sūtra* would presuppose either literacy and access to a copy of the text or proximity to a teacher who could instruct one in recitation and memorization. Sūtra recitation as a deathbed practice would also have carried the risk that one might fall unconscious or die in mid-sentence, a death that one imagines would have been viewed as both inauspicious and unaesthetic.[44] In contrast, one could die at any point while chanting the nenbutsu and it could still be said of that person that he or she died in admirable fashion, invoking the Buddha's name.

However, while some *ōjōnin* relied solely on the chanted nenbutsu, this was not yet linked to a doctrine of the nenbutsu's exclusive validity, such as would emerge in the Kamakura period with Hōnen, founder of the independent Japanese Pure Land sect. The mainstream of early medieval Pure Land thought recognized a spectrum of practices as efficacious for achieving birth in the Pure Land, and both *ōjōden* as well as court diaries and other historical accounts describe the use of a range of deathbed invocations.[45] Sacred texts other than the *Lotus* were also employed; Genshin himself, when near death, in addition to chanting the nenbutsu, is said to have recited from the "Twelve Salutations" (Chn. *Shi-er li,* Jpn. *Jūnirai*), twelve verses in praise of Amitābha attributed to Nāgārjuna, a practice that may also have been adopted by some members of the Nijūgozanmai-e and others.[46] Deathbed invocations included *dhāraṇī*s believed able to dissolve karmic hindrances, such as the name of the bodhisattva Kokūzō (Ākāśagarbha) or the *dhāraṇī* of the Augustly Victorious One (Skt. *uṣṇīṣavijayā dhāraṇī,* Jpn. *sonshō darani*). Also employed were so-called "hell-harrowing texts," or *hajigokumon,* sūtra passages believed to protect the reciter against falling into hell. A famous example is taken from the *Flower Garland Sūtra (Avataṃsaka sūtra):* "One who desires the knowledge of the Buddhas of the three time periods should contemplate the dharma-realm as being entirely mind-created."[47] Others derive from the *Lotus Sūtra* (for example, "One who with a pure mind believes and reveres and does not give rise to doubt will not fall into [the realms of] the hells, hungry ghosts, or beasts but will be born in the presence of the Buddhas of the ten directions"), or from the *Larger Sūtra:* "By the power of that Buddha's [Amitābha's] original vow, those who hear his name and desire birth in his Pure Land shall at once arrive at that land, where they will achieve [the stage of] non-retrogression."[48] The efficacy of *hajigokumon* is also stressed in some deathbed ritual texts; Ryōchū recommends several examples to be recited by the *chishiki* should the dying person become deranged by extreme pain.[49]

Such vocalization practices were accompanied by other ritual acts, such as holding a five-colored pennant or cord tied to the hand of a Buddha image, recommended by Daoxuan and specified in instructions for deathbed practice from the *Ōjō yōshū* on. Alternatively, some *ōjōnin* are described as forming mudras on their deathbed or holding ritual implements, such as *vajra*s or incense burners or, in some cases, a written vow to be born in Pure Land or a record of the good deeds they had performed in their lifetime.[50] Here again we find a resonance between descriptions in *ōjōden* and instructions in *rinjū gyōgi* texts. Both Tanshū's *Rinjū gyōgi chūki* and the *Kōyōshū* (Collection on filial conduct), a collection attributed to Kakuban and containing a set of instructions for deathbed practice, specify that a record should be made of the dying person's good deeds in that lifetime, which is then to be read aloud and praised at the deathbed to encourage that person.[51]

Ishida Mizumaro writes: "Right mindfulness in one's last moments is a subjective matter, and whether or not the sick person had in fact achieved it could not easily be known. . . . To inspire confidence in those attending, some more immediately recognizable, outwardly visible sign of a good death was required."[52] This helps account for the fact that "right thoughts at the last moment," or *rinjū shonen,* quickly came to be understood, less in terms of the dying person's inward state of mind, inaccessible to outward observers, than as a matter of conformity to prescribed ritual behavior, which was assumed to reflect a proper mental attitude. Dying calmly, holding a cord attached to the hand of a Buddha image with the name of Amitābha on one's lips, was itself deemed proof of *ōjō*. However, additional evidence was sought, and three kinds of indicators are particularly stressed in *ōjōden*. First are wondrous signs appearing at the time of death or shortly after. Yasutane records that when the prelate Zōmyō, chief abbot *(zasu)* of Enryakuji, passed away: "That evening a golden light suddenly illuminated the place, and purple clouds arose of themselves. Music spread through the heavens and a fragrance filled his room."[53] Mysterious fragrance or radiant light in the death chamber, music of unearthly beauty heard in the air, or purple clouds rising in the west all appear in Yasutane's Chinese prototypes and became staples of Japanese *ōjōden* and other deathbed accounts. Sometimes these signs were described as perceptible only to the dying person, but in other cases they were depicted as objectively evident to bystanders or even unrelated persons at a distance.

The second and most widely reported index to a person's *ōjō* was the revelatory dream, examples of which were recorded in immense variety.[54] Such dreams could be precognitive, indicating that the dying person would reach the Pure Land and appear either to the individual concerned or to other parties. More common were dreams after the fact, indicating that the dead person had indeed achieved *ōjō*. Dreams of this variety recall the charter oath of the Nijūgozanmai-e, which mandated that deceased members should make contact with those still living and inform them of their postmortem fate. Dreams appearing to more than one person were deemed especially reliable. An example is the case of the monk Ryōhan, a member of the Nijūgozanmai-e, who died while still a very young man. Both his parents subsequently dreamed that he appeared to them and announced, "I am now in the land of Utmost Bliss, where my name is Bodhisattva Benevolent Wisdom (Ninne)."[55] As in this case, dreams could reveal not only the fact of *ōjō* but the level of birth achieved: Ōe no Masafusa (1041–1111), in whose *ōjōden* collection this account appears, concluded that Ryōhan must have achieved the ninth and highest grade of birth, presumably because he referred to himself as "bodhisattva." The dreams and the visions reported by the dying, and their artistic and literary representations in *raigōzu*, *ōjōden* and, other sources, probably stood in a circular relationship: reports of dreams and deathbed visions would have informed the representations, and the representations in turn shaped the dreams and visions; people saw what they knew they were supposed to see.

A third class of indicators was the appearance of the corpse. Numerous accounts tell of *ōjōnin* whose bodies did not decay but emitted wondrous fragrance. Even in the crematory fires, their bodies retained the posture of meditation and their hands, the mudras they had formed. In the liminal period right before and after death, the body, normally opaque, became in effect a lens opening onto the individual's postmortem fate. *Ōjōden* report only success stories, but behind such accounts lurked the specter of a bad death and consequent rebirth in the evil realms, which, it was thought, could also be known from the manner of dying and the subsequent appearance of the body. "When those who do evil are about to die," Genshin had written, "the wind and fire elements depart first, so they are restless and feverish, and suffer greatly. When those who do good are about to die, the earth and water elements depart first, so they are calm, and experience no pain."[56] Passages in canonical Buddhist texts dealing with corporeal indices to a dying person's realm of rebirth attracted considerable interest in the late Heian and Kamakura periods. For example, Kakuban's instructions for deathbed practice cite the Chinese esoteric scripture *Shouhu guojiezhu tuoluoni jing* (Sūtra of the *dhāraṇī* for protecting the ruler of the realm), which enumerates fifteen signs that the dying will fall into the hells (such as crying aloud with grief or choking with tears, urinating or defecating without awareness, refusing to open the eyes, foul breath, or lying face down); eight signs that the dying will fall into the realm of hungry ghosts (such as burning with fever or suffering from hunger or thirst); and seven signs presaging a descent into the bestial realm (such as contorting of the hands and feet, foaming at the mouth, or sweating from the entire body)—all signs requiring the *chishiki*'s immediate ritual intervention.[57] Although further evidence is needed, one suspects that the emphasis on dying with right mindfulness may have served in part to counter fears about *onryō* (vengeful ghosts), the products of painful or untimely deaths, who could vent their resentment on the living in the form of sickness or other disasters. The manner of death of both worldly and religious leaders was appropriated for a variety of polemical agendas. The epic *Tale of the Heike,* for example, represents the usurper Taira no Kiyomori as dying in an agony of fever and convulsions, while his wife dreams that horse- and ox-headed demons arrive to carry him off to the Avīci hell.[58] The treatise on poetics *Nomori no kagami,* attributed to Minamoto no Arifusa, criticizes the death of the Jishū founder, Ippen:

> Beforehand, people insisted that [when Ippen died,] purple clouds would rise and lotus blossoms would fall from the skies, but when the time actually came, there was no sign of Amitābha's descent. His body was in such a state that his disciples' expectations that he would achieve the Pure Land were completely thwarted, and they had to hurry to cremate him before others could see it.[59]

The monk Nichiren (1222–1282), who preached exclusive devotion to the *Lotus Sūtra* and opposed Pure Land practices in any form, argued his case not only on doctrinal grounds but by charging that, among the leaders of the exclusive nenbutsu movement in particular:

> There are some who have died without [auspicious] signs appearing [even] in two weeks' time, or who have broken out in evil sores, or spit blood, or had hot sweat pour from their entire bodies. In general, of Hōnen's more than eighty disciples, not one has died a good death.[60]

Nichiren also lamented the frequency with which his contemporaries concealed the facts of a teacher's or parent's inauspicious death and instead claimed that the deceased had achieved birth in the western Pure Land[61]—thus hinting indirectly at a crisis of interpretation that must have arisen with some frequency when a deceased loved one's reputation for virtue or piety was not borne out by the manner of his or her death.

The Last Nenbutsu and the *Ōjō* of Evil Men

Many of the *ōjōden* biographies simply tell how virtuous persons died exemplary deaths, and thus offer no moral or soteriological surprises. But these collections also include accounts of the *ōjō* of persons who, according to ordinary social morality or conventional understandings of karmic causality, might be thought to face great, even insurmountable hindrances to achieving the Pure Land. By including such cases, *ōjōden* reinforce the notion of life's final moment as a realm of unique liberative potential, radically discontinuous with society's values, ordinary moral codes, and even the efficacy of everyday practice. One notes, for example, accounts of female *ōjōnin,* both nuns and laywomen. Although not barred from Buddhist liberation, in being bound by the "five hindrances and three obediences" and subject to the pollution restrictions associated with menstruation and childbirth, women were often thought to constitute a soteriologically challenged category. The treatment of women in *ōjōden* is ambivalent; not infrequently, they are represented as potential hindrances to the deathbed contemplation of men.[62] Nonetheless, by including tales of women *ōjōnin,* these collections underscore the point that, by right mindfulness at the last moment, anyone—even those thought to have severe karmic limitations—could at once escape the round of rebirth and achieve the Pure Land.

Also significant in this regard are accounts celebrating the *ōjō* of people who deliberately reject conventional values, including those of the religious establishment. Examples include *hijiri,* or holy men who leave their Buddhist temples, renouncing the possibility of high monastic office, fame, and remuneration to lead an ascetic life or practice in reclusion; monks like Zōga and Ninga who deliberately feign madness to avoid the snares of clerical promotion and worldly honor;[63] and the nun Myōhō, who defies her noble parents' plans for her marriage in order to take the tonsure.[64] Laypeople, too, although on more modest a scale, are sometimes depicted as subverting social norms in their aspiration for the Pure Land. A woman from Nara stubbornly ignores her household duties despite her husband's rebukes and spends her time reciting the *Lotus Sūtra.* Her death is calm and exemplary, and her body emits fragrance for several days.[65] Such nonconformist *ōjōnin* may flaunt this-worldly conventions, but they know how to prepare for the last moment, whose rules are clearly not those of quotidian reality.

But the strongest emphasis in *ōjōden* on the extraordinary soteric potential of the last moment lies in their examples of the *ōjō* of "evil men" *(akunin).* Yasutane's original *ōjōden* collection contains no such examples, although he notes that one of his sources of inspiration, the Tang-dynasty collection *Ruiying zhuan,* includes cases of people who butchered cattle or sold chickens and yet still were able to achieve *ōjō* by meeting a "good friend" and completing ten deathbed thoughts of Amitābha.[66] By the latter Heian period, however, accounts of evil men achieving the Pure Land *(akunin ōjō)* begin to appear with some frequency. The emblematic "evil men" of these

Japanese collections are not butchers or poultry dealers but warriors *(bushi)*, a group emerging as a powerful force within medieval society but whose professional obligation to engage in killing—of animals in the hunt, as a form of war training, and of men on the battlefield—was seen from a traditional Buddhist perspective as deeply sinful.

The first two examples of evil men's *ōjō* in Japanese *ōjōden* occur in the second such collection, compiled more than a hundred years after Yasutane's by Ōe no Masafusa. An official, Minamoto no Noritō no Ason, governor of Tajima, amasses great wealth and is stingy; nevertheless, he reads the *Amitābha sūtra* forty-nine times a day and dies in a state of right mindfulness, being welcomed by the Buddha.[67] In the second example, Minamoto no Yoriyoshi no Ason, former governor of Iyo and an outstanding military leader ("the number of heads he cut off and exposed and the lives he took were beyond calculation") repents of his sins and practices the nenbutsu: his birth in the Pure Land is confirmed by the dreams of many. Masafusa comments: "Thus we may surely know that even those who commit the ten evils and five perverse offenses may be welcomed into the Pure Land. All the more so, those who are guilty of other [that is, lesser] offenses! In considering these two cases, we may be greatly reassured."[68] Some tales make explicit that the power of the deathbed nenbutsu is what enables such sinful men to achieve the Pure Land. *Sange ōjōki* tells of Tanba no Taifu, a warrior from Kai province who hunts and exacts harsh tribute from the peasants on his estates; his atrocities are "too many to record." But in later life, he repents his evils and dies calmly, after having chanted the nenbutsu. Renzen, the compiler, remarks: "Surely this shows that even those who commit the ten evils and five perverse offenses can achieve birth in the Pure Land, by the power of the last nenbutsu!"[69]

Obara Hitoshi has argued that the evil of warriors as described in *ōjōden*—that is, their identification as *akunin*—is inseparable from their social status and occupation and so reflects an aristocratic bias on the part of the compilers; warriors themselves did not necessarily regard their profession as sinful.[70] It may be, as Masafusa's comment suggests, that the *ōjō* of warriors who kill served in these collections as extreme examples, reassuring in their very extremity to the merely ordinarily sinful aristocratic reader: If even such evil men as these can attain the Pure Land, surely one's own hopes for *ōjō* are not unreasonable! But in fact, most *ōjōden* compilers were aristocrats of rather low rank, and a majority of the *ōjōnin* whose deaths are described in their collections come, not from the highest social levels, but from the lesser nobility and literati down to local officials, nameless monks and warriors, and even servants. These facts have led some scholars to argue, in a manner opposite to Obara's view, that *ōjōden* reflect an attitude critical of the aristocracy and a nascent religious egalitarianism.[71] Although this argument has sometimes been carried to excess, the presence in these collections of many humble *ōjōnin* does suggest both the spread of Pure Land practices in the Heian period among a range of social groups and a growing belief in the possibility of liberation for anyone who could face death with a mind fixed reverently on the Buddha, even the lowly and evil. It should also be noted that *ōjōden* contain examples, although very few, of persons whose wrongdoings cannot be attributed to their social circumstances but appear to be gratuitous. A notable case is the monk Jungen. An accomplished scholar, he is clever in exegesis but gives no sign that he ever meditates or chants the nenbutsu. At one point, he engages in sexual relations with his daughter. When reproached, he responds speciously: "Haven't you read the Buddha's teachings? All women are our mothers and children, our elder and younger sisters. How should one distinguish who is a relative, and who a stranger?" But when death comes, he meets it well, chanting the nenbutsu and facing west, and the god Bishamon (Vaiśravaṇa) escorts him to the Pure Land.[72]

In short, in these collections, the last moment is represented as a realm apart: its rules are not those of this world, nor can it be calculated by ordinary standards. An ideal death is not the monopoly of the highborn, the virtuous, or the socially conforming. Especially in accounts of the *ōjō* of evil men, we see an implicit questioning of a direct causal relation between morality or merit-accumulation and salvation, which was to become one of the dominant themes of Kamakura-period Buddhist thinkers.[73]

Anxieties and Extreme Acts

As suggested above, the notion of life's last moment as a unique window of liberative opportunity was on one hand a hopeful one; it was linked to, and helped promote, popular doctrines of universal salvation, especially for those unable to keep the Buddhist precepts or perform demanding practices. Yet precisely because the last moment was seen as discontinuous with ordinary karmic causality, it was also deemed potentially dangerous. That is, even a virtuous Buddhist who had practiced devoutly throughout life could inadvertently negate such accumulated efforts at the last moment by a stray doubt or distracted thought. Hōnen eloquently voices such concerns:

> Even though you may have admirably accumulated the merit of the nenbutsu over days and years, if you should meet with some evil influence at the time of death and in the end give rise to evil thoughts, you will lose [the opportunity of] birth in the Pure Land immediately after death and be swept away to suffer in the currents of samsara for another lifetime or two lifetimes. How vexing that would be![74]

In other words, one had to be concerned that, whether due to insufficiency of training in practice or to a lack of good roots, one might not be able to focus on chanting the nenbutsu when death overtook one. In this sense, the demand for right mindfulness at the last moment could be terrifying.

Sudden or distractingly painful death might, of course, come upon anyone. But for some groups of people this posed a particular danger. Most obvious were the *bushi*, who could be cut down suddenly in battle with no time to fix their minds on the Buddha. We see such concerns reflected in the recorded teachings of religious leaders who counted many warriors among their following, such as Hōnen or Ippen's successor, Shinkyō. Such writings may of course reflect the efforts of Buddhist proselytizers to convince warriors that they were in fact "evil men" in need of salvation, as well as the warriors' own spontaneous concerns. But in either event, Buddhist teachers addressing themselves to *bushi* were often willing to abridge many of the conventions of deathbed ritual. Hōnen, for example, is said to have counseled the samurai Amakasu Tadatsuna as follows:

> Since [A]mitābha's original vow was made entirely for the sinful, the sinful person just as he is can achieve birth in the Pure Land by chanting the name. . . . Even someone born into a warrior house who loses his life on the battlefield, if he dies having said the nenbutsu, then, in accordance with the original vow, Amitābha will come to welcome him and he will achieve birth in the Pure Land.[75]

Tadatsuna, a retainer of the Minamoto, is said to have achieved *ōjō* on the battlefield, fighting against the armed monks of Mt. Hiei.[76]

Shinkyō, too, taught his warrior patrons that many of the conventions of deathbed practices could be dispensed with: one need not be reclining or sitting upright, nor was it necessary to place the palms together. One need only chant the nenbutsu, even once:

> When you face [the enemy's] military camp, or when you are about to fight a hated foe, your desire to destroy your opponent at all costs must indeed be very powerful. Such [feelings] are karmic causes which should make you fall immediately into the evil realms. But for those who faithfully practice the nenbutsu, since they end their lives after having chanted the name, their sins are extinguished by its sound, and they definitely achieve birth in the Pure Land.[77]

Parenthetically, it should be noted that the sufficiency of a single battlefield nenbutsu was not an idea altogether original to these Kamakura-period teachers. Two twelfth-century *ōjōden* include the example of the warrior Sukeshige, who is struck down by an arrow from behind but achieves birth in the Pure Land by uttering a single *Namu-Amida-butsu.*[78]

While willing to simplify greatly the ritual requirements of the last moment, both Hōnen and Shinkyō stressed the importance of chanting up until the moment of death; Shinkyō in particular is explicit about the absolute necessity of chanting at least one last nenbutsu as one's final conscious act.[79] This very simplification throws the ambivalence of the *rinjū shōnen* ideal into stark relief: So great is the power of one's dying nenbutsu that it can remove even a warrior's grave karmic hindrances; but if he fails to chant that single nenbutsu, he will at once be dragged down into the evil realms. Fears about inability to chant even a final nenbutsu in the thick of battle led to the emergence, in the Muromachi period, of the *jinsō* mentioned above, who followed their warrior patrons to the battlefield and conferred on them the ten nenbutsu—the traditional basic requirement of *ōjō*—in advance of the fighting.[80]

How could one maximize one's chances of dying with one's mind serenely fixed on the Buddha? Probably the most common strategy was to accumulate enough religious merit during one's life that one would be predisposed to right thoughts at the last moment. Genshin had cited Daochuo on this point: "If a person accumulates good practices, then at death there will be no evil thoughts. When a tree leans and topples over, it inevitably falls the direction in which it has been bent."[81] This accounts in large measure for what art historian Willa Tanabe has termed the "merit of surfeit," a quantitative approach to merit-making seen in an emphasis on reciting the *Lotus Sūtra* hundreds of times, or chanting millions of nenbutsu, or, if one had the means, commissioning dozens of Buddha images or sūtra transcriptions, or tens of thousands of miniature votive stupas.[82] All such efforts were geared, ultimately, to the final moment, in the hope that virtue accumulated in this life would enable one to meet one's end with a calm and focused mind. Examples abound: Shōnen, a member of the Nijūgozanmi-e mentioned above, is said to have practiced the Amitābha offering rite *(Mida kuyōhō)* twice daily and chanted the nenbutsu ten thousand times at each of the six divisions of the day and another hundred times together with prostrations at each of the twelve divisions of the day, every day for fifteen years, during which period he also recited the *Lotus Sūtra* 4,200 times.[83] Miyoshi no Tameyasu, compiler of two twelfth-century *ōjōden,* is said to have recited the *Heart Sūtra* three hundred times, the nenbutsu ten thousand times, the smaller *Amitābha sūtra* nine times, the *Diamond Wisdom Sūtra* (Skt. *Vajracchedikā-prajñā-pāramitā sutra,* Jpn. *Kongō hannya kyō*) three times, and the invocation of *nyoirin* Kannon a thousand times, every day for the last twelve years of his life.[84] This quantitative emphasis is especially marked in later Heian *ōjōden:* A monk of Kuramadera chants the nenbutsu twelve thousand times daily for four thousand days (about thirteen years), counting his recitations with small beans. At the end of the period, he has accumulated 287 *koku,* 6 *to* of beans—an amount that Frederic Kotas has calculated at about thirteen thousand dry gallons.[85] Even Hōnen, while insisting that *ōjō* is achieved through the power of Amitābha's compassion and not by one's own amassed merit, nevertheless stressed continual chanting of large quantities of nenbutsu as the practice conforming to Amitābha's original vow and essential to ensuring that one would be able to chant the nenbutsu at the moment of death. He himself for years chanted the nenbutsu first sixty thousand, and then seventy thousand, times a day. He is even said to have remarked: "Sometimes one dies from choking on food while eating. You should chant *Namu-Amida-butsu* whenever you chew and *Namu-Amida-butsu* whenever you swallow."[86]

The demand for a proper death encouraged such unremitting efforts in continuous practice and merit accumulation while at the same time undercutting any certainty that such efforts would ultimately be efficacious. The resultant anxiety sheds light on the obsessive quality of much of late Heian aristocratic Buddhist practice. The Pure Land devotions of the nobility have often been characterized as overly aestheticized, preoccupied with ceremony and outward display. But as Nishiguchi Junko writes:

> Behind the proliferation of Amida halls, the various Buddhist ceremonies that were conducted, the cultivation of good deeds, the burial of sūtras, pilgrimages, nenbutsu chanting, and sūtra recitation, lay the severe demands of *ōjō*. Unless we understand such phenomena in this light, we do no more than skim the surface of aristocratic Pure Land devotion. Similarly, the quantitative approach to faith that spread among ordinary people should be understood in the same way. For those who chanted the nenbutsu so many hundreds or thousands of times daily, counting their recitations with small beans, such efforts did not in themselves translate into a guarantee of *ōjō*. In the figures of these people, fully aware of this uncertainty and yet continuing to count their beans, we cannot fail to see the distress of those who aspired to the Pure Land.[87]

Some individuals are said to have turned to even greater extremes in coping with the uncertainty of the last moment. Rather than await a natural death, when senility or the pain of illness might interfere with deathbed contemplation, they literally took matters into their own hands and deliberately ended their lives while in full possession of their faculties. The reasoning behind such acts is voiced by a *hijiri* of Mt. Shosha described in the *Hosshinshū* (A collection of religious awakenings) by Kamo no Chōmei (1155–1216), who embarks on a terminal fast: "Although I am deeply resolved to meet death with right mindfulness and so achieve birth in the Pure Land, it is impossible to know how one will die. So I am resolved to cast aside this body now, while no particular deluded thoughts are troubling me and I am free from bodily illness."[88] Religious suicide, committed in hopes of quickly achieving the Pure Land *(jigai ōjō)*, is especially well documented around the late Heian period, and a range of methods was employed.[89] Among the most widely publicized was auto-cremation, which has its textual basis in the *Lotus Sūtra*, where a bodhisattva called Beheld with Joy by All Living Beings (Skt. Sarvasattvapriyadarśana, Jpn. Issai Shujō Kiken) burns his body in offering to the sūtra. Auto-cremation in Japan is attested from the late tenth century and was soon assimilated to aspirations for birth in Amitābha's Pure Land, much more consistently so than on the continent.[90] The *Hokke genki,* for example, relates the case of an unknown monk from Satsuma who resolves to immolate himself as an offering to the three treasures, in emulation of the bodhisattva described in the *Lotus Sūtra.* As he approaches the act, he vows:

> "By virtue of my thousand recitations of the [*Lotus*] *Sūtra,* I will surely be born in the land of Utmost Bliss. After my body has burned, there will be marvellous signs." Though no wind was blowing, as his body burned, the smoke rapidly drifted toward the west, and though the skies were clear, purple clouds rose in the east. The monks, nuns, laymen, and laywomen who had assembled all shed tears of rejoicing.[91]

Drowning was another common method of religious suicide. A preferred spot was in the sea off Shintennōji, a temple founded by Prince Shōtoku on the shore at Naniwa, now Osaka. According to tradition, the western gate of this temple, which faced the ocean, communicated directly with the eastern gate of Amitābha's Pure Land. Devotees habitually gathered there to chant the nenbutsu, and *ōjōnin* would sometimes row out from the western gate and throw themselves into the sea. Again, people gathered to watch, and wondrous signs were recorded.[92] A particularly poignant case, also described in *Hosshinshū,* is that of a woman of the court, who, grieving over the untimely death of her daughter, goes to Shintennōji and practices intense nenbutsu recitation for twenty-one days. Telling the landlord where she lodges that she wishes to see the famous coast at Naniwa before returning to the capital, she persuades him to row her out to sea, where she faces west, chants the nenbutsu, and flings herself into the waves. Purple clouds rise and envelop the boat, and there is a strange fragrance. A dream diary, discovered in her room, reveals that on the successive weeks of her stay she had dreamed of being welcomed, first by Jizō (Kṣitagarbha) and Ryūju (Nāgārjuna), then by Fugen (Samantabadhra) and Monju (Mañjuśrī), and finally, by the Tathāgata Amitābha and his retinue.[93]

Religious suicide for the stated purpose of quickly achieving the Pure Land, including such forms as fasting, auto-cremation, self-burial, drowning, and the like, clearly exhibited continuities with earlier forms of ascetic practice, of both Buddhist and non-Buddhist traditions. Tales such as that of the grieving mother who drowns herself in the sea off the Shintennōji also suggest that the explanatory net of "aspiration for the Pure Land" was drawn around suicides that were prompted primarily by grief and thus could otherwise be understood only as delusive and tragic.

Acts of religious suicide did not escape criticism. "Such a thing is not to be done," says the monk Tōren in *Hosshinshū,* voicing a common objection as he remonstrates with the *hijiri* Rengejō against drowning himself. "You would do better to [remain alive and] accumulate the merit of the nenbutsu, even by a single day."[94] Other critics, however, did not condemn religious suicide per se but raised questions about underlying motives and mental states. In his diary, the courtier Nakayama Tadachika (1131–1195) criticized contemporaneous acts of burning the body as heretical. He argued that the bodhisattva whose self-immolation is described in the *Lotus Sūtra* had already achieved the stage of acquiescence to the unbornness of the dharmas, so such an act was appropriate for him. But when deluded people attempt it, he said, it merely results in karmic retribution.[95]

Witnessing the death of an *ōjōnin,* including an act of religious suicide, was thought to create a karmic tie that would assist one's own birth in the Pure Land. Those intent on such acts would sometimes announce their intentions in advance, drawing crowds of spectators. However, the presence of observers inevitably lent the death an aspect of performance. Concerns were voiced that this performative aspect of religious suicide could lead to egotistic motives of display and the desire to be seen as holy, which could interfere with one's salvation. Tadachika's criticism may in fact have been prompted by the auto-cremation of an ascetic at Funaoka on the fifteenth day of the seventh month, 1174, which "high and low gathered in a crowd" to watch.[96] By the Kamakura period, cautionary tales began to appear about suicides that go wrong when the individual concerned loses right mindfulness at the crucial moment. Mujō Ichien (1226–1312), in his *Shasekishū* (Collection of sand and pebbles), offers two paired accounts illustrating first the wrong attitude, and then the right attitude, in which to go about religious suicide.[97] In the first account, a monk of Ōhara, eager to abandon this wretched world, decides to hang himself after observing thirty-seven days of silence. He announces his intentions, and the abbot of his temple, deeply impressed, arranges for several special nenbutsu services so that others can establish a karmic tie with this holy monk, and also issues invitations to ranking prelates. When the day arrives, the monk's resolve fails him, but, ashamed to back out after all the publicity, he hangs himself anyway. Six months later, the abbot falls ill. He has been possessed by the spirit of the dead man, who has fallen into the demonic realms for his deluded thoughts and is nurturing a grudge because no one prevented his reluctant suicide.

In the second story, an unnamed monk resolves to drown himself in order to quickly reach the Pure Land, and prevails on a companion to row out onto a lake with him to render assistance. He worries, however, that under the discomfort of drowning, delusive thoughts might arise at the last moment and impede his salvation. He has his companion fasten a rope to him, instructing that he will jerk on it if he changes his mind. Once in the water, his resolve wavers; he tugs on the line and is hauled out, dripping. After some days' interval he makes a second, and then a third, unsuccessful attempt. Finally, the day arrives when he dives in and does not jerk on the rope. "In the sky, celestial music was heard and a purple cloud trailed over the waves. When his friend beheld these auspicious signs, tears of gratitude fell with the water dripping from the oars." Here, dignity of performance is humbly sacrificed in the interests of insuring death with right mindfulness, and the monk achieves the Pure Land.

Contestation and Routinization

The beginnings in Japan of concern with a properly ritualized death, leading to birth in Amitābha's Pure Land or other ideal realm, are fairly easy to pinpoint in the *Ōjō yōshū* and the regulations of the Nijūgozanmai-e. Identifying its end, however, is more complex. Deathbed rituals continued to be performed, and instructions for deathbed practice to be compiled and published, throughout the early modern period (1603–1868). It may even be the case that, under the Tokugawa system of mandatory temple registration, deathbed rituals became available at this time to all social classes, as one of the standard ritual functions provided by local priests to their parishioner families. However, concern for dying in a state of right mindfulness does not figure as prominently in early modern literature as it did during the medieval period. Tokugawa-period texts of deathbed ritual instruction are for the most part simply collections or reworkings of early medieval *rinjū gyōgi* texts and show little new development of content. Although the postmedieval development of deathbed practice requires further study, one might say, at least as a preliminary thesis, that it became routinized.

By the Kamakura period, a number of fault lines and points of contestation were becoming evident in the discourse of death with right mindfulness. A major social factor in this process, as suggested above, was the emergence of warriors as a new and influential body of religious consumers, whose needs mandated some modification of traditional deathbed ritual. Another was the appearance of doctrinal challenges to one or another fundamental component of the *rinjū shōnen* ideal, leading to loss of consensus.

Hōnen, for example, as noted above, maintained the necessity of chanting the nenbutsu up until the moment of death; nevertheless, his conviction that *ōjō* is achieved solely through wholehearted reliance on the "other power" of Amitābha's vow led him to deemphasize the ritual aspects of deathbed practice, especially in his later teachings.[98] In a famous letter to the nun Shōnyo-bō (d. 1201), a daughter of the retired emperor Goshirakawa, Hōnen—having just embarked on an intensive nenbutsu retreat—declined her request that he visit her in her final illness, explaining that Amitābha would come to welcome those who chanted the nenbutsu in all sincerity, whether a *zenchishiki* was in attendance or not. "You should abandon thought of a *zenchishiki* who is an ordinary worldling, and rely on the Buddha as your *zenchishiki*," he said.[99] Contrary to the accepted idea that right mindfulness on the part of the dying practitioner is what brings about Amitābha's welcoming descent, Hōnen argued that Amitābha comes to welcome the dying person because he or she has practiced in accordance with the original vow all along, and that it is rather the appearance of Amitābha and his retinue before the dying that induces in them the state of right mindfulness.[100] This reversal of traditional ideas about the *raigō* is linked to Hōnen's radical denial of the by then traditional position that one's deathbed nenbutsu possessed a particular efficacy that it did not have at ordinary times. "How could the nenbutsu at ordinary times be in any way distinguished from the nenbutsu at the moment of death? If one dies while chanting nenbutsu as one's ordinary practice, then that is the deathbed nenbutsu, and if one's deathbed nenbutsu were to be prolonged, it would be the nenbutsu of ordinary times."[101] Hōnen's reading thus allowed for an abridgment of deathbed formalities, and he understood the deathbed nenbutsu—as he did the nenbutsu in general—less in terms of exerting personal control over one's last moments than of entrusting oneself to the compassionate power of Amitābha's vow. According to some biographical accounts, on his own deathbed, Hōnen refused up until the end to seize hold of the cords fastened to the hand of the Buddha image, saying, "That is people's usual way of practice, but it is not necessarily appropriate for me."[102] This may have been the reason why his contemporary Jien (1155–1225), the eminent Tendai prelate, criticized Hōnen's manner of death, saying, "People gathered there [at Ōtani], saying over and over that he had attained the Pure Land, but it is by no means a certain thing. There was nothing remarkable about his deathbed observances, as there was in the case of Zōga Shōnin and others."[103]

Hōnen's disciple Shinran, revered as the founder of Jōdo Shinshū, denied the necessity not only of the *chishiki* but of deathbed nenbutsu altogether. In keeping with his understanding of Hōnen's teaching as one of absolute reliance on the absolute "other power" of Amitābha's original vow, Shinran understood the decisive moment in one's salvation to be, not the moment of death, but the moment when—abandoning all calculation and reliance on personal effort and entrusting oneself wholly to Amitābha—one is seized by the power of the Buddha's compassion, never to be let go, and faith arises in one's heart: "When faith is established, one's attainment of the Pure Land is also established; there is no need for deathbed rituals to prepare one for Amitābha's coming." He also wrote, "Those whose faith is not yet established are the ones who await Amitābha's coming at the time of death.[104]

The Jishū organizer Shinkyō, as seen above, insisted on the need for both a *chishiki* and the final nenbutsu. But, as Jonathan Todd Brown has noted, Shinkyō also undercut the tyranny of inauspicious signs by ingeniously arguing that the good or evil omens accompanying a death reflect, not the dead person's success or failure in achieving the Pure Land, but the good or evil of that person's deeds in this samsaric realm:

> When purple clouds form and flowers fall from the sky, this [indicates] the *ōjō* of a good person. When there are bad omens, this [indicates] the *ōjō* of an evil person. In either case, if the person died

> chanting the nenbutsu, then he or she achieved birth in the Pure Land.[105]

By shifting the referents of good and evil omens from one's post-mortem destination to relatively insignificant matters of this life, Shinkyō mitigated some of the fears associated with demands for an ideal death.

Such innovations met with criticism, even within the new Pure Land movements, from those who took a more conservative stance. For example, Benchō (also known as Ben'a or Shōkō, 1162–1238) of the Pure Land Chinzei lineage, the second Jōdoshū patriarch, understood his teacher Hōnen as having mandated the deathbed presence of a *zenchishiki*.[106] Benchō's own view of deathbed signs was traditional and severe:

> A good death is when [the pain of] the last illness abates, so that the dying do not suffer but pass away as though sleeping, with a composed mind and palms pressed together, or when they die saying *Namu-Amida-butsu* as their final words. Or, if purple clouds gather, or if the dying see radiant light or behold a manifestation of the Buddha, that is the highest form of death. . . . A bad death is when they thrash about, spit blood, or become deranged before dying. . . . All such persons fall into the three evil paths. One hears of those who say that whatever the manner of their death, nenbutsu practitioners achieve the Pure Land. But theirs is a distorted understanding of the nenbutsu.[107]

Benchō's very vehemence, along with his reference to those of distorted understanding, suggests that traditional understandings of *rinjū shōnen* were now being contested.

Such contestations did not mean that deathbed practice declined, simply that unanimity on the subject was fragmenting and mechanisms were being devised for coping with some of the more acute anxieties surrounding the demand for right thoughts at the last moment. By the end of the Heian and early Kamakura periods, although stories of ideal deaths continue to appear in tale collections, they are increasingly accompanied by others, some clearly intended to amuse, of people whose death fell short of the mark—suggesting that the ideal was now subject to criticism. By the latter part of the thirteenth century, *ōjōden* ceased to be produced as a genre.[108] This same period also saw the proliferation of great variety of mortuary rituals *(tsuizen kuyō)* performed by survivors on behalf of the deceased, a development linked to the spread of Buddhism among an increasingly wider social range.[109] Especially among the *bushi,* one notes the growing popularity of *gyakushu,* or "preemptive funerals"—services performed for an individual's postmortem welfare but held while he or she was still alive.[110] Both *gyakushu* and mortuary ritual aimed at ensuring postmortem welfare but did not depend on the person involved dying in a state of right mindfulness. This was equally true of the standardized funerals that began to spread among people of all classes in the late medieval and early modern period.[111] Increasingly, the energy of ritual efforts to influence the postmortem state shifted from deathbed practice to funerary ritual. Deathbed practices aimed at birth in the Pure Land, and the ideal of a good death, remained important throughout the medieval and early modern periods, but in a more routinized way, and accompanied by new ritual forms.

Notes

This essay is preliminary to an in-progress booklength study of deathbed practices in medieval Japan. I would like to thank Yasuko Makino, Gail Chin, and Sarah Horton for helping me obtain relevant sources.

1. *Ryōgon-in nijūgozanmai konpon kesshū nijūgonin rensho hotsuganmon,* in *Nijūgozanmai shiki, Dainihon Bukkyō zensho* (hereafter, *DNBZ*), ed. and pub. Suzuki Gakujutsu Zaidan (Tokyo: 1970–1973), 49.31b. Though this text has been attributed to Genshin, his name does not appear on the list of founding members; thus this attribution was probably made retrospectively.

2. On the Nijūgozanmai-e in English, see Richard Bowring, "Preparing for the Pure Land in Late Tenth-Century Japan," *Japanese Journal of Religious Studies* 25, nos. 3–4 (1998): 221–257; Paul Groner, "Japanese Tendai Pure Land Organizations in the Late Tenth Century," in *The "Earthly" Pure Land and Contemporary Society: The Proceedings of the Third Chung-Hwa International Conference on Buddhism,* ed. Sandra Wawrytko (Westport: Greenwood Press, in press); Robert F. Rhodes, "Seeing the Pure Land in Heian Japan: The Practices of the Monks of the Nijūgo Zanmai-e," *The Eastern Buddhist,* n.s., 33, no. 1 (2000): 56–79; and Sara Johanna Horton, "The Role of Genshin and Religious Associations in the Mid-Heian Spread of Pure Land Buddhism" (Ph.D. diss., Yale University, 2001), 91–149.

It is not clear whether the group was so named because it had twenty-five members or whether the number of members was set at twenty-five to correspond to the "twenty-five *samādhis*" *(nijūgozanmai).* The "twenty-five *samādhis*" originally referred to twenty-five contemplations aimed at escaping the twenty-five realms of samsaric existence (*Da banniepan jing,* T 12.690b; see also Zhiyi's *Ssujiaoi,* T 46.755c–758b, which correlates the twenty-five *samādhis* with stages of the bodhisattva path). Eventually, however, they came to be associated with twenty-five bodhisattvas who protect the believer in Amitābha *(Foshuo shiwangsheng Amituofo guo jing, Xu zangjing* 1, 87.292b *verso*–293a *recto),* a view also found in Genshin's *Ōjō yōshū,* in *Genshin, Nihon shisō taikei* 6, ed. Ishida Mizumaro (Tokyo: Iwanami Shoten, 1970), 235. In time, these twenty-five bodhisattvas were identified with the bodhisattvas who accompany Amitābha when he descends to escort the dying person to his Pure Land. Against prevailing scholarly opinion that places this development in the Muromachi period (1392–1568), Fujii Chikai argues that its origins can be traced to Genshin's time ("Nijūgo bosatsu raigō ni tsuite," *Indogaku Bukkyōgaku kenkyū* 12, no. 1 [1964]: 118–123).

3. In 964 Yasutane had played a leading role in establishing an earlier association called the Kangaku-e (Society for the Promotion of Learning), comprising both lay scholars of Chinese history and literature and Tendai monks of Mt. Hiei. The members met twice yearly for lectures on the *Lotus Sūtra,* nenbutsu recitation, and the composition of Chinese poetry, often on Buddhist themes. Since the Kangaku-e ceased to meet around the time of Yasutane's ordination, the Nijūgozanmai-e has often been considered a successor group to the earlier Kangaku-e, although organized with more explicitly religious aims. However, the relationship between the two societies is far from clear, and, though Yasutane has traditionally been considered the author of the eight-article regulations, he himself appears never to have joined the Nijūgozanmai-e. For a summary of the Japanese scholarship on these issues, see Horton, "The Role of Genshin and Religious Associations," 94–103.

4. The two sets of regulations are the eight-article *Kishō hachikajō* (*DNBZ* 49.28c–30b; T 84.878b–880b) and the twelve-article *Yokawa Shuryōgon-in nijūgozanmai kishō* (a.k.a. *Jūnikajō*) (*DNBZ* 31.301–305; T 84.876b–878b). The printed versions of these texts are all ultimately derived from a manuscript, possibly dating to the Kamakura period, held at the Chūshōin at Tōdaiji, but they contain numerous discrepancies in titles, misprints, and other errors. These have been detailed in Koyama Masazumi, "Tōdaiji Chūshōin shozō *Yokawa Shuryōgon-in nijūgozanmai (Eshin, Yasutane) rinjū gyōgi* no saikentō: Sōshobon no goshoku ni yoru mondaiten," *Bukkyōgaku kenkyū* 53 (1997): 56–95. Koyama also provides a critical edition of the two sets of regulations based on the Chūshōin manuscript; the titles *Kishō hachikajō* and *Yokawa Shuryōgon-in nijūgozanmai kishō* as used here follow Koyama's edition.

5. It has often been assumed that articles four and five of the eight-article regulations, which deal with treatment of the dying, represent a summary of the "deathbed practice" *(rinjū gyōgi)* section of the *Ōjō yōshū.* However, Koyama Masazumi notes that these articles of the *Kishō hachikajō* draw primarily, not from the *Ōjō yōshū,* but from the *Fayuan zhulin* by Daoshi (d. 668?) (ibid., 63–65; see also n. 8 below). Yet, even though the exact nature of the connection between Genshin's *Ōjō yōshū* and the Nijūgozanmai-e documents remains obscure, both clearly reflect an emerging concern with deathbed practice aimed at achieving birth in the Pure Land

6. *Ōjō yōshū,* in *Genshin,* 206–217. For a partial translation, see James C. Dobbins, "Genshin's Deathbed Nembutsu Ritual in Pure Land Buddhism," in *Religions of Japan in Practice,* ed. George J. Tanabe, Jr. (Princeton: Princeton University Press, 1999), 166–175.

7. *Sifenlü shanfan buque xingshi chao,* T 40.144a; cited in *Ōjō yōshū, Genshin,* 206.

8. *Fayuan zhulin,* T 53.987a; cited in *Ōjō yōshū, Genshin,* 206, although Genshin does not mention this text, or its author, Daoshi, by name. Daoshi and Daoxuan were

close associates, and Daoshi's *Fayuan zhulin* contains a description of purported deathbed practices at the Jetavana monastery very similar to that occurring in Daoxuan's *vinaya* commentary.

9. *Guannian Amituofo xianghai sanmei gongde famen,* T 47.24b; cited in *Ōjō yōshū, Genshin,* 207. Translation from Dobbins, "Genshin's Deathbed Nembutsu Ritual," 169, slightly modified.

10. Ibid., T 47.24b–c, cited in *Ōjō yōshū, Genshin,* 207.

11. *Anluoji,* T 47.11b, cited in *Ōjō yōshū, Genshin,* 208. Translation from Dobbins, "Genshin's Deathbed Nembutsu Ritual," 170, slightly modified.

12. *Wuliangshou jing,* T 12.268a.

13. *Guan wuliangshou fo jing,* T 12.346a.

14. *Ōjō yōshū, Genshin,* 214. Translation from Dobbins, "Genshin's Deathbed Nembutsu Ritual," 174, slightly modified.

15. The calligrapher Fujiwara no Kōzei (972–1027) records in his diary that in 1005, he returned to Michinaga his personal copy of the *Ōjō yōshū,* from which Michinaga had asked him to make a new transcription (*Gonki,* entry for Kankō 2/9/17, in *Zōho shiryō taisei,* ed. Zōho Shiryō Taisei Kankōkai [Tokyo: Rinsen Shoten, 1965], 5:39).

16. *Eiga monogatari,* ed. Matsumura Hiroji and Yamanaka Yutaka, *Nihon koten bungaku taikei shinsōban* (Tokyo: Iwanami Shoten, 1993), 2:325–328; William H. and Helen Craig McCullough, trans., *A Tale of Flowering Fortunes* (Stanford: Stanford University Press, 1980), 2:762–764. However, Michinaga's serene and dignified death as described in *Eiga monogatari* is at variance with the rather grim account of his agonized last days given by the contemporary diarist Ononomiya Sanesuke (see *Shōyūki* VIII, entries for Manju 4 [1027], 11/10 to 12/4, in *Dainihon kokiroku,* ed. Tōkyō Daigaku Shiryō Hensanjo [Tokyo: Iwanami Shoten, 1959–1976], 37–45). For discussion, see G. Cameron Hurst III, "Michinaga's Maladies: A Medical Report on Fujiwara no Michinaga," *Monumenta Nipponica* 34, no. 1 (Spring 1979): 101–112; and Hayami Tasuku, *Jigoku to gokuraku: Ōjō yōshū to kizoku shakai* (Tokyo: Yoshikawa Kōbunkan, 1998), 141–145. Michinaga's case illustrates the broader problem of disjuncture between reality and representation in descriptions of idealized deathbed scenes.

17. See Inoue Mitsusada, *Shintei Nihon Jōdokyō seiritsushi no kenkyū* (Tokyo: Yamakawa Shuppan, 1975), 189–197.

18. According to a collection of Pure Land biographical accounts compiled around 1134, Genshin inscribed a mandala depicting Amitābha's coming for Taira no Koreshige to use in his deathbed contemplation. The compiler, Miyoshi no Tameyasu, notes: "Probably this was the origin of the spread in our country of mandalas depicting Amitābha descending and welcoming [the dying]" (*Goshūi ōjōden* II:15, in *Ōjōden, Hokke genki, Zoku Nihon Bukkyō no shisō* 1, new edition of the 1974 *Nihon shisō taikei* 7, ed. Inoue Mitsusada and Oosone Shōsuke [Tokyo: Iwanami Shoten, 1995], 659). This account in turn probably derives from Genshin's biography in the obituaries of the Nijūgozanmai-e, which says that he drew a picture of the *raigō* based on his study of scriptural passages (*Ryōgon-in nijūgozanmai kesshū kakochō, Zoku Tendaishū zensho,* ed. Tendai Shūten Hensanjo [Tokyo: Shunjūsha, 1987–], *Shiden* 2:289a). For discussion of Genshin's relation to *raigōzu,* see Hayami Tasuku, *Genshin* (Tokyo: Yoshikawa Kōbunkan, 1988), 216–220.

19. An example is the famous Kamakura-period "Amitābha crossing the mountain" *(yamagoe no Amida)* painting held by Konkaikōmyōji in Kyoto. For an introduction to Japanese Pure Land art, see, for example, Murayama Shūichi, *Jōdo geijutsu to Mida shinkō* (Tokyo: Shibundō, 1966); and Ōgushi Sumio, *Raigō geijutsu* (Kyoto: Hōzōkan, 1983).

20. *Dainihonkoku Hokekyō kenki* (hereafter, *Hokke genki*) III:83, *Ōjōden, Hokke genki,* 160. For discussion of other early medieval references to the *mukaekō,* see Itō Shintetsu, "Mukaekō no ichi kōsatsu," *Bukkyō bunka kenkyū* 4 (1966): 65–87; and Horton, "The Role of Genshin and Religious Associations," 179–195.

21. *Ryōgon-in nijūgozanmai kesshū kakochō, Zoku Tendaishū zensho, Shiden* 2:288b.

22. *Rinjū gyōgi, Eshin Sōzu zenshū,* ed. Hiezan Senshūin and Eizan Gakuin (Kyoto: Shibunkaku, 1971), 1:589–600.

23. *Ryōgon-in nijūgozanmai kesshū kakochō, Zoku Tendaishū zensho, Shiden* 2:285b. Variant accounts occur in *Shūi ōjōden* III:28; *Ōjōden, Hokke genki,* 387–388; and in *Sange ōjōki* 12, ibid., 673–674. This monk's name appears in these sources variously as Shōnen, Shōkin, or Shōzen.

24. *Ōjō yōshū, Genshin,* 209. Translation from Dobbins, "Genshin's Deathbed Nembutsu Ritual," 170, slightly modified.

25. This work was discovered by Ishii Kyōdō at the Chūshōin of Tōdaiji in Nara. It is part of a composite text, a transcription possibly dating to the Kamakura period with the outer title *Yokawa Shuryōgon-in nijūgozanmai (Eshin, Yasutane) rinjū gyōgi,* consisting of Tanshū's instructions preceded by the two sets of regulations for the Nijūgozanmai-e mentioned in n. 4 above. Its existence suggests a close connection between Tanshū's work and the deathbed protocols of the Nijūgozanmai-e; it also refers explicitly to the *rinjū gyōgi* of "Yokawa Sōzu," or Genshin (*Rinjū gyōgi chūki, DNBZ* 49.48a).

26. A version of the *Rishukyō,* an esoteric sūtra recited in a number of ritual contexts. Its recitation was said to remove sins and karmic hindrances and to protect the practitioner from falling into the hells. See Ian Astley, *The Rishukyō: The Sino-Japanese Tantric Prajñāpāramitā in 150 Verses (Amoghavajra's Version)* (Tring, England: The Institute of Buddhist Studies, 1991).

27. *Rinjū gyōgi chūki, DNBZ* 49.48a–49b.

28. *Byōchū shugyōki, Shingonshū anjin zensho,* ed. Hase Hōshū (Kyoto: Rokudaishinbōsha, 1913–1914), 2:781–785. For discussion, see Ōtani Teruo, "Jichihan *Byōchū shugyōki* ni tsuite," *Bukkyō bunka kenkyū* 13 (1966): 43–58; and Marc Bunjisters, "Jichihan and the Restoration and Innovation of Buddhist Practice," *Japanese Journal of Religious Studies* 26, nos. 1–2 (Spring 1999), 65–69.

29. *Ichigo taiyō himitsu shū, Kōgyō Daishi senjutsu shū,* rev. ed., ed. Miyasaka Yūshō (Tokyo: Sankibō Busshorin, 1989), 1:172. Although some researchers have questioned Kakuban's authorship, scholarly consensus generally holds this work to be authentic.

30. On this theme see Ikemi Chōryū, "Rinjū nenbutsu kō: Kiku, kikaseru," *Nihongaku* 10 (Dec. 1987): 199–208.

31. *Ichigo taiyō himitsu shū, Kōgyō Daishi senjutsu shū,* 1:173–174. This represents Kakuban's esoteric reading of the *nissōkan,* or contemplation of the [setting] sun, the first of sixteen meditations leading to birth in Amida's Pure Land set forth in

the *Guan wuliangshou fo jing* (T 12.341c–342a). On Kakuban's deathbed instructions, see Tachibana Nobuo, "*Ichigo taiyō himitsu shū* ni okeru 'rinjū gyōgi' ni tsuite," *Indogaku bukkyōgaku kenkyū* 36, no. 2 (1988): 611–613. On the *himitsu nenbutsu* tradition generally, see James H. Sanford, "Breath of Life: The Esoteric Nenbutsu," in *Esoteric Buddhism in Japan*, ed. Ian Astley (Copenhagen and Aaarhus: Seminar for Buddhist Studies, 1994), 25–52.

32. This text has been reproduced in Itō Shintetsu, *Nihon Jōdokyō bunkashi kenkyū* (Tokyo: Ryūbunkan, 1975), 440–461; and in Tamayama Jōgen, "Ryōchū no *Kanbyō yōjin shō* ni tsuite," in *Ryōchū Shōnin kenkyū*, ed. Ryōchū Shōnin Kenkyūkai (Kamakura: Daihonzan Kōmyōji, 1986), 339–355. For discussion, see, for example, Suzuki Jōgen, "*Kanbyō yōjin shō* ni tsuite," *Nihon rekishi* 139 (Jan. 1960): 105–118; Kuge Noboru, "Ryōchū Shōnin ni okeru rinjū gyōgi no sōshō," in *Genchi, Benchō, Ryōchū: San shōnin kenkyū*, ed. San Shōnin Goonki Kinen Shuppankai (Kyoto: Dōbōsha, 1987), 245–274; and Sasada Kyōshō, "*Kanbyō yōjin shō* no ichi kōsatsu: Mitori no ishiki to *zenchishiki* no yakuwari o megutte," ibid., 361–394.

33. *Kanbyō yōjin*, in *Nihon Jōdokyō bunkashi kenkyū*, 456; Tamayama, "Ryōchū no *Kanbyō yōjin shō* ni tsuite," 348. The text says "one or two hours": the day was divided into twelve hours, so this would be two to four hours by our current way of measuring time. Scholarly discussions of the *Kanbyō yōjin shō* sometimes note a similar passage in the *Rinjū no yōi* attributed to Gedatsu-bō Jōkei (1155–1213): "When the dying person's life has ended, you should chant in his ear for at least two hours. Although he may to outward appearances be dead, consciousness may remain, or the spirit may not have departed but be lingering near the dead person. Even if he should be destined for the evil paths, because he hears the name, he may be born in the Pure Land even from the interim state" (*Nihon daizōkyō*, 51 vols., ed. Naka Takkei et al. [Tokyo: Nihon Daizōkyō Hensankai, 1914–1919], 64:25b). However, Jōkei's authorship is problematic, and this may be a considerably later text (see Mitake Moritsuna, "Chūsei no rinjū gyōgi to Myōe," *Ōkurayama ronshū* 44 [1999]: 22–25).

34. *Ichigo taiyō himitsu shū, Kōgyō Daishi senjutsu shū*, 1:173.

35. *Kanbyō yōjin, Nihon Jōdokyō bunkashi kenkyū*, 447; Tamayama, "Ryōchū no *Kanbyō yōjin shō* ni tsuite," 340.

36. Hōnen is said to have acted as *chishiki* at the deathbed of his disciple Shinkan-bō Kansei (see *Shōkō-bō ni shimesarekeru onkotoba* and *Jakue Shōnin tsutaekiki no onkotoba, Shōwa shinshū Hōnen Shōnin zenshū*, ed. Ishii Kyōdō [Kyoto: Heirakuji Shoten, 1955], 747, 769). The diary of Kujō Kanezane records that Hōnen ("Kurodani Shōnin") served as *zenchishiki* to a courtier and lay monk known as Kunitsuna Nyūdō (*Gyokuyō*, entry for Jishō 5 [1181], 2 (intercalary)/23, ed. and pub. Kokusho Kankōkai [Tokyo: 1906], 2:490a). According to the forty-eight fascicle biography, Hōnen attended the deathbed of the retired emperor Goshirakawa and of Fujiwara no Tsunemune, Minister of the Left, and also dispatched his disciples Anraku and Jūren to serve in this capacity for Gon-no-daibu Takanobu no Ason (*Jōdoshū zensho* [Tokyo: Sankibō Busshorin, 1970–1972], 16:201b, 214a–b, 215b–216a). However, Tamura Enchō has noted that the monk who attended Goshirakawa as *zenchishiki* was not Hōnen but one Honjō-bō Tankyō (a.k.a. Tangō) of Ōhara (*Hōnen Shōnin den no kenkyū* [Kyoto: Hōzōkan, 1972], 143–144).

37. Jonathan Todd Brown, "Warrior Patronage, Institutional Change, and Doctrinal Innovation in the Early Jishū" (Ph. D. diss., Princeton University, 1999). See, for example, pp. 198–210, 400–407.

38. On the battlefield practice of Jishū clerics, see Ōhashi Shunnō, *Ippen to Jishū kyōdan* (Tokyo: Kyōikusha, 1978), 143–151; Imari Masaharu, *Chūsei shakai to Jishū no kenkyū* (Tokyo: Yoshikawa Kōbunkan, 1985), 365–378; Sybil Anne Thorton, "The Propaganda Tradition of the Yugyō Ha: The Campaign to Establish the Jishū as an Independent School of Japanese Buddhism (1300–1700)" (Ph.D. diss., University of Cambridge, 1988), 76–111; and Brown, "Warrior Patronage, Institutional Change, and Doctrinal Innovation in the Early Jishū," 444–446.

39. *Nihon ōjō gokurakuki* is translated in Peter Michael Wetzler, "Yoshishige no Yasutane: Lineage, Learning, Office and Amida's Pure Land" (Ph.D. diss., University of California, Berkeley, 1977), 193–266. For a recent study, see Hirabayashi Moritoku, *Yoshishige no Yasutane to Jōdo shisō* (Tokyo: Yoshikawa Kōbunkan, 2001), 71–98.

40. In the Heian period, Yasutane's *Nihon ōjō gokurakuki* was followed by Ōe no Masafusa's *Zoku honchō ōjōden;* Miyoshi no Tameyasu's *Shūi ōjōden* and *Goshūi ōjōden;* Renzen's *Sange ōjōki;* and Fujiwara no Munetomo's *Honchō shinshū ōjōden,* all from the twelfth century. These collections are included in *Ōjōden, Hokke genki,* cited in n. 18 above), as is the *Dainihonkoku Hokekyō kenki,* which, while not exclusively an *ōjōden* collection, contains many such stories. Kamakura-period *ōjōden* include Nyojaku's *Kōyasan ōjōden* and Shōren's *Mii ōjōden,* dealing with accounts of the *ōjō* of monks of Mt. Kōya and Onjōji, respectively, and also Gyōsen's late thirteenth-century *Nenbutsu ōjōden,* which appears to have been influenced by Hōnen's thought. The *Kōyasan* and *Nenbutsu ōjōden* appear in *Ōjōden, Hokke genki; Mii ōjōden* is in *Zoku Tendaishū zensho, Shiden* 2. Individual *ōjōden* accounts also appear in various *setsuwa* (tale) collections, such as *Hosshinshū* and *Konjaku monogatari shū* (vol. 15).

41. *Jingtu lun,* T 47.97a, cited in Yasutane's introduction to *Nihon ōjō gokurakuki, Ōjōden, Hokke genki,* 11. Yasutane's wording of this passage differs slightly from the Taishō verion of the *Jingtu lun.* On the perceived value of compiling such accounts for strengthening one's own merit conducive to birth in the Pure Land, see Frederic J. Kotas, "Ōjōden: Accounts of Rebirth in the Pure Land" (Ph.D. diss., University of Washington, 1987), 35, 302–305.

42. *Ōjō yōshū, Genshin,* 296.

43. *Takagi Yutaka, Heian jidai Hokke Bukkyōshi kenkyū* (Kyoto: Heirakuji Shoten, 1973), 451–463.

44. Takagi notes that *ōjōden* accounts of *Lotus Sūtra* recitation as a deathbed practice always describe the dying person as completing recitation of the sūtra, or of individual chapters, before passing away. Takagi suggests that, whether this was indeed the case or the product of editorial intervention, it reflects an importance placed on proper completion of the deathbed practice (ibid., 462).

45. See Ishida Mizumaro, *Ōjō no shisō* (Kyoto: Heirakuji Shoten, 1968), 237–246.

46. Ibid., 229–230, 238. The *Shi-er li* verses (*Xu zangjing* 1, 2:195a *recto*–a *verso*) were incorporated into influential Pure Land texts, including Shandao's *Wangsheng lizan ji* (T 47.442a–c) and the *Nijugozanmai shiki* (*DNBZ* 49.32a–33c).

47. *Dafangguang fo huayen jing* (T 10.102a–b). This is an example of a subset of *hajigokumon* whose content deals with the emptiness of the dharmas. As *hajigokumon,* however, they were understood less as philosophical propositions than as magical incantations able literally to "empty" situations of fear and suffering.

48. *Miaofa lianhua jing,* T 9.35a; *Wuliangshou jing,* T 12.273a.

49. *Kanbyō yōjin, Nihon Jōdokyō bunkashi kenkyū,* 454; Tamayama, "Ryōchū no *Kanbyō yōjin shō* ni tsuite," 346. Ryōchū's *hajigokumon* consist of verses taken from Shandao's *Wangsheng lizan ji* (T no. 1980) and *Banzhou ji* (T no. 1981).

50. For examples, see Ishida, *Ōjō no shisō,* 235–236.

51. *Rinjū gyōgi chūki, DNBZ* 49.48c; *Kōyōshū, DNBZ* 43.28a. Kakuban's authorship of the *Kōyōshū* is unlikely, and this is almost certainly a later text, perhaps from the Kamakura period.

52. Ishida, *Ōjō no shisō,* 228.

53. *Nihon ōjō gokurakuki* I:6, *Ōjōden, Hokke genki,* 21. Translation from Kotas, "Ōjōden," 325.

54. In surveying the 346 accounts contained in the six major *ōjōden* collections, Nishiguchi Junko finds 72 examples of precognitive dreams and 116 examples of revelatory dreams after the person's death ("Jōdo ganshōsha no kunō: Ōjōden ni okeru kizui to mukoku," *Ōjōden no kenkyū,* ed. Koten Isan no Kai [Tokyo: Shindokushosha, 1968], 140). For discussion of dreams as indices to *ōjō,* see also Ishida Mizumaro, *Ōjō no shisō,* 266–273; and Kotas, "Ōjōden," 272–279.

55. *Zoku honchō ōjōden* 19, *Ōjōden, Hokke genki,* 241.

56. *Ōjō yōshū, Genshin,* 53.

57. T 19.574a, cited in *Ichigo taiyō himitsu shū, Kōgyō Daishi senjutsu shū,* 1:174–176.

58. *Heike monogatari,* ed. Takagi Ichinosuke et al., *Nihon koten bungaku taikei* 32 (1959; reprint, Tokyo: Iwanami Shoten, 1974), 1:406–410; Helen Craig McCullough, trans., *The Tale of the Heike* (Stanford: Stanford University Press, 1988), 209–212.

59. *Nomori no kagami, Gunsho ruijū* (Tokyo: Zoku Gunsho Ruijū Kanseikai, 1939–1943), no. 484, 27:481a.

60. Fragment no. 200, *Shōwa teihon Nichiren Shōnin ibun,* rev. ed., Risshō Daigaku Nichiren Kyōgaku Kenkyūjo (Minobu-chō, Yamanashi prefecture: Minobusan Kuonji, 1988), 4:2925.

61. *Myōhō-ama gozen gohenji, Shōwa teihon Nichiren Shōnin ibun* 2:1535.

62. An extreme case concerns a monk from Higo who achieves the Pure Land despite the intentions of his wife, who confesses to having served him over many lifetimes solely in order to obstruct his enlightenment (*Shūi ōjōden* III:20, *Ōjōden, Hokke genki,* 375; Kotas, "Ōjōden," 508–509). Nishiguchi Junko has also called attention to other *ōjōden* accounts of men who abandon their wives shortly before dying or bar their daughters from their deathbed (*Onna no chikara* [Tokyo: Heibonsha, 1987], 10–11).

63. *Zoku honchō ōjōden* 12 and 13, *Ōjōden, Hokke genki,* 237–238.

64. *Sange ōjōki* 36, ibid., 678–679.

65. *Hokke genki* III:121, ibid., 205–206; *Shūi ōjōden* II:29, ibid., 347.

66. *Nihon ōjō gokurakuki, Ōjōden, Hokke genki,* 11. Yasutane is probably referring to accounts 38 and 39 (*Wangsheng xifang jingtu ruiying zhuan,* T 50.107c).

67. *Zoku honchō ōjōden* 35, *Ōjōden, Hokke genki,* 249–250.

68. *Zoku honchō ōjōden* 36, ibid., 250. The claim that even those who commit the ten evils and five perverse offenses can achieve birth in the Pure Land if they complete ten deathbed thoughts of the Buddha appears in the *Guan wuliangshou fo jing* (T 12.346a). However, this contradicts the text of the eighteenth vow, which specifically excludes from the Pure Land those guilty of the five perverse offenses (*Wuliang-*

shou jing, T 12.268a). For an example of the struggles of Pure Land thinkers to reconcile the two positions, see Chap. 10 of the *Ōjō yōshū, Genshin,* 292–296). Although he cites a range of interpretations, Genshin himself declined to make a categorical pronouncement as to whether or not those guilty of the ten evils and five perverse offenses can achieve *ōjō.* However, the more lenient position would eventually prevail in the Japanese Pure Land tradition.

69. *Sange ōjōki* 40, *Ōjōden, Hokke genki,* 679.

70. Obara Hitoshi, "Heian makki ni okeru akunin ōjō shisō ni tsuite," *Nihon bukkyō* 49 (1979), esp. 8–12.

71. See, for example, Kikuchi Ryōichi, "Inseiki ōjōden setsuwa," *Bungaku* (March 1954): 53–60. This issue is linked to the broader and much disputed question of social factors contributing to the spread of Pure Land practices in the latter Heian. For a summary of some of the major arguments, see Hayami Tasuku, *Jōdokyō shinkō ron* (Tokyo: Yūzankaku, 1978), 89–104.

72. *Shūi ōjōden* III:5, *Ōjōden, Hokke genki,* 363–364.

73. Because *ōjōden* tend to identify evil with outward behaviors often specific to particular professions or classes, the *akunin ōjō* thought implicit in these collections has sometimes been compared unfavorably with the doctrine that the evil person is the chief object of Amida's compassion *(akunin shōki),* associated with the exclusive Pure Land movements of Hōnen and Shinran, which sees evil as a universal existential condition. See Obara Hitoshi, "Heian makki ni okeru akunin ōjō shisō ni tsuite," and Kunisaki Fumimaro, "Akunin ōjōbanashi," in *Ōjoden no kenkyū,* 30–48. Although such differences in the definition of "evil" between Heian-period *ōjōden* and later Kamakura-period thinkers must certainly be acknowledged, this evaluation readily lends itself to an evolutionary model of Japanese Pure Land thought that privileges the Kamakura founders as normative. Both *ōjōden* accounts of the salvation of evil men and the later *akunin shōki* doctrine are linked to an increasingly widespread trend in medieval Japanese Buddhism that regarded salvation or liberation as transcending a strict moral calculus of ordinary good and evil deeds—a development by no means limited to the Pure Land tradition.

74. *Shichikajō no kishōmon, Shōwa shinshū Hōnen Shōnin zenshū,* 814.

75. *Amakasu Tarō Tadatsuna ni shimesu onkotoba, Shōwa shinshū Hōnen Shōnen zenshū,* 717.

76. For an account of Tadatsuna's *ōjō,* see *Hōnen Shōnin denki, Jōdoshū zensho* 17:172b–175a. This account was later incorporated into the forty-eight fascicle biography, *Hōnen Shōnin gyōjō ezu,* and is translated in Harper Havelock Coates and Ishizuka Ryūgaku, *Hōnen the Buddhist Saint* (Kyoto: Chion-in, 1925), 475–477.

77. *Ta-a Shōnin Hōgo,* ed. Ōhashi Shunnō (Tokyo: Daizō Shuppan, 1975), 237. Translation from Brown, "Warrior Patronage, Institutional Change, and Doctrinal Innovation in the Early Jishū," 327, slightly modified.

78. *Goshūi ōjōden* III:8, *Ōjōden, Hokke genki,* 664–665; *Honchō shinshū ōjōden* 8, ibid., 684–685.

79. For Shinkyō's insistence on the final nenbutsu, see Brown, "Warrior Patronage, Institutional Change, and Doctrinal Innovation in the Early Jishū," 330–340.

80. See n. 38 above. One also wonders whether the demand for a ritually correct death affected women of childbearing years. Mortality in childbirth was high, and a woman went to her delivery not knowing if she would survive. Difficulties in labor

were attributed to malevolent possessing spirits, and childbirth sometimes was ritualized as a scene of exorcism. A symbolic tonsure—a slight shaving of the head—was sometimes administered to imperial women undergoing difficult delivery, presumably with the idea that, should they die in labor, it would be advantageous to their salvation to die as nuns. (See, for example, *Murasaki Shikubu nikki,* in *Makura no sōshi, Murasaki Shikibu nikki, Nihon koten bungaku taikei* 19, ed. Ikeda Kikan, Kishigami Shinji, and Akiyama Ken [Tokyo: Iwanami Shoten, 1958], 449–450; Richard Bowring, trans., *The Diary of Lady Murasaki* [London and New York: Penguin, 1996], 55. I am indebted to Hitomi Tonomura for calling this passage to my attention.) This seems to have been part of a broader practice among Heian aristocrats of "deathbed tonsure," or *rinjū shukke* (see Mitsuhashi Tadashi, *Heian jidai no shinkō to shūkyō girei* [Tokyo: Zoku Gunsho Ruijū Kanseikai, 2000], 597–668). In cases of childbirth, however, ritual attention appears to have been directed primarily to the child's safe delivery. Although some *ōjōden* describe the ideal deaths of young women occuring some days or weeks after delivery (e.g., the wife of Minamoto no Tadaomi, *Zoku honchō ōjōden* 42, *Ōjōden, Hokke genki,* 252–253), thus far, I have yet to find any early medieval discussion of death in childbirth in direct connection with ritualized deathbed practice; my suspicion, to be tested against further research, is that the aims of safe childbirth and of death with right mindfulness belonged to separate fields of ritual concern.

At the same time, one finds very few explicit references from the period under discussion suggesting that death in childbirth was thought in itself to hinder a woman's salvation. The early Heian text *Nihon ryōiki,* tale III:9, mentions a woman who died in connection with pregnancy and fell into hell, but does not make clear whether the two events were causally related (*Nihon ryōiki, Nihon koten zensho* 96, ed. Takeda Yūkichi [Tokyo: Asahi Shinbunsha, 1954], 205; Kyoko Motomochi Nakamura, trans., *Miraculous Stories from the Japanese Buddhist Tradition: The Nihon Ryōiki of the Monk Kyōkai* [Cambridge: Harvard University Press, 1973], 234). Hōnen, when asked whether death in childbirth constitutes a sin, is said to have replied only that such a woman would achieve the Pure Land if she chanted the nenbutsu (*Ippyaku shijūgokajō mondō, Shōwa shinshū Hōnen Shōnin zenshū,* 664). Hank Glassman sees such scattered references as constituting a "pre-history" to the notion that death in childbirth is sinful, which would become established around the fifteenth century and develop during the early modern period in connection with the cult of the *Blood Pool Sūtra (Ketsubonkyō)* ("The Religious Construction of Motherhood in Medieval Japan" [Ph.D. diss., Stanford University, 2001], 141; see also Glassman's essay in this volume).

81. *Anluoji,* T 47.11b (a near identical statement occurs earlier in Tanluan's [c. 476–542] *Lüelun anluo jingtuyi,* T 47.3c). Both texts represent this as a statement made by the Buddha. Cited in *Ōjō yōshū, Genshin,* 208; translation from Dobbins, "Genshin's Deathbed Nembutsu Ritual," 170, slightly modified.

82. Willa J. Tanabe, *Paintings of the Lotus Sutra* (New York: Weatherhill, 1988), 24–28.

83. *Ryōgon-in nijūgozanmai kesshū kakochō, Zoku Tendaishū zensho, Shiden* 2:285a–b.

84. *Honchō shinshū ōjōden* 22, *Ōjōden, Hokke genki,* 687. Frederic Kotas suggests that Tameyasu's compilation of two *ōjōden* collections was also motivated in part by

personal anxieties about achieving birth in the Pure Land and a desire to establish proof that *ōjō* was indeed possible ("Ōjōden," 149–150).

85. *Honchō shinshū ōjōden* 25, *Ōjōden, Hokke genki,* 688; Kotas, "Ōjōden," 185.

86. *Tsune ni ōserarekeru onkotoba, Shōwa Shinshū Hōnen Shōnin zenshū,* 493. See also the very similar statement attributed to Hōnen in *Ichigon hōdan, Gunsho ruijū* no. 840, 28 (1): 290a.

87. "Jōdo ganshōsha no kunō," 156–157.

88. *Hosshinshū* III:7, *Hōjōki, Hosshinshū, Shinchō Nihon koten shūsei* 25, ed. Miki Sumito (Tokyo: Shinchosha, 1976), 143.

89. See Yoshida Yasuo, "Shashingyō no tenkai to sono shisō," *Nihon kodai no bosatsu to minshū* (Tokyo: Yoshikawa Kōbunkan, 1988), 187–222. The appropriateness of the word "suicide" in this context is much disputed, given its modern pathological overtones. Here it is used in the minimalist sense of a death whose proximate cause is the individual's own action; no assumptions about agency, intent, or inner states are implied.

90. According to Chingen, compiler of the eleventh-century *Hokke genki,* the first case of auto-cremation in Japan was that of the monk Ōshō, an ascetic of Mt. Nachi, who burned himself as an offering to the *Lotus Sūtra* (*Hokke genki* I:9, *Ōjōden, Hokke genki,* 64–65; Yoshiko Kurata Dykstra, trans., *Miraculous Tales of the Japanese Buddhist Tradition: The* Dainihonkoku Hokekyō kenki *of Priest Chingen* [Osaka: Kansai University of Foreign Studies, 1983], 38–39). However, since Ōshō's dates are unknown, this claim is difficult to verify. For several cases attested prior to the compilation of *Hokke genki,* see Yoshida, *Nihon kodai no bosatsu to minshū,* 209; these are mentioned in court diary entries that give no indication as to motive. In the account of Ōshō's auto-cremation, the only suggestion of a connection to Pure Land devotion is that he seats himself on the pyre facing west. Subsequent accounts, however, almost invariably present burning the body as a practice directed toward *ōjō.* For auto-cremation in the Chinese Buddhist context, see Jacques Gernet, "Les suicides par le feu chez les bouddhists chinoise du Ve au Xe siècle," *Mélanges publiés par l'Institut des Hautes Études Chinoises,* no. 2 (Paris, 1960), 527–558; Jun Yün-hua, "Buddhist Self-immolation in Medieval China," *History of Religions* 4, no. 2 (1965): 243–268; and James A. Benn, "Where Text Meets Flesh: Burning the Body as an Apocryphal Practice in Chinese Buddhism," *History of Religions* 37, no. 4 (1998): 295–322; and "Burning for the Buddha: Self-Immolation in Chinese Buddhism" (Ph.D. diss., University of California, Los Angeles, 2001).

91. *Hokke genki* I:15, *Ōjōden, Hokke genki,* 72.

92. Kubota Jun, "Tennōji to ōjōtachi," in *Ronsan setsuwa to setsuwa bungaku,* ed. Nishio Kōichi Kyōju Teinen Kinen Ronshū Kankōkai (Tokyo: Kasama Shoin, 1979), 215–229.

93. *Hosshinshū* III:6, *Hōjōki, Hosshinshū,* 139–142.

94. *Hosshinshū* III:8, ibid., 149.

95. *Kirei mondō, Gunsho ruijū* no. 139, 9:450a–b.

96. *Hyakuren shō* 8, entry for Shōan 4 (1174), 7/15, *Shintei zōho kokushi taikei,* ed. Kuroita Katsumi and Kokushi Taikei Henshūkai (Tokyo: Yoshikawa Kōbunkan, 1929–1966), 12:90. Ishida Mizumaro has suggested that the timing of this incident corresponds to Tadachika's criticism (*Ōjō no shisō,* 299, n. 44).

97. *Shasekishū* 4:7, 4:8, *Nihon koten bungaku taikei* 85, ed. Watanabe Tsunaya

(1966; reprint, Tokyo: Iwanami Shoten, 1973), 190–193; Robert E. Morrell, trans., *Sand and Pebbles (Shasekishū): The Tales of Mujū Ichien* (Albany: State University of New York Press, 1985), 148–150.

98. Hōnen's teachings on this point are not entirely consistent; in some cases he is on record as approving both the presence of a *chishiki* and the traditional accoutrements of deathbed ritual, such as the five-colored cords. However, especially in the period of his life following the writing of the *Senchaku hongan nenbutsu shū*, Hōnen's declaration of the invocational nenbutsu as the only valid path of salvation in the Final Dharma age, he seems to have denied the need for such outward formalities. For Hōnen's understanding of deathbed nenbutsu, see, for example, Suzuki Jōgen, "Rinjū gyōgi ni tsuite," *Jōdogaku* 27 (1960): 393–419; Itō Shintetsu, "Jōdokyō girei to Hōnen Shōnen," in his *Nihon Jōdokyō bunkashi kenkyū*, 46–65; and Nabeshima Naoki, "Hōnen ni okeru shi to kanbyō no mondai," parts 1 and 2, *Ryūkoku Daigaku ronshū* 434–435 (1989): 137–155; 436 (1990): 272–299. These studies, however, stress Hōnen's rejection of deathbed formalities but do not address his emphasis on the need to continue chanting up until the last moment, as suggested in the passages cited in nn. 74 and 86 above.

99. *Shōnyo-bō e tsukawasu onfumi, Shōwa shinshū Hōnen Shōnin zenshū*, 545. See also *Ippyaku shijūgokajō mondō*, ibid., 657, which denies the need for a *zenchishiki* at one's deathbed.

100. See, for example, *Gyakushu seppō, Ōgo no Tarō Sanehide e tsukawasu gohenji, Ōjō jōdo yōjin, Jōdoshū ryakushō*, and *Seizanha Gyōkan Gyōe shoden no onkotoba, Shōwa shinshū Hōnen Shōnin zenshū*, 276, 520–522, 562–564, 596–597, and 778, respectively.

101. *Nenbutsu ōjō yōgi shō, Shōwa shinshū Hōnen Shōnin zenshū*, 686. See also *Sanjin ryōkan oyobi gohōgo*, ibid., 453.

102. See, for example, *Gorinjū no toki montei tō ni shimesarekeru onkotoba, Shōwa shinshū Hōnen Shōnin zenshū*, 724–725. However, the nine-fascicle biography says that Hōnen held the cords only for the sake of others (*Hōnen Shōnin denki, Jōdoshu zensho*, 17:210b). Another staple feature of accounts of Hōnen's last hours is his awareness of the presence of Amitābha, invisible to his disciples, on whom he focused, rather than on the Buddha image enshrined by his bedside. For variant accounts, see *Hōnen Shōnin den no seiritsushiteki kenkyū*, vol. 2 *(Taishōhen)*, ed. Hōnen Shōnin Den Kenkyūkai (Kyoto: Rinsen Shoten, 1991), 271.

103. *Gukanshō, Nihon koten bungaku taikei* 86, ed. Okami Masao and Akamatsu Toshihide (Tokyo: Iwanami Shoten), 295. The reason for the specific reference to Zōga is not clear. Zōga's ideal death is described in *Hokke genki* III:82, *Ōjōden, Hokke genki*, 158–159; *Zoku honchō ōjōden* 12, ibid., 238; and *Konjaku monogatari shū* XII:3, *Shin Nihon bungaku taikei* 35, ed. Ikegami Jun'ichi (Tokyo: Iwanami Shoten, 1993), 3:183–185.

104. *Mattō shō* 1 and 18, *Shinran chosaku zenshū*, ed. Kaneko Daie (Kyoto: Hōzōkan, 1964), 580, 608.

105. *Ta'a Shōnin hōgo*, ed. Ōhashi Shunno (Tokyo: Daizō Shuppan, 1975), 184. Translation from Brown, "Warrior Patronage, Institutional Change, and Doctrinal Innovation in the Early Jishū," 328, slightly modified.

106. "At the time of death, *ikkō* practitioners should make use of a *zenchishiki*.

That is what Hōnen Shōnin instructed" (*Shōkō-bō ni shimesarekeru onkotoba, Shōwa shinshū Hōnen Shōnin zenshū,* 747).

107. *Nenbutsu myōgishū* 3, *Jōdoshū zensho* 10:380a–b.

108. *Ōjōden* collections were again compiled in the Edo period. However, my cursory impression—to be tested by further research—is that these early modern collections reflect a very different ethos from those of the Heian period, stressing conformity to moral and social norms as characteristic of *ōjōnin.* For early modern *ōjōden,* see for example Kasahara Kazuo, *Kinsei ōjōden shūsei,* 3 vols. (Tokyo: Yamakawa Shuppansha, 1978–1980).

109. For a survey of these developments, see Janet Goodwin, "Shooing the Dead to Paradise," *Japanese Journal of Religious Studies* 16, no. 1 (1989): 63–80.

110. On the development of *gyakushu,* see for example Kawakatsu Shōtarō, "Gyakushu shinkō no reikishiteki kenkyū," *Ōtemae Joshi Daigaku ronshū* 6 (1972): 147–165. Kawakatsu argues that, with increased patronage by well-to-do warriors and local landholders, the form of *gyakushu* shifted in the Kamakura period from the elaborate ceremonies sponsored by nobles to the erection of small commemorative stone tablets or Buddha images. "Preemptive funeral" is Willa Tanabe's translation (*Paintings of the Lotus Sutra,* 40).

111. On the development of late medieval and early modern funerals, beginning with the Zen sect, see, for example, Tamamuro Taijo, *Sōshiki Bukkyō* (Tokyo: Daihōrinkaku, 1963); William M. Bodiford, "Zen Funerals," in *Sōtō Zen in Medieval Japan* (Honolulu: University of Hawai'i Press, 1993), 185–208; and Duncan Ryūkan Williams, "Representations of Zen: An Institutional and Social History of Sōtō Zen Buddhism in Edo Japan" (Ph.D. diss., Harvard University, 2000), esp. Chap. 5, "Funerary Zen," 162–207.

4

Amida's Secret Life

Kakuban's *Amida hishaku*

JAMES H. SANFORD

The predominant understanding of Japanese Pure Land Buddhism derives from the Jōdo Shinshū (True Pure Land sect) established by Shinran (1173–1262) and further extended under the leadership of the "second founder," Rennyo (1415–1499).[1] This version of Pure Land is characterized by several key, defining features. First, the notion that inasmuch as the world has entered an age of decay *(mappō),* the only possibly salvific practice available to humanity is to rely on Amida's compassionate response, which undeserved reward comes in the form of our being granted birth (*ōjō*) in a "pure land" *(jōdo)* that is free of all sorrow, and wherein all activities are conducive to nirvanic attainment. Second, the conviction that the locus of such birth will, in fact, be Gokuraku (Sukhāvatī), the western paradise over which Amida holds dominion and which is virtually transcendent to this dirty world *(edo)* in which we live. Third, the belief that translation to the Pure Land will be effected by the nenbutsu, or calling out to Amida, and that this call-and-response model signals the fact that salvational power comes to us from a source that is fundamentally outside ourselves, an "other power" (*tariki,* as opposed to "self power," or *jiriki*). Although this model of Pure Land Buddhism has become normative, there are several forms of Japanese Pure Land thought that diverge from it. There are five that are especially worthy of notice.

The first of these are the rivals of Shinran's True Pure Land, which also derive from Hōnen (1133–1212). Shinran was only one of Hōnen's disciples, among whom there was disagreement as to which elements of the master's teaching were central. Differences arose, for example, regarding the exact nature of nenbutsu invocation, over how many invocations were necessary for or helpful to salvation, about Amida's exact relationship to the salvation of stupid, foolish beings (*bonbu*, Skt. *pṛthagjana*) such as ourselves and so on. Full concern with Japanese Pure Land ideology would have to take into account not only the familiar genealogy (which includes such figures as Shandao, Hōnen, Shinran, Rennyo), but also the teachings of other disciples such as Zennebo, the founder of the Seizan school of Pure Land Buddhism.

Hijiri-related Pure Land practice would be the second divergent form requiring consideration. There were a number of links between Pure Land ideas and the somewhat shamanic, sometimes itinerant, figures known in Japanese as "*hijiri*," often rendered into English as "holy men." The phenomenon of "Pure Land" *hijiri* would include many of the apparently rather settled "Kōya *hijiri*" hermits, who took up residence on the slopes of Shingon's sacred peak, Kōyasan. Some, if not all, of these Kōya *hijiri* were devotees of Amida and have been specifically referred to as "nenbutsu *hijiri*." Two individuals from among these Pure Land–oriented *hijiri* attained sufficient importance to become familiar names in the standard histories of Japanese religion: Kūya Shōnin (tenth century), who is credited with being the founder of dancing nenbutsu *(nenbutsu odori)*, and Ippen Hijiri (1239–1289), the "founder" of the Ji sect of Japanese Buddhism.

A third strain of Pure Land thought distinct from the mainstream form is secret nenbutsu *(himitsu nenbutsu)*, found within the esoteric Shingon school. The early shapers of this tradition predate Hōnen, and their views diverge in important ways. They tended to immanentalize the location of the Pure Land, arguing that, rather than being an alternate world of unalloyed purity set at some enormous—and functionally transcendent—distance from us and our "dirty" world of samsara, the Pure Land was, in fact, located in the human heart, mind, or body. Amida, the central buddha of normative Pure Land thought, was taken to be but a reflex of, or an alternate name for, the primary buddha of Shingon, Dainichi (Skt. Mahāvairocana). The nenbutsu was seen not as an invocation to some external divinity, but rather as a constituent element of the human body, innate, perfect, inherently pure. The nenbutsu was identified with breath, life force, or both at once, so that to live at all, simply to produce the two-part instinctual rhythm of breathing in and out, becomes a constant intoning of the nenbutsu.[2]

A number of Shingon prelates figures in the history of this secret nenbutsu movement, but the most important is Kakuban, who is usually construed as its founder. Interestingly enough, Kakuban seems to have emerged from, or at least been deeply influenced by, the ranks of nenbutsu *hijiri* hermits on Kōyasan. It is Kakuban's notions of Amida and his Pure Land that are considered in more detail below.

Fourth of the divergent forms are True Pure Land heresies. True Pure Land thought after the time of Shinran's leadership developed some unexpected options. One wave of such "heretical" views was the so-called *hiji bomon* (secret dharmas) that emerged around the time of Rennyo. A second divergent form emerged in the Tokugawa era as part of the *kakushi nenbutsu* (hidden nenbutsu) and *kakure nenbutsu* (hiding nenbutsu) movements.[3] Both of these appearances of Jōdo Shinshū "heresy" seem to have been heavily influenced by secret nenbutsu ideas.

The fifth divergent form that can be identified is that of Pure Land thematics found in other Buddhist schools. Pure Land ideology in Japan is often depicted—as are the two other main forms of "Kamakura New Buddhism," Zen and Nichiren—as having emerged from the matrix of Tendai Buddhism, and discussion of the specific impact of Tendai ideas on proto–Pure Land figures is sometimes at least hinted at.[4]

If we move beyond Tendai and into Zen venues, however, Pure Land language and imagery does show up. Three examples from Rinzai Zen leap fairly quickly to mind. The first is a short prose work attributed to Ikkyū Sōjun (1349–1481) entitled *Amida hadaka* (Amida laid bare), an "exposé" of the true nature of Amida that presents a view of the Pure Land quite close to the ideas found in *himitsu nenbutsu* texts. A second Zen example is a passage in the *Orategama* of Hakuin (1685–1768) that seems an almost unseparable fusion of Zen, normative Pure Land, and esoteric notions about the Pure Land.[5] The third is Ungo Kiyō's *Ōjōyōka,* discussed and translated by Richard Jaffe in this collection.

It may also be the case that further Pure Land–Zen connections are to be found within the context of the Ōbaku Zen school. Ōbaku, a late arrival on the Japanese scene, is often characterized as being an especially Chinese-style form of Japanese Buddhism. Thus one might reasonably speculate that the fusion of Pure Land and Chan that took place in China might have been mirrored in the Ōbaku school—a worthwhile topic requiring further investigation. In his essay in this volume, Richard Jaffe discusses the role of the newly introduced and more inclusive Ōbaku teachings in provoking established Rinzai monastics to "purify" their own school of any traces of nenbutsu practice.

Kakuban

Kakuban Shōnin (1095–1143, also known as Kōgyō Daishi) is generally accredited with being the founder of the Japanese Shingon school's major "schism," the Shingi (New Doctrine) school. For this (and for other reasons, including his influential theory of the place and nature of the buddha Amida),[6] he is arguably the most important figure in the Shingon school after its founder/transmitter, Kūkai (Kōbō Daishi, 774–835).

Kakuban began his religious career at the young age of thirteen at Ninnaji, where he began the study of Esoteric Buddhism *(Mikkyō)* under the tutelage of the Shingon monk Kanjo (1052–1125). Throughout his late teens and early twenties Kakuban went on to add to his repertoire the doctrines of a wide range of Buddhist schools through study at a number of temples in Nara and Kyoto, on Kōyasan, and elsewhere. By his thirties he had attracted the patronage of ex-Emperor Toba. As a result of this connection, in 1134 Kakuban was simultaneously made the head of the Daidemboin hall, which he had himself established on Kōyasan, and Kōyasan's principal temple, Kongōbuji. The latter appointment met with stiff resistance on the part of the monks of Kongōbuji and their sympathizers at Tōji and Daigoji.

The Kongōbuji clerics were especially outraged at Kakuban's appointment because it was out of lineage, but they doubtless also had objections to his strong *fu ni* (non-dualist) leanings and to his willingness to associate "non-dually" with persons of less than sterling social and educational backgrounds, in particular the largely self-ordained *Amida hijiri* (saints of Amida), who were then gathered in large numbers on Kōyasan. James Foard traces this movement to Kyōkai (Odawara Hijiri), who arrived on Kōyasan about 1073 and says of Kakuban that "he arose among the *hijiri* to provide them with a unity of Pure Land and Shingon doctrines, and to lead them in nearly wresting the mountain from the established clergy."[7]

However close Kakuban may or may not have come to taking over Kōyasan, he was almost certainly in debt to the *Amida hijiri* movement for some of his ideas.[8]

After about a year under trying circumstances Kakuban withdrew from both posts and retired in seclusion to his Mitsugonin hall, where he undertook a thousand-day silent meditation ritual. In 1140, however, soldiers of the Kongōbuji faction destroyed both the Daidemboin and the Mitsugonin. Kakuban and a number of his followers fled to Mt. Negoro, where they established Emmyoji. Kakuban never returned to Kōyasan and died at Negoro in 1143 at the relatively young age of forty-nine years. He left behind a quite substantial body of writings.

Kakuban's Understanding of Amida and the Pure Land

Kakuban was a proponent of the radically non-dual *honne* (or *fu ni*) wing of Shingon as opposed to the more "gradualist" *shusho* (or *ni ni*) wing. Consistent with this position he made little distinction between the various schools of Buddhism or between Buddhist, Shintō, and Taoist ideas. Because every sound in the universe is the voice of Shingon's primary buddha, Dainichi (literally, Great Sun), the properly attuned ear can hear the truth anywhere. Kakuban's voluminous writings are, in fact, replete with "non-Buddhist" notions and voices—as well as the properly attuned interpretations of them.

After his role as titular founder of Shingon's New Doctrine school, Kakuban is best known for promoting the view that the Buddha Amida, the central divinity of the Pure Land school, and Shingon's own principal buddha, Dainichi, were the same and that the true nature of the Pure Land was not transcendent but immanent. This theory was not only important in the formulation of Shingon's *himitsu nenbutsu* tradition, but also maintained itself as a persistent "heresy" within the Jōdo Shinshū tradition—especially among the underground *kakure nenbutsu* movements of the Tokugawa period.[9]

Just as the *Amida hishaku* (examined and translated below) tells us something of what Kakuban thinks of Amida, so the *Mitsugon Jōdo ryakkan* gives us his Shingon reading of the essential nature of the Pure Land, namely Dainichi's *Mitsugon Jōdo*. As it turns out, Kakuban posits neither the distant "pocket-universe" of normative

Pure Land texts nor the internalized corporeal realm that can be seen in the renditions of Ikkyū and Hakuin—although it is fairly close to these. Rather, Kakuban mandalizes the *Mitsugon* Pure Land, renders it into something very like a conventional Shingon expression of the *Garbhadhātu maṇḍala.* Here is a representative passage:

> The *Mitsugon* Pure Land is the Lotus family of the Heart-King Dainichi and is the Golden Pagoda of that broadly shining dharma-ruler. It is the abiding place of secret embellishments and the pure and wondrous realm of the mandala. Its form is broad and wide, like space itself. Its essential quality is everlasting and overspans the entire universe.

The text goes on to describe the *Mitsugon* realm in terms quite like those used in normative Pure Land works for Amida's *Gokuraku* paradise, namely, the *Amitāyur-dhyana sūtra* and the two *Sukhāvatīvyuha* sūtras. Here one finds jeweled trees, beautiful pavilions, perfumed breezes, and magical, dharma-playing musical instruments. But there are also five gates, each of which is associated with one of the five standard mandalic buddhas. One passage deploys the *Mitsugon* Pure Land as if it were a tantric visualization:

> In the center of a heart-altar is the *mandala* of the Heart-King; in its center is a lotus seat; atop the lotus seat sits a lion; next there is a great jeweled lotus blossom; then a full moon; then an eight-petaled lotus flower; atop this is the seed-syllable *dharmakāya,* blazing with light.

Of course, insofar as the location of any visualized mandala is the heart-mind, and insofar as the heart-mind is coexistent with the body, we can also say that the instantiation of the *Mitsugon* Pure Land is, once again, an expression of Shingon's epitome of enlightenment, *sokushin jōbutsu* (bodily buddhahood), or to anticipate a term that will come to be used in the full-blown secret nenbutsu tradition, *sokushin ōjō*—perhaps translatable, despite the ugliness of the English, as "rebirth in the Pure Land of one's very own body." If the "A" of Amida is the same as the "A" that is the central seed-syllable of Dainichi's *Garbhadhātu maṇḍala,* and if the key setting-sun meditation of the *Amitāyur-dhyana sūtra* is emblematic of the literal meaning of *"dai-nichi"* (great sun), then why not *sokushin ōjō?*[10]

For Kakuban, the notion of Pure Land is a fairly conventional rendering of standard *Mikkyō* thematics: Amida is a manifestation of the *dharmakāya,* Dainichi, in a fashion that seems almost one with the Buddhist-Shintō conflations that go by the name *honji suijaku.* That is, in a wholly intra-Buddhist context, Dainichi is the *honji* (primordial ground) of a *suijaku* (trace) called Amida; the nenbutsu is less a call to some external divinity than the evocative mantra that stirs individual *bodhicitta* to awareness of its own innate buddha-nature; the residence of Dainichi–Amida turns out to be not an alternate universe, but a pleromatic mandala, of which Dainichi–Amida is the central object of devotion *(honzon).*

Kakuban puts forth his notion of the non-duality of Dainichi and Amida in a number of places. The most elaborate treatment is given in his *Gorin kuji* [*myo*] *himitsusu shaku* (Esoteric explication of the mantras of the five *cakras* and the nine syllables), a text that eventually took on virtually canonical status in some *kakure nenbutsu* groups.[11] But at least as important—in part because of its brevity—was Kakuban's widely circulated *Amida hishaku* (The esoteric explication of Amida).

Amida Hishaku

The *Amida hishaku* consists of three segments. In the first Kakuban equates three rather noumenal-seeming categories (the *dharmakāya,* the one mind, and the Buddha Dainichi) with the minds of ordinary sentient beings. Kakuban's formulation takes place against the background of Shingon's complex doctrines concerning the ontological status of the buddha. Within Shingon the most usual version of the Mahāyāna theory of the three bodies of the buddha *(trikāya)* actually comprises four (or five) bodies. Highest among these is the *jisho hosshin* (Skt. *svabhava dharmakāya*), or "self-nature dharma-body" among whose primary "manifestations" is *jishochi* (Skt. *svabhava jñāna*), the "wisdom of self-being," or omniscience. This body/wisdom represents reality at its fullest; the view that Dainichi is the *dharmadhātu* (universe); the notion that the innate union of principle *(li)* and wisdom *(chi)* is the presence of Dainichi as fundamental consciousness (that is, the immanent buddha-nature in all sentient beings); and the theory that the essenceless essence of Dainchi and all dharmas is emptiness *(śunyatā).* The derived bodies are all secondary forms of the *dharmakāya.* First comes the *juyu hosshin* (Skt. *sambhoga dharmakāya*) mode of enlightened sentient beings. This has two varieties: the *jijuyu hosshin* (Skt. *svasambhoga dharmakāya*), who enjoys the fruits of his own enlightenment; and the *tajuyu hosshin* (Skt. *parasambhoga dharmakāya*), who preaches for the benefit of bodhisattvas at the final stages of their spiritual careers. Third is the *hengeshin hosshin* (Skt. *nirmanakāya dharmakāya*), or historical buddha, who teaches lesser bodhisattvas, saints, and ordinary persons. Finally comes the *tōru hosshin* (Skt. *nisyanda dharmakāya*), who manifests salvational bodies throughout samsara. Shingon claims that the teachings of other schools of Buddhism are derived from the lower bodies, while Shingon's own secret teachings come directly from the highest form of the *dharmakāya,* Dainichi himself.

The split between the highest *dharmakāya* and its lower manifestations is mirrored in Kakuban's text in the differentiation of the one mind and the minds of sentient beings. In the end these are non-dually one, but in the short term one takes a preliminary, dualistic view. The logical inconsistency of a program of enlightenment in a framework that denies the enlightened-deluded distinction confounds Kakuban's rhetorical line—a not uncommon difficulty for non-dualist writers. A full blown non-dualism at the practical level would, of course, erase both Buddhism as a system and Kakuban's need for any literary expression of it.

Despite these logical problems, Kakuban denies such antinomies as the contrast between buddha and sentient being, and the differentiation of the samsaric world of dharmas versus nirvana. For Kakuban, buddhahood is innate and part and parcel with the phenomenal world; even enlightenment and delusion cannot really be differentiated. Kakuban goes on to suggest that, given this, the propositions made by many Pure Land thinkers serve only to extend false dualisms onto some distant other world (the Pure Land) and to posit there a virtually transcendent Amida. The propagation of such notions comprises a particularly delusive piece of spiritual mischief. In actual fact, both Amida and his right-hand bodhisattva, Kannon (Avalokiteśvara), are, like all divinities, one with sentient beings, one with the phenomenal world of dharmic occurences, and one especially with the highest *dharmakāya* embodiment of buddhahood, Dainichi.

In the second section of his text, Kakuban systematically analyzes the secret meanings of thirteen names or epithets of Amida in terms of Shingon doctrinal categories and in each case concludes, once again, that Amida and Dainichi are identical. Finally, Kakuban analyzes the constituent syllables of Amida's name: "A," "mi," "da." These syllables are correlated with various rubrics and in each case their use, whether as mantra, nenbutsu, or encoded philosophical message, testifies to the truth that Amida is immanent, fully embedded in this world, and non-different from sentient beings.

Issues Affecting Translation

Amida hishaku, like hundreds of other Japanese Buddhist texts, was written in a form of classical Chinese influenced by Japanese vocabulary habits and syntactical considerations. Most editions are both punctuated to show where phrases or sentences end and provided with *kundoku* markings that allow the trained reader to rearrange the order of the text and read it as Japanese, with explicit nouns, verbs, adjectives, and so on. Sometimes these indicators are useful to the translator; sometimes they are not. Additionally, while not a difficult piece, *Amida hishaku* is, like most such works, full of Buddhist technical terms. Some of these have the feel of specialist language; others are composed of common terms whose meaning is a fairly transparent reading of their constituent parts. As much as possible, I have tried to render the English version in similarly transparent language and have provided notes only when meanings seem less than self-evident. A few very common Buddhist terms for which no good English equivalents seem to exist have been "restored" to Sanskrit (for example, "dharmas," "*tathāgata*"). Proper names are given their Japanese pronunciation. As the translation itself is of a religious text, I have rendered a number of seminal Shingon terms in initial capital letters, despite the danger of offending some modern sensibilities. And at rare points I have altered the syntax of long Chinese compounds to produce a more fluent English text.[12]

Kakuban's *The Esoteric Explication of Amida*

The Buddha Amida constitutes the Wisdom Body of the Intuition of the Self-Nature *dharmakāya,* the support of enlightenment on which all sentient beings depend. When we witness the One Mind for ourselves, we see the absolute nature of all dharmas.[13] When we ourselves witness the multitudinous dharmas, we know the quality of every sentient being's mind. Thus the fundamental nature of the One Mind partakes of the two truths[14] yet is without discriminations.[15] In the nine [lower] realms,[16] forms and minds alike flourish like a dense forest with [innate] possession of the Five Wisdoms.[17] Indeed, all the divine beings of the four kinds of mandala[18] have, from the outset, always dwelt within temporary bodies of five *skandhas*. The various worthies of the Three Secrets[19] have always been limitlessly present within the delusive mind and its nine consciousnesses.[20] Since the One Mind is, in fact, the multitudinous dharmas, the realm of the Buddhas and the realm of living beings comprise a non-duality that is yet dual. Since the multitudinous dharmas are, in fact, the One Mind, the realm of the Buddhas and [the realm][21] of sentient beings comprise a duality that is yet non-dual. Again, these minds [of ours] and the Buddhas are from the outset of one substance. This mind needs not seek transformation into a Buddha. As soon as one withdraws from delusion, Wisdom emerges and one attains Buddhahood in this very body.[22]

To assert that there is a [Buddha][23]-body outside of one's own body, or to represent [the existence] of some Pure Land beyond this soiled world, is to encourage profound fools and to bring profit to the evilest of men. The accomodated teachings hide the true meanings and let only the surface show, while the true words of the *dharmakāya* open up True Wisdom even as they obstruct grasping passions.[24] Therefore, if one awakens to the deep wellspring of the One Mind, the lotus-terrace [blossoms] of the nine kinds of mind and the nine consciousnesses of the Pure Mind are all laid open.[25] If one stands witness by awakening to the Three Secrets in the present [lifetime], the "marks" of the Five Buddhas will be complete in this physical body and its five senses.[26] Who, then, would gaze into the distance [seeking] some jewel-embellished land?[27] Who, then, would patiently await [the arrival of] its subtle aura? Enlightenment and delusion are found in ourselves. There is no Buddha-[body][28] outside of the three actions. Since truth and error are of one quality, the Land of Bliss is to be obtained within the five [samsaric] realms.[29] If one awakens to the guiding principle, then in that very moment one's name becomes Kanjizai Bosatsu [Kannon; Skt. Bodhisattva Avalokiteśvara]. Within both the conditioned dharmas and the unconditioned dharmas one awakens to the principle of the equanimity that dissolves all obstructions.[30] This mind is the epitome. Because this [mind] is far from discrimination and grasping, and because it witnesses the natural virtues of the One Mind, it is to be called "Amida Nyorai" [Tathāgata Amitābha or Amitāyus]. This is the great meaning.

We next come to an explication of the Name.[31] In India they say "Amida." In China this was translated as "Immeasurable Life" (Wu-liang Shou; Jpn. Muryoju), "Immeasurable Light" (Wu-liang Kuang; Jpn. Muryoko), and so on.[32] Generally, thirteen translations of the Name are used. At least that is the usage of the exoteric schools. But according to the understanding of the esoteric school [Shingon], all names are, without exception, secret denominations of the Tathāgata [Dainichi Nyorai]. Just so, we next come to the true meaning of each of the thirteen translation names.

1. Immeasurable Life. The Dharmakāya Tathāgata dwells within the Dharmadhātu Palace,[33] beyond birth, beyond destruction.[34] Therefore, some call Dainichi Nyorai "the Buddha of Immeasurable Life."

2. Immeasurable Light. Because the light of the Dharmakāya Tathāgata's Wondrous Intuitive Wisdom[35] shines broadly on limitless sentient beings and limitless worlds, eternally dispensing profit, some call Dainichi Nyorai "the Buddha of Immeasurable Light."

3. Limitless Light. Because the Dharmakāya Tathāgata's Wondrous Intuitive Wisdom discriminates between no realms and is without any boundaries, some call Dainichi Nyorai "the Buddha of Limitless Light."

4. Unobstructed Light. Because the Wondrous Intuitive Wisdom of the Dharmakāya Tathāgata exists within both created and uncreated dharmas; within higher truth and common sense truth, all the way up to Absolute Reality and Absolute Nature;[36] within the various minds of all sorts of sentient beings; within the dharmas of grass and trees, mountains and rivers; some call Dainichi Nyorai "the Buddha of Unobstructed Light."

5. Unmatched Light. The Wondrous Intuitive Wisdom of the Dharmakāya Tathāgata is beyond verbal comparison. This is because it is from the outset free of all delusive thoughts. Since true awakening to that which is beyond verbal comparison is far distant from the insight wisdom that

compares truth and delusion, some call Dainichi Nyorai "the Buddha of Unmatched Light."

6. Flaming Regal Light. The Wondrous Intuitive Wisdom of the Dharmakāya[37] is a burning conflagration that illuminates minds [plunged in] the darkness of ignorance. Because he burns away the defilements of the passions like a flaming light, Dainichi Nyorai is called "the Buddha of Flaming Regal Light."

7. Light of Bliss. The Light of the Dharmakāya Tathāgata's Wondrous Wisdom destroys the darkness of sentient beings' ignorance. Because when one begins to manifest inner witness within the palace of the mind,[38] one begins to awaken to the joy of primordial non-birth, some call Dainichi Nyorai "the Buddha of the Light of Bliss."

8. Light of Knowledge and Wisdom. Because, according to the Wondrous Wisdom of the Dharmakāya Tathāgata one can, with care, determine the true meaning of the twin Absolute and common sense truths and can, with care, clearly judge the created and uncreated dharmas, Dainichi Nyorai is called "the Buddha of the Light of Knowledge and Wisdom."

9. Indestructible Light. Because the Intuitive Wisdom of the Dharmakāya Tathāgata consists of the personal enjoyment[39] of the bliss of the Dharma and is eternal, unchanging, and indestructible, Dainichi Nyorai is called "the Buddha of Indestructible Light."

10. Incomprehensible Light. Because the Wondrous Wisdom of the Dharmakāya Tathāgata is even more difficult to comprehend than the ten stages and Complete Enlightenment,[40] some speak of "the Buddha of Incomprehensible Light."

11. Uninvoked Light. Because the Wondrous Wisdom of the Dharmakāya Tathāgata is beyond the reach of the wisdom of ordinary persons, sages, and saints alike and also beyond their capacity to invoke and praise, some speak of "the Buddha of Uninvoked Light."[41]

12. Pure Light. Because the Wondrous Wisdom of the Dharmakāya is from the outset unstained by the defilements of the six senses, some speak of "the Buddha of Pure Light."

13. Light Surpassing the Sun and Moon. Because the shin-

> ing brilliance of the Wondrous Intuitive Wisdom of the Dharmakāya is from the outset everlasting and always removed from day and night, time and space; and yet there is no place over which it does not shine, no season through which it does not shine; and because it surpasses the worldly sun and the worldly moon, some speak of "the Buddha Whose Light Surpasses Sun and Moon."[42]

Therefore the names of the Buddhas and Bodhisattvas of the ten directions and the three ages [are all bynames of the Singular Great Dharmakāya. Furthermore, these Buddhas and Bodhisattvas of the ten directions and the three ages][43] are all individualized wisdom-seals[44] of Dainichi Nyorai. Of all the words uttered by sentient beings, there is not one word but that it is such a secret name. Deluded, we say "sentient being." But with enlightenment we speak of "Buddha Wisdom." Therefore, when one intones the three syllables—"A," "mi," "da"—ageless heavy sins are wiped away; when one invokes the singular Buddha Amida, endless rich wisdom is produced. Just as within a single pearl of Indra's Net there suddenly appears an infinity of reflected pearls, so too that singular Buddha Amida promptly fills with limitless innate virtues.

Next comes the explication of the structure and meaning of these syllables.[45] "A" stands for the One Mind's equanimity in primordial non-arising;[46] "mi" stands for the One Mind's equanimity as the selfless Great Self;[47] "da" stands for the multitudinous dharmas of the One Mind, which are both absolute and tranquil.

Further, "A" stands for the Buddha-family.[48] For it represents the non-duality of Principle and Wisdom[49] and the substance of the Dharmadhātu of One Mind. "Mi" stands for the Lotus-family. For Wondrous Intuitive Wisdom reveals that the Absolute essence of the "twin Emptinesses of sentient beings and dharmas"[50] is from the outset unstained by the six dusts [of senses and their passions] and thus like a lotus blossom [that rises unsullied by the mud below it]. "Da" stands for the Vajra-family. For the Wondrous Wisdom of the Tathāgata has an adamant self-nature that easily destroys all delusive foes.

Further, "A" stands for Emptiness. For the dharmic constructs of the One Mind[51] are from the beginning empty and unreal. "Mi" stands for the provisional. For the multitudinous dharmas of the equanimity of the One Mind have but a provisional reality like that of a mirage. "Da" is the Middle Way. For the One Mind's equanimity with the multitudinous dharmas leaves it far from dualistic extremes and without any attainable fixed nature.

"A" is being. For the substance and nature of the One Mind are unextinguished, innate, non-arising. "Mi" is emptiness, because the self-nature of the multitudinous dharmas of the One Mind cannot be attained. "Da" means non-emptiness. For the multitudinous dharmas of the One Mind represent the ceaseless merits of the Primordial Dharmakāya.[52]

Further, "A" is primary cause. For Buddha-realms and sentient beings are alike caused in accordance with whether the One Mind is awake or deluded. "Mi" stands for conduct. For it attains the fruit [result] of Buddhahood by cutting off the [false] views of "twin selves in persons and dharmas" and stands witness to the "twin Emptinesses of sentient beings and dharmas."[53] "Da" is fruit [result]. For it manifests the non-dual absoluteness of Principle and Wisdom of the One Mind. Therefore, it is indeed the fruit of Buddhahood.

Thus the discipline that makes [linguistic] distinctions *(shabetsu)* is called *jiso,* the shape of syllables. Further, that the shape of syllables is without fixed characteristics,[54] is like the fact that Indra's net does not take or reject any particular pearl. For the equanimity of the One Mind cannot be attained. This is, in fact, also *jigi,* the meaning of syllables. Therefore, if one departs from the meaning of words, there is no shape. If one departs from the shape of words, there is no meaning.[55] To take that and reject this, or to take this and reject that, constitutes the discrimination of a deluded mind.[56] To loathe this Shaba *(sahā)* world and to take joy in Paradise, to hate one's "soiled body" and pay honor to the bodies of the Buddhas may be called ignorance or delusion. Even though some [Pure Land proponents] may speak of a "dirty world" and a [decayed] "age of latter days," how could those [Shingon followers] who constantly contemplate the equanimity of the Dharmadhātu fail to enter the way of Buddhahood?

Notes

1. For a statement of this view, see Akihisa Shigematsu, "An Overview of Japanese Pure Land," trans. Michael Solomon, in *The Pure Land Tradition: History and Development*, Berkeley Buddhist Studies Series, no. 3, eds. James H. Foard, Michael

Solomon, and Richard K. Payne (Berkeley: Berkeley Buddhist Studies, 1996), 267–312.

2. See James H. Sanford, "Breath of Life: The Esoteric Nenbutsu," in *Esoteric Buddhism in Japan,* ed. Ian Astley (Copenhagen and Aarhus: Seminar for Buddhist Studies, 1994), 65–98.

3. See Chiba Jōryu, "Orthodoxy and Heterodoxy in Early Modern Shinshū: *Kakushi Nembutsu* and *Kakure Nembutsu,*" trans. Whalen W. Lai, Richard H. Shek, and Eisho Nasu, in Foard et al., *The Pure Land Tradition,* 463–496.

4. Whether there are other late developments in the opposite direction, i.e., modifications of Tendai thought that can be considered to be direct responses to Pure Land ideology, I do not know. Probably the place to begin such an investigation would be within secondary studies of Tendai ritual practice.

5. Philip B. Yampolsky, trans., *The Zen Master Hakuin* (New York: Columbia University Press, 1971), 128–129.

6. The abbreviated transliteration, Amida, indistinguishably represents two Sanskrit names of this buddha: Amitāyus (Infinite Life) and Amitābha (Infinite Light).

7. James H. Foard, "Ippen and Pure Land Wayfarers," in Foard et al., *The Pure Land Tradition,* 370.

8. For more on the *Amida hijiri,* see Gorai Shigeru, *Kōya hijiri* (Tokyo: Kadokawa, 1984). For more on Kakuban, see Kushida Ryoko, *Kakuban no kenkyu* (Tokyo: Yoshikawa Kobunkan, 1975); and Miura Akio, ed., *Kogyo Daishi denki shiryo zenshu,* 3 vols. (Tokyo: Pitaka Publishers, 1974).

9. The *kakure nenbutsu* movement is also called the *kakushi nenbutsu* movement; *"kakureru"* implies in hiding from repression, while *"kakusu"* suggests something deliberately hidden, such as esoteric secrets. For more on these groups, see Chiba, "Orthodoxy and Heterodoxy," 462–496; and Takahashi Bonsen, ed., *Kaskushi nenbutsu ko,* 2 vols. (Tokyo: Maruzen, 1969). For the broader impact of *himitsu nenbutsu* thought in brief, see Sanford, "Breath of Life," 65–98. Kakuban's ideas—or at least parallel notions—were also found in less radical venues. James C. Dobbins points out, for instance, that both Ippen Hijiri's Jishu school and the Seizan branch of Pure Land thought "regarded the *nembutsu* as the union of believer and Buddha through which birth in Pure Land becomes an immediate reality" (*Jodō Shinshū: Shin Buddhism in Medieval Japan* [Bloomington and Indianapolis: Indiana University Press, 1989], 107). Since both Hōnen and Shinran were born within a few years of his death (1143), Kakuban cannot have been resisting their form of Amidism directly. Nonetheless, the ideas he attacks in *Amida hishaku* and elsewhere seem very close to those that later became normative in the Shinshū mainstream. One occasionally finds Shingon-esque ideas about Amida in provenances outside of either Shingon or Pure Land. One important example would be the text attributed to the Zen monk Ikkyū Sojun, *Amida hadaka,* for which see James H. Sanford, trans., in *Zen-man Ikkyu* (Chico, Calif.: Scholars Press, 1981), 216–229.

10. From there, of course, it is only a hop and a skip to a more fully tantric "exchange of bodily mantras," which did indeed happen. One is reminded that in Daoism *"ho-chi"* means "spiritual orgy," and *"kimyō,"* which translates the *"namu"* of *Namu-Amida-butsu,* literally means "return life"; "life" in secret nenbutsu usage can stand for "breath," "semen," or both.

11. The most useful version of this work is in Nasu Seiryu, ed., *Gorin kuji hishaku no kenkyu* (Tokyo: Rokuyaen, 1970).

12. My translation of *Amida hishaku* basically follows the *Taishō* Tripitaka version (T 79.48), but I have also looked at the version in Kobayashi Seijo, ed., *Kogyo Daishi zenshu* (Tokyo: Kaji Sekkai Shisha, 1909), 1:58–61. I have taken into account as well the modern Japanese rendering of Miyasaka Yusho, ed., *Kogyo Daishi senjutsushu* (Tokyo: Sankibo, 1977), 1:149–152. The Taishō terms its main text the *Temmei* 3 (1783) version, but it footnotes variants from a second version called the *Kongōsammai-in* text (hereafter, *Temmei* and *Kongō*). I note most of these, generally quite minor, variants. The Kobayashi version is virtually identical with *Temmei,* save for some alternative punctuation choices. I believe that *Temmei* is both earlier and more accurate than *Kongō.*

13. Shingon uses several terms for "enlightenment," but perhaps its favorite is *sho.* This term has the sense of personal experience to which one can testify. I have consistently translated it here with some variant of "witness," even though that rendering may carry just a hint of Christian usage that is not really very appropriate to Kakuban.

14. The two truths of the Mādhyamika school are the provisional and the absolute, the latter of which both subsumes and abolishes the former.

15. For "discriminations" *Temmei* has *"sa"* and *Kongō* its virtual synonym, *"betsu."* It seems not unlikely that these both derive from some earlier version that had the common compound form *"sabetsu"* (also read *"shabetsu"*).

16. If to the six realms *(rokudo)* of samsara (*deva*s, *asura*s, humans, hungry ghosts, animals, and hell-dwellers) one adds *śrāvaka*s, *pratyekabuddha*s, bodhisattvas, and buddhas, one obtains the ten realms *(jikkai).* Separate off the realm of buddhas, and nine lower realms remain.

17. *Shinra* ("like a forest") is part of a rather elegant four-character Shingon compound, *shinra bansho* ("ten thousand forest-dense images" for the universe as *dharmakāya,* or as Dainichi—Dainichi being identical with the *dharmakāya.* The five wisdoms of Shingon are: *hokkai taishōchi (dharmadhātu svabhāva jñāna),* the omniscience of Dainichi and its four manifestations; *daienkyōchi* (great mirror wisdom, *ādarśa jñāna*), pure mind; *byōdōshōchi* (awareness of equanimity wisdom, *samatā jñāna*), non-discriminating mind; *myōkanzatchi* (wondrous intuition wisdom, *pratyavekṣaṇā jñāna*), mind directed toward sentient beings and dharmic multiplicity; and *jōshosachi* (accomplishment wisdom, *kṛtyanuṣṭhāna jñāna*), transformations made practical. The Five Wisdoms are systematically correlated with the five buddhas of the *vajra* mandala *(Kongōkai mandara):* Dainichi, Akṣobhya (Ashuku), Ratnasambhava (Hōshō), Amitāyus (Amida), and Amoghasiddhi (Fukūjōju).

18. Any mandala can be reproduced in any of four formats. A *mahāmaṇḍala* represents *dharmakāya* as *dharmadhātu.* Its iconography pictures the Shingon divinities as living beings (buddhas and bodhisattvas). The remaining three formats are iconographically distinct submanifestations of the *mahāmaṇḍala.* The *samayamaṇḍala* replaces images of divinities with their iconographic attributes: flowers, swords, wheels, etc. (or more rarely with the phenomena of nature). It emphasizes the transformation of insight into wisdom. The *dharmamaṇḍala* replaces the divinities with their *bīja* mantras, or "seed-syllables." These represent the dharma as communicable meaning. Finally, the *karmamaṇḍala* represents images of the divinities (e.g., statues). It stands for the efforts necessary to generate enlightement.

19. Dainichi revealed three secrets to Shingon. These transform three sorts of karmic acts ("the three actions"): those of body, those of speech, and those of mind

into salvational activities. The process toward enlightement then is embodied as ritual gestures (mudra), is given voice in the form of incantations (mantras), and transmutes the mind via the contemplation of mandalas and the like. Mudras, mantras, and mandalas are multiple in form, but non-dual in essence, samsaric in structure, nirvanic in quality.

20. The Yogācāra school's standard eight levels of mind from sense data up to the *ālaya-vijñāna* (storehouse consciousness) to which has been suradded the *amala-vijñāna* (immaculate consciousness), thus "nine consciousnesses."

21. *Kongō* omits "the realm of."

22. The term *"sokushin jōbutsu,"* or "buddhahood in this very body," is a key feature of Kūkai's systematization of Shingon. The term is sometimes rendered "buddhahood in this very lifetime" because it guarantees the claim that Shingon esoteric procedures constitute a magically rapid path to enlightenment. In addition, the notion certifies Kūkai's belief that enlightenment has no possible locus save the material universe, that Dainichi, like us, consists of a body (the universe) eternally enmeshed with nirvanic mind.

23. *Kongō* omits "buddha."

24. *Zuiki seppo* are *upāya*-laden teachings given out to ordinary human beings in accordance with their limited capacities. These contrast with Dainichi's higher secret teachings, which are designated for buddhas, bodhisattvas, and initiated followers of Shingon. Usually this contrast simply signals the teachings of all the "exoteric" schools of Buddhism versus Shingon esotericism, but here I wonder if Kakuban doesn't want to include some of his Shingon rivals within the *zuiki* cohort. *Kongō* omits the *"-po"* of *"zuiki seppo."* This imparts a slightly less formal, less technical tone to the term.

25. Rebirth in Amida's Pure Land comes in nine grades. The wise and faithful are born in open lotus flowers, where they can immediately experience the magnificent wonders all around them. At the other end of the scale are those who, but for their deathbed utterance of the nenbutsu, might well have landed in hell. They are born in closed lotus blossoms that slowly (over eons) open as the hearts and minds of these former sinners ripen to maturity.

26. For the five buddhas, see n. 17 above. The "marks" are the unusual physical characteristics that are said to embellish the bodies of buddhas. I doubt that Kakuban means that these literally appear on the bodies of sentient beings. But their metaphoric attribution shows that buddhas and sentient beings are fundamentally alike. Kakuban freely interchanges the five-sense and six-sense models of Buddhism (the latter including a coordinating common sense).

27. *Kongō* has "truth," *Temmei* "jewel."

28. *Kongō* omits "body."

29. The six realms are made five by conflating *devas* and *asuras*.

30. "Equanimity" translates *"byodo."* This term regularly renders Sanskrit *"samatā,"* for which "sameness" might be a better choice. Because it seems an especially important word throughout Kakuban's text, I have tried to maintain a consistent English equivalent. The term implies universality and non-differentiation.

31. In this context "Name" refers to Amida and the nenbutsu invocation of his name as a prelude to rebirth in the Pure Land.

32. These are the Sino-Japanese translation equivalents of Amitāyus and Amitābha.

33. I assume this signals Dainichi's Vajra Dharmadhātu Palace, the setting of the *Mahāvairocana sūtra.*

34. *Fushō fumetsu.* Not mentioned in *Amida hishaku* but clearly of significant import is the fact that "A," the first syllable of "Amida" is both the seed-syllable of the womb mandala and the central focus of Shingon's ubiquitous *A-ji kan,* "meditation on the syllable A." In the latter, the meditator visualizes the letter "A" emerging from a white moon disk, a symbol that suggests Amida as well as Dainichi (see n. 42 below). For a discussion of the various understandings of *A-ji kan,* see Taiko Yamasaki, *Shingon: Japanese Esoteric Buddhism* (Boston and London: Shambhala, 1988), 190–215. (The last item presented in Yamasaki's discussion of *A-ji kan* is a poem by Kakuban.) See also Richard K. Payne, "*Ajikan:* Ritual and Meditation in the Shingon Tradition," in *Re-Visioning "Kamakura" Buddhism,* Kuroda Institute Studies in East Asian Buddhism, no. 11, ed. Richard K. Payne (Honolulu: University of Hawai'i Press, 1998).

35. Kakuban makes *myōkanzatchi* the center of his argument in these paragraphs partly because this wisdom is regularly associated with Amida in his role as fourth of Shingon's five buddhas, but also because this wisdom realizes the intuition that phenomena and sentient beings—just as they are and in their full multiplicity—are the *dharmakāya* Dainichi, a main theme of *Amida hishaku.*

36. *"Jissō"* and *"jisshō"* often translate *"dharmakāya"* and *"bhūtatathatā,"* respectively. Here they are virtual synonyms.

37. *Temmei* omits "Tathāgata." *Kongō* retains the formulaic structure completely.

38. I suppose we are to take this "palace of the mind" to be the microcosmic equivalent of Dainichi's own Vajra Dharmadhātu residence. See n. 33 above. "Inner witness" translates *"naishō,"* the key Shingon term for enlightenment.

39. *Jiju hōraku* is enlightenment enjoyed by Dainichi for his own pleasure in contrast to his distribution of this energy for the sake of others. Cf. the two kinds of *juyu hosshin* in the discussion of "derived bodies" on p. 127.

40. The ten stages (*jūji;* Skt. *daśabhūmi*) of a bodhisattva's journey to enlightenment come almost at the end of the entire fifty-two stage program. They are followed by complete enlightenment *(tōgaku)* and wondrous enlightenment *(myōgaku).*

41. The use of the term "uninvoked" as a descriptor for Amida seems quite unexpected, indeed almost unnatural.

42. Although Dainichi/Amida may surpass both sun and moon, sunlight is still an emblematic image of Dainichi, the Great Sun. In similar fashion, moonlight aligns with Amida, who, in *yamagoshi raigō* paintings, approaches the dying nenbutsu petitioner like a moon rising over distant mountains. The association of these two buddhas with the sun and moon also neatly indicates the priority of Daininchi over Amida for Kakuban—all in spite of their non-dual unity. (See also n. 34 above.)

43. *Kongō* omits the entire passage bracketed in the translation. This very common type of copyist's error strongly suggests that *Kongō* is derived from a prior *Temmei*-like manuscript.

44. "Individualized" renders *"shabetsu."* "Wisdom-seal" is *"chi-in,"* "seal" being the common translation of "mudra." Shingon sometimes uses the compound *"chi-in"* to mean "heart/mind."

45. The Tantric tradition's close interest in mantras led it to pay serious attention to Indian linguistic theories, such as those generated by Panini (fourth century B.C.) and his followers, scholars whose scientific understanding of language was two and

one half millennia ahead of Western hypotheses and is even today not fully assimilated in the Western academy. Kūkai (who, unlike most later Shingon figures, could probably actually read Sanskrit) brought aspects of this discipline to Japan. It was soon, however, largely lost, but Kakuban here appears to be fairly knowledgeable—although he could be citing boilerplate cliches. In this piece he contrasts *jisō* (the phonetic/phonemic structure of language, perhaps including orthography as well), with *jigi* (its semantic elements). See also nn. 54 and 55, below.

46. *Hombushō;* Skt. *anutpada.*

47. "Selfless Great Self" is *muga daiga,* the notion that the doctrine of non-self (*muga;* Skt. *anatman*) does not foreclose the existence of a Great Self for enlightened beings, whose innermost nature is emptiness.

48. Shingon organizes its major womb mandala *(taizōkai mandara)* in terms of three families: the Buddha family, the Lotus family and the Vajra family. In Indo-Tibetan tantrism such families commonly represent different personality types of aspirants, but in Shingon they seem limited to use as handy taxonomic headings. In this framework Buddha is equated with meditation, Lotus with compassion, Vajra with wisdom, and so on.

49. "Principle and Wisdom" (*ri* and *chi;* Chn. *li* and *shih*) constitute a key pair of terms in Shingon. They encode a number of the preliminary dualisms that are to be non-dually united in awakening. For example, Principle is equated with the universe that is to be known and Wisdom with the knower, or Shingon aspirant. Or, again, Principle is associated with the womb mandala and Wisdom with the *vajra* mandala.

50. *Shōbō nikū* ("living beings and dharmic things: two emptinesses") indicates that emptiness is the core of everything. The difficulty is how one understands emptiness. For Kakuban it is an innermost reality beyond all qualities and all distinctions, but present in everything.

51. For *"isshin"* ("One Mind"), *Kongō* has *"issai"* ("all"). This would render the translation "For the dharmic constructs are all empty and unreal."

52. [This paragraph resonates with the Tiantai "three truths" theory. *RKP*]

53. Kakuban rejects the theory that there is a substantial self either for persons or things *(ninbō niga)* and against this notion reaffirms the *shōbō nikū* idea that emptiness is the core essenceless essence of buddhas, persons, and things alike.

54. I.e., the phonemic shape of a given morpheme is (1) ultimately arbitrary and (2) a form that may vary phonetically according to its environment.

55. Words without semantic content *(jisō)* would not be words at all and cannot therefore be spoken of as having any linguistic structure. Words with a variable phonemic structure *(jigi)* would no longer distinguish meaning and therefore would not be words at all. So too no mind can exist without a body, no nirvana without samsara. Structure and content are codependent.

56. Any choice of one thing over another is arbitrary and unfounded. Expressions that condemn "choosing this and rejecting that" are very common in Shingon, especially among *fu ni*-oriented authors.

5

"Show Me the Place Where My Mother Is!"

Chūjōhime, Preaching, and Relics in Late Medieval and Early Modern Japan

Hank Glassman

In medieval Japan, Buddhist storytellers used text, image, and sound to transport audiences of the faithful and the curious to other worlds. These religious narrative performances gave flesh to the skeleton of doctrine and endowed the sylphs of legend with real-world solidity. With pictures and words the skillful preacher sent his or her listeners to other places in time and space: to the depths of hell and back, to the remote historical past of Japan or Buddhist India, to the eternal Pure Land of Amida Buddha in the west. Although canonical Buddhist scripture and orthodox ritual were integral to the lives of people in medieval Japan, perhaps an even greater role can be ascribed to the popular performances by itinerant troupes of specialists who entertained festival and market crowds with their reenactments of sacred legends. These preachers used illustrated scrolls, painted banners, and cosmographic maps known as *mandara,* as well as statues, relics, and the surrounding landscape, to bring their words to life—to make the stories they told real. In the pages that follow, this rich and synthetic liturgy of multimedia spectacle will form the background of my discussion. Preachers of the Pure Land sect, especially those of the Seizan branch, used the compelling legend of an orphan girl named Chūjōhime to attract a base of believers, solicit donations, and transmit their message of salvation through faith in Amida Buddha and faith in one's own future birth in his Pure Land. As we shall see, the preachers played a key role in the development of Chūjōhime's legend and the production of the relics associated with her cult. In doing so, they created a Pure Land Buddhism not glimpsed in the sūtras or the doctrinal debates of the scholar monks.

The Legend of the Taima *Mandara* and Its Medieval Transformation

> Later I went to Hōryū Temple and then to Taima Temple, where the daughter of Lord Yokohagi had dedicated herself to the worship of the Buddha. Once a strange nun came to her and said, "Bring me ten bundles of lotus stems, and I will weave you a maṇḍala depicting paradise." The nun took strands from the lotus stems and dyed them various colors, simply by dipping them in water from Dyeing Well. When the fibers were ready for weaving, a court lady appeared, requested some oil for her lamp, and wove from ten that night until four the next morning. As the two strangers were about to leave, Yokohagi's daughter said, "Will we ever meet again?"
>
> She was told, "Long ago Kashō preached the Buddhist law; then, reincarnated as Hōki Bodhisattva, he came here to the Taima Temple and inaugurated Buddhist services. We have come because you sincerely believed in the Western Paradise. If you trust in this maṇḍala, you will not suffer." Then the two women disappeared into the western sky. I found inspiration in this tale, which has been transmitted in written form.[1]

This passage appears in the thirteenth-century diary of Lady Nijō, a concubine of the cloistered Emperor Go-Fukakusa who renounced the world to become a wandering nun. In this description of her visit to Taimadera in 1290, Nijō notes that the story had been "transmitted in written form," and it is believed that she indeed read it as text or had it read to her at Taimadera while viewing the *mandara*[2] (see Plate 5.1). We can imagine that perhaps she saw a more subdued predecessor to the dynamic preaching performances mentioned at the beginning of this chapter. Over the course of the next two centuries this tale developed considerable complexity and depth, becoming a poignant medieval saga of loss, struggle, and redemption. The story Nijō summarizes is that of Chūjōhime, the legendary woman whose faithful desire to see the Pure Land resulted in the miraculous creation of the Taima *mandara*. In Nijō's account, the heroine is anonymous and her life before her entry into Taimadera obscure. Had Nijō been able to hear this tale in its more developed form, it would have no doubt captured her imagination and inspired her further, for her own story bears striking similarities to the life of the Chūjōhime of later legends.[3]

Chūjōhime, known to Nijō only as Lord Yokohagi's daughter, had, like Nijō lost her mother at a tender age and had demonstrated promise in becoming the emperor's favorite and her clan's pride and joy. However, she rejected this privilege (and duty) from the beginning, steadfastly refusing to become a concubine, and devoted herself instead to Buddhist practice on her late mother's behalf. This dedication to her mother's memory inspires and preoccupies her, making secular life impossible. As we shall see, Chūjōhime's maternal fixation was her mother's dying wish.

The stories of Nijō and Chūjōhime are also linked by the motif

Plate 5.1. Taima Mandala *(mandara)*, 1750. Hanging scroll. The Metropolitan Museum of Art, Charles Stewart Smith Collection, Gift of Mrs. Charles Stewart Smith, Charles Stewart Smith, Jr., and Howard Caswell Smith in memory of Charles Stewart Smith, 1914. (14.76.54)

of the aristocratic lady wandering and in exile. The great folklorist Orikuchi Shinobu identified the wayfaring of the fallen noble, or *kishu ryūri,* as a principal motif of medieval Japanese literature and noted that the role of wanderer was especially associated with women. Orikuchi called this folklore type the "wandering princess" *(sasurai himegimi).*[4] A large part of Chūjōhime's appeal for a medieval audience was her vulnerability and marginalized status as a daughter wrongly accused, hiding in the mountain's fastness, her days spent absorbed in *nenbutsu zammai* (single-minded concentration on Amida Buddha), copying one sūtra in particular again and again for the sake of her dear mother. She has no skills or means to sustain herself in this wild place and must rely on her father's escaped retainer and his wife to support and care for her. It is Chūjōhime's weakness and vulnerability that make her such a compelling figure.

In time, the Taima *mandara* itself would recede into the background as the nameless daughter of Lord Yokohagi moved upstage. Once the miraculous image had been the focus of the legend; now the woman for whom it had been created became the tale's true protagonist and was given the title Chūjōhime.[5] The wellspring of Chūjōhime's religious devotion and her deep faith is now the memory of her late mother. It is these painful memories of her separation, through death, from the mother she never knew that form Chūjōhime's principal motivation toward holiness.

In its broadest outlines, the story of Chūjōhime runs as follows. Born to Yokohagi no daijin and his wife, Chūjōhime was only three years old when her mother fell ill and died. On her deathbed, the mother was unable to concentrate on the rituals necessary for salvation, so concerned was she about her daughter's fate. She threw down the five-colored strings linking her to an image of Amida Buddha and cursed her daughter, saying she wished she had never had a child. With her dying breath, she charged the little girl with rescuing her from damnation. As Jacqueline Stone demonstrates in her contribution to this volume, the final moments of a Buddhist's life were thought to be of the utmost importance for salvation. Although from the mid-Kamakura period on, as Stone points out, there were those who denied the crucial nature of one's final state of mind, Chūjōhime's story demonstrates that, at least as a literary trope, the idea of a "bad death" was still a readily recognizable conceit at the end of the medieval period. The implication of the mother's agitated condition is clear: she will not attain birth in the Pure Land. Her daughter must strive to save her.

After her father's remarriage, Chūjōhime went through childhood loathed by her stepmother. When she was invited to enter the service of the emperor, her stepmother created the appearance of sexual impropriety on the girl's part and turned her own father against her. He ordered Chūjōhime to be executed on desolate Hibariyama, but his retainer did not have the heart to carry out the deed. Having disobeyed his master's direct order, the warrior could not return home, so he took Chūjōhime and his wife to live in the mountains. Here the girl copied a sūtra describing Amida Buddha's Pure Land a thousand times and dedicated the merit accrued thereby to her late mother's memory. Eventually Chūjōhime was reunited with her father, who once again attempted to send her to the imperial palace, but she escaped to Taimadera. At this point the earlier legend of the *mandara* begins.[6]

The textual history of the Chūjōhime legend is quite complex and need not concern us here.[7] Various types of texts survive—from notes on sermons to scripts for the puppet theater, from nō plays to illustrated books. The details contained in these narratives differ, often substantially. For our purposes, the essential shift to note is one that occurred over the course of the fourteenth century, during the transition from the Kamakura to the Muromachi period. The exact date is of course hard to determine because we are concerned with the development of an oral tradition, one that was not fixed in writing until after the fact. The Taima *mandara* legends of the former period are primarily concerned with the creation of the *mandara* and do not discuss Chūjōhime's childhood, while those of the latter center around Chūjōhime's abuse at the hands of her stepmother and her abandonment in the mountains. This shift can be attributed to the active role of Pure Land preachers in the expansion of the *mandara*'s narrative.

The earliest known text relating the story of Chūjōhime the stepchild and orphan is Zeami's play *Hibariyama* from the end of the fourteenth century. Zeami's play does not even mention the *mandara,* and instead focuses completely on Chujohime's exile in the mountains and her reunion with her father. It adds elements not seen in any of the earlier versions, such as details of Chūjōhime's life before she became a nun and her mother's death. In *Hibariyama,* she lives in the mountains with her wet-nurse, not the retainer and his wife. Another play by Zeami, *Taema,* excludes these elements and centers on Chūjōhime's relationship to the *mandara.*[8] Where did Zeami get the material for his two stories? The Taima *mandara,* which was not well known during the Nara and Heian periods, was rediscovered and adopted by Hōnen's disciple and founder of the Seizan branch of the Pure Land sect, Shōkū (1177–1247) during the thirteenth century and used widely and enthusiastically as an aid to preaching. We have a record of the content of sermons (which like Shōkū's were based on the Taima *mandara*) in a 1436 text by the Pure Land monk Shōsō (1366–1440).

Shōsō's 1436 work, the *Taima mandara sho,* marks a turning point in the development of the Chūjōhime legend.[9] It is the earliest surviving written version in which all of the key elements of the legend take shape. Here we find the name of Chūjōhime's father, the locations of two mountains purported to be Hibariyama (the site of her near-execution), her wicked stepmother, and the rest. It is very clear that Shōsō's text is a record of his sermons at Taimadera: it is interspersed with references to "this Taima temple," compares the *mandara* at hand to others, and contains phrases to jog the memories of his listeners, such as "as I explained yesterday."[10] As we shall see preaching was essential to the creation and development of Chūjōhime's legend and cult. Zeami almost certainly had as his source for *Hibariyama* the performances of itinerant preachers lecturing on the Taima *mandara.*[11] As the legend continued to expand over the following centuries, the proselytizing monks of the Seizan branch of the Pure Land sect had an enormous influence on its direction and content.

This essay traces the transformation of the Chūjōhime story in the medieval period and illuminates the role that preaching played in the recasting of the story of the *mandara.* More than one scholar has stressed the point that this tale was from the beginning a story of women's salvation.[12] This is indeed true; in fact two women are saved—Queen Vaidehī, the heroine of the *mandara*'s narrative, and Chūjōhime of the framing tale. One could include also the women who would have constituted a good part of the preachers' audiences. Ultimately, the story is about the salvation of the hearer of the text, the witness to the exposition of the *mandara* and its story. However, the tale of Chūjōhime was from the start and remained throughout its history an account of women's salvation through birth in the Pure Land. It is through engagement with the story of an individual woman and her suffering that salvation is offered to women.

The development of Chūjōhime as a character was the key to her story's widespread popularity in the medieval period. It also made the tale a powerful tool for propagating the Pure Land teachings through faith in the *mandara* and in the Land of Bliss it represents. Every step of this development was shaped and guided by the professional preachers who lectured on the *mandara* using the practice known as *etoki* (literally, "picture explaining" or "picture preaching"). The Chūjōhime legends of the medieval period were always created through performance. As Tokuda Kazuo has said, "It is precisely when the iconography of doctrine is explained through *etoki* that it becomes concretely understood."[13] It is through performance that the "iconography of doctrine" becomes flesh and blood.

Witnessing the Pure Land: Chūjōhime's Vision of a "Living Amida"

When the medieval audience saw the *mandara* and heard its details explained, they were reenacting the role of Chūjōhime as she listened to the preaching of the apparitional nun, or *keni,* who had manifested herself to create the *mandara* in response to Chūjōhime's supplications. When Chūjōhime prayed to see Amida Buddha in his living form, he revealed himself to her in the body of a woman and created a map of his Pure Land for her: "Since you are a woman, I have transformed myself into a nun and come to you as a woman."[14] Thus was Chūjōhime made the conduit for the revelation of the Pure Land in this world. The texts are explicit: whoever sees the *mandara* and worships it is guaranteed birth in Amida's paradise upon death, regardless of his or her religious attainment.[15] Through her resolve to see a living vision of Amida Buddha, Chūjōhime forges a link between this world and the next world, not only for herself but for all.

Shortly after entering Taimadera to escape marriage, Chūjōhime prays for a vision of the living Amida Buddha. Zeami describes this in his play *Taema:*

> Although the plan to have her installed as empress was ready, a matter such as this never entered the mind of Princess Chūjō. She thought only about enlightenment in the future world. Secretly she slipped away from the capital at Nara, and came to this temple. Here she cut off her hair and prayed that she might worship Amida in his living form *(shōjin no Amida nyorai wo ogamitaku to go-ryūgan o okoshitamō).*[16]

Chūjōhime ensconces herself in a room for seven days and single-mindedly pursues her goal. It is at this point, on the sixth day of her seclusion, that the original narrative as recounted by Lady Nijō—that of the visit by the apparitional nun and apparitional weaver woman—appears in the *otogizōshi* versions.[17] As we shall see, these versions emphasize Chūjōhime's life before her entry into Taimadera. The miracle of the *mandara* is, of course, still the denouement, but it completes a drama different from the one Lady Nijō heard. In the *otogizōshi* versions, the weaving of the *mandara* is not simply the fulfillment of a pious woman's desire to worship a living Amida, but the realization of Chūjōhime's long-cherished wish to see her dead mother's dwelling place. After the vision has been granted through the weaving of the tapestry, the apparitional nun mounts the *mandara* on two pieces of jointless bamboo and proceeds to explain its details to Chūjōhime, pointing out with a bamboo rod the places she is explicating. The practice of preaching on the *mandara* is thus established at the moment of the image's creation. The nun explains to Chūjōhime that her wish to see a vision of Amida in the flesh has indeed been fulfilled because the nun herself is Amida in female form. The nun disappears, borne on purple clouds to the western sky, the apparitional weaver vanishes, and Chūjōhime is left alone. As they depart, they tell her that they will return to welcome her into the Pure Land in thirteen years. Chūjōhime takes up the mantle of explaining the *mandara,* first to her attendants, and later to monks of the Taimadera and various high-ranking monks and noblemen.[18] True to the promise, Amida returns with his entourage of twenty-five bodhisattvas thirteen years later to welcome Chūjōhime into the Pure Land. Chūjōhime dies at the age of twenty-nine and is led into the Pure Land in the very body—a female body—she occupied in this life.[19]

The Taima *mandara,* a transformation tableau *(hensō)* of Amida Buddha's Western Paradise, Sukhāvatī, was created for the purpose of preaching on the *Sūtra on the Contemplation of Immeasurable Life,* the *Kanmuryōjukyō* (hereafter, *Kangyō*).[20] It was precisely this process of preaching on the *mandara* that led to the elaboration of the Chūjōhime legend. In the Kamakura period, the story had been a simple miracle tale in which an unnamed woman of aristocratic birth, perhaps an old nun, living at the Taimadera, was visited by an apparitional nun who, asking her to gather cartloads of lotus stems, dyed them five colors and directed an apparitional woman in the weaving of the *mandara*. The story was then utterly transformed leading up to the Muromachi period. From this time on it became a truly medieval story. One could call this the "*hime*-ization" of the Taima legend: the anonymous heroine is transfigured into a fairy-tale princess. The motifs of the beautiful girl's evil stepmother, near beheading, and banishment to the mountains are well represented in other stories of the medieval period, but it is not unlikely that the Chūjōhime legend served as the classical source for a number of later legends.[21] These elements served to make what had always been a story of women's salvation through Pure Land devotion more appealing, more convincing, more exciting for a medieval audience, who, it must be remembered, heard and saw the Chūjōhime legend as a performance created by the man or woman preaching the sermon on the *mandara* and birth in the Pure Land.

Preaching, the Taima *Mandara,* and the Creation of the Chūjōhime Legend

The Taima *mandara,* a sumptuous tableau of the splendors of the Western Paradise of Amida Buddha, is one of the great monuments of Pure Land art.[22] The eighth-century original is a tapestry, probably of Chinese origin, now largely in tatters and barely decipherable. Many copies were made however, from the thirteenth century on, so its content has not been lost to us.[23] The *mandara* is composed of four zones; the largest, central zone is the hieratic, symmetrical view of the court of Amida Buddha in the Pure Land, enclosed on three sides by cloisters to the left, right, and bottom. These cloisters explicate the content of the *Kangyō,* or, more specifically, they elucidate in visual form a seventh-century commentary on the sutra written by the great Chinese Pure Land patriarch Shandao.[24] For centuries, the *mandara* was a central element in the transmission and cultivation of Pure Land faith and practice in Japan. It gives eloquent testimony to the fact that medieval Pure Land believers enjoyed a wide range of religious expression and were not limited to the recitation of the nenbutsu (that is, the recitation of the Buddha's name, *Namu-Amida-butsu*) in their religious praxis.

As splendid as the *mandara* itself is, the spectacular legend surrounding its creation by Chūjōhime is every bit as iconic as the transformation tableau. What had begun in the Kamakura period as a simple tale of the miraculous weaving of the tapestry in response to the desire of an old nun to see the Pure Land became, during the Muromachi period, a riveting tale of a stepchild slandered and abandoned, nearly executed, and wholly dedicated to a lifelong wish for reunion with her mother, whose face she could not even remember.

The Taima *mandara* was never a mere art object, appreciated for its visual qualities or the technical skill that produced it. It was an instrumental and dynamic icon, the relic of a miraculous event containing stories within stories. Although mere contact with the image was sufficient for salvation, the *mandara* was used as an illustrated manual for meditation as well as in preaching and teaching Buddhism. As we have seen, the legend of the creation of the *mandara* explicitly notes its use by the *keni,* whose first act upon completing the tapestry was to explain its content to Chūjōhime. Preaching the *mandara (mandara kōsetsu* or *mandara etoki)* was widespread in medieval Japan. Around the Taima *mandara* centered a whole system of preaching, an entire culture of reception that allowed for elaboration, extemporaneous composition, and embellishment.[25]

This practice led to the creation of the Chūjōhime legend as it came to be known in the fifteenth century. Preachers brought to life the world of the *mandara,* with its depiction of Queen Vaidehī and the glories of the Pure Land as explained in the *Kangyō*. They extolled the merit of the *mandara* and its miraculous origins. Before long, the sufferings of its patron and de facto creator, Chūjōhime, had also become an integral part of the performance. The focus of the preaching shifted from the content of the *mandara* itself to the story of its creation and from there to the travails of its legendary patron. Originally, the *mandara* was seen as a map of a place of purity and refuge offered to a mother (Vaidehī) suffering unspeakable mistreatment at the hands of her only son, an illustration of a sūtra; in time it became a relic, a testament to the power of the faith manifested by a daughter in dire straits who longs to meet her mother beyond the grave.

The preaching/performance of the *mandara* and of the Chūjōhime legend—whether through illustrated hand scrolls *(emaki),* hanging scrolls, relics, or statues—adapted itself to the religious themes of the day. The story of women's salvation took various forms and emphases at different times. Some versions stressed the cruelty of the stepmother, some Chūjōhime's defiance of the Taima monks who refused to admit her to the temple because she was a woman. One Tokugawa-period work inexplicably concluded that the moral of Chūjōhime's tale was good girls should obey their stepmothers.[26]

From the late Muromachi period, the Chūjōhime legend was drawn into a larger cultural discourse that pathologized, in both the medical and spiritual realms, female biology, linking menstruation and related functions to sin and disease. Part of this recasting of Chūjōhime as a savior from "female troubles" culminated in her becoming the poster girl for a gynecological patent medicine known as Chūjōtō.[27] As we shall see below, Chūjōhime's implication in this misogynistic medicalization of women's fertility was by no means solely the creation of the drug company Tsumura Juntendō, which produced Chūjōtō. The association between our heroine and the regulation of menstrual flow and vaginal discharge had older and deeper roots in local legend. In a certain sense, this later recasting was encoded in the tale of Chūjōhime from the start.

Tanaka Takako has pointed out that Chūjōhime is the quintessential suffering savior so familiar in Japanese folk literature. In Chūjōhime's case the suffering inflicted on her as a result of her sexuality (latent though it is) transforms her into the savior of her sex: her vulnerability makes her transcendent. In Tanaka's words, she is the "abandoned goddess."[28]

The trials of lost or abandoned children play a very prominent role in medieval Japanese folktales and fiction.[29] In this context, the scenes in the Chūjōhime narrative that come to mind are those of her desertion by her stepmother at Mt. Katsuragi's Jigokudani and her planned execution on Hibariyama. However, Chūjōhime suffers a more fundamental abandonment earlier in the tale, one that sets the stage for her future suffering and redemption: the loss of her mother at a young age. Her mother's death makes her aware of impermanence and causes her mind to take a religious turn and is also the indirect cause of the pain inflicted on her by her evil stepmother. It is because her mother dies that Chūjōhime ultimately becomes a holy person. The fact that Chūjōhime's entire religious career is inspired and sustained by concern for her dead mother's salvation and a wish to be reunited with her is largely ignored in the secondary literature. However, this aspect of the legend, as told in the *otogizōshi* versions, makes Chūjōhime a convincing model for women's religious practice and explains her rise to sainthood. To better understand this element of the story, let us step back into the world of the *mandara* to look at another suffering savior and exemplar for women engaged in Pure Land practice.

Queen Vaidehī

During the Muromachi period, the Chūjōhime tale continued to be one of women's salvation and Pure Land faith as it had been during the Kamakura times, but its heroine became much more human. In the expansion of the narrative, Chūjōhime was given a name, a face, and a body. Part of the inspiration for her story as a woman in dire straits comes from the *mandara* itself. In its left border we find illustrated the tribulations and salvation of Queen Vaidehī, the protagonist of the *Kangyō*. Vaidehī's story contains a ready supply of the pathos demanded by a medieval audience.

Vaidehī is a mother oppressed by her wicked son, while Chūjōhime is a daughter sentenced to death by her father because of the machinations of her stepmother. What ties these two heroines together is their role as mediators of divinely inspired visions of the Pure Land. Both are saved by a buddha (Śākyamuni in Vaidehī's case, Amitābha in Chūjōhime's) through his revelation of the Pure Land to them and both take on the task of transmitting this revealed splendor to others. Vaidehī and Chūjōhime pray to see and know a place free from suffering and evil; each becomes a conduit for the saving vision she has received. Because of the suffering and salvation of these two women, anyone who gazes on the world represented in the *mandara* will be reborn in the Pure Land.

As explained above, the Taima *mandara* is a visual representation of the *Kangyō,* or the *Contemplation Sūtra.* This sūtra is set in a cell where the queen of the ancient Indian kingdom of Magadha has been imprisoned by her son. The queen's name is Vaidehī, or Idaike in Japanese. She has been placed in irons by Prince Ajātaśatru (Ajase) for the crime of conspiring to keep her husband alive when it was the prince's intent to starve his father to death. On her daily visits to the king, Vaidehī spread a paste of flour and honey over her body and filled her silver body ornaments with grape juice for the king to eat and drink. (In the early 1930's, Japan's first psychoanalyst, Kosawa Heisaku, took Freud's Oedipus complex and applied it to this story cycle, dubbing it "the Ajase complex." The complex refers to the unresolved animosity that Kosawa and his followers contend many Japanese [men] feel toward their mothers and the psychological problems caused by Japanese society's inclination toward the "maternal principle.")[30]

For her deception, Ajātaśatru came close to killing his mother until his hand was stayed by his ministers, who threatened to leave his service. They exclaimed that while cases of patricide were not uncommon in the annals of the royal families of India, never once had such a heinous act as the execution of one's mother been recorded. Ajātaśatru settles for imprisoning his mother to keep her out of the way while he kills the king. As she languishes in her cell, the queen is brought to the depths of despair and asks aloud what karma could have brought her such an inimical child and wonders if there is not a better world somewhere. Śākyamuni's disciples Maudgalyāyana (Mokuren) and Ānanda (Anan) miraculously appear before the queen and her attendants, stating that the Buddha is at present preaching a sermon on Vulture Peak but will manifest himself in the cell straight away to answer the queen's prayers. The Buddha presently does appear before her eyes and shows her a wide and vast array of lands dazzling beyond imagination. He asks Vaidehī to choose from this display one land in particular that appeals to her. She of course immediately settles on the Western Pure Land of Amitābha (Amida) Buddha, Sukhāvatī (Gokuraku, Ultimate Bliss). She is then able to behold with her own eyes every detail of this paradise: jeweled trees, enormous flowers, placid lotus pools, shimmering pavilions, and extraordinary, chimerical avian life.

Vaidehī takes heart in this vision of the perfect world to come and rejoices, but she is concerned, as she tells the Buddha, that future beings unable to have visions inspired by the transcendent power of the Buddha will have no means of beholding Amida's Land of Ultimate Bliss. Implicit in this statement is the understanding, already mentioned above, that to see the Pure Land in this life causes one to be born there in the next life: Vaidehī's salvation comes through seeing. In the sūtra narrative that follows, the connection between sight and salvation is made quite explicit.[31] The efficacy of seeing is a fundamental aspect of the logic of the *mandara* and its ritual explication. The Buddha explains to Vaidehī, her attendants, Ananda, and future generations a visualization technique that builds up the Pure Land in the mind's eye methodically, one step at a time. He goes on to say that beings are born into the Pure Land at different stages of progress in the path and through different physical processes according to their abilities and their acts in the present life.

The *mandara* illustrates all of this. On the left border there are scenes of Lady Vaidehī having visions of splendor in her cell. This is not a single tableau but is illustrated in a set of eleven frames. The right border illustrates the content of the visualization in its thirteen stages. The bottom cloister of the *mandara* depicts the birth of beings of nine grades of spiritual attainment into the Pure Land. The central portion of the *mandara,* the main body of the work, is a detailed vision of the Pure Land itself. Here we see the jewel-encrusted towers, the celestial musicians, Amida and his retinue, the "stage" where pure beings newly born from lotuses come before the Amida triad to receive instruction, the limpid ponds, and the other splendors of this paradise. The ritual performance of displaying the *mandara,* explaining its content, and telling the story of its creation was absolutely central to the propagation and practice of Pure Land Buddhism in medieval and early modern *(kinsei)* Japan.

Preaching and the Relics of Chūjōhime

The primary occasion for the retelling of the Chūjōhime story was, naturally, the explication of the *mandara* of the Pure Land, created by Chūjōhime's deep faith and through her encounter with Amida Buddha provisionally manifested in a female body. The *mandara* is evidence of Chūjōhime's vision. Although Queen Vaidehī was a remote figure from Buddhist mythology, Chūjōhime provided a more proximate connection to Amida Buddha and the Pure Land depicted in the *mandara.* She was, after all, a woman situated in Japan's historical past whose life followed contours common in Japanese literature. Her real presence in this world, and by extension in the next, was further reinforced by the ritual display of her bodily relics and contact relics, such as the sūtras she copied, her writing brush, her razor, her monastic robes. Many statues of her were also used to assert her real historical existence and her continuing accessibility, creating for the saint Chūjōhime many duplicates, images like the *chinsō* of Zen masters, which Bernard Faure has called "substitute bodies"[32] (see Plate 5.2).

Connections between relics and the transmission and elaboration of Chūjōhime's story were essential. One concrete example of this can be found in the sixteenth century. A critical moment in the history of the development of the Chūjōhime legend was the creation of the *Taima mandara engi* of 1531, the so-called Kyōroku-bon. This *emaki* would serve as an important model for all later hand scroll versions of the tale.[33] The text was created through the efforts of the Pure Land preacher Yūzen, whose activities were centered at Taimadera. In 1530 Yūzen brought a version of the story called *Chūjōhime monogatari* to the residence of the great literatus, Sanjonishi Sanetaka (1455–1537). He made numerous visits to Sanetaka to show him a collection of Chūjōhime's personal effects—her inkstone, her brush, her surplice, and so on—all of this to coax him to

Plate 5.2. Seventeen-year-old Chūjōhime at the time of her tonsure (seventeenth century, wood). Reprinted courtesy of Naka no bo, Taimadera.

agree to lend his calligraphic skills to the *emaki* version of the story.[34] No doubt Yūzen's efforts were also instrumental in gaining the services of the famous artist Tosa Mitsushige, the son of Mitsunobu, and painter of the celebrated *Kitano tenjin engi,* to illustrate the Kyōroku-bon.[35]

Over the centuries, the display of relics continued to be central to the spread of the Chūjōhime cult. And, as Sekiyama Kazuo has maintained, the popularization of the legend and cult of Chūjōhime was a major factor in the widespread influence of the Pure Land sect in late medieval Japan.[36] The most central of the relics was of course the image itself, the *mandara,* the physical manifestation of Chūjōhime's faith and her personal vision of the Pure Land. (Naturally, the *mandara* on display was in almost every case a copy of the original, but no less efficacious, no less legitimate a relic for that fact.) The *mandara* was created expressly for her in response to her heartfelt prayers. What is more, it was conceived by Amida and executed by the bodhisattva Kannon, appearing for Chūjōhime's benefit in female bodies as the apparitional nun and the apparitional woman. The ritual exhibition of Chūjōhime's relics, the *mandara* foremost among them, was the principal context for the dissemination of her story. In addition to those mentioned previously, other relics included a hanging scroll illustrating Chūjōhime's birth into the Pure Land and embroidered with *Namu-Amida-butsu* in her own hair, and bodily relics.[37] An essential aspect of this display was the preaching on statues representing Chūjōhime as a nun—another type of relic. Many of these still exist today, most having been created in the seventeenth century. Several purport to have been carved by Chūjōhime herself. One of these in particular, the one housed at Seirenji in Uda-gun, Nara prefecture, displaced a statue of Amida to become the principal object of worship at this small Pure Land sect convent.[38]

Chūjōhime's relics were taken on tours of the entire Yamato region and beyond, always acting as referents to their place of origin—where the events described in the Chūjōhime legend unfolded, including Taimadera and associated temples along the pilgrim's road to Kumano. The most dramatic event in the Chūjōhime narrative is the moment of her near beheading on Hibariyama. At least three sites are purported to be the original Hibariyama, and the legends surrounding each refer to the others in their claims to primacy.

As Gorai Shigeru has pointed out, real geographical sites were crucial points of reference for medieval preachers and audiences. Preachers could not simply tell their story without some proof of the physical reality of their tale. Writing, relics, robes, and statues played a part in this, but so did the landscape itself. Peaks and valleys were renamed to correspond to the topography of the legends.[39]

The practice of telling the Chūjōhime story with an exhibition of relics continued until quite recent times. It is essential to emphasize that the retelling and exhibition were in themselves religious ritual and that those who saw the relics and heard the story were promised birth in the Pure Land due to their karmic affinity *(kechien)* with Chūjōhime. In fact, there is evidence that, during the medieval period, some of the legend texts themselves functioned as records documenting this karmic connection. Their final pages consisted of alms records *(kanjinchō)* listing the names of donors from the audience.[40]

In the *kinsei* period, touring exhibitions of relics known as *degaichō* formed a kind of reverse pilgrimage wherein the treasures of the mountain would descend to meet the people of the plain, the townspeople. The famous tenth-century prelate Jie daishi Ryōgen is said to have brought relics down from Mt. Hiei so that his mother in the capital could worship them. As we shall see below, a comparison between the Taimadera *degaichō* and Ryōgen's relic ceremony is apt given the practice of *nyonin kinsei,* or the banning of females from holy sites, in some medieval Chūjōhime narratives. However, my focus here is on the *degaichō* of the personal effects of Chūjōhime and the treasures of Taimadera. These missions of proselytization, which were also fund-raising tours for specific building and renovation projects, became very popular in the *kinsei* period.

We are fortunate to have an illustrated book, the *Kaichō danwa* by the artist and writer Saru-an Takariki Tanenobu, that vividly captures the sights and sounds of one of these roadshows.[41] It is the spring of 1829. A five-year travelling exhibition of the treasures of the Okunoin at Taimadera has come to Nagoya for the first time. The curious and faithful flock to Seianji, a branch temple of Kyoto's Chion-in, to see what there is to see. Although our source is of a relatively late date, it documents a practice that had already been in place for centuries and is invaluable in understanding one context of the performance of the *mandara* lectures and the telling of the Chūjōhime legend. Tanenobu illustrates the day's events in detail: a man is taking tickets; a weaving exhibition is in progress; families meander with small children in tow; the *edokishi,* like modern museum docents, point out each item of interest from their stations behind the low bamboo railing that guides the pilgrims and tourists through the exhibit. The role of the *edokishi* in helping people understand and contextualize the objects on view cannot be overemphasized.

Tanenobu refers to their explanations as *"edoki"* and makes it clear that the words he transcribes are mere encapsulations or extracted portions of much longer speeches. It seems that the *edoki* concerning Chūjōhime's statue of herself along with the retainer who saved her and his wife was particularly detailed. At this station the story was told in full, under the gentle gaze of Chūjōhime herself.[42]

One particularly fascinating aspect of the exhibition, made clear in the illustrations only, is that nuns were exclusively responsible for displaying and explaining the personal effects and bodily relics of Chūjōhime. One nun leans over the railing to give an interested man a closer look at a crystal reliquary, while another uses a bamboo baton to part the curtain of a portable shrine revealing to a young couple Amida's name, embroidered by Chūjōhime with the hair shorn at the time of her religious vows. The man sits on his heels and clutches a rosary, the woman cranes forward for a better view. Also on display in the nun's section in the temple's main hall is the *Shōsan jōdokyō,* the sūtra Chūjōhime copied one thousand times, along with her brush and inkstone.[43] Just before entering this room the visitors pass a hanging scroll of the six-character invocation of Amida's name *(myōgō),* one of forty-eight copies (one for each of Amida's vows in his past life as the bodhisattva Dharmakāra) written by the Tendai Pure Land patriarch Ryōgen in his mother's memory. The message of women's salvation implicit here is not a simple one and needs to be unpacked further. You will recall that Ryōgen brought the relics ceremony to his mother because as a woman she was not allowed on Mt. Hiei. As Ryōgen brought the relics down from the mountain and into the public sphere, so the traveling exhibition of the treasures of Taimadera widens the scope of access to these relics, making them available to women. In the case of the *degaichō,* a woman's relics tour the country and are brought before men and women, but women are still not allowed to visit the inner sanctum of the temple where the relics are kept.[44] In point of fact, however, it was the telling of Chūjōhime's story occasioned by this ritual display that made the place of exhibition holy, not the purity of an all-male milieu, as the pilgrims were brought into the presence of the vulnerable saint. An essential part of this story is her diligence in producing copies of a certain sūtra.

The *Shōsan jōdokyō*

Among the relics of Chūjōhime are the many copies of the *Shōsan jōdokyō* she was said to have produced. This association with writing made her a kind of patron saint of calligraphy; she is even said in some accounts to have been Kūkai's tutor. Although this sūtra was not a popular or well-known one, copies of it are central to the Chūjōhime cult. In one of the earliest references to Chūjōhime by name, the thirteenth-century Pure Land saint and Kumano pilgrim Ippen shōnin receives one of the one thousand copies.[45] What is this text, and how did it come to be an essential feature of the Chūjōhime cult? To answer these questions, let us return to the medieval narrative of the heroine and undertake an examination of the unique history of this sūtra in Japanese Buddhism. As we shall see, this is a case in which a legend was constructed to incorporate relics at hand.

In Muromachi prose *(otogizōshi)* versions of the story, we find a seven-year-old Chūjōhime playing in gardens to the south of her palatial residence one fine spring day, accompanied by her devoted nurse, Jijū. The girl remembers nothing of her mother's death, having been shielded from this painful event by her father and those in his service. In the garden, Chūjōhime sees a little boy and a little girl of humble rank reaching into the blooming cherry trees to collect sprays of blossoms. A man and a woman enter the garden and take the children away in their arms.[46] Chūjōhime asks her nursemaid who these people are and the surprised servant replies that the adults are the mother and father of the two children and that the father carried the son and the mother carried the daughter. Chūjohime is perplexed by this response and asks why, if these children have both a father and a mother, does she have only a father and no mother. The nurse is overcome by grief and blurts out the story of Chūjōhime's mother's death.

Chūjōhime is profoundly unsettled by this revelation and has an awakening experience through a direct apprehension of impermanence. She aspires to renounce the world and seek enlightenment. From this moment on, she is also possessed with a burning desire to know her mother's current whereabouts and to be reunited with her. She leaves her father's compound without telling a soul and goes to see a holy man, a renowned seer.[47] In the Hiroshima University Chūjōhime manuscript, Chūjōhime demands of this clairvoyant monk, "Show me the place where my mother is!"—an echo of Vaidehī's request that Śākyamuni Buddha show her a perfect world without suffering. The man picks up a beautiful silk brocade pouch and draws from it a sūtra scroll. He tells Chūjōhime that her mother's dwelling place is described in detail in the sūtra and that she should read it over and over if she wishes to see her mother. He hands her the sūtra; she bows three times and accepts it. The sūtra given to Chūjōhime is the *Shōsan jōdokyō.*

The *Shōsan jōdokyō* is Xuanzang's seventh-century translation of the smaller *Sukhāvatīvyūha sūtra.* It was never as popular as Kumarajiva's earlier translation, known in Japanese as the *Amidakyō,* and was hardly ever used in China or Japan. However, it did enjoy considerable popularity during the Nara period due to the powerful Hossō sect's association of the sūtra with the school's founder, Tripitaka master Xuanzang. More importantly, it was this sūtra that was copied eighteen hundred times by the scribes of the national network of convents and temples, the Kokubunji and Kokubun niji, to commemorate the death of Empress Kōmyō in 760. Most of the sūtra scrolls ascribed to Chūjōhime, judging from the paper, ink, and calligraphy, are in fact Nara-period copies.[48] So it seems that when the Chūjōhime legend was expanded at the end of the Kamakura period, there were many Kōmyō memorial copies still in circulation—ready-made relics with an air of authenticity to back up the Chūjōhime legend. The eighteen hundred sūtras copied for the empress' memorial became the one thousand sūtras Chūjōhime copied for her mother's salvation. They were the source of the *nenbutsu zammai* that sustained her in the lonely fastness of Hibariyama.

The sūtras copied for the Nara empress underwent a transformation at the hands of the Pure Land priests during the medieval period. These men created a new legend for the Taima *mandara,* one that infused an existing artifact with a new identity and meaning and at the same time created a new context for the worship of the *mandara* itself. Now the *mandara,* and the Pure Land it represents, became inseparable from the story of Chūjōhime and her lifelong desire to work toward her mother's salvation. The sūtra is the glue that binds the hagiography to the icon.

To the medieval Japanese imagination, entry into the religious life for the sake of a missing parent was the most laudable goal imaginable. Chūjōhime was not the only abused stepdaughter to miss her mother and long for a reunion. In the world of medieval Japanese religious legend, even the Buddha himself was inspired in his religious quest by the absence of his loving mother and by his deep sadness and sense of obligation occasioned by her death.[49] The elaboration of the motif of a child's sudden apprehension of her mother's death goes hand in hand with what I described above as the "*hime*-ization" of the Chūjōhime story. Key to the transformation of the tale into a genuinely medieval one was the addition of Chūjōhime's dedication to her mother's memory. This humanization of the *mandara* story's protagonist was undertaken by the itinerant lecturers on the Taima *mandara,* who modeled themselves on Shōkū's thirteenth-century example and were sensitive to the ever-changing needs of their audience. As Iwaki Takatoshi has suggested, the idea that Chūjōhime's *hosshin* was inspired by the news of her mother's death was almost surely introduced during the preaching performance of the *mandara.* This idea was then spread by preachers who focused their lectures on birth in the Pure Land and especially on women's salvation.[50] The ancient copies of the *Shōsan jōdokyō* were used by preachers to bring this element of the story to life. Pointing to a real object in the world, a genuine Nara-period copy of the sūtra, they could proclaim, "Here before you is one of the thousand copies Chūjōhime made in her mother's memory."

Similarly the geography of the legend was superimposed on places at hand, places already known to local audiences. As previously noted, at least three sites were identified as the infamous Hibariyama and Chūjōhime's cult was associated throughout the medieval period with that of Mt. Kumano (sites relevant to the narrative, such as Hibariyama, lay along the major pilgrimage route to that important center of religious activity). Kumano was, of course, famous for its welcoming attitude toward female pilgrims and for its army of itinerant female preachers, the *Kumano bikuni.*[51]

The *Kumano bikuni,* like Chūjōhime and Vaidehī, were mediators to other worlds through their explanation of visions. From the late medieval period on, these nuns took an active role in bringing to life through words and pictures the joys and terrors of the afterlife. But the stories told by the *Kumano bikuni* and the propagators of the Chūjōhime cult were deeply ambivalent.[52] Chūjōhime is a holy woman, but at the same time, because of her female body she is in need of redemption. Elsewhere I have discussed the lessons on gender, sexuality, and salvation imparted to women through the Chūjōhime legend and cult. Among the relics associated with Chūjōhime kept by Hibariyama Tokushōji is a woodblock for the *Ketsubonkyō*, the *Blood Pool Sūtra*, said to have been carved by her hand.[53] At one convent, Hibariyama Seirenji, a statue of Chūjōhime, formerly used on travelling fund-raising campaigns, came to displace the image of Amida Buddha in the main worship hall. This happened early in the twentieth century through the sponsorship of a drug company producing a gynecological preparation that borrowed Chūjōhime's name, legend, and image.[54] Vaidehī, Chūjōhime, and Chūjōhime's mother all gain birth in the Pure Land, Amida's Land of Sukhāvatī, where there are no women. The status of their female bodies—impure because of menstruation and prohibited from the Pure Land—thus remains problematic in that process of salvation.

Performance and the Transformations of Chūjōhime

In the preceding pages, I have attempted to demonstrate some of the ways in which the exposition of stories embedded in graphic images, the exhibition of texts and objects, and the generative reenactment of a narrative of salvation, undertaken by preachers, served to make real the legend of an abused stepchild who became an honored saint. In the course of this discussion, it has become clear that the image of Chūjōhime was never static. She was constantly re-created and re-imagined by each new generation of preachers and their patrons. The legend's capacity for reformulation through the addition of new components (such as the *Shōsan jōdokyō*, statues, or the carved woodblock of the *Ketsubonkyō*) kept the story of Chūjōhime compelling for generations. In studies of the legends and cults of medieval and *kinsei* Japan, it is essential to bear in mind the creative power of performance, through which preachers made saints flesh and blood and touched the hearts and minds (and purses) of those gathered.

Notes

Abbreviations

NKBT: *Nihon koten bungaku taikei.* 100 vols. Tokyo: Iwanami Shoten, 1957–1969.

CSCK: *Chūjōhime setsuwa no chōsa kenkyū hōkoku sho.* Nara: Gankōji bunkazai kenkyūjo, 1983.

MJMS: *Muromachi jidai monogatari shū.* 5 vols. Edited by Yokoyama Shigeru and Ōta Takeo. Tokyo: Inoue Shobo, 1962.

MJMT: *Muromachi jidai monogatari taisei.* 14 vols. Edited by Yokoyama Shigeru and Matsumoto Ryūshin. Tokyo: Kadokawa Shoten, 1973–1988.

I would like to thank the various people who read and commented on this article, including J. Todd Brown, David Moerman, Duncan Williams, Keller Kimbrough, and two anonymous reviewers. Their observations and corrections have improved it greatly. Any remaining errors are mine alone.

1. Karen Brazell, trans., *The Confessions of Lady Nijō* (Stanford: Stanford University Press, 1973), 205–206.

2. See Tokuda Kazuo, "Kyōroku-bon 'Taimadera engi' emaki to 'Chūjōhime no honji'" in his *Otogizōshi kenkyū* (Tokyo: Miyai shoten, 1988), 362. Also I have followed Elizabeth ten Grotenhuis in referring to the Taima *hensō* as a *"mandara"* throughout this essay to emphasize its difference from the orthodox mandala of the Vajrayāna. See ten Grotenhuis, *Japanese Mandalas: Representations of Sacred Geography* (Honolulu: University of Hawai'i Press, 1999), 3.

3. It is possible that Nijō was told the name of the heroine and did not record it. In the 1299 *Ippen jijiri e,* there is an account of a 1287 pilgrimage to Taimadera by Ippen that mentions the name "Hongan Chūjō no hime" (see Komatsu Shigemi, ed., *Ippen shōnin eden, Nihon no emaki,* vol. 20 [Tokyo: Chūō kōronsha, 1998], 225). Had Nijō heard of the girl's orphanhood and her invitation into imperial service, she would have mentioned it. This is conjecture, but the similarities to her own life are undeniable. Nijō writes, in a diary entry from earlier that same year:

> I persisted in dwelling on the past. I could not recall my mother's face, for she had died when I was only two. When I turned four I was taken, toward the end of the ninth month, to the palace of Retired Emperor Go-Fukakusa. His Majesty graciously bestowed his favors on me from the time my name was entered on his roll of attendants, and I experienced the feel of worldly success. During the years that I was well received at the palace I cherished the secret dream of becoming the pride and joy of my clan. Such expectations did not seem unreasonable, yet I decided to give up everything and enter the path of renunciation. This seemed in accordance with my fate. The sūtras say, "Neither family, nor wealth, nor rank can accompany you in death." I thought that I had renounced all such worldly attachments, but still I found myself longing for the palace of my youth and recalling His Majesty's great kindness. Reminded of these things, my only solace was to weep until tears darkened my sleeves. (Brazell, 196)

It should be noted that Nijō's decision to give up her position and become a nun was at least in part precipitated by her failure to bear surviving children to Go-Fukakusa.

The children mentioned in her diary were all fathered by other men, her secret lovers.

4. Although the Japanese word *"hime"* does not correspond directly to the English "princess" (the *hime* need not be the daughter of a ruler) I will nevertheless translate it as such and will also refer to Chūjōhime as a princess. See Orikuchi Shinobu, "Shōsetsu gekyoku bungaku ni okeru monogatari no yōsu," in *Orikuchi Shinobu zenshū* (Tokyo: Chūō kōronsha, 1972), 7:263–270; and Tanaka Takako, "Suterare-hime no monogatari: Chūjōhime to 'onna no yamai,'" in *Sei naru onna: saigu, megami, Chūjōhime* (Tokyo: Jinbun shoin, 1996), 23, 45–46. Also see Miyata Noboru, *Hime no minzokugaku* (Tokyo: Seidōsha, 1987).

5. A similar process occurred in the history of European religious art. See Sixten Ringbom, *Icon to Narrative: The Rise of the Dramatic Close-up in Fifteenth-century Devotional Painting,* rev. ed. (Doornspijk, The Netherlands: Davaco, 1983).

6. For a detailed reading of the legend in its late medieval form and a discussion of sources, see Hank Glassman, "The Religious Construction of Motherhood in Medieval Japan" (Ph.D. diss., Stanford University, 2001). The story as described here can be found in, e.g., the Nara *ehon,* "Chūjōhime," *MJMS* 4.342–358. A 1651 woodblock printed version is translated by Kelly Kimbrough in Haruo Shirane, ed., *Japanese Literature: Beginnings to 1600* (New York: Columbia University Press, in press).

7. On the development of the Chūjōhime legend and cult, see Elizabeth ten Grotenhuis, *The Revival of the Taima Mandala in Medieval Japan* (New York: Garland, 1985); and ten Grotenhuis, "Chūjōhime: The Weaving of Her Legend," in *Flowing Traces: Buddhism in the Literary and Visual Arts of Japan,* ed. James H. Sanford et al. (Princeton: Princeton University Press, 1992), 180–200. Also see Tokuda, "Kyōroku-bon," and Gankōji bunkazai kenkyūjo, eds., *Chūjōhime setsuwa no chōsa kenkyū hōkoku sho* (Tokyo: Gankōji bunkazai kenkyūjo, 1983).

8. See ten Grotenhuis, *Revival of the Taima Mandala,* 188–190; and Tokuda, "Kyōroku-bon," 364–366. For translations of *Taema* see Kenneth Yasuda, trans., *Masterworks of the Nō Theater* (Bloomington: Indiana University Press, 1989), 437–459; and Thomas Rimer, trans., *"Taema," Monumenta Nipponica* 25, nos. 3–4 (Autumn–Winter 1970): 431–445.

9. Iwaki Takatoshi, "Chūjōhime densetsu no seiritsu to rufu," in *CSCK,* 9, 16. For the text of the *Taima mandara sho,* see *Jōdoshū zensho,* vol. 13 of *Jōdoshū Kaishū Happyaku-nen Kinen Keisan Junbikyoku,* ed. Jodōshū zensho (Tokyo: Sankibō busshorin, 1971).

10. Tokuda, "Kyōroku-bon," 370–372.

11. Sekiyama Kazuo, "Chūjōhime no keifu," in his *Shomin bukkyō bunka ron* (Tokyo: Hōzōkan, 1989), 28.

12. Tokuda Kazuo, "Etoki, toku ni *Kangyō hen* to Chūjōhime densetsu o megutte," in *Sōden, jisha engi, emaki, eden,* Bukkyō bungaku kōza, no. 6, eds. Itō Hiroyuki et al. (Tokyo: Benseisha, 1996), 383–385. Also see Tokuda, "Kyōroku-bon," 372. Here Tokuda quotes Shōsō's text, which explicitly states that the *mandara* tells a story of women's salvation in which both the woman represented in the *mandara* and the woman whose faith caused the creation of the *mandara* are saved by Amida despite "the thick clouds of the five obstacles and the three subjugations." Shōsō also makes the point that the apparitions that appear in response to Chūjōhime's desire to see

the Pure Land take on female shape out of compassion for her. See Abe Yasurō, "Chūjōhime setsuwa to bungaku," in *CSCK,* 49–50.

13. Tokuda Kazuo, "Etoki to engi emaki" in *Issatsu no kōza: etoki,* Nihon no koten bungaku, no. 3, eds. Etoki no kenkyū-kai (Tokyo: Yūseidō, 1985), 381. Tokuda suggests that the transition from sūtra text to illustration to *etoki* performance to written text in the form of *otogizōshi* or *engi* was quite common. On the role of preaching practices in the development of the legend, also see Sekiyama Kazuo, "Chūjōhime densetsu to Taima mandara," in Etoki no kenkyū-kai, eds., *Issatsu no kōza,* 127–133; and Gorai Shigeru, "*Taimadera engi* to Chūjōhime densetsu" in his *Jisha engi kara otogi banashi e,* Shūkyō minzoku shūsei, no. 6 (Tokyo: Kadokawa shoten, 1996), 87–119.

14. *Chūjōhime no honji,* in *MJMT* 9.297: *Nanji, nyonin nareba ama to genji nyonin to natte, kireru nari.* In his essay in this collection, James Sanford describes the Shingon theory of the Five Buddha bodies. Among these are the *tōru hosshin,* capable of manifesting in various forms throughout the six realms, and the *henge hosshin,* or the transformation body of the buddha who preaches in the earthly realm. Here the "transformed nun," the *keni,* is understood to be a living manifestation of Amida Buddha.

15. See, for example, *Chūjōhime no honji,* in *MJMT* 9.297: *Kore o ogamu tomogara ha. Bonnō wo, danzesu shite. Mujō bodai wo shōka shi, shōji wo, itowazu shite nehan no kishi ni itaru to* ("Those who gaze with devotion upon this [*mandara*] will, without cutting off the defilements, be confirmed in the fruit of ultimate enlightenment, and will, without despising samsara, arrive on the opposite bank of nirvana"). Also see *Chūjōhime,* in *MJMS* 4.355, where the *mandara* is described as "the main image for assured Birth in the Pure Land, for the deluded people of the future evil age who are burdened with sin" *(mirai akuse no, zaishō bonbu, ketsujō ōjō no honzon).* The idea that Birth *(ōjō)* takes place regardless of the efforts of the beholder of the *mandara* is a very important point of doctrine. Birth is achieved through the grace of Amida Buddha alone. After Ippen shōnin visited the Taimadera in 1287 and saw the *mandara,* he is said to have remarked, "The revelation I received from the Taima Mandala declared: 'Your long-accumulated merits are not merits, virtues not virtues.' All dharmas of good and evil should be understood in terms of this." Translation from Dennis Hirota, *No Abode: The Record of Ippen* (Kyoto: Ryūkoku University Translation Center, 1986), 174.

16. Yasuda, *Taema,* 454. Also see, for example, *MJMS* 4.532 and *MJMT* 9.295.

17. *Otogizōshi,* or *Muromachi jidai monogatari,* refers to a very broadly defined corpus of texts and includes many subgenres. See Chieko Mulhern, "*'Otogi-zōshi:* Short Stories of the Muromachi Period," *Monumenta Nipponica* 29, no. 2 (1974): 181–198; and Barbara Ruch, "*Otogi bunko* and Short Stories of the Muromachi Period" (Ph.D. diss., Columbia University, 1965).

18. These details are illustrated in the *Chūjōhime eden* owned by the Okunoin at Taimadera. I wish to express my gratitude to the resident priest of the Okunoin, the Reverend Kawanaka, for his generosity in allowing me access to this work. The images in this set of four hanging scrolls are based on the seventeenth-century work *Chūjōhime gyōjōki.*

19. Birth of women into the Pure Land is a vexed and much discussed topic in the

history of East Asian Buddhism. See Taira Masayuki, "Nyonin ōjō ron no rekishiteki hyōka o megutte," in his *Nihon chūsei shakai to bukkyō* (Tokyo: Hanawa shobo, 1992), 427–450. James Dobbins has suggested that although the idea that women were barred from the Pure Land was emphasized at a doctrinal level, in the minds of individual believers, especially women, women were assumed to be born into the Pure Land as women. See James Dobbins, "Women's Birth in the Pure Land: Intimations from the Letters of Eshinni," *The Eastern Buddhist*, n.s., 28, no. 1 (1995): 108–122. Also see Paul Harrison, "Women in the Pure Land: Some Reflections on the Textual Sources," *Journal of Indian Philosophy* 26, no. 6 (December 1998): 553–572. Although it is possible that the term *"sokushin ōjō"* in this context could mean, as it often does, that Chūjōhime was born into the Pure Land (i.e., assured of birth in this life rather than after her death), in at least some contexts it is quite clear that the intended meaning is birth into the Pure Land without transformation first into a male body. See, for example, *MJMS* 4.349: "Let the sins of the five obstacles and the three subjugations be erased, and lead me in this body into the western Pure Land" *(Goshō sanjū no tsumi wo metsu shi, saihō jōdo ni, kono mi wo indō shi tamaihite).*

20. *Guan wuliangshoufo jing* (T 365). The organization of the *mandara* is based on the seventh-century monk Shandao's commentary on the *Guan Wuliangshoufo jing shu* (T 1753). On the sūtra, see Jonathan Silk, "The Composition of the *Guan Wuliangshoufojing:* Some Buddhist and Jaina Parallels to Its Narrative Frame," *Journal of Indian Philosophy* 25, no. 2 (1997): 181–256. For a translation, see Ryūkoku University Translation Center, trans., *The Sūtra of Contemplation of the Buddha of Immeasurable Life as Expounded by Śākyamuni Buddha* (Kyoto: Ryūkoku University, 1984). On Shandao's commentary see Julian F. Pas, *Visions of Sukhāvatī: Shan-Tao's Commentary of the Kuan Wu-Liang-Shou-Fo Ching* (Albany: State University of New York Press, 1995).

21. For a review of the legends, see Marion Ury, "Stepmothers in Japanese Folk Tales" in *Children's Literature* 9 (1981): 61–72. Also see Chieko Mulhern, "Cinderella and the Jesuits: An *Otogizōshi* Cycle as Christian Literature," *Monumenta Nipponica* 34, no. 4 (1979): 409–447; and Chieko Mulhern, "Analysis of Cinderella Motifs, Italian and Japanese," *Asian Folklore Studies* 44, no. 1 (1985): 1–37.

22. For photographs, description, and a detailed discussion of the iconography of the Taima *mandara*, see ten Grotenhuis, *Japanese Mandalas*, 13–32. For a "clickable" version of an eighteenth-century reproduction with links to details, see <<http: //www.ne.jp/asahi/pureland-buddhism/amida-net/con-ex.htm >>.

23. Many of the copies were made in reduced sizes: half, one-quarter, one-sixth, and one-eighth the size of the original. Also a great number were made from woodblocks, printed and then colored by hand. In the fourteenth-century production of copies of this *mandara* was at its peak. See Machida-shi kokusai hanga bijutsukan, ed., *Han ni natta e, e ni natta han: chuusei Nihon no hanga to ega* (Paintings into woodcuts, woodcuts into paintings: Woodcuts and paintings of medieval Japan) (Machida: Benrido/Machida City Museum of Graphic Arts, 1995), 6–12, 26–27.

24. See n. 20.

25. On *mandara kōsetsu* and the development of the legend, see Sekiyama, "Chūjōhime no keifu," 25–38. Also see Tokuda, "Etoki to engi emaki," 83–85. For discussion of the culture of performed religious literature in the Muromachi period, see Barbara Ruch, "Medieval Jongleurs and the Making of a National Literature," in

Japan in the Muromachi Age, eds. John Whitney Hall and Toyoda Takeshi (Berkeley: University of California Press, 1977), 269–309.

26. Aoyama Tadakazu, *Kanazōshi jokun bungei no kenkyū* (Tokyo: Ōfūsha, 1982), 291.

27. Chūjōtō is dissolved in bath water and is still on the market. For old advertisements for this medicine and its relationship to bathing, see *Yu: Ofuro no bunkashi* (Omiya: Saitama kenritsu hakubutsukan, 2000), 44. Also see Dana Levy et al., *Kanban: Shop Signs of Japan* (New York: Japan Society, 1982), 70–72, 150–152. For the connection between bathing, blood pollution, and women's salvation in the *kinsei* period, see Miyazaki Fumiko and Duncan Williams, "The Intersection of the Local and the Translocal at the Sacred Site: The Case of Osorezan in Tokugawa Japan," *Japanese Journal of Religious Studies* 28, nos. 3–4 (2001): 399–440.

28. Tanaka, "Suterare-hime no monogatari," 23–24. See ibid., 45–57, on the role of Chūjōhime's sexuality in the nature of her suffering. On the theme of the helpless savior in medieval temple *engi* and *otogizōshi,* see Hamanaka Osamu, "*Kumano no honji* kō: muryoku to higo," in his *Muromachi monogatari ronkō* (Tokyo: Shintensha, 1996), 202–210.

29. Examples include the medieval stories of Izumi shikibu and Dōmyō ajari, *Kumano no honji, Asagao no tsuyu, Tsukihi no honji,* and the popular hagiographies of Shaku Ryōben and Hōkongō-in Dōgyo, as represented in the nō play, *Hyakuman.*

30. On the Ajase complex, see Kosawa Heisaku, "Zaiaku ishiki no nishu: Ajase conpurekkusu," in *Seishin bunseki: Freud igo,* Gendai no esprit, no. 148, ed. Okonogi Keigo (Tokyo: Shibundō, 1979), 166–173; originally appeared in *Seishin bunseki kenkyū* 1, no. 1 (1954). See also Okonogi Keigo, *Nihonjin no Ajase compurekksu* (Tokyo: Chūō kōronsha, 1982); Okonogi Keigo, "Ajase complex," in *Psychotherapy Handbook,* ed. H. Richie (New York: New American Library, 1979); and Kawai Hayao, *Bosei shakai Nihon no byōri* (Tokyo: Chūō kōronsha, 1976). On the Ajātaśatru legend, see Hubert Durt, "Quelques aspects de la légende du roi Ajase (Ajātaśatru) dans la tradition canonique bouddhique," *Ebisu: Etudes japonaises* 15 (1997): 13–27.

31. I thank J. Todd Brown for bringing these passages to my attention. (See T 12.342a26–29; 342c11–13; 343c2–3.)

32. On the creation of memorial images of male and female Zen masters that functioned as religious icons, see Barbara Ruch, "The Other Side of Medieval Japanese Culture," in *The Cambridge History of Japan,* ed. Kozo Yamamura (Cambridge: Cambridge University Press, 1988–), 3:502–511; and Bernard Faure, *The Rhetoric of Immediacy: A Cultural Critique of Chan/Zen Buddhism* (Princeton: Princeton University Press, 1991), esp. 169–174. According to the origin legend of one Chūjōhime temple, Kyoto's Tenshōji, their statue of the saint was carved by Eshin sōzu Genshin himself (*Tenshōji yurai,* in *CSCK,* p. 101).

33. Tokuda, "Kyōroku-bon," 375–381.

34. Abe, "Chūjōhime setsuwa to bungaku," 59, and esp. Tokuda, "Kyōroku-bon," 369–384. On the same visit of 1530, when he showed Sanetaka the Chūjōhime text, Yuzen also brought a work called *Eshin sozu,* a hagiography of the great prelate Genshin. Legends about Genshin strongly emphasize his mother's influence on his monastic career.

35. Uchida Takako, "Chūjōhime densetsu to bijutsu," in *CSCK,* p. 32.

36. Sekiyama, "Chūjōhime densetsu to Taima mandara," 128.

37. These relics will be discussed in more detail below. The use by nuns of hair shaved or cut at the time of ordination to create religious images was not uncommon. For other examples of nuns' embroidery using their own hair and a fascinating meditation on the history and meaning of nuns' hairstyles, see Kastūra Noriko, "Ama sogi kō," in her *Onna no shinjin* (Tokyo: Heibonsha, 1995), 11, 15–57, and esp. 38. (Also see the translation of this article by Virginia Skord in *Engendering Faith: Women and Buddhism in Pre-Modern Japan,* ed. Barbara Ruch [Ann Arbor: University of Michigan Center for Japanese Studies, in press]). Images of Chūjōhime's tonsure can be found on p. 31 of Katsūra, *Onna no shinjin.* For an example of hair used in calligraphy, see Maribeth Graybill et al., eds., *Days of Discipline and Grace: Treasures from the Imperial Buddhist Convents of Kyoto* (New York: Institute of Medieval Japanese Studies, Columbia University, 1998), 3, 18.

38. Tanaka, "Suterare-hime no monogatari," 10; Gorai, "Taimadera engi," 90.

39. Gorai, ibid., 102–106. Michel DeCerteau has noted the importance of place in European hagiography. Here, too, we can see the saint's life firmly anchored in locales. Michel DeCerteau, *L'ecriture de l'histoire* (Paris: Gaillimard, 1975), 286; cited in Bernard Faure, "Bodhidharma as Textual and Religious Paradigm," *History of Religions* 25, no. 3 (1986): 187–198.

40. Tokuda, "Kyōroku-bon," 373–375.

41. The discussion that follows is based on the transcription, analysis, and photographic reproduction of the *Kaichō danwa,* contained in Hayashi Masahiko, *Edo o itohite, jōdo e mairamu: Bukkyō bungaku ron* (Tokyo: Meicho shuppan, 1995), 277–340. Traveling exhibitions gained popularity from the end of the medieval and through the *kinsei* period. Eventually other, less edifying, forms of entertainment traveled with the show, leading to the application of the name *"kaichō,"* or "peep-shows," which featured female strippers (Iwamoto Yutaka, *Nihon bukkyōgo jiten* [Tokyo: Heibonsha, 1988], 128). For a discussion of an ancestor of the *degaichō,* see Janet Goodwin, *Alms and Vagabonds: Buddhist Temples and Popular Patronage in Medieval Japan* (Honolulu: University of Hawai'i Press, 1994), 116–117.

42. Chūjōhime as a nun, that is. Her religious name appears variously in different texts as Hōnyo, Honganni, Chūjō Hōni, or Zenni. In this exhibition she was called Chūjō Hōni.

43. This sūtra (T 367) is Xuanzang's 650 translation of the smaller *Sukhāvatīvyūha sūtra.* For an English translation, see Inagaki Hisao, trans., "Hsuan-tsang's Version of the Smaller *Sukhāvatīvyūha sūtra,*" in *Ryūkoku daigaku ronshū* 442 (1993); and Inagaki Hisao, trans., *The Sūtra on Praise of the Pure Land and Protection by Buddhas* at <<http://www.net0726.or.jp/~horai/amida-sūtra-b.htm>>. Kumarajiva's translation (T 366), known in Japanese as the *Amidakyō,* is the standard one. The author of the *Kaichō danwa* notes that the sūtra is not on indigo paper and includes the *edokishi*'s observation that Xuanzang's translation was preferred over Kumarajiva's in Chūjōhime's lifetime. See n. 48 below.

44. Women were also forbidden to climb Tateyama, a site famous for women's salvation, and could only gain indirect access to it through the *degaichō* of the Nyoirin Kannon image. See Kodate Naomi's discussion of two mid-nineteenth-century *degaichō* in "Ketsubonkyō no juyō to hatten," in *Onna to otoko no jikū,* ed. Okano Naoko (Tokyo: Fujiwara shoten, 1996), 3:108.

45. Gorai, "Taimadera engi," 97. This reference from the *Ippen hijiri e* (1299) suggests that this aspect of the Hibariyama legend was in place at least by the thirteenth century. Also see n. 3 above.

46. *MJMT* 9.273–274, 288–289; *MJMS* 4.344–345, 360–361. The texts vary in some details, such as the sexes of the children and the specificity of the ages of the parents; in one version, "around thirty" is given as the man's age, "twenty-six or seven" as the woman's. For a detailed analysis of this scene as it relates to the medieval hagiography of the Buddha, see Glassman, "The Religious Construction of Motherhood."

47. For Chūjōhime's encounter with the holy man, see *MJMS* 4:345. Both the desire to be reunited with her mother and the visit to the clairvoyant monk are reminiscent of story of the girl Bright Eyes in the *Jizō hongan kyō*. See Hank Glassman, "The Nude Jizō at Denkōji: Notes on Women's Worship in the Kamakura Period," in Ruch, ed., *Engendering Faith*.

48. See n. 43 above. On the failure of the *Shōsan jōdokyō* to gain popularity in China, see Nomura Nobuo, "*Shōsan jōdo kyō* to *Amida kyō* rufu," *Shinshū kenkyū* 36 (1992): 130–142. On its popularity in the Nara period and its use in Kōmyōshi's memorial, see Matsushima Ken and Kawahara Yoshio, *Nihon no koji bijutsu 11: Taimadera* (Tokyo: Hoikusha, 1988), 196–198. Matsushima and Kawahara record the number of sūtras copied as one thousand. More recently, Yamashita Yumi has put the number of sūtras copied for the memorial at eighteen hundred. See Yamashita, *Shōsōin monjo to shakkyōjo no kenkyū* (Tokyo: Yoshikawa kōbunkan, 1999), 114–116; and Miyazaki Kenji, "Kōmyōshi shichi-shichi-nichi shakkyō o meguru hitotsu, futatsu no mondai," *Ōtani gakuhō* 75, no. 4 (1996): 46–59. On the empress' calligraphic reputation and the Nara-period provenance of the Chūjōhime sūtras, see Uemura Wadō, "Kōmyō kōgō hatsugan no issaikyō" and "Chūjōhime hitsu to tsutaeru *Shōsan jōdo setsu butsuju kyō*" in his *Nihon no shakkyō* (Tokyo: Rikusha, 1981), 89–104. See also *Nara jidai no shakkyō to dairi* (Tokyo: Haniwa shobō, 2000).

49. See the sixteenth-century tale *Shaka no honji, MJMT* 7.90–117, 118–162. On Śākyamuni as a model for dedicating oneself to the religious life for the sake of one's mother in late medieval Japanese hagiography, see Glassman, "The Religious Construction of Motherhood." This theme is also invoked in the Chūjōhime narrative that became the convent Seirenji's origin tale (see *CSCK,* 99); here the heroine is compared to Prince Siddhartha (Shitta taishi). A further similarity can be found in the late Kamakura- and Muromachi-period *nehan-zu* (death portraits) of the Buddha laid out on the same plan as the Taima *mandara* (the bottom border and left and right edges are used to portray scenes of the Budddha's life in a series of cells). It is quite probable that these images were used in preaching and took the Taima *mandala* as their model. See, for example, Hyakubashi Akio, *Nihon no bijutsu 8: Butsuden zu,* no. 268 (Tokyo: Shibundo, 1988), plates 118 and 119.

50. Iwaki, "Chūjōhime densetsu no seiritsu to rufu," in *CSCK,* 10. As Iwaki notes, the 1614 work of the Pure Land monk Taichū, *Taima hakki,* was inspired by these preaching performances and in turn greatly influenced them.

51. See Gorai, "Taimadera engi," 90–106. On *Kumano bikuni* and women's faith also see, for example, Ruch, "Medieval Jongleurs"; Hagiwara Tatsuo, *Miko to bukkyōshi* (Tokyo: Yoshikawa kōbunkan, 1983); and Hayashi Masahiko, "*Kumano*

bikuni no etoki," in his *Zōho Nihon no etoki* (Tokyo: Miyai shoten, 1984). Also see David Moerman, "Localizing Paradise: Kumano Pilgrimage in Medieval Japan" (Ph.D. diss., Stanford University, 1999).

52. As mentioned above, Ippen shōnin is said to have received a copy of the *Shōsan jōdokyō* in Chūjōhime's hand; he also had a famous poetic exchange with the Zen master Kakushin (Hottō kokushi), whose mother founded Myōhōzan, the home temple of the *Kumano bikuni.* See Hagiwara, *Miko to bukkyōshi,* 247–248; and Abe, "Chūjōhime setsuwa to bungaku," 75. For more on Hottō kokushi, father of the Kaya dō, and preaching, see Gorai, "Taimadera engi," 101; and Gorai Shigeru, "Ippen shonin to Hottō kokushi," *Indogaku bukkyōgaku kenkyū* 9, no. 2 (1961): 96–105. The exchange between Ippen and Kakushin is also alluded to in the nō play *Taema*'s retelling of the Chūjōhime story. It is noteworthy that this was an anecdote carried throughout Japan by the *Kumano bikuni,* who also lectured on *Kumano no honji,* the *Blood Bowl Sūtra,* and displayed *mandara*s to their female patrons.

53. This supports Matuoka Hideaki's assertion that preachers of the Pure Land sect had an important role in disseminating the *Ketsubonkyō* with its teachings on the blood pollution of menstruation and childbirth. See Matsuoka Hideaki, "Waga kuni ni okeru *Ketsubonkyō* shinkō ni tsuite no ichi kōsatsu," in *Josei to shukyō,* Nihon joseishi ronshū, no. 5 (Tokyo: Yoshikawa kōbunkan, 1998), 269.

54. See Glassman, "The Religious Construction of Motherhood," 208–215.

6

"Just Behave as You Like; Prohibitions and Impurities Are Not a Problem"

Radical Amida Cults and Popular Religiosity in Premodern Japan

FABIO RAMBELLI

THERE HAVE BEEN several Amitābha cults in premodern Japan, often in competition with each other. In addition to the Jōdo and the Shin sects, Tendai, Shingon, and even Zen developed their own teachings concerning Amida and his Pure Land.[1] Traditionally, Amida cults are considered only in terms of religiosity and spirituality—as forms of "popular Buddhism" in tune with the "spiritual needs" of most Japanese—as opposed to esoteric Buddhism, which appealed to only a restricted number of learned aristocratic aesthetes.[2] Scholarship usually distinguishes between the Pure Land beliefs of the aristocracy, which were aimed at preserving one's lifestyle in the next life in Amida's Pure Land, and the beliefs of the masses, who were trying to find consolation in the promise of a better afterlife. Whereas the former is usually associated with Tendai and, more rarely, with Shingon doctrines concerning Amida, the latter is identified with the teachings of the Kamakura reformers such as Hōnen, Shinran, and Ippen. However, this distinction is problematic for various reasons. Firstly, elites and masses often shared the same beliefs and practices and participated in the same rituals. Secondly, Tendai and Shingon Pure Land teachings were not only for the aristocracy; on the contrary, Pure Land teachings based on Amida's vows were the most important tools in the spread of Shingon and Tendai among the common people.[3] Thirdly, and more fundamentally, the received distinction between Amida cults of the aristocracy and those of the masses ignores the social and ideological contexts in which Pure Land movements developed. Amida cults, in fact, played an important role in the political and ideological debates and struggles in medieval Japan. In other words, received interpretations of Pure Land movements operate a systematic misremembering of their original oppositional potential and revolutionary role in the history of Japanese culture, religion, and thought. In fact, Amida's cults were also at the heart of numerous peasant revolts (*ikkō ikki* in particular) and strenuous resistance against religious and secular establishments—a resistance that lasted for centuries.

A fundamental distinction can be made between Pure Land doctrines and practices that supported dominant ideology (normative Amidism) and Pure Land teachings that offered instead transgressive, and potentially revolutionary, ideological elements against the dominant system (radical Amidism). Normative teachings were developed mainly by Tendai and Shingon. The existing order was maintained by providing consolation—that is, ideological justification for existing forms of exploitation and social distinctions. Commoners *(bonbu)* were described as ignorant, immoral, and in need of the strong and compassionate guidance of Buddhism in the form of enlightened emissaries of dominant religious institutions if they were to be saved from hell. In exchange, they would participate in rituals and perform social obligations of various kinds (pay tithes, provide labor and corvées for temples, and so on). Amida was presented as a savior figure for everyone but especially for those who lacked high spiritual capacities; the invocation to Amida's holy name *(nenbutsu)* was marketed to evil and ignorant common folk as the best option for salvation. More sophisticated doctrines and practices concerning the ontological and cosmological status of the buddha Amida and his Pure Land were developed by the leading Tendai and Shingon intellectuals; these represented the other side, so to speak, of the simple teachings for subordinates.

The teachings of the Buddhist establishment, commonly known as the exo-esoteric system *(kenmitsu taisei),* were remarkably supple and accomodating: they made room for all sorts of doctrines and practices (and transgressions) provided they never questioned the fundamental assumptions of the system—namely, that ruling and intellectual elites were such out of karmic necessity (which at the same time created for subordinates a sort of ontological bondage to their subjection).[4] In presenting the nenbutsu as an easy path for "the lowest," religious institutions reinforced the spiritual as well as the social inferiority of commoners.[5]

However, Hōnen began to question dominant assumptions about Amida, his Pure Land, the practice of the nenbutsu, and the philosophical anthropology in the "final period of the dharma" *(mappō)*. We will discuss Hōnen's ideas later. Here I would like to note that his thought triggered an unexpected response: a proliferation of radical movements that openly challenged dominant Buddhism's ideas of morality, behavior, and social order. These movements, commonly referred to by the name of their shared doctrinal view, *ichinengi* (the belief that a single thought of Amida leads to birth in the Pure Land), spread all over Japan, from Kyūshū in the west to Tōhoku in the east. Often engaged in iconoclastic and anticlerical acts of rebellion, they were the target of doctrinal criticism and repressive measures on the part of the establishment. One of the most brutal and effective moments of repression was the so-called "Ken'ei Dharma Persecution *(hōnan)*" of 1207, triggered by the alleged secret love affair between one of Hōnen's radical disciples and an imperial concubine. In the present essay I will examine the reasons for the anti-Amidist persecutions, the thought and ideology of radical Amidists, and the importance of radical Amidist movements for the study of Japanese cultural history. In particular, I argue that radical Amidist movements represent the irruption on the public scene of medieval Japan of an alternative discursive mode that expressed the mentalities of the voiceless *bonbu*. It redeployed strategically fundamental elements of dominant culture in ways that closely resemble Bakhtin's concept of the "carnivalesque." In this sense, radical Amidism is an important window on popular mentalities.

The "Secret Love Affair Incident" of 1207 and the Persecutions against Radical Amidists

In the second month of Ken'ei 2 (1207), Anrakubō and Jūren, two of Hōnen's most prominent followers, were accused of lèse-majesté against retired emperor Go-Toba. They were captured and tortured, and their trial ended with the passing of a severe sentence: Anrakubō, Jūren, and two other comrades were sentenced to death, and Hōnen and seven other followers, including Shinran and Kōsai, were exiled to faraway places.[6] Many pages have been written on this dramatic moment of the history of Japanese religions, and the dynamics of the incident are still not completely clear. Jien's *Gukanshō* gives one of the most neutral accounts:

> While the [*ichinengi*] movement was spreading throughout the capital and the countryside . . . a Lady-in-Waiting at the Retired Emperor's detached palace, as well as the mother of the princely-priest of Ninna Temple, became believers. These ladies secretly called Anraku and other *nembutsu* priests into their presence to explain their teaching. Anraku seems to have gone with some colleagues to see these ladies, even staying overnight. Because this was an unspeakable affair, Anraku and Jūren were eventually beheaded. Saint Hōnen was banished [in 1207] and not allowed to reside in the capital.[7]

Jien does not mention explicitly any "love affair," as many other accounts do; he merely stresses the intolerable breach of etiquette that offended Go-Toba. However, it is hard to believe that such a harsh sentence was the result of the priests' violations of the precepts or of Go-Toba's jealousy, as some historians have argued. The mounting pressure on the court from Enryakuji and other centers of institutional Buddhism for an exemplary punishment of Hōnen's radicals may have played a role. And yet, a few months earlier the court had refused to punish Anrakubō and others for their religious activities, at the explicit request of Enryakuji. It is possible that the "secret love affair incident" *(mittsū jiken),* as it is commonly known, was perhaps the final act of rebellion and transgression on the part of the Pure Land radicals. Given his direct involvement, Go-Toba could no longer defend the radicals and his office punished them severely.[8] But why had the centers of institutional Buddhism been so angry with the radical Amidists? What had they been accused of?[9]

In 1204 Enryakuji had submitted a petition to the court calling for a ban on Hōnen's nenbutsu. Although Hōnen received reassurances from the office of the retired emperor, he responded to Tendai's petition in his "Pledge Sent to Enryakuji" *(Sō Sanmon kishōmon).* In it he strongly urged his followers to refrain from actions that would offend the sensibility of the dominant Buddhist establishment. However, the situation deteriorated rapidly, and a few months later, in the tenth month of 1205, several prominent members of the religious world, led by Jōkei of the Kōfukuji, petitioned the retired emperor—an act virtually unprecedented in Japan. The "Kōfukuji Petition" vehemently requested the dissolution of Hōnen's movement and severe punishment for its members.[10] The petition accused Hōnen's followers of spreading teachings that were "Māra's concoctions." Hōnen's disciples were called "devils" *(tenma)* and "enemies of the diffusion of Buddhism" *(buppō guzū no onsō)*. They were accused, among other things, of lacking respect and consideration for the clerical precepts, of refusing to worship the Buddhas and the *kami*, and of slandering the true Dharma. Dominant religious institutions felt threatened by the new nenbutsu groups, who refused to recognize the moral and ideological supremacy of dominant orthodoxies and were not afraid to engage in highly symbolic gestures bordering on blasphemy. All these things, maintained the establishment, would result in the end of Buddhism and calamities for the state.

The accusations were probably not unfounded. Several contemporary documents accuse Hōnen's Amidist radicals of polluting temple compounds, blaspheming the scriptures and the holy images of the Buddha, and insulting representatives of dominant institutions.[11] Hōnen himself had addressed the criticism levelled by the religious establishment in two documents directed to his followers, the previously mentioned *Sō Sanmon kishōmon*[12] and the *Shichikajō seikai* (Regulations in seven articles).[13] In the first document, Hōnen made clear, using strong language and an unusually strict tone, that his followers should stop all free interpretations of his teachings and cease any actions and speeches against dominant religious institutions and their followers. He also threatened the recidivists with terrible punishment of rebirth into hell by quoting a proviso in Amida's eighteenth fundamental vow, which excludes from the benefits of his vow the slanderers of the True Law and those responsible for the five heinous crimes *(gogyaku)*[14]—a proviso that Hōnen had ignored previously.[15] In the more detailed *Shichikajō seikai,* Hōnen urged his followers to refrain "from denigrating other buddhas and bodhisattvas and from attacking Shingon and Tendai" (article 1), "from indulging in disputes with men of wisdom or when encountering people with other religious practices" (article 2), and from "wanton ridicule" of "people of other persuasions or practices" (article 3). As far as doctrinal issues were concerned, Hōnen ordered his followers to "refrain from saying that there is no practice of clerical precepts in the nenbutsu path; from avidly encouraging sexual indulgences, liquor, or meat eating; from occasionally calling those who adhere to the precepts 'men of indiscriminate practice'; and from teaching that those who rely on Amida's principal vow have no reason to fear committing evil *(zōaku)*" (article 4). In matters of interpretation his followers should "refrain from deviations from the scriptures, from what is not the teaching of your master, from arbitrarily putting forward your own doctrines, from needlessly seeking out disputes, from being laughed at by the wise, and from leading the ignorant astray" (article 5). Concerning behavior, they should "refrain from delighting so much in rhetoric, from knowing nothing of the true teachings, from expounding various heresies *(jahō),* and from converting ignorant priests and lay people to them" (article 6). Finally, Hōnen urged his disciples to "refrain from expounding heresies, which are not Buddhist teachings, and from regarding them as true teachings. Refrain from the deception of calling them the teachings of your master" (article 7).[16]

These documents describe a very interesting phenomenon triggered, directly or indirectly, by Hōnen himself: subalterns expressing their ideas, formulating their own interpretations of Buddhism, passionately arguing their positions, and relentlessly countering the establishment. But here Hōnen makes a vehement attempt to prevent any free activity of interpretation, thought, and argument against dominant religious ideas and their followers. He describes the radical Amidists as "ignorant being[s] who [are] unable to distinguish between right and wrong," as having "mind[s] ignorant and biased." As such, they are not entitled to free thinking: they should abstain "from arbitrarily putting forward [their] own doctrines, from needlessly seeking out disputes," show respect for Shingon and Tendai (the religious and political establishment), refrain from criticizing the dominant religious ideas and practices connected to exploitation and social control, and adhere strictly to orthodoxy. We will return to the paternalism and authoritarianism of this position at the end of the essay. What concerns us at present is the connection of Hōnen's thought with the revolutionary activity of some of his followers, a connection that has always troubled historians of Japanese religions.

Why did Hōnen's teachings result in such a revolutionary activism? Did they contain explicit radical elements? No existing document proves that Hōnen openly and explicitly supported his radical followers. On the contrary, as we have seen, he strongly criticized any heterodox interpretation of his teachings. Yet some of his followers were not impressed with the "Regulations in Seven Articles":

they claimed "the words of Master Hōnen always have two sides" (as noted in the "Kōfukuji Petition"), implying that the document was intended to placate the establishment, not rein in his followers. As several authors have pointed out, Hōnen's doctrines do contain some potentially revolutionary elements, in particular the concepts of "radical choice" *(senjaku)* and "only practice" *(senju)*. "Radical choice" refers to Amida's choice of the nenbutsu as the only path to salvation; "only practice" to Amida's choice at the level of popular devotion. Taira Masayuki has argued that Hōnen's ideas were never absolute but applied to his disciples alone and not to *all* Buddhists; in other words, only his followers were required to adopt the nenbutsu as the only and exclusive practice.[17] Still, Hōnen's cautious attitude was enough to trigger a domino effect that resulted in a radical questioning of the dominant religious institutions' moral authority.

According to Hōnen, Amida chose the nenbutsu; he did not choose any of the other practices upheld by the *kenmitsu* system. It is well known that the teachings of dominant religious institutions involving the worship of countless buddhas, bodhisattvas, and local *kami,* were organically connected, for example, to the mechanisms of domination of land holdings *(shōen)*. From a radical perspective, Hōnen's teachings led to the refusal to worship *kami (jingi fuhai)* and other buddhas, a refusal that also resulted in the destruction of sacred images *(habutsu),* concrete symbols of the *kenmitsu* system of domination.[18] Radicals also engaged in criticism of (and perhaps even in acts of violence against) followers of dominant religious teachings.

Hōnen's teachings offered, indirectly at least, a powerful alternative to the elitism of Buddhist institutions in general. In the eyes of the *kenmitsu* elites, society was hierarchically organized on the basis of a systematic correlation between power and spiritual capacities: at the top were the emperor and the priesthood, whose status was determined by virtuous actions accomplished in previous lifetimes;[19] at the bottom were lepers, mendicants, and people with physical disabilities, whose sad fate was the consequence of wicked deeds against religion.[20] Commoners, as ignorant, immoral beings, were considered essentially "evil" *(akunin)* and in need of religious guidance to better themselves and become enlightened. Thus religious elites are presented as the model: everyone else must strive to become like them by following a process that, when successful, would take several lifetimes. The Buddhist precepts played a fundamental role in enforcing this vision, and it is not surprising that Hōnen, Shinran, and the radical Amidist movements explicitly ignored these precepts.[21]

Hōnen, and later Shinran, reversed the dominant perspective: Shinran in particular relativized the dominant concept of evil by making it universal. In the final period of the dharma, he argued, everyone is intrinsically evil, incapable of detached and disinterested good deeds. There is no distinction between the enlightened, morally pure elites and their ignorant and corrupt subordinates: in the final period only evil, common folk exist.[22] Those who think that they are better than others are actually worse than the worst criminals because while sinners are aware of being sinners, elites delude themselves by believing in their innate goodness.[23] This position, which was shared by most radical Amidists, prompted a dramatic transformation in the interpretation of the concept of evil *(aku)*. Evil became the essential characteristic of *all* beings: the *kenmitsu*'s lowest are now the anthropological paradigm. In this way, radical Amidists were able to offer an alternative vision—an essentially egalitarian one not completely unrelated to Hōnen's emphasis on rebirth in Amida's Pure Land *(ōjō)* as a revolutionary way of salvation—that is, rebirth in a world ruled by principles held by common folk.[24]

The rejection of dominant religious practices, belief in Amida's salvific power, and fundamental egalitarianism led radical Amidists to conclude that there was simply no need for religious practice. Here was perhaps another instance of the rejection of all repressive interference from religious institutions in the everyday lives of people. Taira Masayuki has argued that for Hōnen practice had "zero value" in the sense that it did not determine salvation. After all, the nenbutsu was recommended not because it was easy (as the *kenmitsu* ideologues maintained) but because it was chosen by Amida.[25] Once Amida is established as the only foundation of soteriology and the nenbutsu as the only practice, it is easy to stress equality under Amida and reject *kenmitsu* religious multiplicity that in fact perpetuated social injustice.[26] Here we have the apparent paradox that whereas the *kenmitsu* establishment's respect for religious diversity masked an ideology of domination based on social stratification, Hōnen's radical egalitarianism based on an exclusive practice functioned as an ideology of liberation.[27]

In this way, dominant religious institutions were challenged on a more mundane level. Their moral supremacy was directly connected to their political and economic power. As Kuroda Toshio, Satō Hiroo, Taira Masayuki, and others have made clear, Hōnen's teachings acted as catalysts for social protest and became a form of resistance ideology for peasants and the urban underclass during the Kamakura period and later.[28] These authors, however, tend to idealize the new nenbutsu teachings in toto and to reduce the *kenmitsu* system to a mere reactionary apparatus.[29] The situation, however, was more fluid and complex than that. As we shall see, members of the *kenmitsu* establishment also produced doctrines with liberational potential that influenced radical thought and popular rebellions: for example, the radical interpretations of Tendai *hongaku* doctrines or Shingon pansexualism that we find in several *ichinengi* texts. And in time, the Jōdo and Shin sects would develop repressive ideologies of their own.

Radical Amidist movements constituted a sort of "theology of liberation,"[30] which often meant freeing oneself from the repressive moral codes used by the establishment to reproduce the conditions of subjugation. This is particularly evident in the radical Amidists' treatment of the problem of evil: if good meant devotion and submission to buddhas and deities associated with the *shōen* system and their emissaries, then the most obvious form of resistance to embrace emphasized "evil"—not in abstract, absolute terms but in very concrete and contextual ways. Evil was by definition the refusal to accept the moral codes and social norms imposed by the *kenmitsu* institutions that formed the basis of their control of vast land holdings.[31] As Satō Hiroo explains, the more one follows dominant moral precepts, the more one is subjugated by the system;[32] the only way out is to refuse the system, and the easiest way to do it is to reverse and negate its principles in carnivalistic and grotesque terms.

Ichinengi Radical Amidism

We have seen that Hōnen's thought lent itself to some radical interpretations that could easily be used as a weapon in struggles against the ruling bloc and its system of domination. Such interpretations were made by several people in various parts of Japan, proof that these were more than simple misunderstandings of Hōnen's teachings. Amidist radicalism was a massive phenomenon for several centuries in many parts of Japan and should not be dismissed (as many sectarian historians are wont to do) as a temporary heresy created by ignorant people who were in no position to reinterpret the master's teachings. One of the most interesting aspects of the entire phenomenon is the extent of its proliferation—the fact that many people throughout the country engaged in religious, political, and philosophical speculation and used their intellectual activity as a tool to change the social order in a liberating way. But what were the ideas of these Amidist radicals? How did they interpret and transform Hōnen's (and later Shinran's) doctrines to suit their life and world view? As can be expected, we know very little of this mass intellectual activity. Most of the participants probably never wrote anything, and many of the texts that were composed were destroyed or circulated secretly. Several texts have been preserved, however, and even though they were written by members of the intellectual elite, they give us a glimpse into the minds of their interpreters and followers. Interestingly, many contain references to another heretical movement, Shingon's Tachikawaryū, which emphasized the body and sex in particular as a tool to attain buddhahood. I will return to the connections between Amidist radicals and the Tachikawaryū later.

Ichinengi is the name given to several alternative approaches to the Pure Land, approaches that I will refer to collectively as "radical Amidism." Official Pure Land literature offers several examples of *ichinengi,* usually ideas presented by anonymous preachers. Even though sectarian documents attempt to minimize the phenomenon, it is clear that Hōnen's ideas triggered the development of a whole galaxy of heterodoxies of this kind. *Ichinengi* is defined as an "aberrant interpretation" *(igi)* of Hōnen's Pure Land doctrines, according to which rebirth in Amida's Pure Land requires only a single act of thought or speech addressed to Amida or, in some cases, simply exposure to Amida's doctrines. As discussed by Hank Glassman in this volume, the belief in the power of Chūjōhime's relics and story to establish a karmic affiliation that assures birth in Amida's Pure Land, although not identified as heretical, appears to share this kind of understanding.

Some *ichinengi* interpreters went even further. In Hōnen's words they "established a new 'no nembutsu' doctrine, whereby they [gave] up even the slightest practice, the single utterance of the nembutsu."[33] Those who followed these movements considered themselves saved and therefore beyond good and evil, beyond social conventions, moral codes and obligations, and social order as defined by the dominant religious institutions. Their opponents accused them of upholding the doctrine of "licensed evil" *(zōaku muge),* according to which immoral acts committed by the followers of the *ichinengi* were not obstacles to their rebirth in the Pure Land. Hōnen repeatedly criticized these interpretations of his doctrines. Shinran and subsequent Jōdo Shinshū leaders were also very critical of this kind of alternative interpretation of Amidist orthodoxy and orthopraxy.[34] The followers of "heresies" were derogatorily called *honganbokori* (flaunting Amida's vow) and *hōitsu muzan* (self-indulgence without remorse). These doctrines and practices continued throughout Japanese premodern history until the late Edo period, in movements variously called *hijibōmon* (teachings of secret affairs), *ianjin* (aberrant cults), or simply *igi* (aberrant interpretations). In spite of various attempts to provide a neat and systematic classification of the various *ichinengi* movements on a doctrinal basis, their texts reflect a galaxy of scattered individuals and groups upholding different ideas and practices. What seems to be common to all (or at least most) is a general antiestablishment stance, a strong liberationist message, a simplification of the Buddhist teachings, a reversal of Buddhist perspectives on various issues (the status of the ignorant masses, the role of precepts, and so on)—all presented in a discursive mode that, as we shall see, reminds one of Bakhtin's "carnival." Philosophically, *ichinengi* are radical filiations of Tendai *hongaku* doctrines or Shingon cosmology and soteriology. The two *ichinengi* theoreticians whose works are still extant, albeit in fragmentary form, are Jōgakubō Kōsai (1163–?) and Hōhonbō Gyōkū (fl. 1207), who explicitly developed Tendai *hongaku* themes.

Only a relatively minor work by Kōsai is still extant, entitled *Kangyō gengi bunshō.*[35] Consequently, Kōsai's thought is known today largely from fragments of his works quoted in other texts, most of which criticize his doctrines.[36] Kōsai in particular is known for his distinction between the original Amida *(honmon no Mida)* and its trace *(jakumon no Mida).* While the former corresponds to original enlightenment *(hongaku),* the latter represents acquired enlightenment *(shikaku).* Kōsai's form of *ichinengi* maintains that it is not necessary to follow the path of Amida's traces, which involves practices protracting for a countless period of time. It is enough to produce a single thought *(ichinen)* of faith in Amida's vow to be saved by virtue of Amida's innate and original enlightenment, which is substantially identical to our own nature as deluded sentient beings. As Gyōnen's *Jōdo genryūshō* argues, for Kōsai the *ichinen* is the wisdom of the Buddha *(butchi);* therefore, *ichinen* is identical with the single universal mind of enlightenment permeating all beings. The realization of this universal mind renders practice irrelevant. In other words, Kōsai creatively utilized in a Pure Land context the Tendai distinction between buddhahood in principle (original enlightenment) and buddhahood as the result of practice (acquired enlightenment) in favor of the former. As a consequence, religious practice was deemed unnecessary for salvation.

Gyōkū, like Kōsai, was exiled in 1207 along with other disciples of Hōnen as a result of the "secret love affair incident" involving Anrakubō and Jūren. Very little is known about his thought; one text reports that he established distinctions between Pure Land as essence *(tai)* and appearance *(sō)* and between chanted nenbutsu *(shōnen shōmyō)* and conceptual nenbutsu *(rinen),* that is, the understanding of the essentials of the Pure Land teachings. Whereas chanted nenbutsu resulted in rebirth in what appeared to be the Pure Land, conceptual nenbutsu determined rebirth in the actual Pure Land.[37] In this way, Gyōkū too appears to have emphasized the essential, innate aspects of Hōnen's doctrines to the detriment of actual religious practice.[38]

Another important trend among *ichinengi* movements is represented in their connection to the Shingon heresy known as Tachikawaryū. The *Nenbutsu myōgi shū* reports of a "certain master" whose teachings were particularly popular in the Higo province (present-day Kyūshū). According to this master, the very word *"ichinen"* has a deep esoteric meaning whose knowledge would disclose the path to quick rebirth into Amida's Pure Land. Such a meaning is inscribed in the characters of the word itself. "Nen" can be broken down into "the heart and mind of two people"; therefore, *"ichinen"* means "the heart and mind of two people become one."[39] Accordingly, when a man and a woman have sexual intercourse, at the moment in which both are experiencing pleasure, they should together chant *Namu-Amida-butsu.* This is the true meaning of *ichinengi,* and heterosexual sex is the only means through which one can be reborn in Amida's Pure Land. All commentators saw in this text the influence of the Tachikawaryū—influence that is also evident in other heterodoxical or heretical texts belonging to the Pure Land canon.[40] For example, the *Hachimanchō no nukigaki: Ajikan no honmi* ("Excerpts from the eighty-thousand doctrines notebook: The original flavor of the letter A visualization"), an apocryphon attributed to Shinran, presents a systematic interpretation of the formula *Namu-Amida-butsu* on the basis of Tachikawaryū pansexualistic logic.[41] What follows is a brief synopsis of the main arguments of the text. Amida, as the Buddha of the Eternal Life, is directly connected to the principle of life (breath) and the generation of life (heterosexual intercourse). In particular, the *dharmakāya* of skillful means generates the two syllables A and UN, representing the two phases of breathing (inspiration and expiration, respectively) and the two fundamental cosmic principles (yang and yin, respectively). "A" and "UN" together further generate the name "Amida," which in turn is interpreted according to Shingon's pansexual logic as mobilizing breathing techniques lying at the source of the life principle and heterosexual sex. The text also says that the place where a man and a woman have sexual intercourse is the threefold buddha body *(trikāya)*. Furthermore, *"namu"* is explained according to the same logic as symbolizing the two sexes: *"na"* the father and *"mu"* the mother.[42] *"Namu,"* probably in the sense of "faith" and "devotion" is a natural, unconditioned *(jinen)* entity. *"Jinen"* is interpreted according to the two series of identities:

> *ji* = water = moon = night = yin = menstruation = mother
> *nen* = fire = sun = day = yang = sperm = father[43]

The *Nukigaki* engages in complex semiotic plays to show the unconditioned nature of nenbutsu and the necessity of salvation: in other words, *Namu-Amida-butsu* contains all the principles of life and the order of the cosmos; birth is equal to rebirth into Amida's Pure Land; sexual intercourse is equal to the recitation of the nenbutsu; accordingly, there is no need for specific religious practices. Salvation can be achieved in this very body, here and now, without effort (and in a pleasurable way):

> Man and woman are originally non-dual; therefore, samsara is pure and there are no defilements to purify; there are no passions to despise; there is no Buddha to pray to for his advent. Therefore, the enlightenment of the Buddha and the rebirth [in the Pure Land] of sentient beings are non-dual, both in name and in substance.[44]

The collection *Shōnin Misōde no uta* is very similar in content.[45] Several sections delve deeply into Shingon esoteric grammatology to expose the profound, hidden principle of phenomena and the essential identity of names and things. In particular, the section entitled "Sokushin buttai shō" interprets Amida and the nenbutsu on the basis of the Shingon mandala of the five viscera.[46] As a result, the substance of *Namu-Amida-butsu* is located in the five viscera—at the very center of the human body. The text is aware of its antinomian potential and concludes with an emphasis on the necessity of performing good deeds; however, this final exhortation could easily be ignored by readers. Another text, entitled *Kōbō Daishi Nenbutsu Kudenshū (kōhon),*[47] presents a vision of Pure Land that is very similar to that of Shingon's *himitsu nenbutsu* (esoteric nenbutsu) tradition.[48]

Tachikawaryū is a little-studied phenomenon in spite of its importance in the history of Japanese religiosity and culture. Extant sources report that the founder of this heretical movement was the monk Ninkan (fl. early twelfth century). When he was exiled to Izu for lèse-majesté, he changed his name to Rennen (thought of the lotus) and began to practice heretical teachings, especially after his encounter with an *onmyōji* (a ritual specialist of yin-yang doctrines) from Tachikawa in the Kantō region who became his disciple, Kenren. Even though there are doubts concerning the attribution of the sect's paternity to Ninkan, the symbolism of traditional narratives on the origin of Tachikawaryū is particularly interesting because they trace it to the fatal encounter between a renegade aristocratic monk from the capital and an exponent of popular religiosity that took place in eastern Japan (which at the time was considered barbaric and exotic). If we take this symbolism seriously, we see a circuit between center and periphery, high and low cultural registers that produced an alternative religious discourse. In fact, Tachikawaryū spread throughout the provinces: according to some accounts nine Shingon followers out of ten in the countryside were actually Tachikawaryū practitioners.[49] These figures are probably grossly exaggerated, but traces of Tachikawaryū cults and doctrines can be found all over Japan, from the top Shingon monasteries down to the remote countryside for at least four hundred years (from the twelfth to at least the late sixteenth centuries). It is no surprise, then, that leading exponents of Shingon sectarian orthodoxy such as Gōhō

(1306–1362) and Yūkai (1345–1416) publicly destroyed Tachikawaryū texts and ritual implements in attempts to stop its influence.

The teachings of the Tachikawaryū are characterized by a radically materialistic cosmology: texts present the universe as the transformation of a golden turtle drifting in the vast ocean into the two fundamental fluids (blood/female and semen/male), the lotus and the *vajra*, and so forth.[50] Overall, Tachikawaryū attempted to make salvation natural, necessary, automatic.[51] They carried to extremes the Shingon tenet that to the initiate each word spoken is a mantra, each gesture a mudrā.[52] In particular, everything is explained in sexual terms; the term "pansexualism," used by Iyanaga Nobumi to define Tachikawaryū doctrines and its related teachings, is therefore particularly appropriate. As Yūkai critically argued in his *Hōkyōshō*, an anti-Tachikawaryū pamphlet, Tachikawaryū adepts "consider the path of yin and yang, of man and woman, as the secret technique to becoming Buddha in this very body, and [think that] there is no other doctrine to attain Buddhahood outside of this."[53] An example of this fundamental attitude is offered by one of the few extant Tachikawaryū texts, the *A-un jigi*. In it, complex Shingon doctrines are reduced to breathing and sexual intercourse, which thus gain cosmological connotations and soteriological import.[54] It is important to note that for Tachikawaryū not only sex, but also gestation was a way to achieve buddhahood.[55] In this sense, Tachikawaryū was literally a "proletarian" religion whose soteriological goal was achieved by bearing children or simply trying to conceive them—an easy means of salvation for those who had nothing other than children as "resources." This soteriology rejected orthodox religious practices: if one is already, naturally and innately Buddha, why wait for the buddhahood that results from religious practices, an artificial and surrogate buddhahood in any case?[56] Moriyama Shōshin blames Tachikawaryū for its exclusive focus on sexual instincts, but this kind of criticism completely misrepresents the Tachikawaryū ideological apparatus.[57] Sex and other transgressions of precepts, far from being the manifestations of brute instincts, were used as tools in the ideological arena of the time to produce an alternative "theology of liberation" that represented the mentalities of common folk against dominant discourses of religion, morality, and order. The intended audience for these teachings becomes clear when we examine the purported goal of

Tachikawaryū practice: the ability "to make birds fall from the sky, reverse the flow of rivers, resuscitate the dead, and to make poor people rich"[58]—powers encountered in miraculous tales but most spectacular of all was the power to bring wealth to the poor. (In orthodox Buddhism, wealth is a karmic retribution for keeping the precepts, not violating them.)

So far we have outlined the two major components of the *ichinengi* galaxy, namely Tendai *hongaku* thought and Shingon pansexualism. In spite of obvious differences in their doctrinal backgrounds, we can detect important commonalities. In both cases, the radical Amidists popularized doctrines aimed at a restricted priestly elite. In fact, the diffusion of initiatory doctrines among people of low status was (and still is) perhaps the most recurring and serious accusation levelled by the establishment against the *ichinengi* and the Tachikawaryū as well. As for radical Amidists' ideas about generalized evil, it is noteworthy that similar doctrines appear in Tendai *hongaku* texts discussing the irrelevance of religious practice (and in particular the precepts) after initiation.[59] In a section of the *Kankō ruijū* concerning the problem of evil, the opponent (the one raising questions) criticizes the textual representative of orthodoxy (the one giving answers) for presenting a degenerated view similar to the "licensed evil" *(aku muge)* heresy. The representative replies:

> At the beginning of the religious education one should not say that evil constitutes the basis of meditative practices *(shikan),* because that would determine the increase of delusory ideas. However, in the advanced stages of religious practice, [it should be taught that] the very essence of deluded mind is the state of awareness attained through meditation.[60]

The opponent asks: "Then, the practitioner of *shikan* meditation should not be afraid of performing himself evil karma such as killing or stealing, should he?" The explanation given in the text is that evil, too, if it is the result of spontaneous, nonintentional, unconditioned actions that are not produced by attachment and delusion, is a kind of meditative practice.[61] According to the *Kankō ruijū,* the initiated one, who by definition has transcended dualism, delusion, and attachment, can perform actions that unenlightened beings may understand as evil because evil too is part of religious practice. In this way, as Tamura Yoshirō has explained, evil is presented by *hongaku* circles as something produced by nonenlightened vision.[62] The *ichinengi* shared the same idea, but reversed its ideological content. Evil is relational and contextual and cannot be defined by the teachings of dominant religious institutions. Those who are saved thanks to Amida's compassion are beyond the distinction of good and evil and are therefore free to act as they please—much like Tendai *hongaku* masters. In this way, the *ichinengi* radically questioned the medieval order of things by proposing an anticlerical "theology of liberation."

The Tachikawaryū played a similar role with respect to Shingon orthodoxy as the *ichinengi* did with their interpretations of Tendai *hongaku* doctrines. Yūkai accused Ninkan of adulterating the Shingon teachings with popular beliefs and of spreading initiatory knowledge among common folk ("married people, meat-eaters, polluted people").[63] Tachikawaryū spread secret initiatory knowledge among rural peasants and urban dwellers all over Japan. This de-emphasized the social order, which was based on the acquisition of secret knowledge and was believed to reflect the cosmic ordering of things. We can see here the transgressive and revolutionary elements of radical Amidism: the most secret doctrines and rituals, known to only a few aristocratic priests and some important members of the ruling class (among them the emperor, for whom sexuality was an important aspect of his symbolic power),[64] were diffused among all orders of society. These doctrines immediately acquired enormous liberatory potential: if everyone is already naturally saved, why bother with religious practice at all, especially given religion's connection with systems of social domination? Thus an eschatological message (salvation can only be achieved in Amida's Pure Land) turned into a potentially revolutionary program aimed at the realization of a perfect equalitarian society in this world.

Chōrenbō and Popular Radicalism

So far I have discussed texts that appropriated elite doctrines from a popular, liberationist perspective but still remained within an elite dimension: most are written in a difficult Chinese, with complex Buddhist terminology. In this section I attempt to trace the popular appropriation of these doctrines. In particular, here I would like to discuss a little-known text, the *Isshū gyōgi shō*, an apocryphon attributed to Shinran and written (supposedly in 1210) to criticize the ideas and the actions of radical Amidists.[65] According to this document, the correct instructions for Pure Land followers were revealed to Shinran by two *kenmitsu* deities, Togakushi Gongen of Shinano and Hakone Gongen of Kantō. According to the *Isshū gyōgi shō,* devout believers should follow received ideas of morality, respect the teachings and the followers of other schools, and worship all buddhas and *kami* because Japan is a sacred land *(shinkoku).*[66] This text contains injunctions to radical Amidists not to criticize the Buddhist establishment and not to go against dominant interpretations of Buddhist doctrines, practices, and morality. They should refrain from deviations from sectarian orthodoxy: ignorant people should not argue with the learned, the wise, the virtuous.[67] The text repeatedly threatens that the transgressors will be subjected to "Amida's punishment" *(Amida no obachi)* and be hurled into hell without possibility of escape; it also mentions the caveat included in the eighteenth original vow of Amida, which threatens to exclude from salvation those responsible for the five heinous crimes and slanderers of the Dharma *(hihō shōbō)*—a warning usually ignored by Hōnen and Shinran but employed in sectarian debates. As the text makes clear, the Pure Land teachings, if understood wrongly, take one to hell.[68]

The main polemical target of the *Isshū gyōgi shō* is a certain Chōrenbō, who was active around the Seiji era (1199–1201) in the Echigo province (present-day Niigata prefecture). Originally from the province of Dewa in northeastern Japan, he was a "master of the Tachikawaryū heresy";[69] among his disciples there were Zenchaku and Jūren, the monk from Sado who joined Hōnen in the capital and was later put to death by the imperial court after the 1207 incident.[70] In the *Isshū gyōgi shō,* Jūren is explicitly accused of being the cause of Hōnen's exile because of the heresies he had learned from Chōrenbō.[71] Chōrenbō, for his part, is accused of causing people to fall into hell.[72] The *Isshū gyōgi shō* contains several passages from a work allegedly written by Chōrenbō entitled *Miya santan* (In praise of shrines)—a clearly ironic title for a book that presents a radical antinomian, if not anticlerical, position. I haven't been able to find any additional information on Chōrenbō, and his *Miya santan* is not mentioned in any other source. It is possible that Chōrenbō and his work were a rhetorical device employed by the author of the *Isshū gyōgi shō* to criticize sectarian heterodoxies. Still, it is interesting that Chōrenbō is presented as Jūren's master, and his text, supposedly influenced by the Tachikawaryū heresy, as a summary of radical Amidists' doctrines. I will argue that, even if such a text did not exist, the ideas quoted from it do represent important aspects of the ideology of the radical Amidists and of popular thinking in medieval Japan. For example, Chōrenbō is quoted as saying:

> The exclusive practice [of the Pure Land school] is the easy practice, and therefore there is no ritual etiquette to it: one should behave as one wishes, keeping well in mind the instructions of one's master: these are the teachings of the nenbutsu school.[73]

More specifically, Chōrenbo states that "in the easy practice there are no precepts: one should not be ashamed of impure acts such as having sex, drinking alcohol, eating meat, or taking life";[74] "just behave as you like; prohibitions and impurities are not a problem" for rebirth.[75] Salvation is presented as something easy and natural: there is "nothing else to do but to chant the nenbutsu or think that Amida will save me" to be saved;[76] actually, "it is enough to listen to just one bit of the fundamentals [of our sect] to be reborn in paradise."[77] In a different passage, however, Chōrenbō offers an even more radical soteriology, a version of the "no nenbutsu" vehemently criticized by Hōnen: "I will certainly be reborn even without chanting the nenbutsu, even without thinking of it; it is enough to listen to the teachings concerning rebirth [into Amida's Pure Land]."[78] Chōrenbō is suggesting that there is no need for religious practice at all: it is enough to be exposed only superficially to the Pure Land teachings to realize that one is already saved and therefore does not have to follow repressive regulations: "the one who chants the nenbutsu is not ashamed of impure acts, does not keep the precepts, does not look at the scriptures spoken by the Buddha, does not worship the image of Amida."[79] Along this line of thought, Chōrenbō is quoted as promulgating iconoclastic ideas: "if you meet the Buddha, don't worship him";[80] "the buddha triad or the Four Heavenly Generals are useless";[81] "the images of the ancestors cause samsara"[82] as does the use of the rosary.[83] In other words, worship and images are either useless or even dangerous. Statements such as these explain the acts of blasphemous disrespect attributed to him: making fun of other sects and Shintō shrines,[84] cooking fish and eating it, and even "eating meat and polluting in front of the Buddha [in a temple]."[85] The same iconoclastic attitude can be found toward the *kami,* who are "all snakes"[86] and "dirty things."[87] Only the ignorant worship them and as a consequence they will fall into hell.[88]

Chōrenbō and Jūren reportedly even went to Gion, an important cultic center in Kyoto affiliated with Enryakuji, and made fun of the powerful religious militia *(jinin),* saying things such as "your deity *(suijaku)* will lead you to hell."[89]

Chōrenbō's ideas appear to be a radical version of the more sophisticated *ichinengi* doctrines discussed above, with perhaps echoes of Zen iconoclasm. If the nenbutsu is the principle of life, sex is no different from nenbutsu: there is no need to chant the nenbutsu if one engages in sex. Thus, salvation is, for those exposed to these teachings, necessary and inevitable. For Chōrenbō, concrete and pleasurable everyday practices (eating, drinking, engaging in sex) are the keys to salvation; there is no need to worship statues, perform religious practices, or be subjugated to the dominant authoritarian morality. In their emphasis on materiality, the body, pleasure, everyday life; in their disregard of organized religion (or religion in general) with its morality and rituals; in their arguments for the sacredness of the body, which renders unnecessary any other manifestation of sacrality; in all this, we hear the voice of medieval Japanese peasants' cultural resistance to hegemonic institutions.

The passages allegedly written by Chōrenbō, with their echoes of an anticlerical peasant culture usually ignored in historical documents, evoke another "heretic" who lived more than three centuries later on the opposite side of Eurasia, the Italian miller Menocchio, whose religious and political ideas have been reconstructed by Carlo Ginzburg.[90] In Menocchio too we find a materialistic cosmology—or, more precisely, what Ginzburg calls a "religious materialism," according to which "only matter imbued with divinity, the mixture of the four elements, exists."[91] This cosmology echoes the thought of radical Amidists, according to whom Amida is everything and can be found solely in the materiality of the body and the universe. A second aspect of Menocchio's thought is an underlying anticlericalism: to him the Church was, in Ginzburg's words, an "enormous edifice built on the exploitation of the poor."[92] This explains Menocchio's antiritualism: in his trial by the Inquisition, he said: "I believe that the law and commandments of the Church are all a matter of business, and they [the priests] make their living from this";[93] he defined sacraments as "human inventions," "business," "merchandise";[94] he believed, therefore, that neither relics nor images should be venerated.[95] Similarly the *ichinengi,* and Chōrenbō in particular, displayed anticlerical and antiritualistic dispositions grounded, as Kuroda Toshio, Satō Hiroo, and Taira Masayuki have demonstrated, in the awareness that dominant religious ideas are organically connected to systems of exploitation and social control. A third feature of Menocchio's world view is what Ginzburg calls "a unilateral insistence on the practical aspects of religion,"[96] or, in other words, "a decided tendency to reduce religion to morality."[97] In particular, writes Ginzburg, interpreting Menocchio's words, "man's relationship to God becomes unimportant compared to his relationship with his neighbor. And if God is that neighbor, why then do we need God?"[98] The *ichinengi* too, despite their focus on evil, emphasized interpersonal welfare rather than individual angst produced by religious and moral guilt.

Popular Religious Materialism, or the Carnivalization of Dominant Buddhism

We have seen many instances of an interesting circuit of center and periphery that marked Japanese intellectual history. Peripheral people (those from distant provinces, the low middle classes, and the peasantry, usually excluded from dominant discourses) appropriated certain ideas of the center with results that were often unpredictable and, at times, revolutionary. These peripheral ideas were eventually taken up by the center (the main religious institutions in the capital, intellectuals, and urban groups), where they were systematized, countered, or amplified and in time found their way back to the provinces and the subordinates. *Ichinengi* radical Amidism and Tachikawaryū pansexual esotericism seems to have followed this path. The "heresies" were so popular and influential that orthodoxy had to define itself against them, as demonstrated in the *Isshū gyōgi shō* or in Yūkai's *Hōkyōshō*. At this point, "orthodoxy" was nothing more than a reaction to a supposed "heterodoxy"—a heterodoxy of heterodoxy, as it were. This fact completely relativizes the respective status of orthodoxy and heterodoxy, whose definitions depend ultimately on the context, the producers of meaning and the interpreters.

As we have seen, a recurring accusation levelled by the orthodox against heretical movements was their creation by people with no deep understanding of the true meanings of the texts and the doctrines of (orthodox) masters. But from a different perspective, these heresies are instances of what Michel de Certeau calls the "capture of speech" by the subalterns, the anonymous individuals outside the official discourse with no effective public voice of their own.[99] In other words, several aspects of radical Amidism and pansexual esotericism can be envisioned as direct interventions by commoners in the religious, political, and intellectual arenas resulting from their appropriation of some elements of Buddhism within popular culture. Heresies allowed the "speechless" from the provinces and the underclass to express their own world view in a language that explicitly challenged the dominant ideology.

The explicitly "popular" nature of radical movements is indirectly recognized even by a critic such as Ishida Mitsuyuki, who writes that *ianjin* (aberrant cults) originated in the "attachment to human nature" in its immediate, bodily aspects.[100] This raises the issue of the status of religiosity in popular culture, a culture that usually takes the form of carnival to express itself. In this connection, the ideas of Mikhail Bakhtin concerning popular culture, carnival, the grotesque, and the quest for liberation are directly relevant here.

As Michael Holquist has written, "Bakhtin's carnival . . . is not only not an impediment to revolutionary change, it is revolution itself."[101] Amidist radicals challenged dominant ideas about religion, morality, and social order and tried to impose alternative models drawn from popular traditional culture. Members of the various *ichinengi* movements were much like Bakhtin's folk: "blasphemous rather than adoring, cunning rather than intelligent; they are coarse, dirty, and rampantly physical, revelling in oceans of strong drink, poods of sausage, and endless coupling of bodies."[102] Blasphemy was the strongest accusation levelled against the *ichinengi;* their doctrines emphasized physicality—strong drink, meat eating, and sex. As for intelligence, the *ichinengi* showed that ignorant folk were capable of expressing philosophical positions in ways that can only be characterized (in the terms of the dominant discourse, the only one available at the time) as "cunning": using tactical reversal of doctrines, paradoxical ideas, desecrating humor. Just as Bakhtin's folk were held in striking contrast with those celebrated by Soviet propaganda, so were those who joined the radical Amidist movements differentiated from the typically decorous and pious members of Japan's religious establishment. The *ichinengi* thus appear to have been an enormous aberration in the history of Japanese religion and culture. It is perhaps for this reason that they have been mostly ignored or, when studied, often criticized as a kind of religious hoax perpetrated by deluded and dishonest individuals.

An important feature of popular culture is what Bakhtin calls "grotesque realism": "The essential principle of grotesque realism is degradation, that is, the lowering of all that is high, spiritual, ideal, abstract; it is a transfer to the material level, to the sphere of earth and body in their indissoluble unity";[103] "all that is sacred and exalted is rethought on the level of the material bodily stratum or else combined and mixed with its images."[104] In particular, debasement and reversal are expressed through a focus on the "material bodily lower stratum," "for it gaily and simultaneously materializes and unburdens. It liberates objects from the snares of false seriousness, from illusions and sublimations inspired by fear."[105] Such a "liberating process" is also applied to religious ideas and moral principles usually expressed in "pitifully" and "menacingly" "serious tones" aimed at producing fear[106]—and subjugation. Radical Amidist movements applied the same principles in their treatment of dominant religious ideas: they ridiculed ordinary morality and piety and reversed principles by focusing on the forbidden, the materiality of the body, and the pleasure of the senses, to liberate people from the "menacingly serious tones" of dominant religious discourse and practice. They clearly saw the subjugating aspects of religion and proposed an alternative model—Satō's "liberation theology"—that would free their members of all religious obligations. *Ichinengi* and other radical forms of Amida cults were not a religious movement but a form of anticlericalism expressed in religious terms. Their emphasis on licensed evil *(zōaku muge)* was not a sign of gratuitous immorality, but it contained a carnivalesque reversal of dominant norms aimed at a critique of the entire social order. And, as in all forms of carnivalesque reversal, licensed evil strongly emphasized the lower parts of the body.

According to Bakhtin, "the grotesque body is cosmic and universal. It stresses elements common to the entire cosmos."[107] Thus it is the material, all-pervasive nature of Amida (or Dainichi) that identifies the individual, grotesque body of the practitioner with the cosmic and perfect body of the Buddha in a vertiginous operation of desecration and reversal. Although Bakhtin was writing about Renaissance Europe, his words apply to medieval Japan as well: "It was in the material acts and eliminations of the body—eating, drinking, defecation, sexual life—that man found and retraced within himself . . . all the cosmic matter and his manifestations, and was thus able to assimilate them."[108] While normative nenbutsu (and Buddhism in general) centered on the upper part of the body (heart/mind, mouth as the locus of speech/invocation, and so on), radical Amidists focused on the lower part of the body (stomach/intestines, sexual organs, mouth as the locus of eating and drinking).[109] What the establishment deemed most difficult and arduous was a simple fact of "ignorant" commoner's everyday life; as a result, religious practice is de-emphasized. While the orthodoxy stressed work and morality as the keys to salvation, the heretics endorsed sex, food, and drink—in other words, enjoyment of the material body.

Humor and ridicule, important features of popular carnival, were present in the actions of radical Amidists. They poked fun at dominant religiosity in all its forms and with a certain dose of autoirony. A striking example concerns the alleged founders of Tachikawaryū, the Shingon monk Ninkan, who renamed himself Rennen, and his disciple, the *onmyōji* Kenren. These two Buddhists, who taught that enlightenment can be achieved through sexual intercourse, both have "lotus" *("ren")* as part of their name (in their doctrine, an explicit metaphor for the female sexual organ): "Rennen" (thought of the lotus) and "Kenren" (looking at the lotus) thus have surprising sexual overtones. The same imagery is present in the names "Chōrenbō" (long lotus) and "Jūren" (abiding in the lotus). Here are instances of "grotesque realism," of the carnivaleque appropriation of religious images in order to transgress and reverse them.

Conclusions

Let us return to Jien's comments on the "secret love affair incident" of 1207, where we began our investigation: "Anrakubō and the others . . . even spent the night there [with the imperial concubines]. Such a thing is unspeakable, so in the end Anrakubō and Jūren were beheaded. Also, Hōnen was exiled."[110] Here Jien suggests that the behavior of Jūren, Anrakubō, and the others offended social sensibilities. Jien also wrote: "The exclusive nembutsu, with its fish, meat, and sexual indulgences, remains largely unchecked."[111]

James Dobbins explains: "As a priest, [Jien] considered the exclusive *nembutsu* corrosive to the clerical precepts and a detraction from the teachings of the eight schools. As a leader in society, he feared that it would seduce the ignorant and lowly and would erode social values and civil order."[112] Dobbins is here displaying for us the traditional rhetoric against radical Amidist positions. The underlying assumptions of this rhetoric are the following: there is a fundamental distinction in society between "leaders," or the cultured elites, and the "ignorant and the lowly." Whereas the former are enlightened and morally pure, the latter are immoral and corrupt. Hōnen himself quoted Kūkai's definition of the mind of common folk as "ignorant sheeplike mentality" *(ishō teiyō shin):* "It is to think of food and sex only, and therefore it is like being a sheep."[113] To those in charge, these sheeplike beings are easy prey to ideas that "erode social values and civil order." But whose social values, whose civil order? Obviously, those of the elites. Hegemonic discourses leave no room for the possibility that subordinate classes have their own morality, their own social order, and their own religiosity, which may be different from, and sometimes opposed to, dominant ones. The study of radical Amidist movements reveals the existence of this separate morality and religiosity.

Furthermore, who spread these dangerous ideas? The "ignorant" themselves? Or traitors of the elites, who sided, so to speak, with the sheeplike enemy? What was the radicals' ideological agenda? Medieval commentators had no doubt: these ideas and practices were the workings of Māra and his retinue in their incessant struggle against Buddhism and legitimate sociocosmic order. As Hōnen wrote, a heresy of this kind "must be the fabrication of demons. It wreaks havoc on the Buddhist teachings, and it throws society into confusion."[114] The symbolism of this medieval logic reveals the ideology of dominant religious institutions: their order and values were the "right" ones; any attempt to disrupt their social order was a threat against the good ordering of the cosmos, an irruption of chaos. The ruling elites obviously tried to give a cosmological foundation to their system of domination. And it was precisely this connection between religion and social order that was the main target of radical Amidist movements.

The above questions also suggest that the adoption of Buddhism in the countryside or outside the ruling elites in general was less uniform and more problematic than previously thought. People did not simply convert to Buddhism, they appropriated and used it according to their own mentalités. They were not simply indoctrinated *(kyōke)*, but in many cases they creatively interpreted and "consumed" Buddhist ideas and rituals according to their needs and desires. As Michel de Certeau would agree, the passive consumer became an active producer of meaning and cultural practices. The issue of popular, extrahegemonic religiosity is usually ignored or silenced: received narratives on the history of Japanese religion—based on sectarian approaches and elite doctrines, what James Scott calls the "public transcript"—are systematically skewed in the direction of dominant institutions and stereotypical images of subalterns. According to Scott: "Any analysis based exclusively on the public transcript is likely to conclude that subordinate groups endorse the terms of their subordination and are willing, even enthusiastic, partners in that subordination."[115] My hypothesis is that the various *ichinengi* groups, together with at least some of the Tachikawaryū cults and other aspects of popular religiosity, are examples of Scott's "hidden transcript," that is, "discourse that takes place 'offstage,' beyond direct observation by powerholders."[116] At times, the hidden transcript emerges on the public scene as an alternative discourse. The *ichinengi* seem to be one such moment in which subordinates capture the scene and are able to spread their own discourse. Hidden transcripts can take several forms: Scott lists "offstage parody, dreams of violent revenge, millennial visions of a world turned upside down."[117] We find several of these elements in the discourse of the *ichinengi:* reversal of dominant religious ideas, rejection of orthodox practices, millennial visions, violent revenge against powerful religious institutions.

What then was the position of radical Amidist movements in the history of Japanese Buddhism? As Antonio Gramsci noted, an institutional religion is a plural, complex entity encompassing several elements often in competition with each other. It is impossible to talk about, for example, Catholicism in abstract terms, since there is a Catholicism of the elites, one of the peasants, one of the urban petty bourgeoisie. James Scott expands on Gramsci's remark in his discussion of European Catholicism:

> The folk Catholicism of the European peasants, far from serving ruling interests, was practiced and interpreted in ways that often defended peasant property rights, contested large differences in wealth, and even provided something of a millennial ideology with revolutionary import. Rather than being a 'general anesthesia,' folk Catholicism was a provocation—one that, together with its adher-

> ents in the lower clergy, provided the ideological underpinning for countless rebellions against seigneurial authority.[118]

In medieval Japan, Buddhism was not merely an ideological tool of the elites used to subjugate the masses. It did serve the interests of the elites, as Kuroda Toshio and others have convincingly argued. However, the "masses" were not ignorant and completely enslaved by the lures of Buddhism; they were able to use it according to their own needs. Radical Amidism and pansexual esotericism are clear examples of the multiplicity of Buddhism and its revolutionary possibilities. In other words, "subordinate groups . . . imagine a counterfactual social order. They do imagine both the reversal and negation of their domination."[119] As we have seen, radical Amidism reversed some basic elements of dominant Buddhism and, in some extreme cases, negated the role of Buddhist institutions and practices for salvation.

Clearly, there is a difference in principle between the inversion of dominant, hegemonic values typical of carnivalistic phenomena and a viable, sustainable alternative set of values. Carnival is, after all, a controlled outburst that essentially serves to strengthen the dominant order it reverses. At least some radical Amidist movements, however, used carnivalistic elements to express not just a temporary reversal of the hegemonic order but deeper characteristics of popular mentalities that could not otherwise find adequate representation in dominant discourses about religion, morality, order, and society. These characteristics can perhaps be identified with an emphasis on materiality, the body, immediate social relations, fundamental equalitarian tendencies, and a concern with morality envisioned not as an abstract adherence to religiously grounded ethical codes but a deep concern for fellow human beings. They can also be found in the refusal of absolute forms of social authority and domination. As such, popular mentalités are often in direct antagonism with dominant discourses; what remains to be seen is how long and to what extent they can sustain themselves as independent cultural formations before they are labeled heresies and eradicated or integrated within the system as "mere" carnivalistic expressions.

Finally, we have seen that radical Amidism and pansexual esotericism were practiced over large areas of Japan and exercised a strong fascination on people of all social classes; as such, they represent an interesting form of interaction of high and low cultural registers. One can understand the popular appeal of these teachings, given their liberating potential; it is harder to understand why such doctrines were upheld also by members of the religious and intellectual elite. Mizuhara Gyōei has made a valuable suggestion in this regard by comparing the intellectual fascination of Tachikawaryū in the middle ages with that provoked by Communism in the first two decades of the twentieth century.[120] Both radical Buddhist movements and Communist organizations appealed to the elites and the masses alike with their promises of liberation and of a better society; both had a strong utopian component that made them utterly fascinating and at the same time practically unrealizable.

Notes

1. For a general introduction to the Amida cults in Japan, see Inoue Mitsusada, *Nihon jōdokyō seiritsushi no kenkyū,* in *Inoue Mitsusada zenshū,* vol. 7 (1956; reprint, Tokyo: Iwanami, 1975).

2. Joseph Kitagawa writes: "The Kamakura period was marked by the rejection of the artificial culture delicately concocted by courtiers and clergy, in favor of a more natural spirit and indigenous forms of culture and society" (Joseph Kitagawa, *Religion in Japanese History* [New York: Columbia University Press, 1969], 88). In fact, during the Kamakura period, George Sansom argues: "There was a pressing need for some simpler faith, easy to explain, easy to practise, offering some consolation in troubled times" (George Sansom, *A History of Japan to 1334* [London: The Cressett Press, 1958], 220). Anesaki Masaharu concludes: "The Buddhist religion of the new age was not one of ceremonies and mysteries but a religion of simple piety or of spiritual exercise" (Masaharu Anesaki, *History of Japanese Religion* [1930; reprint, Rutland, Vt., and Tokyo: Tuttle, 1963], 168). Kuroda Toshio demonstrated the inaccuracy of such a picture of the religious situation of the Kamakura period in his *Nihon chūsei no kokka to shūkyō* (Tōkyō: Iwanami, 1975). This essay will show that several people in medieval Japan also rejected piety and religious experience.

3. On popular Buddhism in medieval Japan, see Kuroda, ibid.

4. On the *kenmitsu* system, see ibid.; see also the essays collected in James C. Dobbins, ed., *The Legacy of Kuroda Toshio,* a special issue of the *Japanese Journal of Religious Studies* 23, nos. 3–4 (Fall 1996).

5. Satō Hiroo, *Nihon chūsei no kokka to bukkyō* (Tokyo: Yoshikawa Kōbunkan, 1987), 110–111.

6. The sentence can be found in *Gensei gokajō saikyo kanpu,* quoted in Takeuchi Rizō, ed., *Kamakura ibun* (Tokyo: Tōkyōdō shuppan, 1971–1997), 4:315, n. 2458.

7. Jien, *Gukanshō, Nihon koten bungaku taikei* (Tokyo: Iwanami, 1967), 8:294–295. The passage quoted is from the English translation in Delmer M. Brown and Ichirō Ishida, *The Future and the Past: A Translation and Study of the* Gukanshō, *an Interpretative History of Japan Written in 1219* (Berkeley, Los Angeles, and London: University of California Press, 1979), 172.

8. For a detailed study of the incident in its historical and social contexts, see Taira Masayuki, *Nihon chūsei no shakai to bukkyō* (Tokyo: Hanawa shobō, 1992), esp. 287–328.

9. Other repressions occurred in 1219, 1224, 1227, 1234, and 1240. In 1227 Hōnen's tomb was destroyed, his major work, the *Senchakushū,* was publicly burned, and several followers, among them Kōsai, were exiled.

10. See *Kōfukuji sōjō* in Kamata Shigeo et al., *Kamakura kyū bukkyō (Nihon shisō taikei)* (Tokyo: Iwanami, 1995), 31–42, 312–316. For an English translation, see Robert Morrell, *Kamakura Buddhism: A Minority Report* (Berkeley: Asian Humanities Press, 1987), 75–88.

11. For a selection of critical sources against Hōnen and his groups, see Taira, *Nihon chūsei no shakai,* esp. 292–300.

12. Takeuchi, ed., *Kamakura ibun,* 3:195, n. 1488.

13. Ibid., 3:196–200, n. 1490. For an English translation, see James C. Dobbins, *Jodo Shinshu: Shin Buddhism in Medieval Japan* (Bloomington: Indiana University Press, 1989), 17.

14. *Daimuryōjukyō,* in *Jōdo sanbukyō* (Tokyo: Iwanami bunko, 1963), 1:136.

15. Taira, *Nihon chūsei no shakai,* 307–308.

16. The translation of the "Seven Articles" is from Dobbins, *Jodo Shinshu,* 17.

17. Taira, *Nihon chūsei no shakai,* 173.

18. On *jingi fuhai* and iconoclasm in medieval Japan, see Kuroda, *Nihon chūsei no kokka to shūkyō,* 257–262; Sato Hiroo, *Nihon chūsei no kokka to bukkyō,* esp. 98–109; and Sato Hiroo, "Habutsu hajin no rekishiteki igi," in *Kami, hotoke, ōken no chusei* (Kyoto: Hōzōkan, 1998), 89–117.

19. In the middle ages the sovereign was often referred to as *jūzen no ō,* the "King of the Ten Good Deeds"; the status of a Buddhist monk was also the result of previous karmic affinities.

20. On the cosmological implications of medieval social hierarchy, see Kuroda Hideo, "Hito, sōryo, warawa, hinin," in *Kyōkai no chūsei, shōchō no chūsei* (Tokyo: Tōkyō Daigaku shuppankai, 1986), 185–216.

21. As Taira has noted (*Nihon chūsei no shakai,* 291–292), the establishment was not concerned with violations of the precepts; these were actually quite common at the time. However, it held that the precepts were important and should be maintained as the main pillars of social order and morality. In contrast, radical Amidists had no respect for the precepts, which they saw as the hypocritical tools of social domination. The *ichinengi* movements were against the fear and guilt produced by doctrines concerning precepts and their violations. In this sense, the *ichinengi* were struggling for a radical liberation of consciousness.

22. See also ibid., 295–296.

23. See Satō, *Nihon chūsei no kokka to bukkyō,* 125

24. Taira, *Nihon chūsei no shakai,* 180. In contrast, Tendai and Shingon were not primarily interested in rebirth into Amida's Pure Land. For these schools, rebirth was only a skillful means *(upāya)* to guide the ignorant or, at best, a secondary form of salvation essentially inferior to the primary soteriological goal, that of achieving buddhahood in the present life.

25. Ibid., 175–176.

26. Ibid., 177.

27. Ibid., 191–192.

28. Kuroda Toshio was perhaps the first to emphasize the ideologically oppositional potential of Hōnen's (and Shinran's) teachings. See, for example, his "Kamakura bukkyō ni okeru ikkō senju to honji suijaku" in *Nihon chūsei no kokka to shūkyō,* 191–218. His interpretation has been developed further by Satō Hiroo and Taira Masayuki.

29. See, for instance, ibid., in particular p. 212, where Kuroda presents the equation *honji suijaku*=reactionary vs. *senju nenbutsu*=revolutionary.

30. Satō, *Nihon chūsei no kokka to bukkyō,* 117.

31. Ibid., 114.

32. Ibid., 114–115.

33. Hōnen, *Ichinengi chōji kishōmon,* translated in Dobbins, *Jodo Shinshu,* 51.

34. Shinran was himself accused of being an *ichinengi.* See Myōzui, *Jōdoshū yōshū gendan,* quoted in *Bukkyō daijiten,* 157a. See also Dobbins, *Jodo Shinshu,* 42–53; on "licensed evil" in Jōdo shinshū, see Dobbins, ibid., 53–61.

35. Found in Kōgo Mōshun, *Jōgakubō Kōsai no Ichinengi* (Utsunomiya: Gonguan, 1990), 41 ff.

36. See, for example, *Hōnen Shōnin gyōjō gazu,* fasc. 29; *Kango tōroku,* fasc. 10; *Jōdoshū myōmoku mondō,* fasc. 2; Chien, *Kannen hōmon shiyō shinshō,* fasc. 4. A relatively neutral presentation of Kōsai's ideas can be found in Gyōnen's *Jōdo hōmon genryūshō,* in *Jōdoshū zensho* (Kyoto: Jōdoshū kaishū happyakunen kinen keisan junbi kyoku, 1974), 15:584–602. For a collection of citations concerning Kōsai's thought and the *ichinengi* movements in general, see Kōgo, *Jōgakubō Kōsai;* see also *Mochizuki bukkyō daijiten,* 157–158.

37. *Chinzei myōmoku mondō funjin shō,* fasc. 1, quoted in *Mochizuki bukkyō daijiten,* 158.

38. See ibid.

39. Shōkō, *Nenbutsu myogishū,* in *Kokubun Tōhō bukkyō sōsho dai 2 shū* (1929; reprint, Tokyo: Meicho tukyūkai, 1991), 3:51–84; see also Dobbins, *Jodo Shinshu,* 48–49.

40. These texts are often attributed to important patriarchs of the Shinshū tradition, such as Shinran or Rennyō, or even Kōbō Daishi, perhaps in an effort to counter sectarian orthodoxies by employing the same legitimizing strategies.

41. *Igishū,* in *Shinshū taikei,* 36:213–216; see also James H. Sanford, "Shinran's Secret Transmission to Nyoshin: Esoteric Buddhism in a Pure Land Context," unpublished manuscript.

42. *Igishū,* in *Shinshū taikei,* 36:213.

43. Ibid., 36:214.

44. Ibid., 36:215.

45. Ibid., 36:364–367.

46. Ibid., 36:369–372. The mandala of the five viscera *(gozō mandara)* is also present in another text, the *Shōbushū,* ibid., 36:404–405.

47. Ibid., 36:405–408.

48. *Himitsu nenbutsu* developed esoteric interpretations of Pure Land teachings on the basis of Shingon doctrines; among its major exponents were Kakuban, Kakukai, Jōhen, and Dōhan. The latter two were even considered by Tachikawaryū sources adepts of the heretical school (see Mizuhara Gyōei, *Jakyō Tachikawaryū no kenkyū,*

in *Mizuhara Gyōei zenshū* [1923; reprint, Kyoto: Dōhōsha, 1981], 125). *Himitsu nenbutsu* had many doctrinal and ritual commonalities with Tachikawaryū; however, there is no proof that *himitsu nenbutsu* per se became a popular movement comparable with those of the *ichinengi* radical Amidists or the Tachikawaryū itself. One could argue that *himitsu nenbutsu* was an elite reappropriation of heterodoxical doctrines alimented by either ideological proximity or, more likely, the fascination with the outside, the forbidden (and at the same time by the desire to domesticate it). In any case, *himitsu nenbutsu* was often on the verge of heresy itself, to the point that today many of its doctrines cannot be immediately distinguished from Tachikawaryū doctrines. For example, Jōhen and Dōhan reduced everything in the universe to Amida in a conceptual operation that bears similarities to the thought of Hōnen's radicals; however, neither Jōhen nor Dōhan seems to criticize the status quo of their time. It is well possible that *himitsu nenbutsu*, together with Tachikawaryū, influenced some aspect of radical Amidism. On *himitsu nenbutsu*, see Kushida Ryōkō, *Shingon mikkyō seiritsu katei no kenkyū* (Tokyo: Sankibō busshorin, 1964), esp. 181–232; see also James H. Sanford, "Breath of Life: The Esoteric Nenbutsu," in *Esoteric Buddhism in Japan*, ed. Ian Astley (Copenhagen and Aarhus: The Seminar for Buddhist Studies, 1994), 65–98.

49. Moriyama Shōshin, *Tachikawa jakyō to sono shakaiteki haikei no kenkyū* (1965; reprint, Tokyo: Kokusho kankōkai, 1990), 116; Zeiganbō Shinjō, *Juhō yōjinshū*, quoted in Moriyama, ibid., 531.

50. See the text quoted in Mizuhara, *Jakyō Tachikawaryū*, 122.

51. See, for example, the *Kakoe menju ki*, quoted in ibid., 128.

52. Ibid., 96.

53. *Hōkyōshō* (T 77), in Mizuhara, ibid., 95.

54. Mizuhara, ibid., 95.

55. On esoteric ideas about embryology and gestation, see James H. Sanford, "Wind, Waters, Stupas, Mandalas: Fetal Buddhahood in Shingon," *Japanese Journal of Religious Studies* 24, nos. 1–2 (1997): 1–37.

56. Mizuhara, *Jakyō Tachikawaryū*, 112–113.

57. Moriyama, *Tachikawaryū jakyō*, 12.

58. Shinjō, *Juhō yōjinshū*, in ibid., 134, 531.

59. On Tendai *hongaku* thought, see Tada Kōryū et al., *Tendai hongakuron, Nihon shisō taikei*, vol. 9 (Tokyo: Iwanami, 1973); Tamura Yoshirō, *Hongaku shisōron* (Tokyo: Shunjūsha, 1991).

60. *Kankō ruijū*, fasc. 1, in *Nihon bukkyō zensho* (Tokyo: Suzuki gakujutsu zaidan, 1970), 17:6.

61. *Kankō ruijū*, fasc. 2, in ibid., 40–41.

62. Tamura, *Hongaku shisōron*, 197.

63. *Hōkyōshō*, in Mizuhara, *Jakyō Tachikawaryū*, 83; see also Moriyama, *Tachikawaryū jakyō*, 132–133.

64. See, for example, Iyanaga Nobumi, "*Ḍākinī* et l'Empereur: Mystique bouddhique de la royauté dans la Japon médiéval," in *Reconfiguring Cultural Semiotics: The Construction of Japanese Identity*, eds. Fabio Rambelli and Patrizia Violi, special issue of *VS (Versus) Quaderni di studi semiotici*, nos. 83/84 (May–December 1999): 41–111; and Tanaka Takako, *Gehō to aihō no chūsei* (Tokyo: Sunagoya shobō, 1993).

65. *Igishū, Shinshū taikei*, vol. 36. According to Kuroda, *Nihon chūsei no kokka to*

shūkyō (210), the text was probably composed in the late Kamakura or the Nanbokuchō periods.

66. *Igishū,* 36:136.

67. Ibid., 36:144.

68. Ibid., 36:135.

69. Ibid., 36:132.

70. Jūren was actually a samurai from the Yamato Genji. See Mita Zenshi, *Seiritsushiteki Hōnen Shōnin shoden no kenkyū* (Kōnenji shuppanbu, 1966), 193, quoted in Taira, *Nihon chūsei no shakai,* 291.

71. *Igishū,* 36:136.

72. Ibid., 36:138.

73. Ibid., 36:132.

74. Ibid., 36:133.

75. Ibid., 36:136.

76. Ibid., 36:152.

77. Ibid., 36:144.

78. Ibid., 36:137.

79. Ibid., 36:140.

80. Ibid., 36:135.

81. Ibid., 36:139.

82. Ibid., 36:141.

83. Ibid., 36:143.

84. Ibid.

85. Ibid., 36:152, 154.

86. Ibid., 36:141.

87. Ibid., 36:141, 156.

88. Ibid., 36:156.

89. Ibid., 36:136.

90. Carlo Ginzburg, *The Cheese and the Worms: The Cosmos of a Sixteenth-Century Miller* (Baltimore: The Johns Hopkins University Press, 1980).

91. Ibid., 68.

92. Ibid., 17.

93. Ibid., 10.

94. Ibid.

95. Ibid., 12.

96. Ibid.

97. Ibid., 39.

98. Ibid.

99. Michel de Certeau, *The Capture of Speech and Other Political Writings* (Minneapolis and London: University of Minnesota Press), 1997.

100. Ishida Mitsuyuki, *Ianjin* (1951; reprint, Kyōto: Hōzōkan, 1978), 18.

101. Michael Holquist, introduction to *Rabelais and His World,* by Mikhail Bakhtin (Bloomington: Indiana University Press, 1984), xviii.

102. Ibid., xix.

103. Bakhtin, *Rabelais and His World,* 19–20.

104. Ibid., 370–371.

105. Ibid., 376.

106. Ibid., 380.

107. Ibid., 318.

108. Ibid., 336.

109. It is important to note, however, that sex and other transgressions of the precepts were the objects of the most secret doctrines and rituals of institutional Buddhism: the radical Amidists raided the *sancta sanctorum* of the religious establishment, thus revealing that the king was naked, as it were. In this way, their doctrines produced a radical critique of the system. Radical Amidists' thought and practice also emphasized the sanctity of everyday actions, which is in keeping with Tendai and Shingon initiatory teachings concerning *musōkan,* the visualization of everyday practices as manifestations of the absolute.

110. Jien, *Gukanshō,* 86:294–295. Translation from Brown and Ishida, *The Future and the Past.*

111. Ibid.

112. Dobbins, *Jōdō Shinshu,* 16.

113. Hōnen, *Ichinengi chōji kishōmon* (Pledge to prohibit the single nenbutsu doctrine), quoted in Dobbins, ibid., 51.

114. Ibid.

115. James C. Scott, *Domination and the Arts of Resistance: Hidden Transcripts* (New Haven and London: Yale University Press, 1990), 4.

116. Ibid.

117. Ibid., 9; see also p. 14.

118. Ibid., 68.

119. Ibid., 81.

120. Mizuhara, *Jakyō Tachikawaryū,* 127.

7

Ungo Kiyō's Ōjōyōka *and Rinzai Zen Orthodoxy*

RICHARD M. JAFFE

SOMETIME IN THE second month of 1649, according to the *Ungo Oshō nenpu* and the *Ungo Oshō kinenroku* (hereafter *Kinenroku*), the Rinzai Myōshinji branch cleric, Nanmyō Tōkō, entered a printer's shop in Kyoto. A dharma heir of the Myōshinji-ha cleric, Ungo Kiyō (1582–1659), Nanmyō purchased the printing blocks of his master's increasingly popular poem, the *Ōjōyōka* (Essential song concerning rebirth in the Pure Land) and proceeded to burn them. On that occasion Nanmyō wrote the following verse: "In order to destroy wrong views from all directions, a debate over true and false rages in the world./At dusk a single torch, then after the smoke rises/the bell peels four or five times, splitting the cold clouds."[1]

As the verse indicates laconically, Nanmyō had been prompted to destroy his teacher's work by the heated controversy over Ungo's use of nenbutsu practice to teach his powerful lay patrons in the Sendai region surrounding the temple he had revived, the Zuiganji, in Matsushima. Composed in 1649 at the request of the Yōtokuin (née Tamura no Megohime, 1568–1653), the ordained widow of the former lord of the Sendai domain, Date Masamune (d. 1658), the *Ōjōyōka* was printed that same year. The work proved remarkably popular, judging from the well-worn printing blocks that survive and the vehement reaction of the Myōshinji establishment.[2] Arguing that the Myōshinji branch of Rinzai was a school of "direct pointing and straightforward transmission" *(jikishi tanden),* the Myōshinji leadership had declared all other teachings, including Ungo's use of the recitation of Amida's name, to be shallow and provisional. Why should Ungo throw away the true teachings of Zen and substitute clearly inferior ones, thereby embarrassing the school, they asked? The Myōshinji leadership threatened Ungo with expulsion from the school and warned him that he would be stripped of his clerical rank and his robes should he continue to disseminate his nenbutsu poem.[3]

Written at a time when there was a growing interest among Japanese Zen clerics in the eclectic Chinese Chan brought to Japan by such expatriate teachers as Daozhe Chaoyuan (1602–1662) and Yiran Xingrong (1601–1668), Ungo's advocacy of nenbutsu chanting for the laity proved incendiary. The hard line rejection of the use of the nenbutsu by a Rinzai cleric should come as no surprise to those familiar with the vociferous debate between the followers of Ingen Ryūki (Chn. Yinyuan Longqi, 1592–1673), who brought Ming-style Chinese Linji Chan to Japan, and the Rinzai Myōshinji leadership. The attempt to combine Rinzai Zen with Pure Land practice also was resoundingly condemned by the great Rinzai systematizer, Hakuin Ekaku (1686–1769), who wrote that those who "combined Pure Land with Zen are as common as hemp and millet." Their distortion of the teachings, however popular, Hakuin noted, would not go unpunished. "How do they feel about the torture of having their flesh pared off and their bones ground to pieces, of drinking molten copper and swallowing balls of iron. If they give it some thought it will make their hair stand on end."[4] No doubt Ungo would have felt he was getting off easy with the threat of mere expulsion from the Myōshinji branch, if Hakuin's predictions concerning the fate of those who mixed nenbutsu and Zen practice were true.

Ungo's advocacy of the use of the nenbutsu preceded Ingen's arrival in Japan by approximately five years. Along with such other well-known members of the Myōshinji branch as Isshi Bunshu (1608–1646), whose Zen was colored by his pre-Zen study of the Vinaya under the Shingon teacher, Kenshun Ryōei (1584–1657), and Daigu Sōchiku (1584–1669), who oversaw the revival of the Daian-zenji in Echizen, Ungo is one of a small, but influential group of Myōshinji branch clerics that attempted to revive the fortunes of their stream of Zen just before Chinese Chan influence reached another apogee in the Japanese Buddhist world. Together, Ungo, Daigu, and Isshi began a series of reforms at the periphery of the Rinzai world, thereby helping to catalyze the formation of modern Rinzai Zen.[5]

Ungo Kiyō began his Zen training during the chaos of the late sixteenth century, as a succession of increasingly powerful warlords struggled to unify Japan. The son of a mid-level samurai in Tosa,

Ungo was ordained in 1596 and began training at a subtemple of the Rinzai Zen temple Tōfukuji in Kyoto the following year. By 1600 Ungo had transferred his allegiances to the Myōshinji branch of Rinzai, moving from the Tōfukuji to Myōshinji to study under Itchū Tōmoku (1552–1621) at the *tatchū* Bantōin, from whom he received certification as a Zen teacher in 1614.

Not entirely satisfied with the training at Myōshinji, Ungo joined a group of young monks, including Gudō Tōshoku (1577–1661) and Daigu Sōchiku, two men who came to dominate the Myōshinji establishment, on a pilgrimage to find an enlightened teacher. It was during his travels through Japan that Ungo met a number of influential samurai who, shortly thereafter, became his patrons, granting Ungo successive abbacies of temples in Wakasa, Shikoku, and Aizu. Ungo's reputation as a Zen teacher, poet, and calligrapher spread among influential samurai and court nobles. By 1621 Ungo had served as abbot of Myōshinji and in 1634 the retired emperor, Gomizuno-o (r. 1611–1629.), an ardent Zen patron, invited him to lecture about Zen at court. In 1636, the lord of the Sendai domain, Date Tadamune (d. 1658), honoring the wishes of his late father, Date Masamune, invited Ungo to assume the abbacy of their family memorial temple *(bodaiji),* the Zuiganji in Matsushima.

The Zuiganji originally was established as a Tendai temple, Enpukuji (a) in 828 and became a Tōfukuji branch temple, Enpukuji (b), in 1259. The name of the temple was changed to Zuiganji shortly after Date Masamune became lord of Sendai in 1600. As part of his effort to consolidate power in Sendai, Masamune and his son-successor, Tadamune, constructed or renovated a number of important ritual-religious centers, both shrines and temples, in the Sendai region. These include the Sendai castle, the Ōzaki Hachiman shrine, Shiogama shrine, and, somewhat later, the branch Tōshōgū shrine. The Date family's efforts to construct a network of religious centers in their domain extended to Matsushima, where they undertook the construction of the Godaidō and the reconstruction of Zuiganji, which began in 1604 and continued until 1609. The renovation of the clan temple was an important component in affirming Date hegemony in the region.

In addition to serving as an important ritual center for the Date clan, Zuiganji also became a monastic training temple. The creation of a monastic center at Zuiganji proceeded with full Date support.

After Ungo arrived in Matsushima in 1636, Tadamune increased the temple's annual rice allotment and sponsored the construction of a residence hall for monks *(sōryō).*[6] At the same time, Ungo attempted to establish strict monastic Zen practice at the temple. One of the first acts undertaken by Ungo after assuming the abbacy at Zuiganji was to promulgate a series of rules to be followed by all monks. These regulations include prohibitions against killing animals, cutting timber on temple lands, consuming liquor or any of the five forbidden plants, disloyalty or unfiliality, and having women within the temple except during *Bon* and *higan.* In addition to banning activities inconsonant with monastic practice, Ungo also urged trainees to energetically engage in the regular periods of Zen meditation, liturgy, and cleaning the temple grounds.[7] Tadamune promulgated the rules suggested by Ungo to the monastic community, an explicit warning that transgressors would have to answer to the domainal as well as the temple authorities.

During his career Ungo took a keen interest in making the Buddhist teachings accessible to the laity and to his female disciples as well as to the male clerics that trained under him. His activities included preaching at the imperial court, distributing calligraphic autographs that summarized the teachings or contained the name of a buddha or bodhisattva, and lecturing. One of the closest relationships that Ungo formed with his patrons in Matsushima was with Masamune's widow, Tamura no Megohime (1567–1652). Following her husband's death in 1636, she entered the Buddhist path *(rakushoku),* taking the name Yōtokuin. In 1640, Tamura was ordained by Ungo and, when Ungo stepped down from the abbacy of Zuiganji in 1648, he became the founding abbot of the Yōtokuin, the eponymous subtemple cum residence for Yōtokuin that was completed in 1650. The *Ōshū meisho zue* relates that the Yōtokuin's name when she entered the Buddhist path following Masamune's death was Eian Jushō Nikō. The text also describes that in addition to the sculpture of the Yōtokuin, which was dedicated by Ungo in 1650, there also was a splendid statue of Amida, which served as Yōtokuin's protective deity. Both sculptures eventually were enshrined within Yōtokuin's mausoleum, the Hōkaden, at the subtemple.[8]

According to both the *Ungo nenpu* and the *Kinenroku,* Ungo's most famous work, the *Ōjōyōka,* was composed on behalf of Yōtokuin. In the tenth month of 1649, according to the *Kinenroku,* Ungo visited Yōtokuin in Edo, where she was in residence. The record continues:

> Yōtoku the wife [of Date Masamune] earnestly requested a quick means to enter the Way. The Master [Ungo], in accordance with the causes and conditions [of rebirth] shown to Vaidehī by the World Honored One, urged her to strive for rebirth in the Pure Land. For this reason, Ungo later composed a didactic poem *(dōka)* of one hundred lines. The poem consists of one hundred eight *waka* divided into three sections. Each section contains [thirty-]six *waka;* at the beginning and end of each section there is homage to the Buddhas and a verse dedicating the merit [accrued by chanting the poem] *(ekō).* At the beginning of each *waka,* the six-syllable sagely name [*Namu-Amida-butsu*] is chanted six times. Thus in the entire one hundred eight *waka* the sagely name is repeated six hundred forty[-eight] times altogether.[9]

In this passage and in the song itself, we see the intersection of notions of the diminished spiritual capacity of women, the stereotyping of *waka* as particularly appropriate for women, and the story of Queen Vaidehī as an archetype of how the Buddhist teaching might be presented to women. Unlike men, for whom such advanced practices as *zazen* and koan became available with ordination, even for ordained women like Yōtokuin, it would seem, such "easy" practices as the nenbutsu were necessary. According to the passage above and Ungo's later writings, Ungo used *waka* poetry in composing the song, because he regarded this as the best way to reach people of lower spiritual potential. In the *Kaigen seijutsu,* Ungo stated: "In teaching and converting sentient beings of middle or low spiritual potential, it is best to use *waka,* which is easy to listen to and readily understandable, rather than using words and phrases that are difficult to realize and difficult to understand."[10] Ungo explained that *waka* was particularly suitable for Yōtokuin because she was somewhat skilled in writing *waka* herself, even having already exchanged poems about the Buddhist teaching with Ungo. According to Ungo's account, recitation of song had the added advantage of being far less tedious than the simple recitation of the nenbutsu or, even, the performance of an assigned number of recitations using *juzu* (prayer beads). He also stressed this was the best way to achieve a state of "unattached, nondiscriminating nenbutsu" *(mujū munen nenbutsu),* which he took to be the ultimate goal of recitation practice.[11]

Describing the form of the *Ōjōyōka,* Ungo wrote that the one hundred eight *waka* corresponded to the 108 passions *(bonnō)* that afflicted sentient beings and that the song was intended to "wake all sentient beings from the slumber of the one hundred eight passions and cause them to achieve rebirth in the Pure Land."[12] The *Kinenroku* goes on to describe that the *Ōjōyōka* was chanted with Ungo seated in the center of a circle formed by Yōtokuin and her attendants, who would chant in chorus and clap to keep the beat. Later, wherever Ungo went, he is reputed to have divided his disciples into four sections in order to chant the poem.

Ungo provided several reasons for his use of the nenbutsu and the *uta/dōka* genre in both the afterword to the *Ōjōyōka* and his defense of the song, the *Kaigen seijutsu,* a text that was composed in conjunction with the 1650 eye-opening ceremony for a sculpture *(juzō)* of Yōtokuin. In the *Kaigen seijutsu* Ungo wrote that the practice of the nenbutsu was well suited for those incapable of understanding more profound teachings, namely, "women, whose spiritual capacity was inferior," and "commoners, whose spiritual capacity was dull." In his choice of methods for the dissemination of the Buddha's teaching to all people, regardless of their spiritual capacity or predilection, Ungo did not limit himself to nenbutsu and Zen alone in his teaching. In the afterword to the *Ōjōyōka,* he notes that in his teaching he would respond to the spiritual capacity and personality of his students appropriately. "To those who meditate on Amida, I give the nenbutsu; to those who uphold the Lotus, I give the *daimoku;* to those who have faith in Śākyamuni, Bodhidharma, Yakushi, or Kannon I give them each the appropriate name; to those who uphold the precepts, I confer the precepts; to those who use *sanzen* and *mondō,* I instruct them with koan."[13]

Ungo elaborated in more detail on this audience-based flexibility in choosing practices for his disciples in the afterword to the *Ise monogatari,* literally, "The Tale of Curing the World." Building on the analogy of the Buddha as the great physician, Ungo wrote, "With great compassion and mercy, the Buddha had great pity for [the unlimited suffering of sentient beings]. He disregarded whether one was noble or base and wise or foolish. Based on their type, he expounded the teaching; responding to their illness he gave them medicine."[14] A prolific calligrapher, Ungo left behind copious evidence of his willingness to provide simple means of practice to his students and disciples. In the Sendai region at temples associated with Ungo, for example the Zuiganji and the Tōshōji in Sendai, are numerous calligraphic autographs created by Ungo for his lay and clerical disciples. These include such inscriptions as *Namu-Amida-Butsu; Namu-Yakushi-Nyorai; Namu-Kanzeon-Bosatsu;* and others.[15]

The *Ōjōyōka* is an interesting combination of verses emphasizing the immanence of Amida; boilerplate Confucian exhortations of frugality, honesty, filiality, and loyalty; and scathing criticisms of Buddhist clerical decadence, including that of Ungo's own head temple, Myōshinji. Although at times a fairly straightforward song, the meaning of a number of the verses must have been extremely opaque to the laity who chanted the song along with Ungo and his disciples. If the various teachings, doctrines, and allusions present in the song were readily understood by Yōtokuin, we must conclude that she was an extremely learned disciple of Ungo.

The first type of verse in the song, emphasizing the immanence of the Western Pure Land and Amida, presents a fairly typical Zen gloss on Pure Land thought and practice. This interpretation can be seen in a number of Zen and other works that mention the Western Pure Land, including the *Amida hishaku* by Kakuban (1095–1143), which has been studied and translated by James Sanford in this collection, the *Amida hadaka monogatari* by Ikkyū Sōjun, and the *Orategama* by Hakuin Ekaku. Each section of the *Ōjōyōka* begins with a verse, alluding to the *Kanmuryōjukyō,* that states, "When one awakens to Amida Buddha then He is not far away, / when one is deluded then He is in the distant West." Similarly, the *Ōjōyōka* contains such verses as "Since both the Pure Land and Hell are within our hearts, / if an evil thought arises, you should think 'Watch out!'"; and "Oh Matsushima, northern country of the Teaching, the waters of your harbor are the same as the Pure Land's pond waters."

In addition to offering this Zen interpretation of Amida and the Pure Land, the *Ōjōyōka* contains numerous verses that are strongly moralistic and supportive of the social order. In these sections of the song one can see the same fusion of Confucian and Buddhist values that is typical of Japanese popular religious life during the Edo period. This sort of moral exhortation was common in the didactic songs of the day, for example the *iroha uta* (didactic syllabary poetry) written by the Myōshinji cleric Gudō Tōshoku and the important leader of the Sekimon Shingaku movement, Teshima Toan (1718–1786).[16] In particular Ungo emphasizes the importance of loyalty, filiality, and obedience as the keys to both worldly and spiritual success. To that end, he cites the examples of samurai noted for these qualities—Fujiwara no Kamatari and Minamoto no Mitsunaka. Ungo reminds his audience that these moral qualities are essential even for those who seek to leave the world: "Those who are disloyal and unfilial while in the world—their leaving home to practice is peculiar./Those who are loyal to their masters and filial to their parents, even while at home may look forward to enlightenment." At the same time, Ungo also stresses acceptance of the truth of cause and effect as the basis for all moral or spiritual progress. Ungo peppers the *Ōjōyōka* with verses that remind the listener "Don't complain that even though you do good acts evil befalls you. It serves to extinguish the evil karma of former lives" and "Since even the Buddha could not escape the retribution of former lives, it is best for one to receive quickly the retribution of cause and effect."

The combination of Pure Land immanentalism and moral suasion that we see in the *Ōjōyōka* is certainly not specific to Ungo. So widespread was this combination that it can even be seen in the didactic song, *Gudō Kokushi Iroha uta,* composed by Ungo's most ardent critic, Gudō Tōshoku. Like the *Ōjōyōka,* Gudō's poem, which consists of sixty-two *waka,* was written to provide the laity with an easily understandable description of Zen practice. Shun'ō Zen'etsu (1773–1845), who published the *Iroha uta* in 1843, more than a century and a half after Gudō's death, wrote in his introduction, "Although in order to make [his teachings] readily understandable to the laity, [he employed] vulgar language, his meaning was extraordinarily profound."[17]

Ungo's and Gudō's songs reflect many of the same concerns. With regard to the immanence of the Pure Land and Amida Buddha, for example, we find the following verses in the *Iroha uta:* "All believe that Amida resides in the west; none understand that he resides in this very body"[18] and "Although we think that he resides in the infinitely distant West, when we look carefully we see that he is right before our eyes."[19] Ungo describes Amida and the Pure Land in almost exactly the same way. At the beginning of each section of the *Ōjōyōka,* he states, "When one awakens to Amida Buddha then He is not far away, when one is deluded then he is in the distant West." And, in an allusion to the *Mumonkan,* Ungo writes "Every day Zen Master Zuigan called the Master. We should call Amida Buddha, who is not different from this very body."

Like the *Ōjōyōka,* the *Iroha uta* contains a strong imperative to practice kindness and compassion in one's daily life. The practice of these two qualities is tied to the future prosperity of one's family and one's own fate in the next life, just as it is in Ungo's poem. Gudō writes, "If one possesses an open heart that is merciful and compassionate toward all without distinction, then the protection of the *kami* and the buddhas will allow one's descendants to prosper"; and "People who possess the good roots of mercy and compassion will achieve in the next life the flower of comfort and ease." Finally, the *Iroha uta* contains an exhortation of honesty and filial piety that is similar to the one found in the *Ōjōyōka*.

For all his theorizing about the immanence of Amida and his Pure Land, Gudō stopped short of endorsing the recitation of the nenbutsu. He was, in fact, strongly opposed to this practice. His antagonism toward it was exacerbated by the arrival of Ingen Ryūki in Japan. As Ingen's influence in Japan grew, Gudō became more outspokenly rancorous about the use of the nenbutsu by members of the Myōshinji faction, lashing out against both Ungo and Ingen.[20]

Ungo's song does not stop with mere reiteration of Zen–Pure Land immanentalism or Zen-Confucian moral suasion. The *Ōjōyōka* also contains a good dose of vitriol aimed at a corrupt Buddhist establishment that even included Ungo's own Myōshinji branch of Rinzai, especially in the third section of the song. Ungo argues in his song that it is precisely the evil actions of the clergy that cause the laity to act immorally, but the transition from the rather pious or philosophical sections of the poem to these punchy critiques of clerical decadence can be jarring at times. In the song Ungo writes, "It is particularly mournful that these worldly-wise evil teachers use the buddha-vehicle as a means to make a living./ They laud themselves saying, 'In all the world, *I* am awakened.' Oh, the people seeking fame and profit are numerous!" Ungo goes on to spell out the fate of these self-glorifying clerics:

> When people see these elegantly attired monks,
> they regard them as those who enjoy the favor of the Buddhas and *kami*—how laughable this is!
> These corrupt, thieving, and elegantly attired monks,
> will inevitably become the dregs of hell.
> Oh Buddha! The monks of this age are, more than an ordinary layperson, ignorant of cause and effect and enlightenment.
> The idiocy of these monks, who, not knowing of the King of Death's transcendental faculty of the heavenly eye, bilk the parishioners.

Ungo even bemoaned the state of his own Myōshinji branch of Zen, lamenting, "Oh Buddha! The Udambara flower does not bloom in this corrupt world, / and the briars of the false teachings proliferate. The grasses and trees on Hanazono's Mt. Shōbō—/I wish that they would be as fine as in the springs of old." In conjunction with the other verses, like those above, condemning clerical corruption, Ungo painted a bleak picture of contemporaneous Zen practice in Japan. Like such other dissatisfied Myōshinji clerics as Ryōkei Shōsen (1602–1670), Isshi Bunshu, and Tangetsu Shōen (1607–1672), Ungo regarded the condition of practice—particularly of the precepts—at Myōshinji with dismay. Unlike these other clerics, however, Ungo did not become an open partisan of Ingen after the Chinese cleric's arrival in Japan in 1654. In fact, Ungo does not mention Ingen in any of his writings, although he did not die until 1659, five years after Ingen's arrival in Japan and at the height of tensions between supporters of Ingen and his opponents within the Myōshinji sect. Given the rather arcane nature of some of Ungo's references to the state of Myōshinji Zen, it is difficult to believe that Ungo's lay followers would have understood them fully. What is clear, however, is that such comments must have goaded some members the Myōshinji establishment to demand the retraction of the *Ōjōyōka.*

Apart from the story mentioned above concerning Nanmyō Tōkō's burning of the printing blocks of the song, little direct evidence exists of hostility toward Ungo and the *Ōjōyōka.* It is clear that Gudō Tōshoku, a very influential leader of the anti-Ōbaku faction that emerged within the Myōshinji sect following Ingen's arrival in Japan in 1654, was dismissive of both Isshi Bunshu and Ungo because of the purported similarities between their understanding of Zen practice and the form of Chan introduced to Japan by Ingen and other Chinese expatriate teachers in Japan. In the *Daien Hōkan Kokushi nenpu,* Gudō is recorded in 1655 to have said to Jikuin Somon, an early supporter of Ingen's, "Ungo already chants the nenbutsu. Ingen also chants the nenbutsu. Even if I were to fall into the bottom of the eighty thousand hells, I would [practice] the Zen of the Teachers and Patriarchs."[21]

Although little remains of the attacks on the *Ōjōyōka* by Gudō and others, Ungo devoted considerable effort to defending his song. Several of his later writings are devoted to arguing for the validity of his use of the *Ōjōyōka* and the nenbutsu. The afterword contained in the Enpō 9 (1681) edition of the *Ōjōyōka;* the lengthy *uta, Ise monogatari* (particularly the prose section entitled "The Perfect Prescription for Curing the Myriad Ills"); and the 1650 *Kaigen seijutsu;* all provide us with ample glimpses of the sorts of criticisms directed at Ungo. To cite one straightforward example, in the concluding section of the *Ise monogatari,* Ungo presents a fictional interlocutor who asks why Ungo has failed to speak of the benefits of Zen teachings but rather has chosen to mislead people with talk of rebirth in the Pure Land. The interlocutor continues, "Do you think that the nenbutsu is superior to *zazen?*"[22] Similarly, in the *Kaigen seijutsu* another of Ungo's fictional interlocutors asks "Bodhidharma came from the West [and advocated] a special transmission outside the teachings; not setting up words and letters; direct pointing at the mind; and seeing one's nature and achieving Buddhahood. Why do you promote reading the *Yōka* to achieve rebirth in the Pure Land?"[23]

In defending the *Ōjōyōka,* Ungo relied heavily on both numerous examples of Chinese advocates of mixed nenbutsu-Chan practice and a handful of Japanese clerics, many of whom were not technically members of the Zen school. In these works, Ungo cites such important figures as Bodhidharma (d. 536?), Huineng (638–713), Yongming Yanshou (904–975), Zhongfeng Mingben (1263–1323), and Myōan Eisai (1141–1215). Hirano Sōjō observes that Ungo was particularly influenced by the two prominent proponents of dual Zen-nenbutsu practice *(Zenjō yūgō),* Yongming Yanshou and Zhongfeng Mingben.[24] Hirano also points out that in composing the detailed afterword of the *Ōjōyōka,* Ungo relied heavily on another important Ming work, the *Guiyuan zhizhi ji,* written by Yiyuan Zongben (Ming), a Tiantai cleric who was a prominent advocate of the dual practice of Chan and *nianfo* recitation.[25] Interestingly, several of the works cited by Ungo—the *Guiyuan zhizhi ji* and Zhongfeng's *Tianmu Zhongfeng Heshang guanglu*—were available in Japanese editions printed during the Kan'ei era (1624–1644). During that period, there appears to have been a spike in interest in Zhongfeng's work, which had at least six separate printings between 1627 and 1643.[26] The republication of these Chinese Buddhist texts, some of which had been in Japan since the Muromachi period, at the start of the Edo period is another indication of the "Chinese turn" in Japanese Zen that culminated with Ingen's arrival in 1654 and the general boom in the commercial reprinting of Buddhist texts.[27]

Ungo does not seem to have been aware of more recent Chinese advocates of dual practice, however. For example, he does not cite such prominent proponents of nenbutsu as Yunqi Zhuhong (1535–1615) and Lin Zhaoen (1517–1598), even though Suzuki Shōsan (1579–1675), another Zen cleric who advocated the use of the nenbutsu and an acquaintance of Ungo's, refers to Lin in his own writings. It is even more surprising that Ungo never refers to the most prominent advocate of Zen-nenbutsu practice in Japan, Ingen, or any of the other Chinese Chan masters that had made their way to Japan during Ungo's lifetime.

In choosing various passages from previous Chan advocates of nenbutsu practice, Ungo emphasized the immanentalist perspective of the *Ōjōyōka* and pointed to the nonsectarian nature of nenbutsu practice. To this end, for example, Ungo quotes Zhongfeng Minben and then elaborates his own position concerning the use of the nenbutsu:

> Master Zhongfeng writes, "that which is called 'Pure Land' is Mind. That which is called 'Zen' is also Mind. Although they are of one substance, they have two names. Those who are deluded cling to their names, those who are awakened achieve [an understanding of] their substance."[28] I "transmit but do not innovate, I am truthful in what I say and do not innovate."[29] Therefore, next to the name [of Amida], I always have written, "If one is deluded then the land is distant; when one is awakened, then it is not far." How could this contradict the intentions of the Patriarchs?[30]

Ungo thus points out that his own understanding of Amida and the Pure Land is in line with the thought of his predecessors, especially as expressed in the *Kanmuryōjyukyō* and the *Rokuso dangyō*. In both of these texts, according to Ungo, the understanding of the Pure Land is encapsulated in the statement "When one awakens to Amida Buddha then He is not far away. When one is deluded then He is in the distant West." As James Sanford notes in his discussion of Kakuban's *Amida hishaku,* the stress on Amida's immanence was central to a diverse group of Pure Land theorists, including Kakuban, Ikkyū Sōjun, and the *kakure nenbutsu* tradition that was an important stream of the Jōdo Shin tradition.[31]

In the *Kaigen seijutsu,* Ungo explicitly defines Amida as no different from absolute wisdom, that is, the *dharmakāya.* He also argues that this nenbutsu is not the property of a particular denomination of Buddhism:

> "Amida" means "limitless life" *(muryōju)* in Sanskrit and in Chinese. "A" is "without"; this means emptiness and is replete with the virtue of wisdom. "Mi" is "measure"; this means provisional [phenomena] *(ke)* and is replete with the virtue of liberation *(gedatsu)*. "Da" is "life"; this means the middle way *(chūdō)* and is replete with the virtue of the *dharmakāya*'s eternal existence.[32] Furthermore, as above [the three syllables] indicate the three bodies—*dharmakāya, saṃbogha-kāya,* and *nirmāṇakāya*—and the three jewels—Buddha, Dharma, and Sangha. In the three characters virtues as numerous as the sands of the Ganges are fully present. When the Three Truths and the Three Bodies, and so on, are present in a single thought, this is Amida residing in the essential nature of a person *(honshō no Amida)*. Again, this can be called the lotus flower of the purity of one's essential nature *(jishō sōjō no renge)*. This Amida is not the Amida of one school or one person. This Pure Land also is not the Pure Land of a particular school or one place. It is the Amida of all sentient beings and the Pure Land of the ten directions and the three worlds.[33]

In addition to defending the immanentalist understanding of the nenbutsu and the use of the nenbutsu as nothing more than a form of skillful means, in both the afterword to the *Ōjōyōka* and the *Kaigen seijutsu,* Ungo stresses the importance of following the precepts and adhering to standards of worldly morality—particularly filial piety *(kō)* and loyalty *(chū)*—if one is to be successful in one's practice of the nenbutsu and Zen. Again turning to Yanshou, Mingben, the Korean cleric Hyeon'eung Hyujeong (J. Gen'ō Kyūjō; 1520–1604), and other predecessors to bolster his argument, Ungo concludes that "if one tries to practice Zen meditation *(zenjō)* without avoiding killing, stealing, sexual relations, and lying, this is like steaming sand to make rice or mincing up feces in order to make incense. Even if one has vast knowledge [of Buddhism] it all becomes the path of devils."[34] In the afterword to the *Ōjōyōka,* Ungo also cites the *Kanmuryōjukyō* approvingly, claiming that without the practice of the three meritorious acts *(sanpuku)*—good worldly acts *(sefuku),* precept observance *(kaifuku),* and Buddhist practice *(gyōfuku)* there can be no benefit in either nenbutsu or *zazen* practice.[35]

Ungo's interest in precept adherence was manifest in more than just his writings. I have already noted that one of his first actions after assuming the abbacy at the Zuiganji was to announce publicly that a strict moral standard for clerical behavior at the temple was now in effect. This emphasis on the importance of the precepts for both the laity and the clergy, no matter how awakened, aligned

Ungo closely with the precept-supporting faction within the Myōshinji sect. As a number of scholars have noted, during the early Edo period, the Myōshinji sect was riven with a dispute over the role of the precepts in Zen practice.[36] On one side, such clerics as Gudō Tōshoku, and Daigu Sōchiku asserted that the formal precepts were superfluous once one had fully penetrated the teachings of Zen. On the other side, a group of clerics that included Isshi Bunshu and Ungo, as well as such prominent Myōshinji supporters of Ingen as Nyosetsu Bungan (1601–1671), Ryōkei Shōsen, Tokuō Myōkō (1611–1681), and Dokushō Shōen (1617–1694), advocated strict adherence to the precepts by all Zen practitioners. According to the authors of the *Zōho Myōshinjishi,* at least in part, it was support for Isshi's precept Zen *(jikai Zen)* that united such diverse figures as Ryōkei, Tokuō, and Dokushō behind Ingen, who advocated the practice of full, Chinese-style *Shibunritsu* ordination for Zen clerics.[37] No doubt, Ungo's emphasis on the importance of the precepts and advocacy of nenbutsu recitation affiliated him with the pro-Ōbaku faction, if not in fact, at the very least in the eyes of Gudō and those other clerics who were adamantly opposed to allowing Ingen to gain a foothold at Myōshinji. These fears that clerics like Isshi and Ungo would be supportive of the Ōbaku movement were not entirely baseless. Although neither Isshi (who died before Ingen's arrival) nor Ungo ever explicitly supported Ingen, disciples of both clerics did establish close ties with Ingen and other Ōbaku clerics after the deaths of their own teachers. Both Isshi's student Nyosetsu Bungan (1601–1671) and Ungo's dharma heir and successor as abbot of the Zuiganji, Tōsui Tōsho (1605–1671), were on good terms with Ingen after the deaths of Isshi and Ungo, visiting the Chinese master and exchanging poetry with him. Following Tōsui's death, Ingen even composed a memorial poem on his behalf in response to a request from one of Tōsui's disciples.[38]

Despite the attacks on the *Ōjoyōka* by members of the Myōshiniji establishment that prompted Nanmyō to burn the printing blocks of the text in Kyoto, the song remained popular and available within the Sendai domain from 1650 onwards. Ungo produced a handful of autographs of the text, of which at least three are extant.[39] One copy of a woodblock edition of the song, which Horino contends was printed in 1649, is preserved in the Miyagi Prefecture Library.[40] In addition, one surviving woodblock edition of the song with a foreword was printed in 1650, another slightly different version was printed in 1656, and a third one, with the afterword cited in this paper, was produced in 1681. The fact that one copy of a 1649 edition exists and the song was reprinted again in 1650 in a different woodblock edition, lends credence to accounts that Nanmyō purchased and burned the printing blocks in 1649, thus necessitating reissuing the printed version just one year later. The 1681 version of the song was reprinted in 1777 in an edition that included another didactic song by Ungo, the *Ise monogatari.* Printing blocks for yet another, undated version of the song, different from the Miyagi Prefectural Library edition, are in possession of the Zuiganji. Although a printed version of that edition is not extant, the blocks were used to reprint a version of the song for inclusion in the 1976 reproduction of several versions of the *Ōjōyōka* that was published by Zuiganji. There are numerous minor textual differences between the various editions of the *Ōjōyōka.* The length of the song also differs, with one edition, the *Zuiganjibon,* containing as many as 112 verses. The 1681 version (reprinted with the same printing blocks in 1777), which I have translated here, contains 111 verses.[41] The frequency with which the work was reissued suggests that the song was in some demand throughout the late seventeenth and eighteenth centuries. Katō Shōshun has observed that it is unusual that slightly different versions were issued in 1650 and 1656, a rather short period of time between the production of a new, slightly different set of printing blocks for the song.[42]

Along with the continued reproduction of the song in various forms, the chanting of the *Ōjōyōka* extended beyond the circle of Ungo's immediate lay disciples and became a popular practice in the Matsushima region, where it eventually became known simply as the "Ungo nenbutsu." In the process of its dissemination in the Matsushima region, the chanting of the song became fused with other Tōhoku traditions of *odori nenbutsu* (dancing nenbutsu), *rokusainichi nenbutsu* (precept-observing-day nenbutsu), and *utau nenbutsu* (singing nenbutsu) that were popular in the Edo period. Travel accounts from 1778 and 1822 note that the song was chanted in the Matsushima area on the six precept-observing days *(rokusainichi)* by groups of laymen and laywomen. Watanabe Yoshikatsu has noted by that time the chanting of the song had fused with other traditions of *rokusai nenbutsu* that predated the composition of the song, but the purpose of chanting the *Ōjōyōka* remained purification of the mind to realize the immanence of the Pure Land in this polluted one.[43] The early-nineteenth-century work, the *Ōshū meisho zue,* also contains a woodblock picture of a group of monks chanting the *Ōjōyōka* and describes how the performance of the song had been transformed into a sort of dancing nenbutsu.[44] By the time the *Ōshū meisho zue* was produced, the performance of the *Ōjōyōka* had shifted from the precept days to Bon. During the Bon period, groups of monks, laymen, and laywomen of all ages would come together playing bells and drums, dancing, singing the *Ōjōyōka,* and making offerings of food to their deceased ancestors. The group, initially small, would move from hamlet to hamlet, heading for Matsushima, chanting and dancing along the way. Rice offerings for the ancestors would be collected en route and then taken to Oshima, a small island connected by bridge to Matsushima, where the food would be offered to the spirits of the dead. As the text accompanying an illustration of the Ungo Nenbutsu in the *Ōshū meisho zue* relates:

> Matsushima Nenbutsu Odori (also known as the Ungo Nenbutsu): Only performed at Obon. The National Teacher's 108-verse song is set to a melody and old and young, male and female, gather together. The song is sung in an interesting way, driven along by the accompaniment of bells and small and large drums, while the group goes singing and dancing to various districts. At that time the fog at last is dispersed by the breeze and the phoenix trees hold a bit of dew. Because it is a time of leisure for the country folk, at this village one person, at another village three people, are added to the group. The young women and little children lead and the old men and old women follow after to Matsushima. The rice and coins collected along the way are gathered on Oshima, where they are offered on behalf of the deceased who still have relatives concerned with them. Although this practice would seem to be no different than worldly sport, one has to say that the merit of this skillful means of forming a karmic connection with the Buddha for those people who "while looking at the water cry out that they are thirsty" is not insignificant.[45]

According to Ōba Obuchi, the author of the *Ōshū meishō zue,* by the nineteenth-century recitation of the *Ōjōyōka* only took place once a year at Bon. Thus the song, written by Ungo to make Zen teachings more accessible to the laity and nenbutsu recitation less tedious, over the course of the Edo period had been transformed into a folk practice for propitiating the spirits of the deceased.[46]

The chanting of the *Ōjōyōka* continued in the Matsushima region until at least 1983, when Watanabe Yoshikatsu met and observed several residents who continued to recite the *Ōjōyōka* on certain occasions. At that time only four elderly women recited the song and, according to Watanabe, there were no people training to continue the tradition. By 1983 the *Ōjōyōka* was only performed at the death of the abbot of Zuiganji or as part of either funeral or memorial services for the parishioners of that temple.[47] Even the practice of reciting the song at Bon had ceased. When I began inquiring about the recitation of the *Ōjōyōka* in Matsushima in the late 1990s, according to my informants, there were no longer any people engaging in the practice.[48] During several visits to Matsushima and the Zuiganji I tried to find someone who remembered the way the song was chanted or possessed a recording of its performance but failed to discover anyone. It seems likely that the practice of the Ungo nenbutsu has disappeared with the generations that grew up with the practice.

Conclusions

The early Edo period was a time of widespread experimentation and diversity within the various streams of Rinzai, particularly within the Myōshinji branch. Judging from the literature concerning Ingen's arrival in Japan in 1654, numerous Myōshinji clerics were interested in reforming Rinzai practice. Their efforts to improve Rinzai practice ranged from Isshi's emphasis on adherence to the precepts; revival of strict standards of monastic life at such regional training temples as Daianzenji and Zuiganji; and advocacy of a variety of novel, simple practices like Ungo's nenbutsu or Bankei's "unborn Zen" *(fushōzen)*. With the pacification of most regions of Japan following the ascendance of the Tokugawa regime, daimyo sponsored the rebuilding of regional training temples and clan temples like Daianzenji (supported by the Matusdaira of Fukui domain) and the Zuiganji (overseen by the Date of the Sendai domain). In their attempts to resuscitate their clan temples, powerful daimyo invited well-known Myōshinji clerics to serve as abbots. It was at the behest of Matsudaira Mitsumichi that Daigu Sōchiku assumed the abbacy of Daianzenji and, as I have discussed, Ungo went to the Zuiganji at the request of Date Masamune and his successor, Tadamune. Given that leading clerics like Ungo often returned to Kyoto to serve terms as abbot of the head temple, Myōshinji, no doubt their experiments at reform in regional temples must have had an impact on the conduct of temple life in Kyoto.

Ungo's construction of a simple method of practice for his female patron and disciple, Yōtokuin, was another result of the patronage of elite clerics by powerful regional daimyo. The *Ōjōyōka* is a product of the close ties between the daimyo rulers of Sendai and one of the elite clerics they invited to the region to add prestige to the clan temple and to enhance the practice of Buddhism. That Ungo chose the nenbutsu as the core of the song for those like Yōtokuin, whom he considered of limited spiritual potential, is notable evidence that Pure Land practice and nenbutsu recitation had reached the bedrock of Japanese Buddhism and was not merely the property of the Pure Land schools and Tendai Buddhism. In his discussion of Ungo's *Ōjōyōka,* Hirano Sōjō suggests that Ungo's incorporation of the nenbutsu recitation into the song was actually no more "syncretistic" than the prominent use of *mikkyō* symbols and practices in Rinzai liturgy during the medieval period.[49] As I have noted in

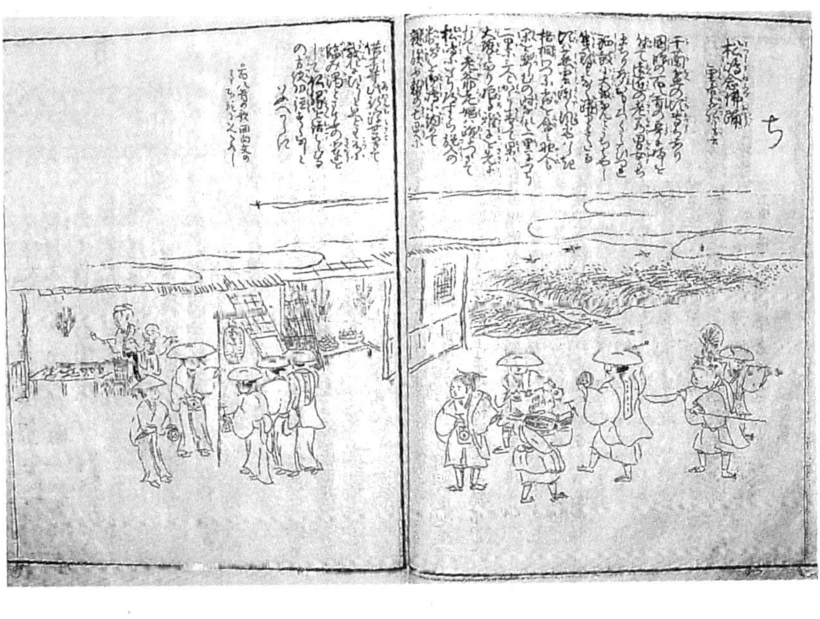

Plate 7.1. Matsushima Nenbutsu Odori. A drawing of the "Ungo Nenbutsu" being performed during Obon. From an autograph manuscript of the *Ōshū meisho zue* by Ōba Obuchi. Courtesy of the Miyagi Prefectural Library.

this essay, Ungo was not the only Rinzai Zen master to incorporate Pure Land imagery or an immanentalist interpretation of Amida in his didactic texts for the laity (the *kana hōgo*). Nor was Ungo the only monk within the Myōshinji faction to employ the *dōka* as a medium of expression. As an image of salvation and easy practice, Pure Land imagery had even penetrated the Rinzai denomination, where such leading clerics as Gudō, Shidō, and Ungo incorporated Pure Land imagery in their didactic songs for the laity.

However, the *Ōjōyōka* could not have appeared at a more unwelcoming juncture in the history of Japanese Zen—just prior to Ingen's arrival, when the allure of Chinese Chan proponents in the Nagasaki area was on the rise. The arrival of a popular, illustrious representative of Chan with legitimate claim to the mantle of Linji forced such Myōshinji leaders as Gudō Tōshoku to define *true* Rinzai practice against the foil of the more all-embracing Chinese Chan. As tensions between the Chinese teacher and his followers and the Myōshinji leadership increased, tolerance for the more inclusive Buddhist practice of Isshi Bunshu and Ungo disappeared. As a result, Ungo's advocacy of the actual chanting of the nenbutsu —as opposed to merely using Amida and the Western Pure Land to illustrate Zen teachings—was denounced as an Ingen-like distortion of the Zen of the teachers and patriarchs.[50]

In recent years a number of scholars have noted the numerous ways that Chinese-style Ōbaku Zen influenced Japanese Zen schools, catalyzing changes in monastic practice and liturgy and rekindling interest in the precepts in both Rinzai and Sōtō Zen.[51] To a degree, the development of "orthodox" Rinzai Zen during the Edo period by members of the one surviving lineage of Rinzai (the Ō-Tō-Kan stream, which flows from Gudō to Hakuin and Tōrei) can be seen as a product of the Myōshinji branch reaction to the Chinese-style Zen brought to Japan by Ingen. Ungo's emphasis on the precepts and monastic reform and his use of writings by numerous post-Song Chinese Chan masters in defense of his use of the nenbutsu is remarkable because it preceded Ingen's arrival in Japan and the struggle between the Myōshinji and Ōbaku partisans by at least five years. In his various defenses of the *Ōjōyōka,* Ungo turned to Chinese Chan and Tiantai works as recent at Yiyuan Zongben's *Guiyuan zhizhi ji,* which was first published in 1553 in China and was reproduced in Japan during the Kan'ei era. As with the Myōshinji-branch partisans of Chinese Chan, Ungo's use of relatively contemporaneous Chinese Buddhist texts demonstrates not only their general availability within early Edo Japan but also their influence within Zen circles.

Despite the rather "unorthodox" practices of Zuiganji's most illustrious abbot, following Ungo's death the temple remained part of the Myōshinji branch. Indeed, at least since the Meiji period the Zuiganji has served as a regional training temple for the Myōshinji branch of Rinzai and the practice there today resembles that of the head temple in almost every important detail.[52] Despite continuing to honor Ungo as the reviver of the Zuiganji and to portray the *Ōjōyōka* as a symbol of the Zuiganji's distinctive history, the song itself is now little more than a historical curio. Ultimately, Gudō's worst fears about Ungo's unorthodox use of the nenbutsu and the threat of Ōbaku Zen were proven wrong. It is therefore fitting that when the Zuiganji reissued a facsimile edition of the undated *Zuiganjibon* woodblock edition of the *Ōjōyōka* in 1976, the printing blocks were sent to the Manpukuji, the head temple of the Ōbaku Zen denomination, to be printed by hand.[53]

The *Ōjōyōka*[54]

I

Homage to the greatly compassionate and greatly merciful
Amida Buddha of the Western Pure Land of Ease and Comfort!
(Namu shihō kirai shikai daizu daihi omitofu)[55]
(repeat three times)

Namu Amida-aa, namu Amidabutsu, namu Amidabutsu, namu Amida-a, namu Amidabutsu, namu Amida-a[56]

When one awakens to Amida Buddha then He is not far away,[57]
when one is deluded then He is in the distant West.
Although the teachings of the three countries are numerous,[58]
none surpasses the teaching of Śākyamuni.
Without exception, in Confucianism, Daoism, and Buddhism,
good receives good retribution and evil receives evil retribution.
From time immemorial people of wisdom have considered the Buddha's Way
to be the teaching that subdues [the passions] in this world and the next.
In every generation among the worthy rulers and subjects of the three countries,
there is no one who does not esteem Śākyamuni's teaching.
Look at those of former generations who have taken refuge in the Three Jewels—

Their nations were at peace and their people were prosperous and happy.
Those who for a single instant enter the True Way,
will have prosperous descendants.
Kamatari Daijin and Tada no Manchū were both
models of those among the nobles and samurai who believed in enlightenment.[59]
For those who are mirrors of people who entered the Way and had future prosperity,
we should look toward the Fujiwara and Minamoto clans.
Models of warriors who left the world to practice
are Dharma Master Saigyō and Kumagai.[60]
Leaving the world means people live in obscurity,
winning fame and achieving *bodai* is [rare like] the udumbara flower.[61]
Look at the merit and virtue of Kumagai's renouncing the world.
He was equanimous toward friends and foes alike; he strove for the accomplishment of buddhahood for both himself and for others.
Those who are disloyal and unfilial while in the world—
their leaving home to practice is peculiar.
Those who are loyal to their masters and filial to their parents,
even while at home may look forward to awakening.
Senjō was filial, loyal and renounced the world.
Truly he was a young samurai without peer.[62]
Leaving the world and practicing the Way are one and the same.
The wise and the foolish both engage in *zazen nenbutsu.*
When I consider the ten monks and eight laymen who were friends,
Mt. Lu of the old days comes to mind.[63]
I have heard that Zen Master Ruman and Bai Juyi of the Tang
both engaged in *zazen nenbutsu.*[64]
Saying that the four great elements and the five *skandha*s are empty—
this is true *zazen nenbutsu.*
In both foreign countries and in Japan becoming a buddha
does not depend on one's sect, but on one's heart.
There are myriad teachings and myriad practices,
so let us each practice our own Way.
Since noble and base, wise and foolish, monk and lay, men and women are all different,
The practice that leads them to awakening should also correspond to each of their needs.
The Buddha's teaching is the true principle of nirvana and enlightenment.
It is the teaching of bliss in this world and the next.
Not knowing the nirvana and eternal bliss of all people,
lamenting the impermanence of birth and death—how pitiful.
Although the buddha-nature is unborn and unextinguishable,
when one is deluded one transmigrates through birth and death.

What is seeing the buddha-nature?
It is understanding the principle of non-arising and non-extinguishing.
When we state what it means to perceive the buddha-nature,
It is grasping the principle of non-arising and non-extinguishing.
When we ask what is awakening to the Buddhist Way,
It is understanding cause and effect and awakening *(bodai)*.
The wise, even when young, diligently practice the Way.
Growing old without knowing enlightenment is folly.
People say "All things are the result of the actions of previous lives,"
but they fail to strive diligently for awakening—how foolish this is.
I have heard that good fortune is brought about by prayer
and misfortune by a failure to enter the door of discretion.
Don't complain that even though you do good acts evil befalls you.
It serves to extinguish the evil karma of former lives.
Even the Buddha and Bodhidharma could not escape the retribution of former lives,
so it is fortunate for one to quickly receive the retribution of cause and effect.
Even people who say "All things are due to the retribution of one's former lives,"
Will be surprised at the moment of truth.
If, however, one has obediently devoted oneself to the single-minded contemplation of Amida's Pure Land,
at the moment of reckoning one's heart will be unshaken.
If people do not even possess the Vow at ordinary times,
how can they cultivate themselves and order their family?
Seeing us now praying for the compassionate vow,
the Buddha criticizes this saying "It is a conditioned thing."
All of the Buddhas have achieved awakening and nirvana
through their compassionate vow.

Ekō: Homage to Śākyamuni Buddha the Original Teacher who eternally abides in the Triple World; to the great saint Mañjuśrī; to the Mahāsattva Samantabhadra; homage to the great compassionate Avalokiteśvara Bodhisattva. We vow to extend the merit [of this recitation] equally to all beings so that they may give rise to an awakened mind-heart and be reborn in the Pure Land.

II

Homage to the greatly compassionate and greatly merciful Amida Buddha of the Western Pure Land of Ease and Comfort!
(repeat three times)

Namu Amida-aa, namu Amidabutsu, namu Amidabutsu, namu Amida-a, namu Amidabutsu, namu Amida-a

When one awakens to Amida Buddha then He is not far away,
when one is deluded then He is in the distant West.
That people who widely disseminate the three teachings of Confucianism, Buddhism, and Daoism
do not enter any path is deplorable.
The failure of people to believe in either cause and effect or enlightenment
is the fault of the monks who violate the precepts.
It is regrettable that the evil monks' sins arise in this manner,
destroying people's aspiration for the Way.
It is particularly mournful that these worldly-wise evil teachers
use the buddha-vehicle as a means to make a living.
They laud themselves saying, "In all the world, *I* am awakened."
Oh, the people seeking fame and profit are numerous!
Seeking fame and profit—this is suffering is it not?
One is used by people and one is used by wealth.
The treasures gathered through immoral action accumulate,
but they cause the body's ruin in this life and the next.
It is said that these treasures cause the body's ruin,
furthermore, this acquisitive heart is fruitless.
Carefully observing those who seek fame and profit,
one sees that they are just creating suffering in this world and the next.
When one changes the heart that seeks fame and profit
and devotes oneself to the truth, then there is enjoyment and bliss in this life and the next.
If one forgets about fame and profit, right and wrong, poverty and wealth, and birth and death,
then for clergy and laypersons alike this very body is Buddha.
When people see these elegantly attired monks,
they regard them as those who enjoy the favor of the buddhas and *kami*—how laughable this is!
These corrupt, thieving, and elegantly attired monks,
will inevitably become the dregs of hell.
Oh Buddha! The monks of this age are, more than an ordinary layperson,
ignorant of cause and effect and enlightenment.
The idiocy of these monks, who, not knowing of the King of Death's transcendental
faculty of the heavenly eye, bilk the parishioners.[65]
Even though one endeavors to uphold the precepts, does *zazen* and nenbutsu,
if one's heart is evil, the karma that results in hell is created.
Those people who uphold the precepts, do *zazen,* and nenbutsu,
and are compassionate and merciful—they will achieve buddhahood.
Compassionate and merciful true patriarchs and teachers who uphold the precepts,
hearing about them, one is deeply moved.

The chap from Shoshadera who picked lice from his robe,
how I long for the days of the venerable monks of the past.[66]
One thought of compassionate truth becomes a seed,
that causes the nine grades of Lotus to blossom.[67]
The spring flower of the three assemblies will also come from the seed of mercy and
compassion in this world.[68]
Oh Buddha! The udambara flower does not bloom in this corrupt world,
and the briars of the false teachings proliferate.
The grasses and trees on Hanazono's Mt. Shōbō—
I wish that they would be as fine as in the springs of old.[69]
Since today the Way of Heaven and Earth is unchanged,
even we of the latter age may also look forward to awakening.
Śākyamuni and Amida were originally people,
and we have human form as well, haven't we?
It is said that Bodhidharma, Baozhi, and Avalokiteśvara
were identical because they all possessed a compassionate and merciful heart.[70]
How unfortunate it is that evil thoughts arise easily, but a compassionate and
merciful heart is difficult to put forth.
Since both the Pure Land and Hell are within our hearts,
if an evil thought arises, you should think "Watch out!"
It is said that although the faults of others are easy to discern,
even a wise person finds it difficult to discern their own faults.
Inquire about the Way from the true person who is merciful and compassionate in
both mundane and supramundane matters.
Even if one says "This does not appeal to me,"
be quick to conform to the admonition of others.
In any circumstance, defying the wishes of others
is an obstacle to both the Buddha's teaching and the worldly law.
I understand that laying down one's life to save birds and beasts
was the practice of Śākyamuni before he became a buddha.
Above all else, clerics laud the practice of Sadāparibhūta,
who was unperturbed by anything.[71]
All of the buddhas and bodhisattvas ride
upon the wheel of their vows, ferrying sentient beings to salvation.

Ekō: Homage to Śākyamuni Buddha the Original Teacher who eternally abides in the Triple World; to the great saint Mañjuśrī; to the Mahāsattva Samantabhadra; homage to the great compassionate Avalokiteśvara Bodhisattva. We vow to extend the merit [of this recitation] equally to all beings so that they may give rise to an awakened mind-heart and be reborn in the Pure Land.

III

Homage to the greatly compassionate and greatly merciful
Amida Buddha of the Western Pure Land of Ease and Comfort!
(repeat three times)

Namu Amida-aa, namu Amidabutsu, namu Amidabutsu, namu Amida-a, namu Amidabutsu, namu Amida-a

When one awakens to Amida Buddha then the Pure Land is not far away,
when one is deluded then He is in the distant West.
When one hears of the teachers of old, they were compassionate, merciful, and equanimous,
When one asks about teachers today, they are prideful, mean, and greedy.
Oh Buddha, the people of today who are said to be awakened,
they are nothing more than nihilists.
People who mistakenly take the defilements to be enlightenment,
and create sins are deplorable.
The defilements are enlightenment—
this is found in a single instant of dedicating the merit of one's practice to others.
Buddha-nature is neither form nor shadow,
where could dust alight?[72]
The buddha-nature and the four great elements combine and the body emerges,
in this way the dusts of the five desires are attracted.[73]
Originally, even the mindless and formless true Buddha
was an ordinary person who was subject to the five desires.
Although one possesses a corporeal body, when the mind of an ordinary person does not exist,
this is the formless true Buddha of the original emptiness.
Regardless of whether the true Buddha has form or not,
because it lacks the four characteristics of existence it is formless.[74]
The heart that does not cling to anything,
is without form, discriminative thought, and abiding.
The patriarchs and teachers say that in the emotions of an ordinary person *(bonjō)* there is discriminative thought,
but in the emotions of the saint *(shōjō)* there is no discriminative thought.
Is the mind-heart not a subtle and divinely possessed thing?
It embraces heaven and earth and penetrates even the subtlest dust.
If the four holy ones and six ordinary type of beings emerge from mind,
then how do we create the action that results in the [three] evil realms?[75]
The evil waters of all people's greed, hate, and delusion,
form a stream of the great river of the three lower destinies.

Depart from the high peak of the road that leads to Yama's Palace,
which is the accumulated dust formed from the sins of the six senses.[76]
In a single instant the cloud of delusion arises,
and this becomes the dark path of transmigration for an eternal *kalpa*.
The nenbutsu that is recited while waiting for the moon of the Pure Land during the night,
is like the west wind of autumn that dispels the clouds and fog.
For the body deeply penetrated by the dew and frost of the karmic obstacles,
zazen and nenbutsu become the sun of wisdom.
The actions with which this old body has passed its days
are offering incense and flowers, chanting the sūtras, *zazen,* and nenbutsu.
When we fail to live up to our words,
in our heart we feel shame.
Even if one fails to conform to the teachings of the sūtras or the teachings of the patriarchs,
be aware that "life and death are a great matter."
Not seeking awakening, not seeking intellectual understanding,
we need only rely on the teachings of all the buddhas.
Refrain from doing all evil, strive to do all good,
purify your own mind, this is the teaching of all the buddhas.[77]
When people rely on the teaching of all the buddhas,
they will return to original emptiness.
"In life one depends [on the body briefly]; in death one returns [to the source],"
this is often seen in the classics of old.[78]
Travel is a painful thing.
How vain it is to deplore the return to the emptiness that is our old home!
Without any hindrances, one returns to original emptiness.
This is commonly called "rebirth in the West."
To be reborn in the original emptiness of the West
and to become the Buddha of Infinite Life—this is propitious.
Our Zen school is a teaching outside the scriptures,
it may seem strange to compose the *Ōjōyōka*.
Since in our school there is no teaching that can be rejected,
why cling to one method for saving beings?
Māyā was [reborn in] Trāyastriṃśa heaven and Vaidehī in the Pure Land,
These are instances of the Buddha preaching in accordance with the spiritual capacity of sentient beings.[79]
When one passes today devoted to merriment,
one necessarily will suffer tomorrow.
The bitter practices and good actions of this existence become seeds
that inevitably will blossom into comfort and bliss in the next life.

The matters of this life—suffering and happiness—last an instant,
but when one is deluded, the future holds in store eons of
transmigration.
Every day Zen Master Zuigan called the Master.
We should call Amida Buddha, who is not different from this
very body.[80]
Oh Matsushima, northern country of the Teaching, the waters of your
harbor are the
same as the Pure Land's pond waters.
Hearing that the ten directions are the mind-only Pure Land,
if sentient beings work diligently, then this body is Amida Buddha.

Ekō : Homage to Śākyamuni Buddha the Original Teacher who eternally abides in the Triple World; to the great saint Mañjuśrī; to the Mahāsattva Samantabhadra; homage to the great compassionate Avalokiteśvara Bodhisattva. We vow to extend the merit [of this recitation] equally to all beings so that they may give rise to an awakened mind-heart and be reborn in the Pure Land.

Notes

Research for this paper was partially funded by a National Endowment for the Humanities Summer Stipend. I thank Horino Sōshun, Kuniyasu Taisen, and the late Hirano Sōjō for their help in gathering materials for my research. I am grateful to Edward Kamens for his generous assistance with this project.

1. *Ungo Oshō nenpu*, in *Ungo Oshō nenpu*, ed. Hirano Sōjō (Kyoto: Shibunkaku, 1983), 109. (Hereafter *KNR.*) A similar account is found in the *Kinenroku*, in the same volume, 227. According to the *Kinenroku*, Nanmyō burned books *(hanmoto)* at the publisher rather than printing blocks *(ita)*.

2. See, for example, the reprint edition of the *Ōjōyōka* in Hirano Sōjō, ed., *Ōjōyōkashū/Ise monogatari* (Matsushima: Zuiganji, 1976). Hirano notes (p. 143) that although no complete printed versions based on the printing blocks at Zuiganji *(Zuiganjibon)* are extant, the blocks themselves are worn from frequent use. A newly printed version of the *Zuiganjibon* is contained in the Hirano book, pp. 3–23.

3. *KNR* 227, 233.

4. Philip B. Yampolsky, *The Zen Master Hakuin: Selected Writings* (New York: Columbia University Press, 1971), 171–172.

5. For a parallel case study that covers the revival of Daianzenji, see T. Griffith Foulk, "The Forgotten History of a Tokugawa-Period Rinzai Monastery" (paper presented at the annual meeting of the American Academy of Religion, Philadelphia, Pa., November 19, 1995).

6. Horino Sōshun, "Zuiganji No Rekishi," in *Matsushima Zuiganji*, ed. Zuiganji (Ichinoseki: Kawashima Insatsu, 1989), 46.

7. Zuiganji, ed., *Ungo Oshō bokusekishū* (Matsushima: Zuiganji, 1985), 67–68. According to the early-nineteenth-century work, the *Ōshū meisho zue*, when it was

composed the five rules were still posted, in Ungo's calligraphy, outside the main gate of the Zuiganji. The prohibition against allowing women on the temple grounds was expanded in that version of the rules, dated 1648, to include several additional days. The author of the *Ōshū meisho zue* records fourteen days monthly, in addition to *bon* and *higan,* when women were allowed into the main temple compound. See Asakura Haruhiko, ed., *Nihon meisho fuzoku zue, Ōshū/Hokuriku no kan* (Tokyo: Kadokawa Shoten, 1987), 1:310.

8. Ibid., 1:318, describes the subtemple Yōtokuin as it existed in the early nineteenth century.

9. *Kinenroku,* 227. Several scribal errors are found in this portion of the text. The *Kinenroku* states that each section of the poem contains sixty-six *waka.* It also records six hundred forty-six as the total number of repetitions of the nenbutsu.

10. Horino Sōshun, "Ungo Kiyō jihitsubon 'Kadai kaigen seijutsu' ni tsuite," *Zuiganji Hakubutsukan nenpō* 9 (1983): 19; Watanabe Yoshikatsu, "Ungo Nenbutsu ni tsuite," *Tōhoku Daigaku Nihon Bunka Kenkyūsho kenkyū hōkoku,* supp. 14 (March 1977): 45. Horino speculates that the *Kaigen seijutsu* was composed in 1650, the year that the eye-opening ceremony of a sculpture of Yōtokuin took place.

11. Horino, "Ungo Kiyō jihitsubon," 9.

12. Ibid.

13. Hirano, ed., *Ōjōyōkashū/Ise monogatari,* 55; Watanabe, "Ungo Nenbutsu ni tsuite," 47.

14. Hirano, ed., *Ōjōyōkashū/Ise monogatari,* 124.

15. See, for example, Ungo's calligraphic autographs of the names of Amida, Kannon, Śākyamuni, Bodhidharma, etc., in Zuiganji, ed., *Ungo Oshō bokusekishū,* 50–58. Hirano notes (p. 181) in the case of the autographs of Kannon's name that these were frequently presented to clerical and lay disciples of Ungo. Many of them are well worn, apparently from use as images of veneration in various altars.

16. For Gudō, see Furuta Shōkin, "Zensō no uta," in *Zensō no seishi, Furuta Shōkin chosakushū* (Tokyo: Kōdansha, 1971), 6:403–407. For Teshima, see Janine Anderson Sawada, *Confucian Values and Popular Zen: Sekimon Shingaku in Eighteenth-Century Japan* (Honolulu: University of Hawai'i Press, 1993), 123–140.

17. The full title of the work is *Gudō Kokushi yonjyūhachiji iroha uta.* The complete text is in Furuta, "Zensō no uta," 403–407. The quote from Shun'ō's introduction is found on p. 402.

18. Ibid., 404.

19. Ibid., 406.

20. Itō Kokan, *Gudō: Nihon no shōto* (Tokyo: Shunjūsha, 1969), 123, 269.

21. Kimura Shungen, ed. *Kundokuhon Gudō roku/Gudō nenpu* (Tokyo: Sekai Seiten Kankō Kyōkai, 1998), 160.

22. Hirano, *Ōjōyōkashū/Ise monogatari,* 121–122.

23. Horino, "Ungo Kiyō jihitsubon," 11.

24. Information on Yanshou's understanding of dual Chan-*nianfo* practice can be found in Heng-ching, Shih, *The Syncretism of Ch'an and Pure Land Buddhism* (New York: P. Lang, 1992), 144–174.

25. Hirano, *Ōjōyōkashū/Ise monogatari,* 145. The *Guiyuan zhizhi ji* is found in Nishi Giyu, Tamaki Kōshirō, and Kawamura Kōshō, 61:424–491. *Shinsan Dainihon*

zokuzōkyō (Tokyo: Kokusho Kankōkai, 1980), For example, Ungo quotes the *Guiyuan zhizhi ji*, 434b, directly in the afterword to the *Ōjōyōka* (Hirano, *Ōjōyōkashū/Ise monogatari*, 59–60). See also, Bandō Shōjun, ed., *Daijō Butten: Chūgoku/Nihon hen, kana hōgo* (Tokyo: Chūō Kōron Sha, 1991), 29:468, n. 145.

26. Komazawa Daigaku Toshokan, *Shinsan Zenseki mokuroku* (Tokyo: Komazawa Daigaku Toshokan, 1962), 64–65.

27. On the republication and importation of Chinese texts in Edo Japan, see, Peter Kornicki, *The Book in Japan: A Cultural History from the Beginnings to the Nineteenth Century* (Honolulu: University of Hawai'i Press, 2000), 153–156, 296–300.

28. According to Katō Shōshun (in *Daijō Butten*, ed. Bandō, 29:469, n. 153), this quotation is found in Zhongfeng's *Tianmu Zhongfeng Heshang guanglu*.

29. *Lunyu*, 7.1. Translation from Confucius, *The Analects*, trans. D. C. Lau (New York: Dorset Press, 1979), 86.

30. Bandō, ed., *Daijō Butten:* 29:299–300; see also, Watanabe, "Ungo Nenbutsu ni tsuite," 47.

31. James H. Sanford, "Amida's Secret Life: Kakuban's *Amida hishaku*," in this collection, p. 124.

32. In this passage Ungo has provided an etymology of "Amida" based on the triple truth *(sandai)* of Tendai: emptiness *(kūtai)*; provisionality *(ketai)*; and the truth of the middle *(chūtai)*. See Hisao Inagaki, *A Dictionary of Japanese Buddhist Terms* (Kyoto: Nagata Bunshōdō, 1984), 275; Nakamura Hajime, Fukunaga Mitsuji, Tamura Yoshirō, and Konno Tōru, eds., *Iwanami Bukkyō Jiten* (Tokyo: Iwanami Shoten, 1989), 323–324. A similar interpretation of the word "Amida" is given by Kakuban in his *Amida hishaku*. See Sanford, "Amida's Secret Life," in this collection, pp. 132–133; and Henny van der Veere, *Kōgyō Daishi Kakuban* (Leiden: Hotei Publishing, 2000), 114–116.

33. Horino, "Ungo Kiyō jihitsubon," 9–10.

34. Hirano, *Ōjōyōkashū/Ise monogatari*, 63.

35. Hirano, *Ōjōyōkashū/Ise monogatari*, 54–55. For the *sanpuku*, see T 12.341c.

36. To cite just a handful of sources that comment on the debate over the precepts in the Myōshinji sect, see Itō Kokan, *Gudō: Nihon no shōtō*, 231; Ogisu Jundō, *Zenshūshi no sansaku* (Tokyo: Shibunkaku Shuppan, 1981), 533–535; Richard Jaffe, "Ingen and the Myōshinjiha," *Komazawa Daigaku Zen Kenkyūsho nenpō* 2 (1991): 17–18, 26; Takenuki Genshō, *Nihon Zenshūshi* (Tokyo: Daizō Shuppan, 1989), 197–204; Helen Baroni, *Obaku Zen: The Emergence of the Third Sect of Zen in Tokugawa Japan* (Honolulu: University of Hawai'i Press, 2000), 128–129.

37. Kawakami Kozan, and Ogisu Jundō, *Zōho Myōshinjishi* (Kyoto: Shibunkaku, 1984), 453–454. Although a number of scholars, including, Itō, Ogisu, and Baroni, have used the term *"jikai zen"* to describe the emphasis on the precepts among such clerics as Ungo, Isshi, Ryōkei, and Ingen, I have not seen that designation used in any of the primary sources about the debate over the precepts within the Myōshinji sect. See, for example, Baroni, *Obaku Zen*, 128–129; Ogisu, *Zenshūshi no sansaku*, 533–535; and Takenuki, *Nihon Zenshūshi*, 197; among others.

38. See Ōtsuki Mikio, ed., *Ōbaku bunka jinmei jiten* (Kyoto: Shibunkaku, 1988), 264–265, for a biography of Tōsui, and 295–297 for a biography of Nyosetsu.

39. At least one autograph of the *Ōjōyōka*, a portion of which is reproduced in

Zuiganji, ed., *Ungō Oshō bokusekishū,* in *Matsushima Zuiganji,* 60–61, is privately held. Another is in the possession of Zuiganji (Hirano, *Ōjōyōkashū/Ise monogatari,* frontispiece) and a third is owned by the temple Tōshōji in Sendai.

40. Horino, "Zuiganji No rekishi," 147.

41. Included in Hirano, *Ōjōyokashū/Ise monogatari,* 3–22.

42. Bandō, ed., *Daijō Butten,* 29:552. In addition to Katō Shōshun's analysis in the Bandō volume, Hirano also describes various editions of the *Ōjōyōka* in Hirano, *Ōjōyōkashū/Ise monogatari,* 143–145.

43. Watanabe, "Ungo Nenbutsu ni tsuite," 49–50; Watanabe Yoshikatsu, "Zuiganji no iō," in *Miyagi no kenkyū, Minzoku/hōgen/kenchikushi hen,* ed. Watanabe Nobuo (Osaka: Seibundō Shuppan, 1983), 7:94–100.

44. Ōba Obuchi, *Ōshū meisho zue,* undated manuscript in the Miyagi-ken Toshokan. The catalog states that the autograph was composed prior to 1821. The picture is found in the fourth volume of the work.

45. *Ōshū meisho zue, kan* 4. The volume is not paginated. The text has been rendered into printed form in Asakura, *Nihon meisho fuzoku zue,* 1:317. Partially cited in Watanabe, "Zuiganji no iō," 98.

46. Watanabe, "Zuiganji no iō," 98–99.

47. Watanabe, "Zuiganji no iō," 94–96.

48. Inquiries concerning the recitation of the song were made during 1996–1997 in Matsushima. I spoke with the former abbot of the Zuiganji, Hirano Sōjō, the current director of the Zuiganji Hakubutsukan, Horino Sōshun, and the staff of the Matsushima Hakubutsukan.

49. Hirano, *Ungo Oshō nenpu,* 23–24. See also Baroni, *Obaku Zen,* 114, 128–129.

50. Kimura Shungen, *Kundokuhon Gudō roku Gudō nenpu* (Tokyo: Sekai Seiten Kankō Kyōkai, 1998), 160.

51. See, for example, Baroni, *Obaku Zen,* 122–164; Michel Mohr, "Zen Buddhism during the Tokugawa Period: The Challenge to Go Beyond Sectarian Consciousness," *Japanese Journal of Religious Studies* 21, no. 4 (1994): 341–72.

52. For a brief description of the practice at the Zuiganji, see Zuiganji, ed, *Zuiganji,* 66–83.

53. Hirano, ed., *Ōjōyōkashū/Ise monogatari,* 143.

54. This translation is based on the annotated Enpō 9 (1681) edition of the *Ōjōyōka* reproduced in Hirano, *Ōjōyōkashū/Ise monogatari,* 24–71. The same text, annotated by Katō Shōshun, is available in Bandō, *Daijō Butten,* 29:279–302. A translation of the afterword is not included here.

55. The publishers of the 1681 edition of the *Ōjōyōka* included *rubi* indicating the Sino-Japanese pronunciation for this sixteen-character phrase. The same exact sixteen-character phrase is used in the *Chokushū Hyakujō shingi* in the sections that cover monastic funerals. See Bandō, *Daijō Butten,* 29:456, n. 3.

56. This six-fold repetition of the name of Amida was to be repeated at the beginning of each verse of the song.

57. The first line of this *waka* is a direct quotation from the *Liuzu Dashi fabao tanjing,* T 48.341b. This line is repeated at the beginning of each section of the poem. The phrase "He is not far away" *(koshi fuon)* is found at the beginning of the *Kanmuryōjukyō,* T 12.341c.

58. India, China, and Japan.

59. Kamatari Daijin is a reference to Nakatomi no Kamako (614–669), better known as Fujiwara no Kamatari. Kamatari, the first patriarch of the Fujiwara clan, was an ardent student of the Chinese classics and an opponent of the Soga clan. The Nakatomi family originally was associated with the recitation of Shinto prayers for the court. Kamatari, however, gave his assent to the use of Buddhism for the protection of the nation during his tenure as advisor *(uchitsuomi)* to the crown prince, Naka no Ōe. Kamatari was a fervent Buddhist who sponsored assemblies for the study of various sūtra and helped fund construction of such temples as Sankaiji, which later became the Kōfukuji.

Tada no Manchū is another name for Minamoto no Mitsunaka (913–997), a military commander during the Heian period. Mitsunaka's descendants prospered during the eleventh and twelfth centuries. Mitsunaka took the tonsure in 970 and founded the Tada no In.

This *waka* should be paired with the subsequent one. Both of these men's families prospered in later generations—according to Ungo this was due to their piety.

60. Saigyō (1118–1190) is one of the most renowned *waka* poets of the late Heian–early Kamakura periods. He was born in the Satō clan as Satō Norikiyo. Although the men in this clan had traditionally become warriors, Saigyō became a monk in 1140.

Kumagai is Kumagai Naozane (1141–1208), a warrior who became a disciple of Hōnen and in 1192 was ordained as a cleric. According to the *Heike monogatari,* Kumagai decided to become a priest after killing Taira no Atsumori during the Battle of Mikusa. See Takagi Ichinosuke, Ozawa Masao, Atsumi Kaoru, eds., *Heike monogatari, Nihon bungaku taikei,* vols. 32–33 (Tokyo: Iwanami Shoten, 1959–1960), 9.16; Helen McCullough, trans., *The Tale of the Heike* (Stanford: Stanford University Press, 1988), 315–317.

61. The udumbara *(udonge)* blossom is a legendary flower that is said to bloom once every three thousand years. The blossoming of this flower is a metaphor for the appearance of the Buddha in the world.

62. This obscure reference to Senjō is probably a reference to Osada Kagemune, son of Osada Tadamune (d. 1180?). Ungo refers to Senjō in a similar verse in the *Ise monogatari* but adds that "Senjō had a father named Osada." See Hirano, *Ōjōyōkashū/Ise monogatari,* 110. According to the *Heiji monogatari,* Tadamune, accompanied by Kagemune, betrays Minamoto no Yoshitomo (1123–1160) by offering him refuge and then murdering him. Tadamune and Kagemune, who is referred to on several occasions in the text as Senjō Kagemune, are both killed by the eventually triumphant Minamoto family. I am uncertain why Ungo cites Senjō as an example of filiality and loyalty here.

63. This is a reference to the Lotus Society of Huiyuan (334–416) and the "eighteen worthies" who were part of that assembly. The Lotus Society was founded in 402 by Huiyuan and 123 monks and laypeople from his community on Mt. Lu. This group gathered on the north slope of the mountain and vowed to be reborn in the Pure Land. For more on the Lotus Society and the "eighteen worthies," see Erich Zürcher, *The Buddhist Conquest of China* (1959; reprint, Leiden: E. J. Brill, 1972), 217–223.

64. Foguang Ruman (d.u.) was a dharma successor to Mazu Daoyi (709–788). He is best known for having been the teacher of the poet Bai Juyi for over nine years. In addition to his involvement with Zen practice, Bai was also an avid practitioner of the nenbutsu. Together with Ruman, he founded the Xianghuoshe, a society for the study of Zen and Pure Land practices. For more on Bai's involvement with Pure Land practice, see Hattori Eijun, *Jōdokyō shisōron* (Tokyo: Busshorin, 1974), 157–158. This pair is often cited in Japanese literature as an example of the confraternity of laypeople and monks. For example, this pair is mentioned in connection with the Kangaku-e (Society for the Promotion of Learning) on Mt. Hiei, a society of monks and laymen that met to discuss sūtras and to meditate. See Edward Kamens, trans. *The Three Jewels,* Michigan Monograph Series in Japanese Studies, no. 2 (Ann Arbor: The Center for Japanese Studies, 1988), 295–298.

65. The transcendental faculty of the heavenly eye *(tengenzū)* enables one to see anything at any distance.

66. Shoshadera is another name for the Engyōji, a Tendai temple in Hyōgo prefecture traditionally held to have been established by Shōkū (917–1007) in 966. Shōkū attracted numerous famous individuals to his temple, including Izumi Shikibu and Fujiwara no Michinaga. The temple became famous for poems commemorating the establishment of a relationship with the teaching *(kechien).* Among the poems created for this purpose is Izumi Shikibu's famous *waka* of the dark path.

67. The Pure Land, like aspirants to the Pure Land, is divided into nine grades. There are nine grades of lotus-seat for the nine grades of aspirants. The lotus plants into which the aspirants are born will bloom slowly or quickly according to their merit.

68. The "three assemblies" is a reference to the *Ryūge san'e,* the three dharma assemblies for the three grades of aspirants (high, middle, and low) that will take place 5,670,000,000 years after the death of the Buddha. This assembly will be presided over by Maitreya Buddha, who will achieve awakening at the foot of a "dragon flower" tree *(ryūgeju).*

69. Mt. Shōbō is the "mountain name" for Myōshinji, the head temple for the Myōshinji faction, to which Ungo belonged. Hanazono refers to the emperor, Hanazono (1297–1348), who sponsored the founding of Myōshinji in 1337. The founder of the monastery was Kanzan Egen (1277–1360). According to a number of Myōshinji branch monks who were Ungo's contemporaries, there had not been a true teacher in Japan since the death of Kanzan. Ungo may be echoing that lament in this verse.

70. Baozhi (Jpn. Hōshi, 418–514) was said to have been a spiritual mentor for Emperor Wu of the Liang dynasty. His biography may be found in the *Jingde chuandenglu,* chap. 27.

This *waka* may be based on a passage found in the *Biyan lu,* case 1 (T 48.140c). After Bodhidharma left the court of Emperor Wu, Baozhi asked the Emperor, "Does your majesty know who that monk is?" The emperor said that he didn't know. Bao responded, "This is the Mahasattva Avalokiteśvara transmitting the Buddha Mind Seal." Yuanwu Keqin's (1063–1135) commentary on this case continues:

> According to tradition, Master Chih died in the year 514, while Bodhidharma came to Liang in 520; since there is a seven-year discrepancy, why is it said

that the two met? This must be a mistake in the tradition. As to what is recorded in tradition, I will not discuss the matter now. All that's important is to understand the gist of the matter. Tell me, Bodhidharma is Avalokiteśvara, Master Chih is Avalokiteśvara, but which is the true Avalokiteśvara? Since it is Avalokiteśvara, why are there two? But why only two? They are legion.

The translation of this passage comes from Thomas Cleary, trans., *The Blue Cliff Record* (Boulder: Prajñā Press, 1978), 5.

71. Sadāparibhūta (Jōfukyō), or the Bodhisattva Never Disparaging, is described in the *Lotus Sūtra (Miaofa lianhuajing),* T 9.50b–51d. This bodhisattva predicted that all would eventually become buddhas. No matter how he was treated by others he would make this same prediction of buddhahood for them.

72. An allusion to the famous verse of the Sixth Patriarch: "Awakening entails no tree at all, / Nor does the clear mirror entail any material frame. / The Buddha-nature is eternally pure; / Where could there be any dust?" (T 48.348b–349a. This translation is from Paul Demiéville, "The Mirror of the Mind," in *Sudden and Gradual: Approaches to Enlightenment in Chinese Thought,* ed. Peter N. Gregory (Honolulu: University of Hawai'i Press, 1987), 13.

73. The four great elements *(shidai)* are earth, water, fire, and wind. In Buddhist cosmology these elements are the basic constituents of the material world. The five desires *(goyoku)* are the five cravings that arise in conjunction with the five sense organs (eyes, ears, nose, tongue, and body [tactile sense]). See the *Miaofa lianhuajing,* T 9.9b. Another list of the five desires lists the craving for wealth, sex, food and drink, fame, and sleep. See the *Dafangguang fohuayanjing,* T 9.426a.

74. The four characteristics of existence (shisō) are birth, abiding, change, and extinction. Another common set of four characteristics is birth, old age, sickness, and death.

75. The four holy ones *(shishō)* refers to the *śrāvaka, pratyekabuddha,* bodhisattva, and buddha. The six ordinary types of being *(rokubon),* or six realms *(rokudō),* are those of hell, hungry ghosts, animals, *asura*s, men, and heavenly beings. The three evil realms *(akushu)* are the animal, hungry ghost, and hell realms.

76. *Shide no yamaji* is the mountain road that the deceased must follow to the palace of Yama, King of Death. Here their sins and merits are weighed and proper retribution is meted out.

77. This aphorism, known as the "the verse of admonishment of the seven buddhas," *(shichibutsu tsūkaige)* is found in verse 183 of the *Dhammapada,* among other places.

78. An allusion to the *Huinanzi,* "Jingshenxun": "People are born from the origins of heaven and earth. They do nothing more than temporarily embody in this transient world. Death is when they leave the transient world and return to the origin."

79. According to legend, one week after the birth of the Buddha, Māyā, his mother, died. Thereupon she was reborn in the Trāyastriṃśa heaven. After his enlightenment, the Buddha ascended to that heaven, where he is said to have expounded the teachings to his mother.

Vaidehī, the wife of King Bimbasara of Magadha, was imprisoned by her son, Prince Ajātaśatru, along with her husband. According to the *Kanmuryōjukyō* (T

12.340–346), Vaidehī was visited in prison by Śākyamuni Buddha, who taught her the meditations needed to visualize the Pure Land. Through these contemplations Vaidehī was enlightened and was promised rebirth in the Pure Land. See Hank Glassman, "'Show Me the Place Where My mother Is!' Chūjōhime, Preaching, and Relics in Late Medieval and Early Modern Japan," in this volume, p. 151.

80. This is a reference to *Mumonkan* (1249), case 12 (T 48.294b). The case reads: "Everday Master Ruiyan Shiyan [Song dynasty] used to call out to himself, 'Oh, Master!' and would answer himself, 'Yes?' 'Are you awake?' he would ask, and would answer, 'Yes, I am.' 'Never be deceived by others, any day, any time.' 'No, I will not.'" This translation comes from Shibayama Zenkei, *Zen Comments on the Mumonkan* (1974; reprint, New York: New American Library, 1975), 93. Ungo's use of Ruiyan is double-edged because the name Ruiyan (Zuigan) is the same as that of Ungo's temple, Zuiganji.

8

From Generalized Goal to Tantric Subordination

Sukhāvatī in the Indic Buddhist Traditions of Nepal

Todd T. Lewis

I did not expect to find any Pure Land Buddhism when I set out for my first research in Nepal Himalayas back in 1979, knowing that scholars had long suggested that the first exponents of Amitābha-Sukhāvatī cosmology were Buddhists of northwest India or Central Asia.[1] I was likewise familiar with the history of Mahāyāna Buddhism, where the evolution of "Pure Land Schools" was a distinctly East Asian development shaped by monastics who assimilated and domesticated Indic textual traditions.[2]

But in 1980, at the close of my second year of fieldwork, a tragedy occurred that brought the "Pure Land" back into view: a vigorous middle-aged man—a leading merchant in the Kathmandu Buddhist community, beloved for his social activism, ecumenical Buddhist faith, and compassionate ways—began losing weight and was diagnosed as having liver cancer. His death within two months was a blow to everyone who knew him. During the procession to the burning *ghat* and at memorial gatherings held in the days following, the heartfelt sentiment expressed by many mourners was formally stated in Newari: *Sukhāvatī bhūvanay lāi he māh* (May he be reborn in Sukhāvatī).[3]

This refrain surprised me. I had never heard any reference to Sukhāvatī spoken by Newar Buddhist householders. I knew belief in Sukhāvatī was certainly not a sectarian orientation in Nepal, nor had it ever been so in ancient South Asia except perhaps for a very small minority. But what were the origins and evolutionary developments associated with Sukhāvatī belief in the Indic Mahāyāna communities? The sad utterances at my friend's funeral indicated that Newar Buddhist traditions might provide insight into this early development or on its place among later Mahāyāna traditions. Accordingly, I sought out other areas in which Sukhāvatī beliefs and practices were found in the surviving traditions of the Kathmandu valley. To comprehend how Sukhāvatī traditions have become domesticated there, the reader must be familiar with Newar Buddhism in its Himalayan context.

Historical Background and Cultural Context

Any scholar who has worked with Indic Mahāyāna texts or later Buddhist iconography knows of the plenitude of Sanskrit manuscripts preserved in the Buddhist and state libraries of the Kathmandu valley. The discovery of these Nepalese manuscripts in the nineteenth century was a landmark in modern Buddhist studies, giving European scholars their first complete overview of Northern Buddhism's vast Indic literary heritage. Because Nepal was largely sealed off from the outside world until 1951, scholars have only recently recognized the value of Sylvain Levi's assertion that other aspects of Buddhist culture *besides texts* might provide insights into the faith's later Indic history, particularly its material culture, rituals, festivals, and the evolution of its Mahāyāna culture.[4]

Despite Newar Buddhism's slow decline over recent centuries, over three hundred Buddhist *vihāra*s (monasteries) still exist,[5] along with *vajrayāna* ritualists, bodhisattva temples, stupas, Mahāyāna festivals, tantric meditation lineages, and pilgrimage traditions related to popular Buddhist stories.[6] Devout Buddhists still form a large proportion of the valley's urban population and being Buddhist remains a vital marker of group identity.[7] This rich cultural survival disproves the old assertion that Indic Buddhism completely died: the Newars in their small but vibrant oasis of tradition continue to practice Indic Mahāyāna-Vajrayāna Buddhism.[8]

Until the modern state's formation in 1769, "Nepal" referred only to a valley roughly twenty miles in diameter and forty-five hundred feet up in the central Himalayan foothills. Safe from military conquest but readily accessible to migrants, monks, and traders, Nepal has welcomed Buddhism since Gupta times. Newar Buddhism is predominantly "Indic," and through Nepal later Indic-Sanskritic Mahāyāna traditions were conveyed to Tibet; at times, Tibetan Buddhist influences have also been strong.[9] In the last four centuries at least, Nepalese Buddhism has had much in common with the domesticated forms of Mahāyāna Buddhism in modern Tibet and Japan—notably, a householder sangha, a special emphasis on death ritualism, and, most preeminently, devotion to the celestial bodhisattva Avalokiteśvara.

Geography shaped the formation of Nepal as an independent state and its predominantly Indicized civilization. The fertility of valley soils allowed for intensive rice and other crop cultivation. The wealth derived from trans-Himalayan trade allowed the people of the Kathmandu valley to import, domesticate, and reproduce many Indic traditions in a distinctive urban civilization organized on caste principles, allowing both Hinduism and Buddhism to flourish. Sanskrit pandits have existed in Nepal for more than a millennium and a half, as well as Hindu temples, Buddhist monasteries, and stupas. The literate elite of the valley also found employment in copying of Sanskrit manuscripts for local patrons as well as Tibetan scholars and their monastic libraries.

After conquest by a Kshatriya dynasty from Gorkha in 1769, state policies favoring Hinduism precipitated the decline of Buddhist traditions, although a great wealth of both devotional and cultural observance still survives. Today, with Kathmandu the capital of the modern state and the center of contact with the outside world, this valley is one of the most complex urban civilizations in Asia. A Mahāyāna-Vajrayāna Buddhist culture is among its most unusual features.

Newar Buddhism

Most Newar Buddhists practice exoteric Mahāyāna devotionalism, directing their devotions to *caitya*s in their courtyards and neighborhoods and to the great stupas such as Svayambhū. They also express a strong devotion to the celestial bodhisattvas and make regular offerings at temples and shrines dedicated to Avalokiteśvara, Tārā, and Mahākāla, among others. Newar Buddhists participate periodically in special ritual and festival observances dedicated to these divinities, who hold the promise of transforming their worldly and spiritual destinies.[10] Most laity also worship other Indic deities: Ganesha, Bhimsen, Shiva, Vishnu, Devī in many guises, *nāga*s, and so on. One strong belief is that worshiping all local deities is the Mahāyāna ideal.

The Newar Buddhist sangha is one of "householder monks" now limited to only two endogamous groups having the surnames Vajrācārya and Shākya. Individual sanghas still dwell in monastery courtyards referred to as *vihāra* (New. *bāhā*), and its members undergo in childhood first the classic celibate ordination, then Mahāyāna-styled initiation into the bodhisattva sangha of householder monks.[11] Like married Tibetan lamas of the Nyingmapa order, as adults the Newar *vajrācārya*s serve the Buddhist community's ritual needs, with some among them specializing in textual study, medicine, astrology, and meditation. David Gellner has aptly characterized Newar Buddhism as a religion dominated by prescribed ritual practices rather than any singular doctrinal formulation.[12] Most Newar Buddhists understand basic Mahāyāna doctrines from the popular *avadāna* and *jātaka* stories about the bodhisattvas and their spiritual virtues (*pāramitā*s). In addition to compiling many recensions of these tales and telling them in public sessions, *vajrācārya*s in the local sangha perform for their community highly sophisticated Buddhist life cycle rites and other rituals at festivals and special observances.

In terms of soteriological practice, the Newar Buddhist tradition also has an esoteric level: *vajrayāna* initiations (Skt. *abhisekha;* New. *dekha*) direct meditation and ritual to tantric deities such as Samvara, Hevajra, and their consorts (*yoginīs*). It is the *vajrācārya* spiritual elite that pass on *vajrayāna* initiations to other high castes, including merchants and artisans; their tantric training forms the authoritative basis of their ritual service to the community.[13]

The Newar laity supports the local *vajrācārya* sangha, which helps them, in return, to look after their spiritual destiny in this world and beyond. In their maintenance of this exchange and in their concern for merit-making, Newars closely resemble lay Buddhists in other countries.

Anthropological Studies in the Modern Study of Buddhism

Drawing on ethnographic research on modern rituals and contemporary Buddhists, this essay intends to contribute to the understanding of faith, death ritual, and paradise rebirth aspiration in the Indic history of Mahāyāna Buddhism. A note on my approach will complete this introductory section.

Buddhist studies has suffered from the limited number of disciplines involved in researching the faith and imagining Buddhist history. The study of Buddhism has been dominated by either philological-textual studies usually distanced and disinterested from the texts' community context(s) or ethnographic studies, growing fewer, that have neglected local literati and literatures.[14] The result has been either highly idealized representations of Buddhism based on a small elite's philosophical definitions and disputations or representations ignoring local literati due to the neglect of the indigenous intellectuals who have translated and interpreted the classical texts for their own specific communities.

The scholarly disinterest in ritual and ritual texts has deprived the field of a key element needed to construct a sociologically informed imagination of Buddhist history. This disinterest has also obscured comprehension of the domestication of texts and how doctrines were applied in the events of "real life," especially childhood, marriage, old age, and after-death contingency.[15] Far from being a "vulgarization" or a "concession" to the masses, ritual in all Buddhist societies has been the fundamental means of applying dharma analysis to acculturate followers (especially the young) or, to use Buddhist terms, to condition individuals consciously and beneficently *(kuśala),* ultimately pointing them toward spiritual maturity and awakening. My hope is that this article will show how the pursuit of data that "flies below the radar" of elite philosophy-centered scholarship can contribute to the development of Buddhist history.

Sukhāvatī Belief in Modern Newar Buddhist Practices

Newar Buddhism, even in its declining state in modern Nepal, is still characterized by a wealth of texts and praxis traditions. Sukhāvatī beliefs are found scattered throughout this Mahāyāna culture in stupa veneration and death rites; they are most evident in the rituals, vernacular texts, and "theology" associated with the celestial bodhisattva Avalokiteśvara (Kwan Yin). Sukhāvatī belief also endures in more distinctly Newar traditions such as old-age life cycle rites and local devotional songs. After surveying these areas in this section, I will describe what seems to have been the historical trajectory of Sukhāvatī beliefs and practices in the context of the Vajrayāna traditions that came to dominate Newar Buddhism over recent centuries.

Stupa Veneration

Thousands of stupas (or *caityas*) mark the urban environment of Newar settlements.[16] Most modern shrines show the later five-buddha symbolism and place each buddha according to a consistent directional orientation. Medieval and modern *caityas* invariably show Amitābha in the west (see Plate 8.1).

Plate 8.1. Typical Newar votive stupa, with Amitābha facing west

As elsewhere in the Buddhist world, a prominent hilltop stupa dominates the local Buddhist landscape. Extant since Licchavi times, Svayambhū stupa to the west of Kathmandu city has been the focus of praxis for Buddhist devotees from throughout the valley as well as across the central Himalayan midhills and Tibet. Hemraj Shākya recorded an oral tradition regarding the original consecration of Svayambhū by Shāntikara, the legendary *siddha* and original Newar *vajrācārya:* "Aparamita Tathāgata, dwelling in Sukhāvatī, came to put into place the Mahācaitya's topmost gold umbrella and its crest jewel *(cūdāmani).*"[17]

Svayambhū has remained a regular destination for pilgrimage and for making offerings at its many associated shrines and *vihāra*s. Today, its ambulatory has niches for the four buddhas, their consorts, and for Vairocana, symbolic of the Adi Buddha. Most Newar patronage at the great stupa, and most *pūjā*s conducted on the hilltop, is done before the Amitābha niche on the west side of the stupa. This preference is also evident in the morning *pūjā* offerings that Buddhist households make at neighborhood *caitya*s: if devotees leave offerings, these are set down before Amitābha and rarely given to any other *tathāgata.* For most Newar laity, the practice is "just our custom." Several commentators did offer a reason for this preference: Amitābha is the *tathāgata* of the current era, the Kali Yuga. This is a point we will return to below.

The Avalokiteśvara Cultus

Besides *caitya* veneration, Newar Buddhism today is focused on devotion to Avalokiteśvara, affectionately called Karunāmaya (Compassionate-Hearted), a celestial bodhisattva who has been integrated into Nepal's devotional life in a variety of ways.[18] Most Newar images of Avalokiteśvara feature the classical Indic iconographic placement of Amitābha affixed on the crown (see Plate 8.2). At major temples images of Avalokiteśvara are located near shrines dedicated to Tārā, reflecting the view, showed in Tibet, that both are emanations from the right and left eyes, respectively, of Amitābha in Sukhāvatī.[19]

Daily veneration of Avalokiteśvara is the most common devotional focus of Newar Buddhists. For most devotees the center of Buddhist activity inside the old city of Kathmandu is the temple in the courtyard of Kanakacaitya Mahāvihāra, called Jana Bāhā in popular parlance. (For this reason, the colloquial term for the bod-

Plate 8.2. Eighth-century image of Padmapaṇi Lokeśvara from a monastery courtyard, Kathmandu

hisattva is *"Jana Bāhā Dyah,"* or "Deity of Jana Bāhā.") Several Sukhāvatī traditions are articulated through rituals, icons, and texts associated with this shrine complex.

The *ratha jātras* of Avalokiteśvara are the most important festivals in the valley, the greatest overall being in Patan-Bungamati and the largest in Kathmandu City, orchestrated for Jana Bāhā Dyah each spring. One reason for assembling a five-story *ratha* and pulling it through the narrow city streets in spectacular fashion is to provide the housebound and the sick with a chance for veneration that will enable them, among other boons, "to be reborn in Sukhāvatī." The Kathmandu Avalokiteśvara tradition is explained by an often-cited story tradition that we turn to next, that of Jana Bāhā Dyah.

A Vernacular Text: Janabāhādyah Bākham

The *Janabāhādyah Bākham,* a Kathmandu-centered Newari-language text that was probably derived from an early modern historical account *(vamshāvalī),* is a story told occasionally in public by Vajrācārya or Shākya storytellers.[20] The narrative explains the origin of Kathmandu's greatest Buddhist temple and festival at the time of Avalokiteśvara's manifestation "from Sukhāvatī." It also positions other sites in the local sacred landscape as having royal origins while ordaining specific Mahāyāna practices with the promise of Sukhāvatī rebirth as the reward for devout observance:

> Maitreya Bodhisattva asked the Buddha, "How did Avalokiteśvara, also called Janabāhādyah, who resides in Kathmandu, arise?"... Shākyasimha Buddha replied, "Once there was a King Yaksha Malla and through the efforts of that king's family, Karunāmaya came down from his Sukhāvatī domain to help the people of Kathmandu . . . to build a *vihāra* at the holy site [called] Kalmochan *tīrtha*. . . .
>
> "If those who are born in Nepal observe the *Gumlā Dharma,* if they show devotion to Svayambhū, if they play five traditional instruments at the festivals, if they revere the Five Buddhas, if they perform the proper worship of Shrī Svayambhū . . . they will get the four fruits: dharma, wealth *(artha),* pleasure *(kāma),* liberation *(moksha),* and be freed from all bad karma *(pāp)*. When they die they will be free from the fear of the King of Death (Yama) and go for rebirth in Sukhāvatī *bhūvana.*"[21]

This story legitimates the month-long Buddhist festival held during monsoon season called Gumlā Dharma. It is a time for myriad devotional observances that, alongside the Avalokiteśvara chariot festival, provide the chief focal points of the Buddhist spiritual year.[22] The *Janabāhādyah Bākham* then recounts a testimonial story describing how in the past local Buddhists did show such devotion and how Yama was "cheated" by their fidelity to Buddhist devotion:

> Once Yama sent his messengers to Nepal but found that as soon as the people stopped breathing they disappeared and went immediately to Sukhāvatī by the favor of Avalokiteśvara. As a result, Yamarāja himself went to Kathmandu . . . the King invited him to the palace, where he was seated on the King's throne and worshiped. . . . The King then summoned [celestial bodhisattva] Vajrapāni, who bound Yamarāja with a mantra after which the King presented a petition that he make the people of the country ever young, never to grow old, never afflicted by diseases, having long life. Yamarāja replied that this was not in his power to give, that the people suffered due to their karma, which could not be erased. The King replied that until the request was granted, he would not release Yamarāja. The latter said, "Nobody can grant this request, except for my guru, Shrī Karunāmaya, who lives in Sukhāvatī." The King commanded Yamarāja to summon his guru and so Avalokiteśvara appeared out of the water at a local pond, with Amitābha on his head, one hand in *abhaya mudra,* the other holding a lotus. . . .
>
> King Yaksha Malla then built . . . a *vihāra* for Karunāmaya. Once the *vihāra* was dedicated, Karunāmaya then vowed, "Whoever comes to this *vihāra* and makes ritual offerings to me will be free from disease and have a full life. The sick who come to read a *dhāraṇī* will be cured. In the next life they will come to reside with me in Sukhāvatī *bhūvana*. . . . Hence you should also establish a chariot festival."[23]

Firmly linking the valley's main celestial bodhisattva, Avalokiteśvara, to this paradise, the story informs devotees that conformity to established Newar Buddhist ritual customs, especially during the Gumlā festival and chariot procession, can ensure their rebirth in Sukhāvatī.

Another ritual tradition associated with Avalokiteśvara promises the same end, and we turn to it now.

"Sukhāvatī Lokeśvara"

The veneration of the bodhisattva Avalokiteśvara in Kathmandu has led sangha members to elaborate on the nature of the divinity and develop myriad devotional practices. Most prominent are the traditions that specify 108 or 360 Avalokiteśvara manifestations. Perhaps unique to Nepalese Buddhism was this articulation of an "Avalokiteśvara cosmology," a theory that the whole of the Buddhist pantheon is in fact an emanation of Avalokiteśvara.[24] The 108 images have been rendered in devotional art, often in sculptures, paintings, illustrated manuscripts, and in modern printed form. Two common hand-copied texts are used by both lay and sangha devotees: the *Lokeśvara Nāma 108 Stotra* and the *Avalokiteśvara Nāma 360 Stotra,* which lists each of the names in chanting order.[25]

Each of the *Lokeśvara Nāma Stotra*s contains an illustration of a "Sukhāvatī Lokeśvara" and lists it as part of the tradition. Plate 8.3 is a rendition from a 1979 publication that shows Lokeśvara seated with Tārā.[26] This form is not specified in the Pala-era iconographic sourcebook the *Sādhanamālā* but is found in the Newari *Dharma-*

Plate 8.3. Image of Sukhāvatī Lokeśvara–Tārā from a Newar devotional publication

kośasaṃgraha.[27] Another iconographic form of Sukhāvatī Lokeśvara from Nepal, described as "solitary," is reproduced in Plate 8.4.[28] No specific Newar *vrata* that I have encountered is dedicated specifically to Sukhāvati Lokeśvara, but his inclusion in paintings associated with the *Bhīma Ratha Jankwa* may indicate a connection with this ritual.[29]

Newar Lay Buddhist Rituals

Other ritual practices in Kathmandu valley households contain numerous references to Sukhāvatī.

Pañca Dāna. Each year during Gumlā, one day is dedicated for each household to make donations directly to members of the san-

Plate 8.4. Solitary form of Sukhāvatī Lokeśvara from an iconographic manual (based on Bhattacharyya, *Indian Buddhist Iconography*)

gha who visit on a "begging round." One common motive articulated by the donor householders is "to be reborn in Sukhāvatī."

Tantric Buddhist Animal Sacrifice. Another reference to Sukhāvatī was made by scattered Newar *vajrācārya* priests and laity with regard to animal sacrifice. Newar Buddhists have long made blood offerings to certain members of their local pantheon, and there are prescribed *pūjā* guidelines for the *vajrācārya*s who perform them. The Buddhist ritualists do not actually wield the knife, however.[30] What does Sukhāvatī have to do with the taking of animal life, a practice that contravenes many early Nikāya and Mahāyāna texts? The answer lies in the local *vajrayāna*-derived explanation of its ritual efficacy: before the animal is dispatched, the *vajrācārya* whispers a mantra into its ear so that, as one of my informants noted, "It can go to Sukhāvatī." This same informant, a priest, commented that, in Buddhist terms, it was a service to liberate animals from their rebirth state. He also noted that the wick lamp placed on the animal's severed head, which is laid before the deity, is said to symbolize this Sukhāvatī destiny. (Bruce Owens has observed that similar comments were made of the sacrifices at the Patan-Bungamati Avalokiteśvara festival.)[31] To be sure, the practice of animal sacrifice and its justification has been much disputed in recent decades.

Burā/Burī Jankwa, or *Bhīma Ratha Jankwa.*[32] This optional Newar rite for elders *(burā-burī),* performed since at least the fifteenth century, is done to mark the occasion of reaching the age of seventy-seven years, seven months, and seven days. The rituals elevate the individual to a new, divine status, as expressed in the dramatic performance of children and grandchildren pulling the elder through the city in a decorated chariot. From this point onward, the elder is also relieved of adult religious responsibilities until death.

Burā Jankwa rites generate blessings that assure both longevity ("strengthening the *āyur*") and excellent rebirth destiny *("pāp cut")* by providing sufficient merit so that the elder will be capable of rebirth in Sukhāvatī. Although this is not proclaimed explicitly in the formal chants or rituals, Sukhāvatī rebirth for the elder is usually cited in the inscriptions on the art commissioned to commemorate the rites and is an especially common motif in local Buddhist painting.[33]

Having performed the *Jankwa,* men (but not women) are entitled to special cremation rites. The body conveyed to the *ghāt* seated in a palanquin that resembles the *bhīma ratha* and is cremated in a seated position. The ashes are molded into sand stupas and left at auspicious places by the family during the *śraddha* rites performed throughout the year of mourning.

Burā Jankwa rites include a repetition of all earlier life cycle rites, the gift of a cow to a brahman *(go dāna),* and offerings to almost every beneficent being in the cosmos as laid out in a series of mandalas.[34] The rituals take two days to perform and there are many kinds of offerings.

The required founding of a *caitya* in the name of the elder is the rite's final connection with Sukhāvatī. This is one of the most meritorious actions that a layman can perform, as recorded in classical Mahāyāna sūtras and in local vernacular texts, and here it is done on behalf of the elder.[35] (In modern practice the *caitya* can be depicted in a painting or a repoussé metal plaque [see Plate 8.5].) In public or private representation, the proper installation of any Newar stupa involves *vajrayāna* ritual, including the reciting of the *Uṣṇīṣavijayā dhāraṇī.* Classified as an emanation of Vairocana "who resides in the womb of the *caitya,*" the goddess *Uṣṇīṣavijayā* personifying the *dhāraṇī* must be established inside the new *jankwa* stupa.

Both the textual and iconographic traditions associated with the goddess are linked to Sukhāvatī. The Sanskrit *Uṣṇīṣavijayā dhāraṇī* text notes that its origins were in Sukhāvatī: there the *dhāraṇī* is revealed by Amitābha.[36] The Newar iconography of the Uṣṇīṣavijayā image places her within the *caitya;* the goddess's solitary iconographic depiction goes back a millennium at least, as it is found in the *Sādhanamālā* three times.[37]

The upper right hand of an eight-armed Newar sculpture shown in Plate 8.6 holds a lotus bearing Amitābha. This form has been noted across the Mahāyāna Buddhist world.[38] With reference to the *bhīmaratha* rites, Lokesh Chandra cites a Tibetan text, the *Rinhbyun Album,* which may explain the origins of the Newar practice: it identifies Uṣṇīṣavijayā as one of the "*āyuhsādhana* deities . . . for prolonging life."[39]

Taking into account its role in Newar ritual and a reference from another Tibetan literary source about Svayambhū, I speculate that this image and its contextual *dhāraṇī* practice point back to an old death-time or after-death *dhārani* recitation ritual that connected Sukhāvatī rebirth to the *Uṣṇīṣavijayā dhāraṇī* practice that was begun (or renewed) through the *bhīmaratha* ceremonies. Although scholarly attention to Uṣṇīṣavijayā as a subject of artistic creation has never related this goddess to actual use by Buddhists at the time of death, at least in the Tibetan literature, a connection exists between Uṣṇīṣavijayā and death ritual in Nepal: Taranatha records that the sage Vasubandhu died in Nepal "after reciting the *Uṣṇīṣa-vijayā dhāraṇī* backwards and forwards twice."[40] Further, Lokesh

Plate 8.5. Family repoussé image from a *bura jankwa* rite showing an Uṣṇīṣavijayā Sukhāvatī Lokeśvara *caitya*

Chandra's terse summary of the Tibetan *Rgyud-sde kun-btus,* a minor tantra, identifies Uṣṇīṣavijayā as one of three long-life deities "who are auspicious at the end."[41] This supports our hypothesis and points to the need for further investigation.

Death and After-Death Rituals. We began this chapter by citing the proper Newar Buddhist pronouncement as cremation processions pass on their way to the *ghāt.* Although the respectful *"Sukhāvatī bhūvanay lāi he māh"* is perhaps the context in which layfolk most commonly invoke Sukhāvatī for respected individuals, it is but one of many other afterlife paradigms that Newar Buddhist tradition applies to the crisis of death. It is noteworthy that Sukhāvatī is not specifically cited in the mandala or *dhāraṇīs* associated with the *Durgatipariśodhana Tantra* traditions that dominate in after-death *vajrācārya* rituals.[42] This is striking today—so much so that one

Plate 8.6. Newar Uṣṇīṣavijayā sculpture showing Amitābha sitting in the upper left on a stupa niche in Dhālisikwa Bāhā, Kathmandu

leading Kathmandu *vajrācārya* ritualist does not even mention Uṣṇīṣavijayā or Sukhāvatī in his book's long and detailed discussion of karma and Newar death rites.[43] Certainly there is no trace in modern Newar tradition of the sort of Sukhāvatī visualization death rituals prescribed in the classic Pure Land sūtras.

For the mourning period, Newar Buddhists in recent times have retained but generally reinterpreted brahmanical *śraddha* practices, making *pinda dāna* food offerings to the dead. Across the Newar towns and cities and among different castes, this practice varies rather widely. The Kathmandu high castes make *pinda* offerings at the *ghāt* before cremation and in the weeks and months following, even performing *śraddha* on a kinsman's death anniversary years later.[44]

The Newars' assimilation of the Indic *śraddha* does, however, still emphasize Sukhāvatī Lokeśvara's witnessing the ritual: the celestial bodhisattva is asked to sit on *kusha* grass and is placed directly in front of the *vajrācārya* priest, as shown in Plate 8.7.[45] In the *laukika pinda* ceremony, Sukhāvatī Lokeśvara witnesses the *guru maṇḍala pūjā,* receives offerings, and remains for the Durgatipariśodhana *dhāraṇī* recitations on behalf of the deceased. For the "Sixteen *Pinda* Rite," performed at riverside sacred sites, Sukhāvatī Lokeśvara is similarly honored. The *śraddha* rite's instrumental orchestration is quite explicit: it seeks this bodhisattva's compassionate, salvific actions on behalf of the deceased.

*Mahāyāna Vrata*s. The *vrata* is another example of an Indic religious practice that has been adapted by later Mahāyāna Buddhism. That *vrata*s date back many centuries in the Newar tradition is confirmed by the antiquity of manuscripts describing the proper forms of observance. *Vrata*s are *vajrācārya*-led worship services that focus devotional attention on an individual deity. Groups of individuals devote one or more days to making offerings while remaining chaste, fasting, abstaining from certain foods, and maintaining a high state of ritual purity. All of these practices earn great amounts of *punya* (merit) and Newar tradition specifies a series of rewards for each.

It is somewhat surprising that Sukhāvatī is not mentioned in the most popular Newar *vrata,* which focuses on Amoghapāśa Lokeśvara. The highest goal in the version of this *vrata* presented by John Locke is *anuttara samyak sambodhi* (complete enlightenment), not

Sukhāvatī. The stories in this text even cite Lokeśvara as "coming from Tushita heaven."[46]

But in the appended story *(vratakathā)* of another Newar *vrata,* the promise of Sukhāvatī rebirth is given as a reward for devotional acts dedicated to Tārā. The story closes with this resolution, as the heroine follows the advice of a sage who proposes that she perform a *vrata* to gain divine aid:

> Hearing this from the sage, the female Brahman climbed up the hill with enthusiasm to have a sacred sighting *(darshan)* of Ugra Tārā Vajrayoginī and thereafter went to the Tārā sacred site. On reaching the *tīrtha,* she bathed and offered *pūjā* and said heartfelt prayers.
>
> In answer to her prayers, the goddess Ārya Tārā took pity on the female Brahman and appeared before her in green complexion and in *abhaya mudrā,* holding a flower in one of her hands. The female Brahman fell prostrate on the ground before the goddess and offered

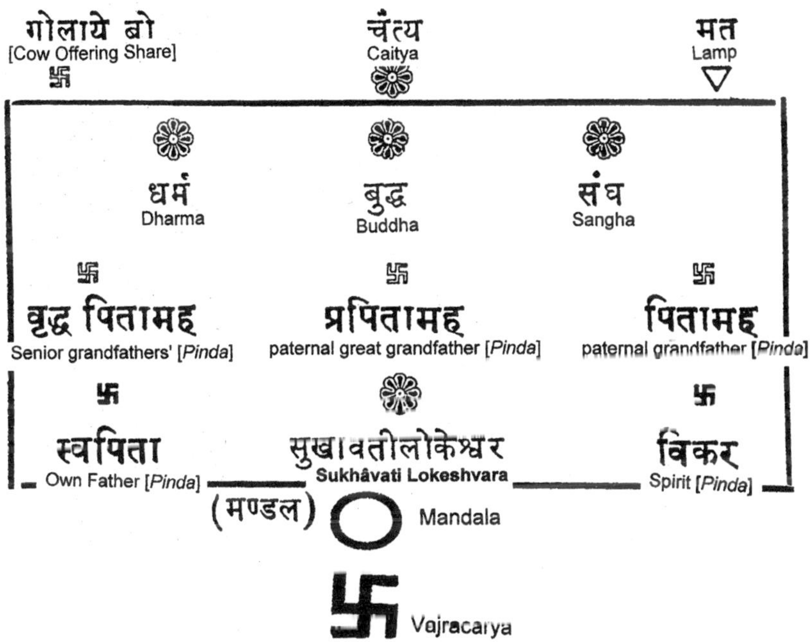

Plate 8.7. A vajrācārya priest's diagram showing part of the ritual setup for a *śrāddha* ritual, with offerings for Sukhāvatī Lokeśvara directly in front of him

> her *pūjā* while chanting devotional songs. The goddess blessed her and vanished out of sight. The female Brahman spent the rest of her life at this Tārā *tīrtha,* living upon fruits and water nearby, meditating and observing the Ārya Tārā *vrata* and offering prayers to the *Tri-Ratna.* When she finally died she was transported to Sukhāvatī *bhūvana.*[47]

This popular ritual thus asserts that devotion to the green Tārā, too, can secure rebirth in Sukhāvatī.[48]

Sukhāvatī in Religious Folksongs

The rich Newar cultural environment includes many song genres, including devotional hymns and compositions, the older *bājans* and more recent *bhajans*.[49] In the former, a few compositions refer to Sukhāvatī. One old song that was until very recently sung by pilgrims while venerating Svayambhū has verses that connect veneration of Svayambhū to rebirth in Sukhāvatī.[50] They mention several themes cited in the *Janabāhādyah Bākham* and the rituals surveyed in this study (assistance in old age, veneration of stupas, aid at the time of death):

> Oh people, pay homage to the feet of the three jewels and show your devotion.
> Days are never the same as long as life lasts for man.
> Life flows on, impermanent. One who does not think of *dharma* in this life will afterwards go to hell.
> Being subject to illusion, veiled by *māya;* one's eyes do not see the *dharma.*
> Not thinking of the next world, not doing good to others, the hour of death approaches.
>
> As a boy he plays; when middle-aged he does not reflect.
> In old age, laziness enters. Separated from everything, he must leave. Love, friends, and wealth do not follow.
>
> Svayambhū, the Light and *Dharmadhātu,* has descended to come to the wonderful hill called Gopuccha.
> If you pay homage to this revered one, you will not need to endure hardships. He will lead his people to Sukhāvatī.[51]

Here the devotional practices at the Svayambhū stupa are interpreted as expressions of non-attachment and insight, with homage to the stupa decisive for Sukhāvatī rebirth.

Another shorter song still sung during the Patan Avalokiteśvara festival provides an example of a disciple begging for the bodhisattva's grace to help him reach Amitābha's paradise:

> Oh Lokanātha, do save me soon!
> To you whose color is like the dawn's, who bears Amitābha on your forehead, who gives gestures of security and of granting a boon, who are Protector of the unprotected and hold in your hand the unfailing snare, to you I, a poor man, have come, full of hope.
>
> . . . .
>
> O lord of the land Sukhāvatī, glorious and endowed with beautiful auspicious marks! Behold, oh Lord: I bid you cast a kind look upon me and take me to Sukhāvatī at that time [of death]![52]

Imported from India in this century, the *bhajan*-style group has inspired Newar devotees to compose hundreds of Buddhist hymns to be sung with a harmonium, tabla, and cymbal orchestra. Some groups gather at resthouses nightly to play and sing together; others assemble only on the auspicious lunar days. In surveying this still quite popular devotional area (many of the different groups that play regularly publish songbooks for their members), the paucity of references to Sukhāvatī is striking. Some songs simply refer to Avalokiteśvara as Sukhāvatīnātha (Lord of Sukhāvatī), although several do praise the bodhisattva for "leading living beings to Sukhāvatī." The rarity of *bhajan* references is no doubt due, in part, to the strong influence of the Theravādin modernist movement.[53] This finding, however, also conforms to the basic pattern evident elsewhere in modern Newar practice: Sukhāvatī rebirth remains an unsystematically articulated goal, merely one of many associations linked to venerating the stupas and bodhisattvas of the country.

Summary and Conclusions

From this survey of Nepalese Buddhist traditions (in particular ritual texts, devotional songs, and modern practices), several summary observations can be made about the role of Sukhāvatī traditions in the history of Indic Buddhism. First, Gregory Schopen is correct in stating that there was no "Sukhāvatī cult" evident in Indic Buddhism and that "hope for rebirth in Sukhāvatī" in the fifth century C.E., when we find the first historical references to Buddhism in Nepal, was a "generalized religious goal."[54] Rebirth in Sukhāvatī did not become a paradigm for understanding death in the Newar tradition, nor was it consistently associated with Avalokiteśvara or Amitābha in Newar *dhāraṇī* practice or other rituals. (Sukhāvatī rebirth is not associated with these divinities alone.)

Sukhāvatī is mentioned in local texts that explain the origins of Svayambhū Mahācaitya as well as the largest Buddhist festival in Kathmandu and other central Buddhist rituals performed by the lay community. Sukhāvatī aspiration is found in scattered devotional songs and articulated as the reward for rituals performed faithfully and directed to Lokeśvara, Tārā, Svayambhū, and Uṣṇīṣavijayā. The view of Sukhāvatī as a "generalized goal" surmised by Schopen primarily from ancient Indic textual sources resonates with what we know about the Newar context: Sukhāvatī is a cliché for a magnificent rebirth locale; rebirth in Sukhāvatī provides a motive for copying texts and making stupas and provides the rationale for local Buddhists making meritorious offerings. Finally, and perhaps these are uniquely Nepalese domestications, rebirth in Sukhāvatī supports the Newar performance of old-age and after-death rituals for kin elders and even the practice of animal sacrifice. Coupled with the view of Amitābha as the buddha who is the best refuge in the Kali Yuga, all these domesticated elements explain the overwhelmingly singular focus on Amitābha in the common gestures of stupa veneration usually visible at Svayambhū and at the valley towns' myriad votive stupas.[55]

Although there is no evidence of a separate "Sukhāvatī cult" in the history of Nepalese Buddhism, Sukhāvatī as a rebirth aspiration may have motivated the copying and veneration of Sanskrit sūtras.[56] Consequently, the Sukhāvatī rebirth paradigm certainly cannot be described in any sense as a Newar "folk tradition"; in fact, it is quite the opposite in that it is the literate and ritual-performing Newar Buddhists who articulate it most often. Indeed, in the *Svayambhū Purāna* (a Newar text recounting the previous world-era origins of the Kathmandu valley and the Svayambū stupa as a Buddhist hierophany), the former buddha Krakucchanda specifically promises Sukhāvatī rebirth to his newly ordained monks if they are devoted to the Three Jewels and follow the ten *pāramitās*.[57]

The nature of Sukhāvatī belief and practice among the modern laity must be considered as part of the Newar case study in late Indic Mahāyāna / Vajrayāna culture. Many Newars today regard the present era as a retrograde spiritual time: some use the Indic and originally non-Buddhist concept Kali Yuga. In my surveys of Buddhist merchants in Kathmandu, the most common view expressed was that Sukhāvatī rebirth is a distant and unrealistic possibility for most.[58] As one man said, "I cannot imagine that anyone living now has such a store of *punya*. Is the rebirth destiny a place called Sukhāvatī; or just a place characterized by *sukha* (happiness)?" In my experience (and also David Gellner's), Newar Buddhists gave disparate answers about how nirvana and Sukhāvatī are related.[59] Despite references having been built into many enduring Buddhist traditions, Sukhāvatī for most Buddhists today is a vaguely understood, distant hope and for many hardly more than a cliché.[60]

The Newar traditions suggest that the emphasis on salvation through faith was limited and ambiguous for Buddhist communities.[61] Some ritualists and monk storytellers certainly did emphasize this path, as in China and Japan;[62] but many others apparently ignored it or envisioned salvation as in the Pure Land sūtras, especially those who regarded true Buddhist realization as *bodhi* on earth (such as, Zen) and those focused on more tantric paradigms.

The Newar traditions indicate that a focal point for Sukhāvatī belief has always been the crisis of death. We have noted narratives from the *Janabāhādyah Bākham* and the *Tārā Vratakathā* in which the Lord of Death, Yama, yields to the authority and grace of the bodhisattvas (Avalokiteśvara, Tārā) *for those who practice.* Several popular songs also express this hope for earning the grace of Sukhāvatī rebirth. In this same manner, Newar *śraddha* rituals compel Sukhāvatī Lokeśvara to witness and act upon rituals performed on behalf of the dead. Here a Newar tradition provides another example of how Indic Buddhism developed ritual practices for all individuals, including monks and nuns, who wanted to exert maximal effort to ensure the best possible rebirth destiny for their departed kinsmen. The concern for aiding kin in their rebirth destiny seems to have been a universal—not solely East Asian—area of concern and ritual innovation for Buddhists.[63]

Finally, Newar Buddhists adopted *vajrayāna* traditions that coexisted with the Sukhāvatī-related rituals described above. More specifically, a *vajrayāna* paradigm and praxis gained supremacy over a more esoteric Mahāyāna orientation. The "Sukhāvatī paradigm" provides another example of the incorporation-subordination process in Vajrayāna Buddhist history[64] made evident in this case by the traditions of the *Durgatipariśodhana Sūtra* that now dominate the rituals performed by Newar *vajrācāryas* in the days, weeks, and months after death.[65] In the history of Newar Buddhism, faith in the powers of freely-acting bodhisattvas or devotion to the great Svayambhū stupa to pull one through to Sukhāvatī was overlaid with a greater faith in the destiny-determining power of tantric *dhāraṇīs*.[66] Just as Sukhāvatī Lokeśvara in the Indo-Newari *pinda dāna* rites has been installed as onlooker in the chanting of the *dhāraṇīs* from the *Durgatipariśodhana Tantra,* so too have the explicit ritual manipulation of the passage to death detailed in the later *vajrayāna* traditions displaced earlier Mahāyāna solutions.

Notes

I am pleased to acknowledge here the generous support that I received toward the completion of the research that informs this paper, especially a Fulbright-Hays Dissertation Fellowship, a Fulbright Senior Research Fellowship, and an American Academy of Religion Research Grant.

An earlier version of this essay appeared in *South Asia Research* as "*Sukhāvatī* Traditions in Newar Buddhism," 16, no. 1 (1996): 1–30. At the request of the editors of the present volume, and in response to issues raised by participants at the 1995 Institute of Buddhist Studies, Berkeley, conference, I have deleted Part 2 of the original essay, edited out many technical South Asian terms, corrected a few minor details, expanded sections on research methodology, and added further data on Newar practices concerned with Sukhāvatī rebirth. My thanks go to the editors at *South Asia Research,* and particularly Michael Hutt, for permission to revise and reprint portions of my article.

Transliterated Newar terms in the text follow the conventions established in David N. Gellner and Declan Quigley, eds., *Contested Hierarchies: A Collaborative Ethnography of Caste in the Kathmandu Valley, Nepal.* (Oxford: Clarendon Press, 1995). I have also used Sanskrit spellings as they are typically employed in Nepal. I dedicate this chapter to my late brother, Jeffrey Meriwether Lewis (1956– 2001).

1. Étienne Lamotte, *History of Indian Buddhism: From the Origins to the Saka Era* (Louvain: Institut Orientaliste, 1988), 435; Fujita Kotatsu, "Pure and Impure Lands," in *The Encyclopedia of Religion,* ed. Mircea Eliade (New York: Macmillan, 1987), 12:90–91.

2. See, for example, Kenneth Chen, *The Chinese Transformation of Buddhism* (Princeton: Princeton University Press, 1973).

3. "Newari" is a modern English neologism for the Tibeto-Burman language spoken in the Kathmandu valley. Two emic terms are preferred by Newars: the colloquial "Newa Bhāy" and the Sanskritized "Nepāl Bhāsā," which suggests the old pre-Shah (before 1769) Nepal when it consisted of the Kathmandu valley only. "Newar" derives from the place name "Nepal."

4. Sylvain Levi, *Le Nepal* (Paris: Leroux, 1905–1908), 1:28.

5. John K. Locke, *Buddhist Monasteries of Nepal* (Kathmandu: Sahayogi, 1985).

6. See Theodore Riccardi, Jr., "Buddhism in Ancient and Early Medieval Nepal," in *Studies in the History of Buddhism,* ed. A. K. Narain (New Delhi: Agam, 1980), 265–281; David N. Gellner, *Monk, Householder and Tantric Priest: Newar Buddhism and Its Hierarchy of Ritual* (Cambridge: Cambridge University Press, 1992); Todd T. Lewis, *Popular Buddhist Texts from Nepal: Narratives and Rituals of Newar Buddhism* (Albany: State University of New York Press, 2000); Michael Allen, "Buddhism With-

out Monks: The Vajrayāna Religion of the Newars of the Kathmandu Valley," *South Asia* 3 (1973): 1–14; John K. Locke, "The Vajrayāna Buddhism in the Kathmandu Valley," in *The Buddhist Heritage of Nepal* (Kathmandu: Dharmodaya Sabba, 1986).

7. David N. Gellner, "Language, Caste, Religion and Territory: Newar Identity Ancient and Modern," *European Journal of Sociology* 27 (1986): 102–148.

8. Siegfried Lienhard, "Nepal: The Survival of Indian Buddhism in a Himalayan Kingdom," in *The World of Buddhism,* eds. Heinz Bechert and Richard Gombrich (New York: Facts on File, 1984), 108–114.

9. See Todd T. Lewis, "Newars and Tibetans in the Kathmandu Valley: Ethnic Boundaries and Religious History," *Journal of Asian and African Studies* 38 (1989): 31–57; Todd T. Lewis, "Newar-Tibetan Trade and the Domestication of the *Simhalasārthabāhu Avadāna,*" *History of Religions* 33, no. 2 (1993): 135–160; Todd T. Lewis and Lozang Jamspal, "Newars and Tibetans in the Kathmandu Valley: Three New Translations from Tibetan Sources," *Journal of Asian and African Studies* 36 (1988): 187–211; Todd T. Lewis and D. R. Shakya, "Contributions to the History of Nepal: Eastern Newar Diaspora Settlements," *Contributions to Nepalese Studies* 15, no. 1 (1988): 25–65; Eberto Lo Bue, "The Newar Artists of the Nepal Valley: An Historical Account of Their Activities in Neighboring Areas with Particular Reference to Tibet," parts 1 and 2, *Oriental Art* 21, no. 3 (1985): 262–277; 21, no. 4 (1986): 409–420; Eberto Lo Bue, "Cultural Exchange and Social Interaction between Tibetans and Newars from the Seventeenth to the Twentieth Century," *International Folklore Review* 6 (1988): 86–114.

10. See John K. Locke, "*Uposadha Vrata* of Amoghapasha Lokeshvara in Nepal," *L'Ethnographie* 83, nos. 100–101 (1987): 159–189; Todd T. Lewis, "Mahāyāna *Vratas* in Newar Buddhism," *Journal of the International Association of Buddhist Studies* 12, no. 1 (1989): 109–138.

11. John K. Locke, "Newar Buddhist Initiation Rites," *Contributions to Nepalese Studies* 2 (1975): 1–23.

12. David N. Gellner, "Monastic Initiation in Newar Buddhism," in *Oxford University Papers on India* 11, no. 1 (1988): 42–112; David N. Gellner, "Ritualized Devotion, Altruism and Meditation: The Offering of the *Guru Maṇḍala* in Newar Buddhism," *Indo-Iranian Journal* 34 (1991): 161–197.

13. William Stablein, "A Descriptive Analysis of the Content of Nepalese Buddhist Pujas as a Medical-Cultural System, with References to Tibetan Parallels," in *In the Realm of the Extra-Human: Ideas and Actions,* ed. A. Bharati (The Hague: Mouton, 1976), 165–173.

14. I have attempted to treat these and associated issues in Todd T. Lewis, "The Anthropological Study of Buddhist Communities: Historical Precedents and Ethnographic Paradigms," in *Shamanism, Altered States, Healing: Essays in the Anthropology of Religion,* ed. Steven Glazier (Westport, Conn.: Greenwood Press, 1997), 319–367.

15. See Lewis, *Popular Buddhist Texts from Nepal,* chaps. 1, 7, where these subjects are treated at greater length.

16. From antiquity, "*stupa*" and "*caitya*" were used in most Buddhist inscriptions and literature as synonyms. They are used in this way in the present essay.

17. My translation from Hemraj Shakya, *Shrī Svayambhū Mahācaitya* (Kathmandu: Nepal Press, 1980), 526. Alexander Rospatt (personal communication, 2001),

in his study of this text and other documents pertaining to Svayambhū, has added further insights: "In the correlation of the [finial} rings, I have found some instances where Sukhāvatī was added as a final member, above all the [ten] *bhumis*, including the *buddhabhumis*. I have also found in the *Svayambhū Purāna* an identification of Nepal (in former ages) with Sukhāvatī."

18. John K. Locke, *Karunamaya* (Kathmandu: Sahayogi, 1980).

19. R. O. Meisezahl, "*Amoghapāśa:* Some Nepalese Representations and Their Vajrayāna Aspects," *Monumenta Serica* 26 (1967): 461.

20. Kamalananda Vajracarya, *Janabāhādyah Bakham* (Kathmandu: Agam Press, 1972). The text here is excerpted from a translation in Locke, *Karunamaya*, 149–154. I have restored a few Sanskrit forms and made minor corrections to keep usages consistent with those in the chapter.

21. Locke, *Karunamaya*, 151–153.

22. Todd T. Lewis, "Contributions to the Study of Popular Buddhism: The Newar Buddhist Festival of *Gumlā Dharma*," *Journal of the International Association of Buddhist Studies* 16, no. 2 (1993): 7–52.

23. Locke, *Karunamaya*, 151.

24. These manifestations include Shrishtikantha Lokeśvara, Ādi-Buddha Lokeśvara, Amitābha Lokeśvara, Amoghapasha Lokeśvara, Maitreya Lokeśvara, Samantabhadra Lokeśvara, Vajrapāni Lokeśvara, Mañjughosa Lokeśvara, Kshitigarbha Lokeśvara, etc. This totalizing construction has also been noted in Tibetan devotional thought concerning Tārā (see Stephan Beyer, *The Cult of Tara: Magic and Ritual in Tibet* [Berkeley: University of California Press, 1973]). Such Buddhist cosmologies mirror the Vishnu *avatāra* theology (see Paul Mus, "Thousand-Armed Kannon: A Mystery or a Problem?" in *Indogaku Bukkyogaku Kenkyo* 11, no. 1 (1964): 438–470).

25. Babu Kaji Shakya, *Mahāyāna Bauddhadevatā Nāmasūci* (Kathmandu: Sankata Press, 1991), 31, 48.

26. A printed book with line drawings of the 108 forms and stories associated with 35 of these emanations was published by Amoghavajra Vajracarya as *Lokeshvarayā Paricaya* (Kathmandu: Madan Printing Press, 1979). See the discussion of the Tārā *vrata* on pp. 253–254.

27. Marie-Thérèse de Mallmann, *Introduction à l'étude d'Avalokiteçvara* (Paris: S. A. E. P. 1948), 55.

28. B. Bhattacharyya, *Indian Buddhist Iconography* (Calcutta: Firma K. L. Mukhopadhyay, 1968), 404.

29. See the discussion of *vrata* on pp. 252–254.

30. The modernist Theravādins in Nepal have spoken out against this practice, and most of the merchants I observed had given up all but egg sacrifices. *Vajrācārya*s still perform these rites during Kathmandu's festivals (e.g., Annapurna *jātra*, in Naradevi's Panchare rituals, and in Patan). Some laity also derided the old and widely heard *vajrācārya* apology for involvement in ritual killing: As one cynical middle-aged man commented, "If such ritual sacrifice leads to Sukhāvatī rebirth, then why don't I sacrifice my mother and father?" On this issue, see Gellner, *Monk, Householder and Tantric Priest*, 124–125; Bruce Owens, "Blood and Bodhisattvas: Sacrifice among the Newar Buddhists of Nepal," in *Anthropology of Tibet and the Himalayas*, eds. Charles

Ramble and Martin Braun (Zurich: Ethnological Museum of the University of Zurich, 1993), 258–269.

31. Bruce Owens, personal communication, 1994.

32. Todd T. Lewis, *The Tulādhars of Kathmandu: A Study of Buddhist Tradition in a Newar Merchant Community* (Ann Arbor: University Microfilms International, 1984), 299–307; Gellner, *Monk, Householder and Tantric Priest,* 198.

33. For examples, see Pratapaditya Pal, "The *Bhimaratha* Rite and Nepali Art," *Oriental Art* 23, no. 2 (1977): 186; Anne Vergati, "Image et rituel: À propos des peintures bouddhiques népalaises," *Arts Asiatiques* 54 (1999): 33–43; Hugo E. Kreijger, *Kathmandu Valley Painting: The Jucker Collection* (Boston: Shambhala, 1999), pl. 28; A. W. Macdonald and Anne Vergati Stahl, *Newar Art: Nepalese Art during the Malla Period* (Warminster, England: Aris and Phillips, 1979); Bernhard Kolver, *Re-Building a Stūpa: Architectural Drawings of Svayambhūnāth* (Bonn: VGH Wissenschaftsverlag, 1992), 35–37.

34. These are the *graha maṇḍala* and *pañcabuddha* (or *duso maṇḍalas*) as specified in Ratna Kaji Vajracarya's ritual guidebook, *Yem Deyā Bauddha Pūjā Kriyāyā Halamjvalam* (Kathmandu: Sankata Printing Press, 1981), 48–49.

35. Todd T. Lewis, "Contributions to the History of Buddhist Ritualism: A Mahāyāna *Avadāna* on *Caitya* Veneration from the Kathmandu Valley," *Journal of Asian History* 28 (1994): 1–38.

36. Rajendralala Mitra, *The Sanskrit Buddhist Literature of Nepal* (Calcutta: Sanskrit Pustak Bhandar, 1971), 263–264.

37. Bhattacharyya, *Indian Buddhist Iconography,* 404.

38. Lokesh Chandra, "Iconography of the Goddess Uṣṇīṣavijayā," *Journal of the Indian Society of Oriental Art,* no. 10 (1979): 17–29; Rob Linrothe, "Xia Renzong and the Patronage of Tangut Buddhist Art: The Stūpa and the Ushnīshavijayā Cult," *Journal of Sung-Yuan Studies* 28 (1998): 91–121. There are two examples of Uṣṇīṣavijayā within a stupa in Beijing: at the Biyun temple west of the city and the Zhenjue temple on the northern boundary of the old city. Both are among the ten Bodh Gaya–modeled, five-stupa monuments in China. The former was built in 1366; the latter in 1473 and perhaps connected with a Nepalese monk who lived in a monastery on Mt. Wu Tai. See *Ancient Temples in Beijing* (Beijing: China Esperanto Press, 1993), 102–109, 113–118.

39. Chandra, "Comparative Iconography of the Goddess Uṣṇīṣavijayā," 14.

40. See Pal, "The *Bhimaratha* Rite and Nepali Art," 186.

41. Chandra, "Comparative Iconography of the Goddess Uṣṇīṣavijayā, 15.

42. See Vajracarya, *Yem Deyā Bauddha Pūjā Kriyāyā Halamjvalam;* Tadeusz Skorupski, *The Sarvadurgatipariśodhana Tantra* (Delhi: Motilal Banarsidass, 1983).

43. A translation of this appears in Todd T. Lewis, "The *Nepal Jana Jivan Kriyā Paddhati,* a Modern Newar Guide for *Vajrayāna* Life-Cycle Rites," *Indo-Iranian Journal* 37 (1994): 1–46.

44. Lewis, *The Tulādhars of Kathmandu,* 314–336.

45. This chant is reproduced from a ritual guidebook by Amoghavajra Vajracarya, *Pinda Vidhānam* (Kathmandu: Sankata Press, 1973).

46. Locke, *"Uposadha Vrata,"* 174.

47. The Newari text is found in Badri Bajracarya, *Shrī Aryya Tārā Devyaih Vrata Vidhi Kathā* (Kathmandu: Popular Printing Press, 1980), and translated in Lewis, *Popular Buddhist Texts from Nepal,* 104–107.

48. Note that the tantric goddess Ugra Tārā Vajrayoginī directs the heroine to continue her devotions to Ārya Tārā.

49. See Todd T. Lewis, "Buddhist Merchants in Kathmandu: The Asan Tol Market and *Urāy* Social Organization," in *Contested Hierarchies,* eds. Gellner and Quigley, 38–79.

50. My guess is that it is in the various song traditions praising "Lokeśvaranāth in Sukhāvatī" that moden Newar laymen frequently encounter this conception of paradise.

51. Siegfried Lienhard, *The Songs of Nepal* (Honolulu: University of Hawai'i Press, 1984), 24.

52. Ibid.

53. On the Theravāda reform movement in Nepal, see Ria Kloppenberg, "Theravāda Buddhism in Nepal," *Kailash* 5, no. 4 (1977): 301–322; Gellner, *Monk, Householder and Tantric Priest,* 321–328; Lewis, *The Tulādhars of Kathmandu,* 494–513; Ramesh Chandra Tewari, "Socio-Cultural Aspects of Theravada Buddhism in Nepal," *Journal of the International Association of Buddhist Studies* 6 (1983): 67–93.

54. Gregory Schopen, "*Sukhāvatī* as a Generalized Religious Goal in Sanskrit Mahāyāna Sūtra Literature," *Indo-Iranian Journal* 19 (1977): 177–210.

55. Jan Nattier has noted that the Kali Yuga framework appeared only sporadically in later Buddhist Sanskrit literature, beginning with the *Lankāvatāra Sūtra* in the Gupta era, and found its most common usage in later tantric literature (see Jan Nattier, *Once Upon a Future Time: Studies in a Buddhist Prophecy of Decline* [Berkeley: Asian Humanities Press, 1991], 280–283). Both this sūtra and the tantras are represented extensively in the Newar tradition.

56. This surmise should be confirmed by examining the colophons of copied texts or scribal passages from other medieval Nepalese documents.

57. A recently published translation of one section of the *Bhadrakalpāvadāna,* a Sanskrit text composed in Nepal, has Gautama Buddha's wife, Yaśodharā, respond to the threats of evil Devadatta with the exclamation, "Send me to Sukhāvatī—chop off my head!" This quote and the point made here also appear in Joel Tatelman's fine article, "The Trials of Yashodharā: Legend of the Buddha's Wife in the *Bhadrakalpāvadāna* [from the Sanskrit]," *Buddhist Literature* 1 (1999): 261.

58. An article summarizing the patterns of Mahāyāna-Vajrayāna belief in the Kathmandu merchant community appears in Todd T. Lewis, "Patterns of Religious Belief in a Buddhist Merchant Community, Nepal," *Asian Folklore Studies* 55, no. 2 (1996): 237–270.

59. Gellner, *Monk, Householder and Tantric Priest,* 131–132.

60. Tatelman, "The Trials of Yashodharā," 261. The same terse, unelaborated reference to "Avalokiteśvara dwelling in Sukhāvatī" is found in the *Kavirkumār Avadāna.* See the published Newari version of the *Bodhisattvāvadānamālā* translated by Asha Kaji Vajracarya (Kathmandu: Bauddha Prakashana, 1982), chap. 11.

61. See, for example, Nalinaksha Dutt, "Place of Faith in Buddhism," *Indian Historical Quarterly* 16 (1940): 639–646; Balkrishna Govind Gokhale, "Bhakti in Early Buddhism," *Journal of Asian and African Studies* 15 (1980): 1–27.

62. Jaraslav Prusek, "The Narrators of Buddhist Scriptures and Religious Tales in the Sung Period," *Archiv Orientahii* 10 (1938): 375–389.

63. Gregory Schopen, "Filial Piety and the Monk in the Practice of Indian Buddhism: A Question of 'Sinicization' Viewed from the Other Side," *T'oung Pao* 70 (1984): 110–126.

64. See Todd T. Lewis, "The Himalayan Frontier in Comparative Perspective: Considerations Regarding Buddhism and Hinduism in Diaspora," *Himalayan Research Bulletin* 14, nos. 1–2 (1994): 25–46. It is also possible that Newar Buddhist priests dropped a practice associated with Tibetan Buddhists, a group disfavored since the rise of the Hindu Shah state in 1769. See Lewis, "Newars and Tibetans in the Kathmandu Valley."

65. Is there a relationship between tantric death ritual traditions in China and Japan and the unprecedented Buddhist innovations in East Asia that led monks and laity to retain the "Sukhāvatī paradigm" and develop death-time ritualism? (See, for example, Stephen F. Teiser, *The Ghost Festival in Medieval China* [Princeton: Princeton University Press, 1988], 107–112.) Charles Orzech has indeed pointed out that the legacy of the *vajrayāna* in medieval China was the creation of rites for the salvation of *pretas* (hungry ghosts); these rituals employ *dhāraṇī* recitations, as some of the relevant texts state that these chants were revealed in Avalokiteśvara's Pure Land. He also notes that the practices became central to the East Asian *avalambana* festival and the patronage economics of Chinese Buddhist monasticism: "These rites for the dead became the principal source of income for small hereditary temples, the most numerous kind of monastic institution" (see Charles D. Orzech, "Seeing Chen-Yen Buddhism: Traditional Scholarship and the Vajrayāna in China," *History of Religions* 29 (1989): 103).

66. Does the nenbutsu belief and practice of later Japanese Pure Land represent a later confluence of *dhāraṇī* practice and a Pure Land paradigm?

9

Buddha One

A One-Day Buddha-Recitation Retreat in Contemporary Taiwan

CHARLES B. JONES

WHILE I WAS IN TAIWAN researching my doctoral dissertation (1992–1994), I spent a great deal of time at one particular Buddhist temple called the Xilian Jingyuan (Pure Garden of the Western Lotus, hereafter Xilian temple). This temple, founded in 1971 by the monk Zhiyu and situated on a mountainside near the town of Sanxia, is known in Taiwan as a place devoted to the practice of Pure Land Buddhism.[1] As part of their program of opportunities for laypersons interested in cultivating this form of practice, the temple offers buddha-recitation retreats of varying lengths: one day, two days, three days, and seven days. These retreats are known as *jingjin nianfo yi* [*er, san, qi*], or "Energetic Buddha-Recitation One [Two, Three, Seven]," usually shortened to the word "Buddha" plus the appropriate number, such as *"fo yi"* (Buddha One), *"fo er"* (Buddha Two), and so on.

I had the opportunity to participate in a one-day buddha-recitation retreat that took place at the Xilian temple on May 1–2, 1994. Although it lasted only a single twenty-four-hour period, its structure was the same as all other such retreats given at the temple regardless of duration, with a few exceptions that we will note as we go. In the sections that follow, I will give a description of the retreat itself, followed by an analysis of its rationale and some conclusions about its significance within the development of modern Chinese Buddhism.

Training for the Buddha One

The Buddha One proper began at 4:00 A.M. on May 2, 1994, but participants began arriving at 3:00 P.M. the previous day. This was necessary not simply because the early wake-up time the following morning made same-day arrival impractical, but also because participants required several hours of training in the procedures of the retreat and conventional temple etiquette before the retreat could begin.

The first item of business was registration and the issuing of robes. Participants who had registered by mail or telephone prior to the start of the retreat simply checked in, while others who came in the hope that there might still be vacancies registered on the spot. At this time participants received name tags and a small booklet published privately by the Xilian temple called the *Handbook of Rituals and Rules for Buddha Sevens and Cultivation (Fo Qi ji Xiuxue Yigui Shouce).* This booklet, small enough for participants to carry around with them, contained a list of rules of conduct and the ritual texts for recitation at various points during the retreat, including the complete text of the *Amituo Jing,* or smaller *Sukhāvatīvyūha sūtra,* as well as mealtime devotions and verses to be chanted during the retreat itself.

The robes, called "ocean purity" *(haiqing),* were to be standard dress for the duration of the retreat. A loose black gown with billowing sleeves, it resembled a baccalaureate graduation gown. Many of the participants brought their own from home, while others borrowed them from the temple. These robes served the purposes of preserving modesty, erasing any social distinctions between participants based on dress, and added a greater air of solemnity and seriousness to the retreat. Upon receiving mine, the nun who fitted me instructed me in the proper way to take it off, put it on, and fold it when not in use. At no time, she said, should it ever touch the floor.

At 5:00 P.M., we all proceeded to the Great Shrine Hall *(Da Xiong Bao Dian)* for evening devotions *(wanke).* Although this technically was not part of the retreat but part of the temple's daily routine, the service was changed in a few respects to accommodate the participants and help prepare them and the site for the retreat to come. The monk serving as the *weinuo* (a term that Holmes Welch translated as "verger") went at the head of the procession that circumambulated the hall with a bowl of water and a small leafy twig. As he went, he dipped the twig in the water and sprinkled it around the hall to purify it for the retreat, a process called *sajing,* or "sprinkling purity."

After this service, the retreatants were free to move into their dormitories, relax, and bathe. The training session began in the New Lecture Hall at 7:00. At this point the participants met the monks who would be running the retreat. Taking overall charge for the conduct of the retreat was the vice-abbot of the temple in the capacity of *zhuyi,* or "master of the one[-day retreat]." It was his job to inspire the retreatants with teachings and safeguard the overall atmosphere of the event. Since the *zhuyi* was not present during the entire retreat, the *weinuo* saw that the *zhuyi*'s directions were carried out and took charge of the actual execution of the retreat. He remained at the front of the Great Shrine Hall throughout the retreat and oversaw its progress. Finally, the *jianxiang,* or "supervisor of the incense," circulated among the retreatants and ensured that all was done in proper form. If anyone fell asleep, slouched on their meditation cushions, or held their hands in the wrong position, the *jianxiang* would nudge them with the incense board *(xiangban)* and correct them. All other support services, such as cooking, cleaning, and supplying incense, were performed by the regular resident clergy with the assistance of lay volunteers who had signed up to serve at the event.

The training was quite detailed. The monk acting as *weinuo* introduced the schedule for the next day's activities as follows:

3:30 A.M.	Get up; wash
4:00–5:05 A.M.	First stick *(zhi),* which includes elements from the usual morning devotion service *(zao ke)* and a recitation of the complete smaller *Sukhāvatī-vyūha sūtra.*
5:20–6:20 A.M.	Second stick
6:30–7:00 A.M.	Breakfast and conferral of the Eight Precepts *(baguan zhaijie)*
7:35–8:35 A.M.	Third stick
8:50–10:00 A.M.	Fourth stick
10:20–11:20 A.M.	Fifth stick
11:30–12:00 A.M.	Lunch
12:00–2:00 P.M.	Rest period, officially called "let each be diligent" *(gezi yonggong)*
2:20–3:25 P.M.	Sixth stick
3:40–4:45 P.M.	Seventh stick
4:50–5:55 P.M.	Eighth, and final, stick
5:55–7:00 P.M.	Evening meal, or "medicinal stone" *(yaoshi),* only for those who did not receive the Eight Precepts. Wash and rest.
7:00–8:05 P.M.	Great Transfer of Merit

In the schedule, "stick" refers to a stick of incense. In the days before the invention of modern clocks, a period of meditation or buddha-recitation was timed by the burning of incense; one stick marked one period of practice.

During a follow-up interview after the retreat, the monk acting as *weinuo* told me that the above schedule would be the same for a buddha-recitation retreat of any length, whether one, two, three, or seven days. During a Buddha Seven, however, additional "sticks" would be added incrementally beginning on the fifth day. Thus there would be nine periods on the fifth day, ten on the sixth, and eleven on the seventh. In this way, retreatants would maintain their practice from 4:00 A.M. to midnight on the last day. He also indicated that participants had to commit to seeing the retreat through; they were not free to come and go at will while the retreat was in progress or stop halfway through.

The next item in the training was the introduction of the Eight Precepts *(baguan zhaijie)*. These are precepts or vows that laypeople may adopt for twenty-four-hour periods during times of intensive cultivation or on significant days such as *uposatha* days. These include the usual Five Lay Precepts (not to kill, steal, lie, engage in illicit sexual relations, or drink intoxicating beverages) plus three more: not to eat after noon (*fei shi shi,* literally, "not to eat at an improper time"), not to adorn the body, and not to sleep on high or luxurious beds. Because the precepts remain in effect for twenty-four hours, the *weinuo* advised participants that they would still be bound to uphold them through the night after they returned home. He also stated that the precept against illicit sexual relations, which normally did not affect sexual relations between legitimate partners, in this context entailed complete abstinence for the entire twenty-four hours.

The *weinuo* went on to explain two further aspects of taking these precepts. First, they were optional. One could freely choose to take all, some, or none of them. Taking them would increase one's religious discipline and the amount of merit accrued during the retreat, but they were not an integral part of the program. Second, if one felt, after returning home, that one is simply not able to maintain the observance of a precept taken, then one need only abandon that precept. For example, a businessman whose job required him to entertain clients with alcohol had only to find a competent witness before whom to declare "I undertook the vow not to drink intoxicating beverages, and now I abandon that vow." The act would still produce the bad karma of drinking, but one would not accrue the bad karma of violating one's vow.

Next the monk assigned the places that retreatants would occupy in the Great Shrine Hall during each "stick." As in all dharma-meetings, the clergy had precedence; the *zhuyi* in particular had a seat on the dais in front of the buddha-altar. After the clergy, those who had received the lay bodhisattva precepts *(zaijia pusa jie)* took the foremost seats and were allowed to wear an additional liturgical garment called a *manyi* over their *haiqing*. They were followed by laypeople who had received the Five Lay Precepts and those who had not taken any precepts. Within each group, participants were further sorted by gender and age, and the last two groups were also arranged by height.[2]

Actually, participants had two places assigned to them in the Great Shrine Hall. They went to the first after entering at the beginning of each "stick." After some preliminary chanting, they would then leave their seats laterally and form another procession to circumambulate the hall, after which they would fill the rows longitudinally, returning to their original positions. This served as each participant's primary spot: in between "sticks," he or she folded up the *haiqing* and laid it on top of the mat in that location with the name badge facing up. Participants also sat in these places during lectures.

During the time in the middle of each "stick" set aside for silent recitation, we were to assume a meditative posture, full lotus for those who could, half lotus for everyone else. (We will discuss the style of meditation used here later.) Each mat also had a large towel on it. During meditation, we were to cover our legs with it under our *haiqing* for warmth. (In other temples, towels are also used for modesty, especially during the hot summer months when many men and women wear shorts or miniskirts.) When coming out of meditation, we were to begin by rubbing our hands together to warm them and then massage our eyes and other parts of the head and legs as needed.

The most detailed training by far had to do with taking meals. For this phase, we moved into the New Lecture Hall, where the resident clergy had actually set up long tables with plates, rice bowls, soup bowls, and chopsticks for hands-on practice. It would be tedious to relate here the proper way to receive food, eat, request help from the waiters, and clean up. We can observe, however, that the regimentation seemed to serve five main purposes: (1) to maintain silence (of both voices and dishes), (2) to keep the billowing sleeves of the *haiqing* out of the food, (3) to provide a set of gestures and arrangements of utensils that would signal the waiters silently of one's needs, (4) to make sure all of the participants' dishes and utensils are in a standard location to help waiters operate efficiently, and (5) to encourage mindfulness and gratitude while eating. After attempting to absorb all of the regulations governing the table, I understood why a nun had once remarked to me that monks and nuns feared mealtimes above all else. Those who had vowed to fast for the duration of the retreat were excused from this part of the training.

After all of this practice and instruction, the last part of the training period consisted of a talk by the *zhuyi* in charge of the retreat. He gave a brief hortatory homily of the kind called *kaishi* ("open and expound") by Chinese Buddhists. He indicated that the retreat's purpose was to train the mind. One's thoughts, he said, may be oriented by habit to the *sahā* world or they could be reoriented through practice to the Pure Land. To achieve this reorientation, the retreatants should reflect on the suffering and ignorance endemic to the former as compared with the bliss, availability of perfect instruction, and ease of practice awaiting them in the latter. The choice was theirs to make.

After this talk, we retired for the night.

The Practice of the Buddha One

The retreat proper began at 4:00 the following morning with the first "stick." Despite this designation, the service followed the same liturgy as an ordinary morning devotion service *(zao ke)*, with the following variations. The service began with the "incense praise" *(xiangzan)*, which opens the liturgy for a seven-day buddha-recitation retreat *(fo qi)* in the *Breviary*.[3] Also, whereas at the Xilian temple morning devotions included the Śūraṃgama mantra on odd days and the Great Compassion mantra on even days, for this service the long recitation consisted of the smaller *Sukhāvatīvyūha sūtra* (or *Amitābha sūtra*).[4] After this, the retreatants all recited the "Mantra for Rebirth" *(wangsheng zhou)* together three times. Both of these latter items normally form part of the evening devotion service.[5]

The second through the eighth "sticks," with the exception of the seventh, all followed the same pattern. A bell signaled the beginning of each "stick," at the sound of which all retreatants entered the Great Shrine Hall, found their primary mats, and stood in readiness. Those on the eastern side of the hall made up the "Eastern Class" *(dongban)*, those on the other side the "Western Class" *(xiban)*. At a signal, everyone moved to their starting position. As the monks handling the musical instruments *(faqi)* began to play, the *weinuo* intoned an invocation together with the participants:

> Amitābha Buddha, with body of golden color,
> his major and minor marks bright and peerless,
> The tuft of white hair entwines five Mt. Sumerus,
> and his dark eyes quell the four great oceans.
> In the midst of this light, *nirmāṇakāya* buddhas in innumerable myriads,
> an unbounded host of transformation-bodhisattvas *(hua pusa)*.
> His forty-eight vows save sentient beings,
> and enable all [those in] the nine grades [of rebirth] to attain the farther shore.[6]

Next the retreatants began to chant Amitābha's name in six syllables *(Na-mo-Ou-mi-tou-fo)* slowly while leaving their seats to form a procession to "serpentine the Buddha['s name]" *(rao fo)*. Each class faced the middle of the hall, and we came out of our classes *(chuban)* by marching straight forward, one rank at a time, to the center aisle, at which point we turned and marched two by two to the back of the hall. At the back wall, we turned right and "inserted classes" *(chaban)* to form a single-file line moving clockwise around the perimeter of the hall. At this point we also changed hand positions. While forming the procession, we held our hands clasped together in front of our chests *(hezhang)*, but upon reaching the back wall, we put our hands at waist level, right over left, palms facing up *(fangzhang)*. The procession generally went around the hall three times.

At the signal, we all went back to our "classes" once again, but whereas we had come out by ranks, we returned longitudinally in files, which led us back to our main mats. The recitation continued at a slow pace until everyone was in place. Then a bell signaled that it was time to sit on the mats, cover our legs with the towels, and prepare to meditate.

The meditation went through phases of oral and silent recitation of the name. The chanting itself went through four distinct phases. First, we chanted the six-syllable invocation slowly. Then, according to the tempo provided by the *faqi,* we dropped the *"na-mo"* and switched to the four-syllable invocation *(Ou-mi-tuo-fo),* put our hands up again in the *hezhang* position, and picked up the pace. At the next acceleration, we put our hands down once again. After one final acceleration, we chanted very quickly. The *yinqing* (small handbell) sounded, and everyone recited the full six-syllable invocation once more very slowly. Then a monk struck the "wooden fish" *(muyu)* three times, another monk dimmed the lights, and we meditated for about twenty minutes.

At our initial training, we were instructed to use this time to recite the Buddha's name silently, taking the opportunity to practice concentrating on the Buddha and his Pure Land with a focused, unperturbed mind *(yi xin bu luan),* and perhaps to attain a direct vision of the Pure Land. We will have more to say about the content of this meditation in just a moment.

At the end of the meditation period, the *yinqing* sounded once again and we practiced the four-tiered *nianfo* once more. After reciting a verse dedicating the merit generated by this "stick" to the attainment of rebirth in the Pure Land, the bell sounded once again, and the "stick" was over.

As mentioned earlier, the seventh "stick" differs from the others in that it includes another instructional and hortatory talk by the *zhuyi,* which sheds light on the method of meditation used during each "stick." The monk acting as *zhuyi* taught that this silent, interior recitation of Amitābha's name was a way of bringing the mind under control and establishing a link with the Buddha and the Pure Land. He also stated that, during this meditation, we could search for the self that was reciting the name and so come to a realization of the truth of no-self. In this way, one could cultivate both wisdom and *samādhi* through Pure Land practice.

Readers may conclude from this that the Xilian temple has inherited the "dual practice of Chan and Pure Land" *(chan-jing shuang xiu)* advocated by the monk-reformer Lianchi Zhuhong in the sixteenth and seventeenth centuries, but this would be incorrect. Zhuhong advocated use of the "Pure Land koan," in which a practitioner in the middle of *nianfo* occasionally stops and asks, "Who is this that is reciting the Buddha's name?" The *zhuyi* of this retreat did not advocate koan practice as such, and on other occasions, when I specifically asked whether this temple made use of the Pure Land koan, I was told emphatically that this was not a Chan temple, but a Pure Land temple and as such made use only of Pure Land techniques. The crucial difference lay in the fact that no one expected to gain a Chan-style enlightenment experience from this meditation. The only goal was to attain rebirth in the Pure Land at the end of one's life, and possibly a vision of the Pure Land and Amitābha Buddha in this life.

The eighth, and final, "stick" ended at 5:55 P.M., after which those who had not taken the Eight Precepts or vowed to fast received permission to go down to the refectory for an informal meal. I was the only one who did. Everyone else took the time to bathe and begin packing their suitcases to return home later that evening. A few, despite injunctions to the contrary, took a nap.

At 7:00 we assembled once more in the Great Shrine Hall for the last observance of the retreat, the Great Dedication of Merit, following the liturgy found in the *Breviary*. Kneeling before the buddha-image with palms joined, the participants said together:

> At this time, the assembly of disciples are worldlings [caught in] birth and death.
> Wrongdoing obstructs us profoundly and heavily, and the suffering of the six paths [of rebirth] is unspeakable.
> Now we have encountered good friends and gotten to hear the name of Amitābha and the merit of his original vows.
> Singlemindedly, we recite and contemplate, seeking and vowing to be reborn [in the Pure Land].
> May the Buddha in his compassion not abandon us, but out of pity gather us in.
> We, the assembly of disciples, do not know the brightness of the major and minor marks of the buddha's body;
> May the Buddha appear to us and lead us to gain a vision [of him] as well as Avalokiteśvara and Mahāsthāmaprāpta
> and all the assembly of bodhisattvas of that realm in their marvellous characteristics of purity, majesty, and brilliance!
> Lead us, one and all, to gain a vision of Amitābha![7]

Next the participants paid homage to Amitābha, Avalokiteśvara, Mahāsthāmaprāpta, and then three times to the "pure, great ocean [assembly] of bodhisattvas."

The retreatants then recited the verses for dedicating the merit of their practice:

> May I be free from obstructions at the end of my life, and may Amitābha come from afar to welcome me.
> May Avalokiteśvara anoint my head with sweet dew, and may Mahāsthāmaprāpta set my foot on the golden terrace.
> In an instant, [I will] leave behind the five kinds of turbidness, and [as easily] as one stretches out one's arm, arrive at the lotus pool.
> After the lotus blossom opens, I will see the Compassionate Worthy, and with my own ears thoroughly hear the sound of the Dharma.
> Having heard, I will awaken to the Forebearance of the Unborn, and, without turning my back on the Pure Land, reenter the *sahā* world, knowing well the expedient means needed to save all beings, and skilfully taking their vexations as a buddha's merit.
> I wish that, as the Buddha automatically knows, at the very end I will achieve this.[8]

The service ended with praises and homage to the buddhas, bodhisattvas, and the patriarchs of the Chinese Pure Land tradition, followed by the Three Refuges and the final exhortation to practice. After this, we were dismissed to return our robes, pick up our things, and depart for home.

The Work of the Retreat

If nothing else, I hope that the reader will understand from my description of the buddha-recitation retreat that, in its Chinese form, the statement that Pure Land practice provides an "easy path" requires extensive qualification. Scholars and laypersons whose understanding of Pure Land Buddhism has been shaped by study of the Japanese model will be impressed by the amount of hard work that Chinese Pure Land practice involves. Participants in this retreat sought to engage in a period of intensified practice that would lead to a transformation of consciousness marked by a direct vision of Amitābha's Pure Land and to habituate themselves to constant mindfulness of the Pure Land so as to solidify karmic links conducive to rebirth there. This emphasis on establishing a karmic connection is similar to the rationale for viewing Chūjōhime's relics and hearing her story as discussed by Hank Glassman in this collection. The retreatants also sought through constant practice to ensure that, at the moment of death, their thoughts would be squarely focused on the Buddha coming to meet and guide them home. The attention paid to the moment of death as key to birth in Sukhāvatī is also found in the medieval Japanese practices examined by Jacqueline Stone in this volume.

Chinese Pure Land thought acknowledges Pure Land practice as the "easy way," but we must put this in perspective. It is easy when compared to its nearest competitor, Chan meditation. The thirteenth patriarch *(zu)* of the Pure Land, the Great Master Yinguang (1861–1947), described the prospects of Chan practice this way:

> As to the line [from Yongming Yanshou's (904–975) *Four Alternatives (Si liao jian)*] "Having Chan but lacking the Pure Land, nine out of ten will stray from the road. When the realm of shadows appears before them, they will instantly follow it": This means that even though a person may be thoroughly enlightened and may have illuminated the mind and seen into their own true nature within a Chan lineage, they still cannot easily cut off the disturbances of views and thoughts. One must practice continually for a long period of time and bring oneself to the point where one is completely and utterly purified; only then can one cut off samsara and find escape. It does not matter if [only] one hair-breadth remains to be cut off. One is still one hair-breadth away from complete purification, and one will revolve around in the six paths as before, and escape will be difficult. . . . The end of their lives comes, and they still have not made it home. Out of ten who have attained a great enlightenment, nine are like this, and that is why the verse says, "nine out of ten will stray from the road."[9]

In Yinguang's reading, Yongming Yanshou had no confidence in Chan meditation as a vehicle to carry the great mass of people to liberation. A great enlightenment took years of hard practice, and if it did not bring about complete purification of the mind in this life, there was no guarantee that one would be able to retain all of one's previous progress and build on it in lives to come.

When Chinese practitioners refer to Pure Land as the "easy way," then, it is in comparison with this. It does not mean that the practice itself is easy. On the contrary, although it is easier than Chan, Pure Land practice still requires constant effort. The twelfth patriarch Chewu (1741–1810) exhorted his followers to make this sustained effort:

> Afterwards, with this mind of faith, hold on to the name [of Amitābha]. One repetition is the seed for a nine-petaled lotus; one phrase is a true cause for rebirth [in the Pure Land]. This mind must directly follow this mind; recollection upon recollection without change, exclusively and exhaustively, without adulteration [from other thoughts] and without interruption. The longer [one maintains this mind] the more solid [it will be]. . . . Longer and longer, the frag-

> ments automatically enter into [the state of] the unified, unperturbed mind. In all sincerity, if one does not attain rebirth in this manner, then the Tathāgata Śākyamuni is a liar, and the World-Honored Amitābha is a vain hope.[10]

The reason for constant practice is that one must attune one's mind to Amitābha and his Pure Land to achieve rebirth. Of especial importance is the concept of *ganying,* a term difficult to translate. Literally, it means "feeling and response," and it denotes the devotee's initiative in cultivating his or her own mind so that it will "resonate" with Amitābha, who will then respond with aid and support. A common image used to illustrate this concept is that of sympathetic vibration. If two strings on an instrument are tuned to the same note, then when one string is struck, the other will begin to vibrate along with it spontaneously. In a like manner, if one "tunes" the mind to vibrate at the frequency of the Pure Land, then Amitabha will respond to this cultivation and a link between practitioner and buddha will come into being.

Those who have not cultivated this frame of mind, or who cultivate it haphazardly or intermittently so that it is not constant, have no strong link with the Pure Land and therefore cannot count on rebirth there after this life. This is the situation of the vast majority of beings. As Chewu says, having a mind means that one must be always thinking of something, and, by the same principle of *ganying* that leads to birth in the Pure Land, one will forge links with other regions of the cosmos and strengthen one's likelihood of being reborn elsewhere.[11] For this reason, constant cultivation becomes necessary; the task is to change one's mind thoroughly so that one is always on the same "wavelength" as the Pure Land.

In particular, Chinese Pure Land Buddhism stresses the importance of the final thought in the last instant of one's life. The abbot of the Xilian temple, the Venerable Zhiyu, once told the following story during a two-day buddha-recitation retreat to press this point:

> There was once an elderly layman whose attainments in buddha-recitation were very good. He enjoyed the things of this world and had two wives. He came down with a grave illness, and his end drew near. Because his practice of buddha-recitation was so good, the Buddha appeared before him, and he said "I can see the Pure Land!" However, an obstruction arose: the junior wife ran up weeping and wailing and said, "How will my son and I live after you are gone?" His mind was disturbed, and he said, "Don't worry. I will write out a will and make sure you are cared for." With this one disturbance, the

> vision of the Amitābha faded away, and the Pure Land disappeared. In front of his eyes he saw only darkness, and then a vision of Hell.[12]

Constant practice increases the likelihood of being able to maintain the "unified, unperturbed mind" right up to the last moment.

Thus, unlike what James Sanford identifies in this collection as the "normative form" of Japanese Pure Land Buddhism, with its emphasis on exclusive reliance on the "other power" of Amitābha and its profound distrust of "self power," Chinese Pure Land Buddhism stresses the need for the practitioner to work actively to set up a resonance that will elicit Amitābha's help and support. The characteristic that most distinguishes the Chinese model from the Japanese is the notion of "the cooperation of self and other power" *(zi ta er li).* While the mainstream of Japanese Pure Land thought from Hōnen to Shinran and Ippen stressed the impossibility of effective religious practice due to the degeneration of human capacities in the age of the Final Dharma *(mappō),* the Chinese have historically been far more optimistic about the human potential for self-cultivation. This optimism carries with it stern injunctions that believers must take responsibility to do what they can to bring about their rebirth in the Pure Land, and buddha-recitation retreats, of whatever length, are a means to this end.

Autobiographical Postscript

There remains one last effect of my own participation in the Budda One to report, and while what follows may not follow strictly the canons of academic writing, I believe that they are still of interest for the study of Chinese Pure Land Buddhism, especially in light of the response this incident engendered at the temple among my informants.

The day after the retreat ended, while I was riding in the back seat of a Taipei taxi and thinking about nothing in particular, I suddenly had a vision of another land. The terrain was completely flat. I could see the sun rising through tall, magnificent trees, and I could hear birds singing in their branches. The sky was a clear, deep blue. There was a pond in the foreground, its surface blue and unruffled. The vision lasted only for an instant, and then I was back in the taxi, blinking in amazement. I have never been prone to visionary experiences, and this was quite a shock to me.

When I returned to the Xilian temple for a follow-up interview with the monk who had acted as *weinuo* for the Buddha One, I reported what had happened. He was quite excited and drew out a copy of the *Breviary*. He reminded me that, in the liturgy of the "Great Dedication of Merit" on page 112, participants prayed for a vision of Amitābha Buddha, his retinue, and (by extension, since the text does not actually say this), the Pure Land. He said that I had simply gotten what I had asked for and earned through my efforts at the retreat. Several laypeople who overheard this conversation expressed a great deal of envy.

A woman who lived at the temple in preparation for ordination as a novice interpreted this experience as the first through the fifth of the sixteen contemplations of the Pure Land as recorded in the *Contemplation Sutra* (*Guan wuliangshou fo jing,* T 365). In the meditative practice recommended by this sutra, one visualizes sixteen aspects of the Pure Land. First, one visualizes the sun setting in the west; second, water covering all the regions of the west; third, the ground; fourth, the jewelled trees; fifth, the streams and ponds.[13] She urged me to persist in my practice and try to complete all sixteen visualizations.

At a later date, the vice-abbot of the temple, who had acted as the *zhuyi,* questioned me quite closely about the experience. That a foreigner and the lone non-Buddhist at the retreat had achieved one of the practice's major goals clearly held much interest for the resident clergy and lay devotees, and all wanted to know why I did not immediately convert.

Leaving that particular question aside, we can observe the following: First, there are some discrepancies between my vision and the description of Pure Land cultivation and content in the *Contemplation Sūtra*. I clearly saw the rising sun, not the setting sun. Also the vision came to me spontaneously, whereas the sūtra indicates that it is something one should deliberately cultivate. Nevertheless, the clergy and laity of the temple immediately identified the content of the vision as the Pure Land of Amitābha because it had followed so closely on the Buddha One and was sufficiently similar to canonical descriptions of the Pure Land to satisfy them. Identifying the vision with a certain step in a graduated program of visualizations allowed them to interpret it as the Pure Land despite the lack of many details, notably the Buddha and his helpers.

Second, the response I received from the clergy demonstrated clearly that they regarded Pure Land practice as *work,* and the granting of a vision of the Pure Land as one of the goals of that work. No one at the temple regarded the vision as a result of Amitābha's free grace. Rather they saw the effort expended in observing the Buddha One as directed toward constructing the kind of karmic links with the Buddha and his land that would naturally lead to just this sort of phenomenon. From their perspective, what happened was nothing extraordinary, but merely what ideally ought to happen to all who intensively cultivate the Pure Land path.

Third, if we place this event in a wider context of religious studies, we may observe the ambiguity and interpretability of religious experience. A skeptic would say that I had just been through a complex ritual that kept me absorbed in deliberately cultivating specifically mapped states of mind for an extended period of time and that predisposed me to certain kinds of experiences. Clifford Geertz, in observing Balinese rituals several decades ago, commented on the role of ritual in making the worldview of particular religions seem "uniquely realistic" precisely by putting participants into a state of passivity and receptivity while presenting them with heightened and focused sensory experiences:

> The dispositions which religious rituals induce thus have their most important impact—from a human point of view—outside the boundaries of the ritual itself as they reflect back to color the individual's conception of the established world of bare fact.[14]

However, even within the religious community there is a need to interpret. As already stated, my vision did not exactly adhere to the canonical ideal. But, for the clergy and laity of the Xilian temple, what I saw had to be the Western Paradise of Amitābha Buddha and nothing else.

My own interpretation of the incident is still in progress.

Conclusions

I have been pursuing two goals in writing about the Buddha One: first, to provide as "thick" a description of the event itself as possible, and second, to use the event to bring out some distinctive features of Chinese Pure Land Buddhist thought and practice. The reader should be able to see by now that Pure Land practice in China is hard work. Amitābha's grace and the power of his original vows are crucial in overcoming the fatal handicaps Buddhists face in the age of the Final Dharma. Nevertheless, in the logic of *ganying*, the believer still takes the initiative in pursuing practices that will transform his or her mind and attune it with the Buddha so as to create karmic links. The ideal remains "the cooperation of self and other power."

This is very distinct from the dominant Japanese model with which Westerners are more familiar. To use a graphic metaphor, the Japanese system is like an elevator in a building without stairs. One merely gets in and rides, and all arrive together; no one can speed up the elevator's progress by his or her own effort. The Chinese model is more like an escalator: believers can ride passively if they wish, but they may still exercise their legs and speed their progress if they choose to walk up. When their legs and the escalator's motor cooperate, they make the most rapid progress possible.

Thus, throughout Chinese Buddhist history, we see the formation of buddha-recitation societies and the recognition as "patriarchs" of those who exemplified arduous practice in Pure Land methods combined with learning, morality, and skill in apologetics. The ideal practitioner recites the Buddha's name constantly so as to reinforce continually the karmic links and the pure state of mind necessary to guarantee rebirth in the Pure Land. Most especially, the goal is to have a "unified, undisturbed mind" focused exclusively on the Pure Land at the moment of death so that at that most critical juncture, Amitābha will respond and come to meet and guide the devotee to the Pure Land, where the real work of enlightenment will finally begin.

Notes

1. Zhiyu relates the story of the temple's founding in "Xilian, Xilian," in his *Chi Pan Lian Chao* (Sanxia: Xilian Jingyuan, 1986), 168–177.

2. Interested readers can find out more about the significance of these arrangements of people at Taiwan Buddhist religious functions in my article "Stages in the Religious Life of Lay Buddhists in Taiwan," *Journal of the International Association of Buddhist Studies*, 20, no. 2 (Fall 1997), 113–139.

3. The Xilian temple, like most Buddhist temples in Taiwan, uses the services found in the *Fomen bibei kesong ben* (A Buddhist breviary), rev. ed., ed. Shi Guangding (Taipei: Fojiao Chubanshe, 1954), 104.

4. Ibid., 3–74.

5. Ibid., 36–45.

6. Ibid., 65.

7. Ibid., 112, 113.

8. Ibid., 114.

9. Yinguang, "Jingtu jueyi lun" ("Treatise resolving doubts about the Pure Land"), in *Yinguang Dashi Quanji* (The collected works of great master Yinguang), ed. Shi Guangding (Taipei: Fojiao Chubanshe, 1991), 1:368–369.

10. Chewu, *Chewu Chanshi Yulu* (The recorded sayings of Chan master Chewu), in *Xinbian wanzhi xu zang jing* (Kyoto: Zōkyō Shoin, 1905–1912; reprint, Taipei: Xinwenfeng, 1993), 10:754b.

11. Ibid, 10:752b.

12. Zhiyu, "Wangsheng Xifang Erli Famen" ("The dharma-gate of the two powers for gaining rebirth in the western region"), in *Shifu de Hua* (The master's talks) (Sanhsia: Xilian Jingyuan Yinhang, 1992), 58.

13. T 365, 12.341c–342c. For reference, see the translation of the *Contemplation Sutra* by Hisao Inagaki and Harold Stewart in *The Three Pure Land Sutras,* BDK English Tripitaka 12-II, III, IV (Berkeley: Numata Center for Buddhist Translation and Research, 1995), 97–101.

14. Clifford Geertz, "Religion as a Cultural System," in *The Interpretation of Cultures* (New York: Basic Books, 1973), 119.

Character Glossary

aku 悪
akunin 悪人
akunin ōjō 悪人往生
akunin shōki 悪人正機
akushu 悪趣
Amakusa Tadatsuna 甘糟忠綱
Amakasu Tarō Tadatsuna ni shimesu onkotoba 甘糟太郎忠綱に示す御詞
Amida 阿彌陀 (阿弥陀)
Amida-dō 阿彌陀堂
Amida hadaka monogatari 阿彌陀裸物語
Amida hishaku 阿彌陀秘釈
Amida no obachi 阿彌陀のお罰
Amituo 阿彌陀
Anluoji 安樂集
Anraku 安樂
Anrakubō 安樂房
A-un jigi 阿吽字義
baguan zhaijie 八關齋戒
Bailian she 白蓮社
Bailiantang ji 白蓮堂記
Bantōin 蟠桃院
Baozhi 宝誌
Benchō (Shōkō) 弁長 (聖光)
Bishamon 毘沙門
bodaiji 菩提寺
bodaishin 菩提心
bon 盆
bonbu 凡夫
bonjō 凡情
bonnō 煩悩
buer famen 不二法門
buppō guzū no onshū 佛法弘通之怨讐
bushi 武士
butchi 佛智
Byōchū shugyōki 病中修行記
Byōdōin 平働等
chaban 插班
Chan 禪
Chang Gong 常公
chan-jing shuang xiu 禪淨雙修
Chewu 徹悟
Chingen 鎮源
Chinkai 珍海
Chinzei 鎮西
chishiki 知敷識
Chokushū Hyakujō shingi 敕修百丈清規
Chōrenbō 長蓮房
chū 忠
chuban 出班
chūdō 中道
Chūshōin 中性院
chūtai 中諦
Da banniepan jing 大般涅槃経
Da fang guang fo huayen jing 大方廣仏華厳経
Da xiong bao dian 大雄寶殿
Daidenbō-in 大傳法院
Daien Hōkan Kokushi nenpu 大圓宝鑑国師年譜
Daigu Sōchiku 大愚宗築
Daihannya rishubun 大般若理趣分
Dainichi 大日
Dainihonkoku Hokekyō kenki (Hokke genki) 大日本国法華経験記 (法華験記)
danmatsuma no kaze 断末摩の風

daochang 道場
Daocheng 道誠
Daochuo 道綽
Daoshi 道世
Daoxuan 道宣
Daozhe Chaoyuan 道者超元
Dasheng qixin lun 大乘起信論
Da Song Hangzhou Xihu Zhaoqing si jieshe beiming 大宋杭州昭慶寺結社碑
Date Masamune 伊達政宗
Date Tadamune 伊達忠宗
Deyun biqiu 徳雲比丘
Ding Wei 丁謂
diyi yidi 第一義諦
dōka 道歌
Dokushō Shōen 独照性圓
dongban 東班
Donglin 東林
Dōsui Tōsho 洞水東初
Eian Jushō Nikō 栄庵寿昌尼公
Eiga Monogatari 栄華物語
Eikan 永観
ekō 回向
Engyōji 圓行寺
Enpukuji (a) 延福寺
Enpukuji (b) 圓福寺
Enryakuji 延暦寺
fangzhang 放掌
faqi 法器
Fayan 法眼
Fayao 法要
Fayuan zhulin 法苑珠林
fo er 仏二
Fo Qi ji Xiuxue Yigui Shouce 仏七暨修學儀規手册
fo yi 仏一
Foshuo shiwangsheng Amituofo guo jing 仏説十往生阿弥陀国経
Fozu tongji 佛祖統紀
Fudarakusan (Mt.) 補陀落山
Fugen 普賢
Fujiwara no Kamatari 藤原鎌足
Fujiwara no Kōzei 藤原行成
Fujiwara no Michinaga 藤原道長
Fujiwara no Munetomo 藤原宗友
Fujiwara no Tsunemune 藤原経宗
Funaoka 船岡
funi 不二
ganying 感應
gedatsu 解脱
Gedatsu-bō Jōkei 解脱房貞慶
Gen'ō Kyūjō 玄応休静
Genshin 源信
gezi yonggong 各自用功
Gion 祇園
Godaidō 御大堂
gogyaku 五逆
Gōhō 果法
Gokuraku jōdo 極楽浄土
Gomizuno-o 御水尾
Gonki 権記
Gon-no-daibu Takanobu no Ason 権大夫隆信朝
Gorinjū no toki montei tō ni shimesare-keru onkotoba 御臨終の時門弟等に示されける御詞
Goshirakawa 後白河
Goshūi ōjōden 後拾遺往生伝
Go-Toba 後鳥羽
goyoku 五欲
Guannian Amituofo xianghai sanmei gongde famen 観念阿弥陀仏相海三昧功徳法門
Guan wuliangshou fo jing 観無量寿法経
Gudō Kokushi yonjyūhachiji iroha uta 愚堂国師四十八字いろは歌
Gudō Tōshoku 愚堂東寔
Guiyuan zhizhi ji 帰元直指集
Gukanshō 愚管抄
guwen 古文
gyakushu 逆修
Gyakushu seppō 逆修説法
Gyōkū 行空
Gyokuyō 玉葉
Gyōsen 行仙
habutsu 破佛
Hachimanchō no nukigaki: Ajikan no honmi 八萬帖之抜書: 阿字觀之本味
haiqing 海清
hajigokumon 破地獄文
Hakuin Ekaku 白隠慧鶴
hanmoto 板本
Han Yü 韓愈
Heike monogatari 平家物語

hezhang 合掌
Hieizan (Mt. Hiei) 比叡山
higan 彼岸
Higo (province) 肥後
hihō shōbō 誹謗正法
hijibōmon 秘事法門
hijiri 聖
himitsu nenbutsu 秘密念仏
Hōhonbō Gyōku 法本房行空
hōitsu muzan 放逸無慚
Hōjōji 法成寺
Hōkaden 法花殿
Hokke genki 法華験記
Hōkyōshō 寶鏡鈔
Honchō shinshū ōjōden 本朝新修往生伝
Hōnen 法然
Hōnen Shōnin denki 法然上人伝記
Hōnen Shōnin gyōjō ezu 法然上人行状絵図
hongaku 本覺
honganbokori 本願ぼこり
Honjō-bō Tankyō (or Tangō) 本成房湛敬(湛教)
honmon no Mida 本門の彌陀
honshō no Amida 本性の阿彌陀
Hosshinshū 発心集
houlai 後來
Huai jingtu shi 懐浄土詩
Huaigan 懐感
hua pusa 化菩薩
Huayan 華嚴
Huayan jing 華嚴經
Huayan shezhu 華嚴社主
Huiyuan 慧遠
Hyakuren shō 百練抄
ianjin 異安心
Ichigo taiyō himitsu shū 期大要秘密集
Ichigon hōdan 一言芳談
ichinengi 一念義
igi 異義
ikkō 一向
ikkō ikki 一向一揆
Ikkyū Sōjun 一休宗純
Ingen Ryūki (C. Yinyuan Longqi) 隠元隆
Ippen 一遍
Ippyaku shijū gokajō mondō 百四十五箇条問答
Iroha uta いろは歌
Ise monogatari 医世物語
Ishida Mitsuyuki 石田充之
Ishida Mizumaro 石田瑞麿
ishō teiyō shin 異生羝羊心
Issai Shujō Kiken 一切衆生喜見
Isshi Bunshu 一絲文守
Isshū gyōgi shō 一宗行儀鈔
ita 板
Itchū Tōmoku 一宙東黙
Iyo (province) 伊予
Izu 伊豆
jahō 邪法
Jakue Shōnin tsutaekiki no onkotoba 寂恵上人伝聞の御詞
jakumon no Mida 迹門の弥陀
Jiacai 迦才
jianxiang 監香
Jichihan 実範
Jien 慈圓
Jiezhu 戒珠
jigai ōjō 自害往生
jikishi tanden 直指単伝
jinen 自然
jingi fuhai 神祇不拝
jingjin nianfo yi [er, san, qi] 精進佛一(二,三,七)
Jingming 淨名
jingxing 淨行
Jingxing she 淨行社
Jingxing dizi 淨行弟子
jinsō 陣僧
Jingtu baozhu ji 浄土寶珠集
Jingtu lijiao zhi 浄土立教志
Jingtu lun 浄土論
Jingtu wangsheng zhuan 浄土往生傳
Jingxing pin 淨行品
jingye 淨業
jishō sōjō no renge 自性清淨ノ蓮華
Jishū 時宗
Jizō 地蔵
jizu 繼祖
Jōdo 浄土
Jōdo genryūshō (a.k.a. *Jōdo hōmon genryūshō*) 浄土源流章(浄土法門源流章)
Jōdoshū ryakushō 浄土宗略称

Jōfugyō 常不軽
Jōgakubō Kōsai 成覚房幸西
Jōkei 貞慶
Jungen 順源
Jūren 住蓮
juzō 寿像
Kai (province) 甲斐
Kaigen seijutsu 開眼誠述
kaishi 開示
Kakuban 覚鑁
Kamakura 鎌倉
Kamatari Daijin 鎌足大臣
kami 神
Kamo no Chōmei 鴨長名
kana hōgo 仮名法語
kanbyō 看病
Kanbyō yōjin shō 看病用心抄
Kangaku-e 観学会
Kangyōsho gengi bunshō 観經疏玄義分抄
Kanjo 寛助
Kankō ruijū 漢光類聚
Kanmuryōjukyō 観無量寿経
Kannon 観音
Kanzan Egen 関山慧玄
Katō Shōshun 加藤正俊
kechien 結縁
Ken'ei (reign name) 建永
kenmitsu 顕密
Kenren 見蓮
Kenshun Ryōei 賢俊良栄
kessha 結社
ketai 假諦
Ketsubonkyō 血盆経
Kirei mondō 貴嶺問答
Kishō hachikajō 起晴八箇条
kō 孝
Kōbō Daishi Nenbutsu Kudenshū (kōhon) 弘法大師念佛口傳集 (廣本)
Kōfukuji 興福寺
Kokūzō 虚空蔵
kōmyō shingon 光明真言
Kongōbu-ji 金剛峯寺
Kongō hannya kyō 金剛般若經
Konjaku monogatari shū 今昔物語集
Kōsai 幸西 (see above: Jōgakubō Kōsai)
koshi fuon 去此不遠
Kōyasan 高野山
Kōyasan ōjōden 高野山往生伝
Kōyōshū 孝養集
Kuaiji 會稽
Kujō Kanezane 九条兼実
Kumagai Naozane 熊谷直実
Kunitsuna Nyūdō 邦綱入道
Kuramadera 鞍馬寺
Kuroda Toshio 黒田俊雄
Kurodani Shōnin 黒谷聖人
kūtai 空諦
Kūya (Kōya) 空也
Kyōkai 教懐
kyōke 教化
Lebang wenlei 樂邦文頁
Lebang yigao 樂邦遺稿
Lianshe zu 蓮社祖
Liu Kai 柳開
Liuzu Dashi fabao tanjing 六祖大師法宝壇経
Lu Shishou 陸師壽
Lüelun anluo jingtuyi 略諭安楽浄土義
Lufu 盧阜
Lushan 盧山
Lunghua sanhui 竜華三会
manyi 縵衣
mappō 末法
Mattō shō 末燈抄
Miaofa lianhuajing 妙法蓮華経
mida kuyōhō 弥陀供養法
Mii ōjōden 三井往生伝
mikkyō 密教
Minamoto no Arifusa 源有房
Minamoto no Mitsunaka 源満中
Minamoto no Noritō no Ason 源章任朝臣
Minamoto no Tadaomi 源忠遠
Minamoto no Yoriyoshi no Ason 源頼義朝臣
Miroku 弥勒
Mitsugon-in 密厳院
mittsū jiken 密通事件
Miya santan 宮讃歎
Miyoshi no Tameyasu 三善為康
mixing 密行
Monju 文殊
Moriyama Shōshin 守山聖真

mujōin 無常院
Mujū Ichien 無住一円
mukaekō 迎講
mujū munen nenbutsu 無住無念念佛
Mumonkan 無門関
Murasaki Shikibu nikki 紫式部日記
muryōju 無量寿
muyu 木魚
Myōan Eisai 明庵栄西
Myōhō 妙法
Myōhō-ama gozen gohenji 妙法尼御善御返事
Nachi san (Mt.) 奈智山
Nakatomi Kamako 中臣鎌子
Nakayama Tadachika 中山忠親
namo Oumitou fo 南無阿彌陀佛
namu Amida butsu 南無阿彌陀佛
namu shihō kirai shikai daizu daihi omitofu 南無四方極楽世界大慈大悲阿弥陀佛
Nancao 南操
Naniwa 難波
Nanmyō Tōkō 南明東湖
Negoro 根来
nenbutsu 念佛
Nembutsu Jōgyōsha 念佛淨行社
Nenbutsu ōjōden 念佛往生伝
Nenbutsu ōjō yōgi shō 念佛往生要義抄
nenbutsu zanmai 念佛三昧
nianfo 念佛
nianfo sanmei 念佛三昧
Nichiren 日連
Nihon ōjō gokurakuki 日本往生極樂記
Nihon ryōiki 日本霊異記
nijūgozanmai 二十五三昧
Nijūgozanmai shiki 二十五三昧式
Ninga 仁賀
Ninkan 仁寛
Ninne 任恵
Nishiguchi Junko 西口順子
nissōkan 日想観
Nōgu 能救
Nomori no kagami 野守鏡
nyoirin Kannon 如意輪観音
Nyojaku 如寂
Nyosetsu Bungan 如雪文巌
Odawara Hijiri 小田原聖
odori nenbutsu 踊念佛
Ōe no Masafusa 大江匡房
Ōgo no Tarō Sanhide e tsukawasu gohenji 大胡の太郎実秀へつかはす御返事
Ōhara 大原
ōjō 往生
Ōjō jōdo yōjin 往生浄土用心
Ōjō yōshū 往生要集
ōjōden 往生伝
Ōjōin 往生院
ōjōnin 往生人
Ōjōyōka 往生要歌
onmyōji 陰陽師
Ononomiya Sanesuke 小野宮実資
onryō 怨霊
Orategama 遠羅天釜
Osada Kagemune 長田景宗
Osada Tadamune 長田忠宗
Ōshō 応照
Ōshū meisho zue 奥州名所図絵
Ōtani 大谷
Ō-Tō-Kan 応灯関
Oumituo fo 阿彌陀佛
Ōzaki Hachiman Shrine 大崎八萬神社
Qian Yi 錢易
Qiantang Bailian shezhu bei 錢塘白蓮社主碑
Qiantang Xihu Jingshe lu 錢塘西湖淨社録
qingliang zhi xiang 濆涼之鄉
Qisong 契嵩
raigō 来迎
raigōzu 来迎図
rakushoku 落飾
rao fo 繞佛
Rengejō 蓮華城
Rennen 蓮念
rensha nembutsu 蓮社念佛
Renzen 蓮禅
rinen 理念
rinjū gyōgi 臨終行儀
Rinjū gyōgi chuki 臨終行儀注記
Rinjū no yōi 臨終之用意
rinjū shōnen 臨終正念
rinjū shukke 臨終出家
Rishukyō 理趣經

rokubon 六凡
rokusainichi 六齋日
Ru fajie pin 入法界品
Ruiyan Shiyan 瑞巌師彦
Ruiying zhuan 瑞応伝
Ryōchū (Nen'a) 良忠（然阿）
Ryōgon-in nijūgozanmai kesshū kakochō 楞厳院二十五三昧結衆過法帳
Ryōgon-in nijūgozanmai konpon kesshu nijūgonin rensho hotsuganmon 楞厳院二十五三昧根本結衆二十五人連署発願文
Ryōhan 良範
Ryōjusen 霊鷲山
Ryōkei Shōsen 竜渓性潜
Ryōō Dōkaku 了翁道覚
ryūgeju 竜華樹
Ryūge san'e 竜華三会
Ryūju 竜樹
Saigyō 西行
sajing 灑浮
sandai 三諦
Sange ōjōki 三外往生記
Sanjin ryōkan oyobi gohōgo 三心料簡および御法語
Sankaiji 山階寺
sanmitsu kaji 三密加持
sanpuku 三福
Sanxia 三峡
Satō Hiroo 佐藤弘夫
Satsuma (province) 薩摩
Seizanha Gyōkan Gyōe shoden no onkotoba 西山派行観尭恵所伝の御詞
Sekimon Shingaku 石門心学
Senchaku hongan nenbutsu shū 選択本願念仏集
senjaku 選択
Senjō 千丈
Senjō Kagemune 先生景宗
senju 専修
Senkan 千観
Shandao 善導
Shancai 善財
Shandao 善導
Shaokang 少康
Shasekishū 沙石集
Shengchang 省常
sheshou 社首
Shibunritsu 四分律
shichibutsu tsūkaige 七佛通戒偈
Shichikajō no kishōmon 七箇条起請文
Shichikajō seikai 七箇条制誡
shidai 四大
shide no yamaji 四手[死出]ノ山路
Shi-er li 十二礼
shikaku 始覚
shikan 止観
Shin 眞（真）
shingi Shingon 新儀眞言
Shingon 眞言（真言）
Shinkan-bō Kansei 真観房感西
shinkoku 神國
Shinkyō (Ta'amidabutsu) 真教（他阿弥陀佛）
Shinran 親鸞
Shintō 神道
Shiogama Shrine 塩釜神社
Shishi yaolan 釋氏要蘭
shishō 四聖
shisō 四相
Shitennōji 四天王寺
shizu 知祖
shōen 荘園
shōjō 聖情
Shōkō-bō ni shimesarekeru onkotoba 聖光房に示されける御詞
Shōkū 性空
Shōnen (a.k.a. Shōkin, Shōzen) 聖念（聖金，聖全）
shōnen shōmyō 稱念稱名
Shōnin Misode no ura 聖人御袖裏
Shōnyō-bō 正如房
Shōnyo-bo e shimersarekeru onkotoba 正如房へつかはす御文
Shōren 昇蓮
Shosha san (Mt. Shosha) 書写山
Shoshadera 書写寺
Shouhu guojiezhu touloni jing 守護国界主陀羅尼經
Shōyūki 小石記
Shūi ōjōden 拾遺往生伝
si liao jian 四料簡
Sifenlü shanfan buque xingshi chao 四分律刪繁補闕行事鈔

sō 相
Song Bo 宋白
Song gaoseng zhuan 宋高僧傳
sonshō darani 尊勝陀羅尼
sōryō 僧寮
Sō Sanmon kishōmon (Pledge sent to Enryakuji) 送山門起請文
Ssujiaoi 四教義
Sukeshige 助重
Sun He 孫何
Suzuki Shōsan 鈴木正三
Ta'a Shōnin hōgo 他阿聖人法語
Tachikawaryū 立川流
Tada no In 多田院
Tada no Manchū 多田ノ満仲
tai 體
Taira Masayuki 平雅行
Taira no Kiyomori 平清盛
Taira no Koreshige 平維茂
Tajima (province) 但島
Takagi Yutaka 高木豊
Tamura no Megohime 田村愛姫
Tamura Yoshirō 田村芳郎
Tanba no Taifu 丹波大夫
Tanluan 曇鸞
Tanshū 湛秀
Tangetsu Shōen 湛月紹圓
tatchū 塔頭
Tendai 天台
tengenzū 天眼通
tenma 天魔
Teshima Toan 手島堵庵
Tianmu Zhongfeng Heshang guanglu 天目中峰和尚広録
Tiantai 天台
Tiantai Deshao 天台徳韶
Tōdaiji 東大寺
Tōfukuji 東福寺
Tō-ji 東寺
Tokuō Myōkō 禿翁妙宏
Tōren 登蓮
Tōshōji 東昌寺
Tōshōgū 東照宮
tsuizen kuyō 追善供養
Tsune ni ōserakeru onkotoba つねに仰せられける御詞
Tuizhi 退之 (a.k.a. Han Yü)
uchitsuomi 内臣
udonge 優曇華
Ŭich'ŏn 義天
Uji 宇治
Ungo Kiyō 雲居希膺
Ungo Oshō kinenroku 雲居和尚紀年録
utau nenbutsu 歌念佛
Wang Dan 王旦
Wang Gu 王古
Wang Yucheng 王禹偁
Wang Wenzheng 王文正 (a.k.a. Wang Dan)
Wangsheng lizan ji 往生礼讃偈
Wangsheng xifang jingtu ruiying zhuan 往生西方浄土瑞応伝
Wangsheng Xifang luezhuan 往生西方略傳
wangsheng zhou 往生咒
wanke 晩課
weinuo 維那
Wenshen 文
Wonjong munllyu 圓宗文類
Wuliangshou 無量壽
Wuliangshou jing 無量壽經
Wutai 五臺
Wu Yue 呉越
Wuyun 五雲
xiangban 香板
xianghao 相好
xiangzan 香讃
xianjue 先覺
Xiangshan yelu 湘山野録
xiban 西班
Xihu Zhaoqing si jie Jingxing she ji 西湖昭慶寺淨行社集
Xilian jingyuan 西蓮浄苑
xingzong 性宗
Xinxiu wangsheng zhuan 新修往生傳
yamagoe no Amida 山越阿弥陀
Yan 顔
yangzhi 楊止
Yanshou 延壽
yaoshi 藥石
yi xin bu luan 一心不亂
Yinguang 印光
yinqing 引磬
Yiran Xingrong 逸然性融

Yiyuan Zongben 一元宗本
Yokawa 横川
Yokawa Shuryōgon-in nijūgozanmai (Eshin, Yasutane) rinjū gyōgi 横川首楞厳院二十五三昧恵心保胤臨終行儀
Yokawa Shuryōgon-in nijūgozanmai kishō (Jūnikajō) 横川首楞厳院二十五三昧起晴（十二箇条）
Yokawa Sōzu 横川僧都
Yongming Yanshou 永明延壽
Yorimichi 頼道
Yoshishige no Yasutane (Jakushin) 慶滋保胤（寂心）
Yōtokuin 陽徳院
yuantong faxing 圓通
Yuanzhao 元照
Yūkai 宥快
zaijia pusa jie 在家菩薩戒
zaijia wu jie 在家五戒
Zanning 贊寧
zaoke 早課
zasu 座生
Zen 禪
zenchishiki 善知識
zenjō 禅定
Zenjō yūgō 禅浄融合
Zhaoqing Monastery 昭慶寺
Zhaoqing si zhi 昭慶寺志
Zhejiang 浙石
Zhe Shousu 翟守素
Zheyou 浙江
zhi 文
Zhifeng 志逢
Zhijue 智覺 (a.k.a. Yanshou)
Zhipan 志磐
Zhishou 智首
Zhiyi 智顗
Zhiyu 智諭
Zhiyuan 智圓
zhongguo benzhuan 中国本伝
Zhuhong 袾宏
zhuyi 主一
zi ta er li 自他二力
zōaku 造悪
zōaku muge 造悪無碍
Zōga 増賀
Zoku honchō ōjōden 続本朝往生伝
Zōmyō 増命
zonggu 宗古
Zongxiao 宗曉
Zuiganji 瑞巌寺
zu 祖
Zunshi 遵式

Contributors

Richard K. Payne is dean of the Institute of Buddhist Studies at the Graduate Theological Union, Berkeley. His research focuses on esoteric Buddhist rituals of the Japanese Shingon tradition and cognitive theory of ritual. He is editor of *Re-Visioning "Kamakura" Buddhism* and *The Pure Land Tradition: History and Development.*

Kenneth K. Tanaka is professor of Buddhist studies at Musashino University in Tokyo, Japan. He specializes in East Asian Pure Land Buddhist tradition. His publications include *The Dawn of Chinese Pure Land Buddhism: Ching-ying Hui-yuan's Commentary on the Visualization Sutra.*

Matthew T. Kapstein is professor of Buddhist studies at the Divinity School of the University of Chicago and directeur d'Études at the École Pratique des Hautes Études, Paris. His recent publications include *The Tibetan Assimilation of Buddhism: Conversion, Contestation, and Memory* and *Reason's Traces: Identity and Interpretation in Indian and Tibetan Buddhist Thought.*

Daniel Getz is associate professor in the Department of Philosophy and Religious Studies at Bradley University. He was a coeditor and contributor to *Buddhism in the Sung* and is continuing research on the Tiantai and Pure Land traditions in the Sung dynasty.

Jacqueline I. Stone is professor of Japanese religions at Princeton University. She is the author of *Original Enlightenment and the Transformation of Medieval Japanese Buddhism,* which received the American Academy of Religion's Award for Excellence in the Study of Religion, Historical Studies Category, and has written numerous articles on Nichiren, Tendai, and other Buddhist traditions.

James H. Sanford is associate professor of religious studies, University of North Carolina, Chapel Hill. He is coeditor of *Flowing Traces: Buddhism in the Literary and Visual Arts of Japan.*

Hank Glassman is assistant professor of East Asian studies at Haverford College. He is currently doing reasearch on the cult of the bodhisattva Jizo in medieval Japan.

Fabio Rambelli is professor of religious studies and semiotics in the Department of Cultural Studies, Sapporo University. He is the author of *Vegetal Buddhas* and coeditor of *Buddhas and Kami in Japan.*

Richard Jaffe is assistant professor of religion at Duke University. He is author of *Neither Monk nor Layman: Clerical Marriage in Modern Japanese Buddhism.*

Todd T. Lewis is professor of world religions at The College of the Holy Cross, where he has taught since 1990. The author of more than thirty journal articles, Lewis has also written numerous books, including *Popular Buddhist Texts from Nepal: Narratives and Rituals of Newar Buddhism* and *The Himalayas: A Syllabus of the Region's History, Anthropology and Religion,* and coauthored the textbook *World Religions Today.*

Charles B. Jones is associate professor in the Department of Religion and Religious Education at the Catholic University of America. He has published in the areas of Buddhism in Taiwan, late imperial Pure Land Buddhism in China, and interreligious dialogue. He is author of *Buddhism in Taiwan: Religion and the State, 1660–1990* and coeditor of *Religion in Modern Taiwan: Tradition and Innovation in a Changing Society.*

Index